Relationships in Organized Helping

Pragmatics & Beyond New Series (P&BNS)

ISSN 0922-842X

Pragmatics & Beyond New Series is a continuation of Pragmatics & Beyond and its Companion Series. The New Series offers a selection of high quality work covering the full richness of Pragmatics as an interdisciplinary field, within language sciences.

For an overview of all books published in this series, please see *benjamins.com/catalog/pbns*

Volume 331

Relationships in Organized Helping. Analyzing interaction in psychotherapy, medical encounters, coaching and in social media
Edited by Claudio Scarvaglieri, Eva-Maria Graf and Thomas Spranz-Fogasy

Relationships in Organized Helping

Analyzing interaction in psychotherapy, medical encounters, coaching and in social media

Edited by

Claudio Scarvaglieri
Ghent University

Eva-Maria Graf
Klagenfurt University

Thomas Spranz-Fogasy
Leibniz-Institute for the German Language Mannheim

John Benjamins Publishing Company

Amsterdam / Philadelphia

The paper used in this publication meets the minimum requirements of the American National Standard for Information Sciences – Permanence of Paper for Printed Library Materials, ANSI Z39.48-1984.

DOI 10.1075/pbns.331

Cataloging-in-Publication Data available from Library of Congress:
LCCN 2022020597 (PRINT)

ISBN 978 90 272 1145 3 (HB)
ISBN 978 90 272 5755 0 (E-BOOK)

John Benjamins Publishing Company · https://benjamins.com

Table of contents

Practices of relationship management in organized helping

Introduction

Eva-Maria Graf, Claudio Scarvaglieri and Thomas Spranz-Fogasy
Klagenfurt University / Ghent University / Leibniz-Institute for the German Language Mannheim

1. Setting the stage: Managing relationships in organized helping

„Der Mensch wird am Du zum Ich"
(Buber 2008)

Helping represents a basic practice of human interaction and is mutually co-constructed by social actors in and through their interaction. Helping exists both across mundane, everyday contexts and across institutional as well as organizational contexts. Unlike the spontaneous, unplanned, often reciprocal, instances of everyday helping, organized forms of helping are characterized by a certain permanency and unilateral structure that imply a stronger commitment, but also higher expectations on the side of the social actors. According to Böhringer, Hitzler and Richter (2022: 16), organized helping is both influenced, pre-structured and delineated by the specific interactive and/or institutional context and concurrently follows – as concrete, locally emerging practice of helping – specific interactional logics that account for its structured organization. I.e., organized helping transpires in the interplay between (pre-)structuring context and locally situated practice; as such it represents a structured situated social action that can be described along its relational, interactive, contextual / situational, and processual dimensions (Böhringer, Hitzler, and Richter 2022: 22ff).
Helping in its everyday as well as institutionalized form is understood here – following the pragmalinguistic conceptualization of Pick and Scarvaglieri (2019; 2022) – as verbal (and non-verbal) helping actions performed by a helper, who takes over these actions instead of and for another person, who is temporarily or permanently unable to perform such actions themselves. Helping thereby relieves these help-receiving persons of the need to decide on the correct action plan and/or to

https://doi.org/10.1075/pbns.331.01gra

act themselves. Particularly in institutional interactions, helping is often preceded by a detailed discussion of the goals of the helping. Moreover, varying degrees of helping can be differentiated, with the helping person performing all actions necessary to achieve the respective goals, performing only parts of them or just making suggestions about how the person in need for help might act themselves (for more details see Pick and Scarvaglieri 2019; 2022).

At the core of helping in both its everyday and (institutionally and professionally) organized forms are the helping person, the person receiving help and the relationship they mutually engage in. A relationship is conceptualized here as the connection between individuals premised on communicative acts (resting on e.g., language, gesture, body posture, facial expression, or gaze), which are performed and concomitantly perceived by the interacting individuals. Interactors construct a mental model of their relationship based on these communicative acts and on social patterns of understanding and interpreting these acts, monitor each subsequent communicative act as regards its possible impact on the relationship and adapt their respective models accordingly (cf. Linke and Schröter 2017: 15). Relationships thus have a historical and developmental dimension; they change over time and are not only locally constructed but also build on previous interaction (cf. Trasmundi and Philipsen 2020: 8). While any relationship then is a psychological phenomenon in its intra-individual interpretation of communication regarding the connection with an interlocutor, relationships – on the other hand – are constructed, maintained and molded by verbal and nonverbal interactive actions and practices: "(…) relationships are dynamically constructed in interaction by the participants" (Locher 2012: 46). These actions and practices of relating can be observed, documented and analyzed in their emergence and situatedness (cf. Arundale 2021: 23) with established methods from the social sciences. The systematic exploration of such overt verbal and non-verbal practices of relationship management across different contexts within the (institutional) helper – helped domain is at the heart of this book.

While building and managing relationships are part and parcel of social interactions in general – Enfield (2009: 65) talks about human societies being relationship-grounded societies – its specific forms and qualities are of particular relevance in social interactions dedicated to helping. The relationship between help giver and help receiver, i.e., the helping relationship, forms the bedrock of helping (Miller and Considine 2009; Graf and Spranz-Fogasy 2018). Helping relations have been defined by Rogers (1951) as relationships in which one of the parties, i.e., the helper, intends and is willing to promote the growth, development, maturity, or improved functioning of the other party, the help seeker. While this definition still holds relevance today, (organized) helping relations have undergone and are still undergoing massive change: As part of the overall societal transformation from a production-oriented to a service-oriented society with its growing emphasis on person-oriented services

(Miller and Considine 2009; Habscheid 2011), helping interactions have become differentiated as well as formalized, regulated and institutionalized (Luhmann 1973; Giddens 1991; Fietze 2011; Graf and Spranz-Fogasy 2018). Various organized forms and formats of person-oriented helping services have emerged and helping services by experts as such represent a prominent characteristic of modern Western societies (cf. Goffman 1983: 310; Miller and Considine 2009).

Such expert-based helping services are offered by professionals, i.e., helpers, who have acquired their profession-specific helping expertise, practices and qualification via specialized and institutionalized education and training, which in turn are built on profession-specific, regulated, and normed standards (Fietze 2015). A helping profession is thereby defined as a professional (and institutional) interaction between a helping expert and a help-seeking client, which is initiated to nurture the growth and learning of a person or to address their physical, psychological, intellectual and/or emotional constitution and problems related with it (cf. Graf et al. 2014: 1). According to the APA, helping professions include "occupations in the fields of psychology, psychiatry, counseling, medicine, nursing, social work, physical and occupational therapy, teaching, and education" (American Psychological Association (APA) 2020) (see also Combs and Gonzalez 1994). Of relevance from a social science and linguistic perspective is how the social actors co-construct their respective roles of 'expert' (e.g., doctor, therapist or counselor) and 'layperson' (client or patient) (Hall, Sarangi, and Slembrouck 1999; Juhila et al. 2003; Graf 2012), what types of knowledge are required to solve the latter's problem(s) and how a shared knowledge-base is co-constructed (Sarangi 2002; Gülich 2003; Brünner 2005; Scarvaglieri 2013): Professional helpers apply their professional vision (Goodwin 1994) based on their professional, clearly delineated objective knowledge, their professional experience as well as institutional perspective, while clients bring their life-world perspective and frame their experience as something subjective, individual and unique. This divergence of perspectives is a vital prerequisite and constitutive characteristic of any kind of therapeutic, consulting, coaching, counseling or medical interaction (cf. Graf 2019: 58).

In helping professions, the relationship between professionals and their patients and clients has proven to be pivotal for the interactive construction of the helping process and for obtaining the respective institutional tasks and goals, i.e., patients' or clients' change, development, or learning (see e.g., Graf et al. (eds.) 2019; Pawelczyk and Graf (eds.) (2019); Scarvaglieri 2020). Originating in (research on) psychodynamics, the 'therapeutic alliance' and its related – at times synonymously used (cf. Horvath and Luborsky 1993: 561) – term the 'working alliance' (first introduced by Greenson in 1965 as the reality-based part of the relationship in contrast to the transference dimension of the relationship) nowadays finds a pantheoretical application to helping professions in general (Bordin 1979; Horvath and Luborsky

1993; Ackerman and Hilsenroth 2003). In addition to broadening its scope, several further developments and adaptations since its origin in the works of Freud (1913) have influenced its current readings. In this vein, e.g., Zetzel (1956) was the first to differentiate aspects of transference from aspects of the 'real relationship' (later termed 'working alliance' by Greenson 1965), and Bordin, in a series of publications (e.g., 1979) elaborated on the concept of the working alliance in its distinction from the unconscious projections of the patients/clients and thereby identified three essential components of the working alliance: *tasks*, *bonds*, and *goals* (cf. Horvath and Luborsky 1993: 563–564). Another adaption was suggested by Luborsky (1976), who introduced the alliance as a dynamic rather than a static entity responsive to the changing demands of different phases of therapy: "Two types of helping alliances [used synonymously with therapeutic and working alliance; EG et al.] were identified: Type 1, more evident in the beginning of therapy, and Type 2, more typical of later phases of treatment" (Horvath and Luborsky 1993: 563).

The therapeutic/working alliance by now represents an established and verified common success factor in therapeutic interactions as well as other helping formats such as coaching and counseling and has inspired much theoretical and empirical work on helping professions from various disciplines within the social sciences (e.g., Horvath 2006; Ardito and Rabellino 2011; Spencer et al. 2019): "The strength of the alliance is arguably the best and most reliable predictor of outcomes [...] and is generally considered one of the most important common factors in therapy" (Ribeiro et al. 2013: 295; see also Horvath and Greenberg 1994; Lambert 2013; Norcross and Lambert 2018; for coaching see Baron et al. 2011; Behrendt 2012; de Haan et al. 2016; Graßmann et al. 2019; for counseling see Thurnherr 2019, in 2022). However, as already claimed by Horvath and Luborsky in 1993, "most studies of the alliance deal with the impact of the quality of the alliance on therapy outcome; we have much less research data on the specific therapist techniques that improve the relationship" (Horvath and Luborsky 1993: 568; cf. Muntigl and Horvath 2014: 328). In a similar vein, Thurnherr argues about 30 years later that "(d)espite its recognized importance for psychotherapy and counseling, how the therapeutic alliance is exactly negotiated has not been extensively researched by psychologists who use qualitative research methods" (2019: 3). And linguistic insights into how the alliance is really 'done' on the interactional micro-level across therapeutic, counseling and coaching interactions are still rare, too (but see Horvath and Muntigl 2018; Scarvaglieri 2020 for psychotherapy or Thurnherr 2019, 2022 for email counseling).

While the ongoing differentiation, specialization, and utilization of helping professions continues as one of the dominant socio-cultural trends in the 21st century (due to the therapeutization of modern society as already outlined by MacIntyre 1987; Giddens 1991; Furedi 2004; Hausendorf 2011, or the related commodification of emotions as outlined in Hochschild 1983 or Illouz 2008), another notable and far-reaching trend is the growing implementation and proliferation of online (professional) help. Computer-mediated or, more generally, electronically mediated professional helping in the realm of e-health, bears far-reaching consequences for the interaction between helper and helped and concurrently, for the verbal and non-verbal practices of establishing and maintaining a helping relationship and the helping itself (see e.g., Locher 2006; Locher and Thurnherr 2017; Stommel 2012; Stommel and te Molder 2015; Stommel and Van der Houwen 2015; Thurnherr 2022). Another, even more radical socio-cultural change in the context of organized helping is the democratization of helping expertise and the growing relevance and presence of online peer support. Such digital self-help formats do not require accredited professional expertise from their participants and are premised on a more variable participation-framework both as regards the roles of help-giver and help-seeker and as regards the timing of the helping itself. This is especially the case in asynchronous formats such as e-mail or Twitter. Although (often) not institutionalized or professionalized in the traditional sense, they nevertheless represent rule-based, situated social helping interactions based on language and other semiotic devices that spill out along their relational, interactive, contextual/situational, and processual dimensions and as such are of core interest for linguistic and pragmatic analysis.

2. Analyzing relationship management: An overview of current linguistic approaches

Documenting and analyzing – from a linguistic perspective – the verbal and non-verbal management of relationships in their respective contextual, processual and temporal embedding across a variety of organized helping contexts is at the core of this edited volume. The volume thereby sheds light on a phenomenon that is ubiquitous and elementary for all forms of social interaction (Goffman 1967; Holly 1979, 2001; Enfield 2009; Linke and Schröter (eds.) 2017) by carving out its specific characteristics across various forms of organized helping with the help of Conversation Analysis, *linguistische Gesprächsanalyse*[1], Discourse Analysis, Pragmalinguistics as well as Interpersonal Pragmatics.[2] Linguistic research on

1. *Linguistische Gesprächsanalyse* is a German research paradigm based on Conversation Analysis, which also draws on pragmatics, discourse analysis and linguistic text analysis (see Deppermann 2008).

2. Following the definition by Locher and Graham (2010: 2), interpersonal pragmatics is concerned with the "relational aspect of interactions between people" since "people adjust their language to their addressees and the situation in order to achieve interpersonal effects".

practices of relationship management in organized helping is still predominantly restricted to the particularities of specific helping formats. A contrasting – and concurrently integrative – view on verbal (and non-verbal) practices of building and managing relationships across different contexts of organized helping is so far missing. In its supra-contextual perspective, the presented research thereby builds on but goes beyond and extends existing research across a variety of related research areas. The individual chapters thereby elucidate how helping relationships are verbally (and non-verbally) initiated and established (Graf and Jautz), managed (Muntigl; Buchholz; Kabatnik et al.; Winkler; Günthner; Thurnherr; Kabatnik), adapted (Graf and Jautz; Kuna and Scarvaglieri), but also challenged (Guxholli et al.; Pawelczyk and Faccio) or repaired (Džanko) along the unfolding interactions by focusing on the respective communicative and discursive practices on the interactional micro- as well as meso-level.

While a theoretical and empirical foundation of relational management in organized helping is still scarce in the wider field of linguistics, relational management in social interaction as such has attracted substantial attention in a variety of related concepts and approaches from Interpersonal Pragmatics and neighboring research areas. In what follows we will give a brief, yet not exhaustive, overview of the most prominent concepts and aspects of this research focusing in particular on their relevance and influence on the present work.

A prominent approach in linguistic pragmatics that tackles the (verbal) management of relationships in interaction is 'rapport management' as introduced in the works of Spencer-Oatey and colleagues. Rapport is understood by Spencer-Oatey most generally as harmony amongst people and as such can be considered part and parcel of any social interaction. Rooted in linguistic politeness theory and face theory (Goffman 1967; Brown and Levinson 1987), rapport management considers (im-)politeness as (dis)harmony in social relations and aims to explore the bases on which people make their social judgements in authentic interaction. While it does aim to examine "the use of language to promote, maintain or threaten harmonious social relations" (Spencer-Oatey 2000: 3), it is more generally interested in the interrelation between language use and the management of interpersonal relations. In this sense, rapport management focuses in particular on intercultural social interactions (see most recently Spencer-Oatey and Kádár 2021). According to Spencer-Oatey (2002: 540) "rapport management involves two main components: the management of face and the management of sociality rights". In contrast to Brown and Levinson (1987), Spencer-Oatey emphasizes the social aspect of face, since she conceives not only of a "quality face" (Brown and Levinson's positive face), but also of a "social identity face" (in place of Brown and Levinson's negative face) that is defined "in terms of social or group roles and is closely associated with our sense of public worth" (Spencer-Oatey 2002: 540). Sociality rights refer to the rights to be "treated fairly" (Spencer-Oatey 2002) regarding costs/benefits as well as personal autonomy and to be able to freely associate or dissociate with or from others. Unlike earlier politeness theories, rapport management thus stresses the way people are treated by others as indicative of their social position in general as well as within the specific group in which they are currently interacting. As such, interactants do not only want to portray their own personal qualities per se (positive face/quality face), they also want to be recognized within their social roles and, vice versa, need to recognize their counterparts in this regard (social identity face, sociality rights).

Explicating the dimensions of polite vs. impolite behavior as facets of harmonious or disharmonious social relations, rapport management delineates the basic and underlying conditions for successful relationship building. In this vein, politeness must also be understood as basis for successfully building and managing relationships dedicated to helping, i.e., polite behavior represents a necessary, but (as the contributions to this volume illustrate) not sufficient condition. While impolite behavior by (professional) helpers and patients/clients would render social interactions as those described in this volume impossible, professional helpers, particularly in the therapeutic contexts at times strategically challenge patients and threaten their "quality face", for instance by infringing on the principles of epistemic authority (Heritage 2013) (see e.g., the contributions by Muntigl or Pawelczyk and Faccio in this volume). As detailed in these contributions, in such moments help-seeker and help-provider employ specific relationship management techniques such as retreating from their initial position or rephrasing their intervention to save face and to repair rapport (cf. Scarvaglieri 2020). (Im)politeness thus forms an essential part of generic relationship management and applying strategies and competencies of rapport management (Spencer-Oatey and Franklin 2009) provides a necessary condition for interaction in helping contexts. Yet, politeness and face-saving strategies do not suffice to build and manage helping relationships in ways that enable and guarantee the clients' development, learning and change.

Relational aspects of communication have also been discussed in (interpersonal) pragmatic and interactional research via the neighboring concept of 'relational work' (see the work of Locher and colleagues and for a summary most recently Thurnherr 2022), which draws on (im)politeness, facework and rapport management in general, but also moves beyond that (cf. Locher and Schnurr 2017: 690). Relational work is defined by Locher and Watts (2008: 96) as "the work invested by individuals in the construction, maintenance, reproduction and transformation of interpersonal relationships among those engaged in social practice". As further argued by Locher and Watts (2005: 10), "[…] human beings rely crucially on others to be able to realize their life goals and aspirations"; concrete aims and goals such as receiving help with a health or emotional issue thereby serves as a prime motivation for humans to seek relationship and cooperation with others.

The concept 'relational work' foregrounds a perspective that perceives interpersonal interaction, face work and rapport not as something that emerges naturally and unintentionally in conversation; instead, relational work is understood by Locher as something that interactants engage in strategically and into which social actors invest time and communicative effort. Pragmatic research on relational work has documented and analyzed practices such as apologizing, criticizing, praising, mitigating, using humor etc. on the basic assumption that interpersonal work is created through discursive practices and that language is always salient in the negotiation of relationships; moreover, research has looked into the impact such strategies have on the ongoing interactions as well as the construction of the participants' identities[3] (cf. Thurnherr 2019: 4). This perspective is relevant in the institutional contexts investigated in this volume because, as evidenced by the contributions, patients/clients and particularly institutional helping agents consciously construct, monitor and manage their relationships and apply various communicative, verbal and non-verbal, techniques to do so. Concurrently, the participants' verbal and non-verbal engagement in relational work is molded by and adapted to the existing social norms in specific contexts (cf. Locher and Watts 2005: 11), i.e., relational work is adapted to what is considered appropriate in a specific therapeutic or medical context, in certain cultural contexts or in certain (social) media (cf. Locher 2012: 47). More recent research applying the concept of relational work in helping contexts has focused e.g., on genetic counseling (Zayts and Schnurr 2011, 2014), email counseling (Thurnherr 2019, 2022 and this volume) as well as (e-)health contexts (Locher and Thurnherr 2017; Locher and Schnurr 2017).

Finally, as regards concrete linguistic and communicative means that bear on relationship management in interactions dedicated to helping and beyond, research in Conversation Analysis and Discourse Analysis has evinced the following findings: Scarvaglieri (2013) claims for psychotherapy that the relationship between therapist and patient is managed on various levels of interaction via different verbal and non-verbal mechanisms on the interactive meso- and micro-level such as e.g., turn-taking, sequentiality, initiation and processing of topics, pauses and intonation as well as the spatial positioning of the participants. These relational

3. While identity construction – as elaborated in the context of Positioning Theory as put forth by Davies and Harré (1990) as well as in socio-constructivist approaches to identity as put forth originally by Bucholtz and Hall (2005) – plays an important role in relationship management due to, among other things, the relational and discursive nature of identity (cf. Thurnherr 2019: 22ff), these concepts are not further detailed here as the focus of this edited volume is on relationship management of the helping dyads themselves, not so much on the individual partners' positioning and identities.

means are used in ways that thoroughly engages and activates the patient. Such "recipient-centeredness" (Scarvaglieri 2017) contributes to building and managing the therapeutic relationship and concurrently prepares the grounds for change (Scarvaglieri 2020) (see Graf and Jautz in this volume and their concept of 'client-centeredness' and its contribution to managing the relationship between coach and client). Also located on the interactive meso-level, Graf (2019) defines "Building a Relationship" as one of the four basic activities of coaching (Graf 2019: 69ff and 127ff). The activity builds on various communicative tasks such as 'Establishing the roles and identities 'coach' and 'client'' (Graf 2019: 130ff) or 'Negotiating hierarchy in an asymmetrical relationship' (Graf 2019: 146ff) and serves as the matrix against which all other activities of coaching transpire. In this sense, building and managing the relationship represents a "permanent task" in helping professional interaction (Spranz-Fogasy 1992) that underlies all other communicative tasks that the participants engage in when doing helping. On the interactional micro-level, research by Muntigl, Horvath and others (e.g., Muntigl et al. 2012; Muntigl and Horvath 2014) addresses practices of dis-/affiliation and dis-/alignment in various forms of therapy as sequential achievements. Such practices of micro-managing the interpersonal relationship are vital for successful therapy, as therapists often carry out actions that violate the principle of epistemic authority (Heritage 2013) and strain the therapeutic relationship (Muntigl et al. 2013; Weiste et al. 2016). Therefore, therapists employ specific conversational mechanisms to uphold an otherwise endangered working relationship such as downgrading, re-framing or explaining their interventions (Scarvaglieri 2020: 11f). In addition, linguistic research has at least in passing documented and analyzed relational management from a temporal and developmental perspective alongside (therapy) sessions and processes (Graf and Jautz 2019; Trasmundi and Philipsen 2020; Scarvaglieri 2020).

In 2010 Arundale claimed that despite prolific discussions of the linguistic and discursive management of relationships in the context of '(im)politeness', 'face-work', 'relational work', 'relating' or 'rapport management' and the fact that "human language use is inextricably linked to phenomena that involve human beings in relationship to one another, however, matters of language use within the relationships that humans create and enact with one another have received comparatively little attention" (2010: 137). In 2022, the gamut and scope of linguistic findings as regards discursive practices of relationship management tells a different story. Yet, a systematic linguistic exploration of how relationships are locally and discursively managed in social interactions both in traditional and innovative formats of organized helping is still missing. This is where the current volume is located.

3. The current volume: Aims and scope, research questions and methodology

Late modern society has witnessed a marked socio-cultural appreciation of the importance of helping professional interactions and more generally, of organized helping, as well as the entailed relationship building as part of its overall therapeutic culture that builds on expert-systems and a commodified emotionality. Against this background, the present volume is both relevant and timely. It brings together research that investigates "the entire gamut of interpersonal effects" (Locher 2012: 45) that linguistic and communicative means have on relationships and thereby contributes to a better understanding of how social agents create relational effects by means of language in organized contexts of helping. According to Enfield (2009: 60), human beings are continually designing and interpreting utterances in view of their relationships with the persons with whom they are engaged and therefore, the forming and maintaining of relationships is "a primary locus of social organization" to be addressed in research on how persons use language in everyday and organized settings.

While health issues in medical and therapeutic interactions build the volume's primary thematic scope (see the contributions by Muntigl, Buchholz, Guxholli et al., Pawelczyk and Faccio, Kabatnik et al., Günthner, Kuna and Scarvaglieri as well as by Džanko), the book also offers a discussion of relationship management in business/executive coaching as a non-health form of organized helping (see the contributions by Winkler and by Graf and Jautz). Beyond detailing "helper – patient/client relationships" in offline helping formats, the discussed organized helping interactions also include professional online help in e-mail counseling (the contribution by Thurnherr) as well as self-help or peer-to-peer help via Twitter (the contribution by Kabatnik). Including such research builds a bridge between the presence and the future of relational practices in formal and informal helping contexts. The volume's overall goal is to deepen our linguistic understanding of the (sequential) co-construction of helping relationships in traditional as well as more recent formats. It focuses in particular on the entailed micro- and meso-level communicative and discursive practices and their unfolding interactive and linguistic morphology within and across the sessions or communicative events. It also aims to carve out commonalities and differences in how psychotherapy, doctor-patient interaction, coaching and counseling "do" helping relationships as emerging situated practice. To this aim, in addition to the individual contributions that focus on the management of particular helping relationships, a synthesizing chapter summarizes and juxtaposes the findings and allows for a more macro-pragmatic perspective on how helpers and helped interactively and communicatively relate with each other (Scarvaglieri and Graf this volume). Such a supra-format understanding of the pragmatics of helping relationships also allows to dovetail these insights into current interdisciplinary research on the more general phenomenon of helping as a social practice as outlined in Böhringer, Hitzler and Richter (2022).

Given the underlying assumption that organized forms of helping in general and helping relations in particular are interactively co-constructed in and through language, a key research question across all contributions in this volume addresses the specific communicative practices that participants apply to manage their relationships. Each contribution identifies particular discursive practices that initiate and build up a new relationship, regulate or maintain an existing relationship or are designed to repair a relationship that has been negatively affected by any specific preceding action. In so doing, all contributions implicitly or explicitly address the progressive dimension of relationship building. Since most of the explored organized helping interactions span the continuum of multiple sessions or contacts, the relationship between helping practitioners and clients/persons receiving help needs to be developed and managed not only within one isolated encounter, but across multiple sessions during the entire organized process. While some contributions focus on first sessions as the onset of the helping relationship and address the particular affordances of these first encounters (e.g., Graf and Jautz), others such as the chapter by Kuna and Scarvaglieri address processes of relationship building across the continuum of the entire treatment. While longitudinal studies on communicative phenomena and how these develop along several sessions in the sense of "supra-session courses of action" (Bercelli et al. 2013; see also Bercelli et al. 2008; Voutilainen et al. 2011, 2018 and Peräkylä 2019) represent a relatively recent and incipient research field, many research gaps still exist. The current volume contributes to closing some of them.

Given the influence of specific media affordances on the type of relation that can be built and on the relational practices that can and must be employed by the participants (Muntigl et al. 2013; Stommel and Te Molder 2015; Linke and Schröter 2017), another empirical focus addresses the medium in and through which the helping relationship materializes (cf. Ekberg et al. 2016; Berger 2017; Van Daele et al. 2020; Kysely et al. 2022). While most contributions draw on face-to-face interaction in the context of verbal communication, embodied practices of relationship building and their combination with verbal practices are at the center of the contribution by Muntigl. In addition to face-to-face settings, the volume also includes studies on the affordances of building and managing relationships in digital discourse (Thurnherr, Kabatnik). There, the lack of a physical co-presence of the interactors and a possible asynchronicity of the interaction necessitate a diverging, often quite sophisticated, handling of the delicate matter of relationships via a variety of semiotic resources (cf. Marx 2019). Forms of digital help and non-professional, peer-to-peer helping (cf. Schmitt 1997; Pick and Scarvaglieri 2019; Wakke and Heller 2022) and helping relationships have recently emerged as a major trend: People thereby receive digital help and support on the internet or through messenger services (Bliesener 2015; Czech et al. 2018) in the forms of e-psychotherapy (Dirkse 2015; Poltrum et al. 2020; Giesler 2019; Thurnherr this volume), e-coaching (Ribbers and Waringa 2015; Weinzinger 2016), or self-help forums (Lindholm 2017; Hünniger 2019) as well as through illness-related networking on social media platforms such as Facebook, Twitter or Instagram (de Choudhury et al. 2014; Andalibi et al. 2017; Scherr and Schmitt 2018; Kabatnik this volume). Research on digital helping not only allows for a comparative view on the influence of the communicative medium on practices of relationship building and management, but also pays theoretical and empirical tribute to processes which will shape helping (professional) interactions to a much greater extent in the (near) future.

A further focus of the volume is on how practitioners and clients and more generally helping dyads link process and practices of relationship building to the pursuit of their respective (institutional) goals. As argued above, the working alliance is regarded as an essential cornerstone for success and effectiveness in helping professions. The contributions in this volume illustrate how relationships are locally managed in the specific interactive format in a way that allows to achieve the respective institutional goals – i.e., the healing of psychic or somatic illnesses, the development of managerial skills, the solving of specific problems or the overcoming of physical restrictions. As such, the volume links current linguistic insights into relationship building in organized forms of helping to research on how change and development, conceptualized as the achievement of goals of helping interactions, are discursively co-constructed by a helping agent and a help-receiving client (Graf and Spranz-Fogasy 2018; Graf et al. 2019; Pawelczyk and Graf 2019). By tackling these key factors in professional forms of organized helping that contribute and secure the attainment of institutional goals, the chapters in this volume are of immense practical value, too. The contributions draw a detailed picture of how specific communicative and interactive practices affect the relationship with a client, which practices are helpful to establish or mold a relationship or how a strained relationship can be repaired on the linguistic micro. or meso-level. Practitioners can thereby find evidence-based and empirically supported stimuli for their own helping work. This practical merit is strengthened by the double competence of several contributors, who not only work as discourse researchers, but also as practitioners across various helping professions (incl. Michael Buchholz, Eva-Maria Graf, and Anssi Peräkylä). Another equally important practical value of such research is its application in the training and supervision context of (future) professionals: discourse-analytic findings as regards the interactive specificities of their professional doing could and should be integrated in trainings and feedback and the respective manuals for doctors, therapists, coaches, counselors etc. (see e.g., Brünner and Pick 2020).

As regards the methods applied, the volume is characterized by a high methodological homogeneity – all contributions work with authentic conversational data and apply established methods from the realms of Conversation Analysis, Discourse Analysis and Interpersonal Pragmatics; in addition, Corpus Linguistics and Interactional Linguistics are drawn upon. The empirical base of (video and audio) recordings of helping interactions used in all contributions documents interactive practices of in-situ construction, managing, and adapting relationships, which allows for a detailed sequential and processual analysis of those practices. The volume thereby addresses a vital methodological desideratum, as most established research on relationships in helping professions is based on "questionnaires or checklist-type measures" (Muntigl and Horvath 2014: 328) about the perceived quality of the relationship, yet not on authentic data that documents the actual performance of relationships (cf. Elvins and Green 2008; Norcross and Lambert 2018; Graßmann et al. 2019). In addition, the volume offers insights into the rewarding combination of both conversational and interview data (Thurnherr) or conversational, discourse and ethnographic data (Kuna and Scarvaglieri) as well as of different (quantitative and qualitative) methods as found in the contribution by Kabatnik (Corpus Linguistics and Interactional Linguistics). And finally, the volume goes beyond documenting and analyzing the pragmatics of relationship building in organized contexts of helping: The contribution by Winkler illustrates how qualitative linguistic insights gained with the help of Conversation Analysis can be turned into a coding material with the practical aim to offer video-based feedback for coaches. Such practice-oriented Conversation Analysis was already promoted by Antaki (2011) and Stivers (2015) and practiced e.g., in Stokoe's Conversation Analytic Role Play Method (CARM) (2014); it represents one of the desiderata where Conversation Analysis and other qualitative linguistic research of (professional) interaction should move into the future.

4. The contributions

The first five contributions of the edited volume by **Muntigl**, **Buchholz**, **Guxholli et al.**, **Pawelczyk** and **Faccio** as well as by **Kabatnik et al.** focus on relationship building in different therapeutic settings.

In *Forging relationships in psychotherapeutic interaction*, **Muntigl** illustrates the central role that talk and conduct play in therapist-client relationship-building; while he presents this relationship as an ongoing interactional achievement, he shows how it is either constituted as part of a focused activity, or as incidental to the main business of the conversation. Analyzing a diverse corpus of video-taped psychotherapy sessions with the help of Conversation Analysis, Muntigl thereby focuses on how therapist-client relationship might be conceptualized in the context of general sociological categories such as 'intimate', 'close' or 'friend', which interactional practices may be 'typically' used to forge such relationships and how shifts in the quality of relationships can be mapped by examining talk.

Buchholz in *Doing We – Working alliance in psychotherapeutic relationships. A recursive model* targets the problem of "larger chunks", i.e., the question how details of narratives and conversation can be brought together not only in, but also between sessions, within the context of the working alliance. Buchholz proposes two approaches to "larger chunks". Following Ginzburg and Poesio (2016), he first analyses hesitation markers as conversational equivalents to embodied pointing gestures. Using the concept of "tacit comparisons", he demonstrates how patients use this to indicate a connection between different stories told. Secondly, Buchholz proposes a recursive model of common ground with four *steps* of (1) pointing to a –perceptual or interactive– object, (2) addressing it, (3) linking it with other conversational objects and, in case of an interactive object, (4) creating a metaphor. Recursion starts when the metaphor is treated *as if* it were a perceptual object; then, the cycle starts with step (1) ("pointing") again. According to Buchholz, the new metaphor thus indicates an important change.

Guxholli et al. in their contribution *What about you? Responding to a face-threatening question in psychotherapy*, discuss patients' efforts to mitigate potential damage to the therapeutic relation. Data comes from 47 video recorded sessions of psychoanalytic, psychodynamic, and cognitive-behavioural psychotherapies conducted in Albanian language. When the therapist questions or challenges the patient's experience of self, this disaffiliating action poses a threat to the patient's face and consequently to the therapeutic relation. Analysis of 24 sequences predominantly occurring in psychoanalytic psychotherapy and psychodynamic psychotherapy reveals that in response to therapists' face-threatening questions, patients resist the transformation of the experience of self by choosing to save their face but not without making considerable efforts to save the therapeutic relation first. The authors conclude that challenging the patient's experience of self is a delicate task in terms of working alliance between the therapist and patient.

The paper by **Pawelczyk** and **Faccio**, *So let's say men can't understand that much: Gender and relational practices in psychotherapy with women suffering from eating disorders*, examines, with the help of Conversation Analysis and Membership Categorization Analysis, how gender is invoked, drawn upon, resisted and interactionally managed in view of the respective session's specific goals. The authors look at three extracts of two psychotherapy sessions, originally in Italian, between a female therapist – working within the interactionist and socio-constructionist approach – and a woman patient suffering from eating disorders and depression. The analyses reveal how the female patient relies on gender as category-sharing to account for her actions and to seek understanding. The therapist, on the other hand, tends to resist the category-sharing, which may jeopardize the evolving therapeutic relationship, yet allows her to accomplish the goals of the session. Concurrently, she is at times engaging the patient in extensive local work around gender categories to foreground her voice and account for her daily struggle with the illness. It is concluded that female psychotherapists should be particularly attuned to the invoking of category-sharing and critically consider its relevance and application against the background of both maintaining a good working relationship and pursuing the institutional goals.

In the final paper on therapeutic interactions, *Relationship management by means of Solution-Oriented Questions in psychodiagnostic interviews*, **Kabatnik et al.** address the eliciting practice Solution Oriented Questions (SOQs) as an interactional tool for relationship building in psychodiagnostic interviews applying Conversation Analysis and German Gesprächsanalyse on 15 videotaped first interviews. Therapeutic alliance results from the concordance of alignment, as willingness to cooperate regarding common goals, and of affiliation, as relationship based upon trust. The authors argue that SOQs particularly allow for both: Solution Oriented Questions are situated at the end of a troublesome thematic unit, which is linked to low agency on the patient's side; yet the formulation of SOQs in a hypothetical, speculative manner serve to relieve the patient of actual responsibilities and to stimulate their self-reflection. SOQs thus lead to an expansion of the patient's agency, to the restructuring of knowledge, and thereby to potential change as a common goal. Concurrently, SOQs reveal understanding of and interest in the patient and their use leads to affiliation via alignment and intersubjectivity, strengthening and securing the therapeutic alliance.

The next two chapters investigate relationship building in the helping format "coaching":

Winkler's contribution, *The role of semi-responsive answers for relationship building in coaching*, is based on the hypothesis that clients' semi-responsive answers are of particular relevance for any coaching process as they reveal ambivalences, (inner) conflicts, uncertainties and/or opposition which ought to be noticed and appropriately addressed by the coach. The chapter first discusses theoretical and methodological aspects in the context of a Conversation Analysis-based manual to study structures of coaching interaction, illustrates a coding-system to identify semi-responsive answers, and, based on transcribed data, analyzes semi-responsive answers with respect to how they are addressed by the coaches. The analysis of 21 face-to-face coaching sessions (64 hours) in Swiss and Standard German reveals that semi-responsive answers are both a valuable source of information and a challenge as they require the coach to maintain a balance between facilitating the process and maintaining a good relationship with the client.

Graf and **Jautz**' paper *Working alliance and client design as discursive achievements in first sessions of executive coaching* explores the coaching alliance as a locally emerging, joint product of coach and clients' negotiation process regarding their relational, procedural, and interactional expectations for their joint coaching engagement. The paper's focus is on the first sessions of two different coach-client dyads, analyzed within an integrative discourse analytic framework. Data stems from a corpus of Emotional Intelligent coaching and is originally in German. Adapting the Basic Activity Model of Coaching (Graf 2019), the authors examine how coach and client use different discursive and relational practices in the context of 'Getting started', 'Voicing expectations regarding coach, coaching and coaching alliance' and 'Negotiating the expectations'. The analyses show how the coach displays a specific 'client design' in the local discursive management of the working alliance: While establishing her own institutional identity as coach by introducing her expertise and managing the coaching agenda, she concurrently attunes her discursive and relational practices to the specificities of the individual clients, their identity constructions and their epistemics of experience and of expertise.

Next, **Günthner**, **Kuna** and **Scarvaglieri** as well as **Džanko's** papers are dedicated to relationship building in doctor-patient interactions.

Günthner in *Relationship building in oncological doctor-patient interaction: the use of address forms as 'tie signs'* focuses on practices of relationship building between oncologists and their patients during oncological consultations when a definitive diagnosis of malignancy must be communicated. In such consultations oncologists have to cope with two tasks: (1) to inform their patients of clinical evidence of the cancer diagnosis and about the details of the disease, and (2) to propose and negotiate treatment therapies. Based on 40 consultations, the article analyzes the sequential construction of the doctor-patient relationship with special focus on physicians' use of terms of address. Drawing on Conversation Analysis and Interactional Linguistics, relationship building is presented as an ongoing task doctors and patients engage in. The data reveal that oncologists frequently address their patients by name in opening and closing sequences as well as during the core part of the interaction. With that doctors document heightened attention to their patients and lend the clinical interaction a more personal and intimate quality. Personalized address forms thus index 'withness' in the sense of Goffman (1971) and serve as a relationship building tool in these clinical contexts.

Kuna and **Scarvaglieri** contribute *Practices of Relationship Building in Hungarian Primary Care. Communicative Styles and Intergenerational Differences.* In doctor-patient interaction they claim a key role for relationship building which unfolds dynamically in the course of interaction and which is subject to larger socio-cultural developments. Using data from Hungarian primary care consultations, they focus on the role of address forms and metapragmatic reflections and discuss intergenerational change in doctor-patient communication. Hungarian physicians (interactively) build different types of relationships: Physicians who have recently participated in communication trainings employ a more flexible and egalitarian style of managing relationships involving the patient in therapeutic decisions and explaining their suggestions. Older physicians who have not received communication training build more hierarchical relationships and adapt less to the individual patient, instead relying on a more personalized style of interaction. The authors correlate the different types of relationship building with the respective socio-political era and with shifts in healthcare communication in general.

Džanko's paper on *Building (dis-)affiliative medical relationships through interactional practices of knowledge management. A comparative study of German and Bosnian medical encounters* sheds light on how building a relationship between doctor and patient is extremely sensitive to possessing and demonstrating epistemic rights. In particular, the paper focuses on (dys-)functional knowledge management indexed by a conflict involving epistemics. Comparing 42 audiotaped conversations of Bosnian and German doctors with their patients with the help of Conversation Analysis reveals that Bosnian patients display an inability to provide the requested information or display reduced access to information they are accountable for. Interactional practices of dysfunctional knowledge management thereby lead to misunderstandings, a break in the progressivity of the interaction, or face threatening actions such as criticism and disciplining of the patient, i.e., bear negatively on the relationship. In contrast, the German data evinces that patients display higher medical knowledge and more personal responsibility. A more patient-centered approach which entails more active patient participation and a higher affiliation of doctors with their patients thereby allows for a functioning knowledge management.

The edited volume ends with two chapters focusing on digital instead of analogical relationship building: In her contribution *How are you getting on with this? Fostering clients' involvement in the therapeutic alliance in email counseling* **Thurnherr** explores how a counselor uses requests to encourage clients to actively participate in the therapeutic alliance in email counseling. Five naturally occurring email counseling exchanges between one counselor and five clients are examined through content and discourse analysis, adding insight from a practitioner interview. Thurnherr investigates different ways a counselor involves her clients in the therapeutic process taking in consideration the affordances of the medium. Analyses reveal that the counselor carefully considers the clients' face-concerns and that she safeguards the therapeutic alliance through intricate relational work. This relational work also constructs clients as active participants in the therapeutic alliance who have expertise not only on their troubles, but also on their resources and who can provide solutions. Whereas some medium affordances such as emoticons are used to carry out relational work, the counselor also deals with asynchronicity that is at times a helpful resource and at times a challenge.

Kabatnik analyzes *in Twitter as a helping medium: Relationship building through German hashtag #depression* the German discourse space #depression on Twitter regarding relationship building. She uses a corpus of #depression tweets as well as follow-up communication as database. In the #depression discourse space, users suffering from depression initiate social exchange surrounding the shared emotional and medical state of being depressed. This is realized interactively via narration, the formulation of wishes, questions or requests, which evoke further reactions of the community. Through (un)commented retweeting, direct addressing and multiple keywording using hashtags, users can express common views and their appreciation, maintain their contacts within the network and be heard in different spaces of discourse. Concurrently, users can reverse the relationship between 'helper' and 'helped' and as such lend or receive support. Twitter thus can act as a helping medium for people in crisis situations through multiple forms of social support from the community in the #depression discourse space.

The final contribution *Relational dimensions of organized helping professions – Findings and Implications* by **Scarvaglieri and Graf** juxtaposes the contributions of this volume as regards overarching relational dimensions and offers these as a potential meta-language of researching helping relationships. Dimensions identified include the participants engaging in a helping interaction ('personal dimension'), verbal and non-verbal techniques and methods of establishing and managing relationships ('linguistic and discursive dimension'), the theoretical and empirical connection between relationships and the purpose of communication in organized helping ('functional dimension'), the development of relationships over time from abstract socio-historical perspectives as well as within the confines of a particular dyad ('temporal dimension'), the medium of interaction/communication and its effects on the relationship ('medial dimension') as well as the influence of social categories on relationship building ('identity dimension'). Based on the research presented here, Scarvaglieri and Graf also suggest a refined definition of relationships from an interactional perspective and point out methodological challenges and options for future language and discourse-based research on relationships.

References

Ackerman, Steven J., and Mark J. Hilsenroth. 2003. "A Review of Therapist Characteristics and Techniques Positively Impacting the Therapeutic Alliance." *Clinical Psychology Review* 23 (1): 1–33. https://doi.org/10.1016/S0272-7358(02)00146-0.

American Psychological Association (APA). 2020. "APA Dictionary of Psychology: Helping Professions." *Accessed January 25th, 2022.* https://dictionary.apa.org/helping-professions.

Andalibi, Nazanin, Pinar Ozturk, and Andrea Forte. 2017. "Sensitive Self-disclosures, Responses, and Social Support on Instagram: The Case of #Depression". *Proceedings of the 2017 ACM Conference on Computer Supported Cooperative Work and Social Computing*, 1485–1500. https://doi.org/10.1145/2998181.2998243

Antaki, Charles. 2011. "Six Kinds of Applied Conversation Analysis." In *Applied Conversation Analysis. Palgrave Advances in Linguistics*, ed. by Charles Antaki, 1–14. London: Palgrave Macmillan.

Ardito, Rita B., and Daniela Rabellino. 2011. "Therapeutic Alliance and Outcome of Psychotherapy: Historical Excursus, Measurements, and Prospects for Research." *Frontiers in Psychology* 270: 1–11. https://doi.org/10.3389/fpsyg.2011.00270

Arundale, Robert. 2010. "Relating." In *Interpersonal Pragmatics* (Vol. Handbooks of Pragmatics), ed. by Miriam A. Locher, and Sage L. Graham, 137–167. Berlin: Mouton. https://doi.org/10.1515/9783110214338.1.137

Arundale, Robert. 2021. "Toward a Pragmatics of Relating in Conversational Interaction." *Journal of Pragmatics* 179: 19–25. https://doi.org/10.1016/j.pragma.2021.04.018

Baron, Louis, Luci Morin, and Denis Morin. 2011. "Executive Coaching: The Effect of Working Alliance Discrepancy on the Development of Coachees' Self-efficacy." *Journal of Management Development* 30 (9): 847–864. https://doi.org/10.1108/02621711111164330

Behrendt, Peter. 2012. "Freiburger Erfolgsfaktoren-Coaching – Vier Erfolgsfaktoren zur Etablierung von Konsistenz bei Coachees Erfolgsstrategien im Coaching." *Zeitschrift für Organisationsberatung, Supervision und Coaching* 19 (1): 391–404. https://doi.org/10.1007/s11613-012-0296-7

Bercelli, Fabrizio, Federico Rossano, and Maurizio Viaro. 2008. "Clients 'Responses to Therapists' Reinterpretations." In *Conversation Analysis and Psychotherapy*, ed. by Anssi Peräkylä, Charles Antaki, Sanna Vehviläinen, and Ivan Leudar, 43–61. Cambridge: Cambridge University Press. https://doi.org/10.1017/CBO9780511490002.004

Bercelli, Fabrizio, Federico Rossano, and Maurizio Viaro. 2013. "Supra-session Courses of Action in Psychotherapy." *Journal of Pragmatics* 57: 118–137. https://doi.org/10.1016/j.pragma.2013.08.001

Berger, Thomas. 2017. "The Therapeutic Alliance in Internet Interventions: A Narrative Review and Suggestions for Future Research." *Psychotherapy Research* 27(5): 511–524. https://doi.org/10.1080/10503307.2015.1119908.

Bliesener, Thomas. 2015. "Das Modellprojekt TKK-ELF: Telekonferenzen für Patienten in Isolation. Anlage, Durchführung, Ergebnisse, Empfehlungen." In *Telekommunikation gegen Isolation*, ed. by Jens Loenhoff and Walter Schmitz, 31–150. Wiesbaden: Springer VS. https://doi.org/10.1007/978-3-658-10646-1_2

Böhring, Daniela, Sara Hitzler, and Martina Richter. 2022. *Helfen. Situative und organisationale Ausprägungen einer unterbestimmten Praxis.* Bielefeld: Transcript Verlag.

Bordin, Edward S. 1979. "The Generalizability of the Psychoanalytic Concept of the Working Alliance." *Psychotherapy: Theory, Research and Practice* 16 (3): 252–260. https://doi.org/10.1037/h0085885

Brown, Penelope, and Stephen Levinson. 1987. "Universals in Language Usage: Politeness Phenomena." In *Questions and Politeness: Strategies in Social Interaction*, ed. by Esther N. Goody, 56–289. Cambridge, New York: CUP.

Brünner, Gisela. 2005. "Arzt-Patient-Kommunikation als Experten-Laien Kommunikation". In *Psychosomatische Gesprächsführung in der Frauenheilkunde. Ein interdisziplinärer Ansatz zur verbalen Interaktion*, ed. by Mechthild Neises, Susanne Ditz, and Thomas Spranz-Fogasy, 90–109. Stuttgart: Wissenschaftliche Verlagsgesellschaft.

Brünner, Gisela, and Ina Pick. 2020. "Bewertungen sprachlichen Handelns und Good Practice in der Angewandten Gesprächsforschung. Methodische Vorschläge für praxisorientierte Forschung." *Zeitschrift für Angewandte Linguistik* 72 (1): 63–98. https://doi.org/10.1515/zfal-2020-2025

Buber, Martin. 2008. *Du und Ich*. Stuttgart: Reclam.

Bucholtz, Mary, and Kira Hall. 2005. "Identity and Interaction: A Sociocultural Linguistic Approach. *Discourse Studies* 7 (4–5): 585–614. https://doi.org/10.1177/1461445605054407

Combs, Arthur, and David M. Gonzalez. 1994. *Helping Relationships: Basic Concepts for the Helping Professions*. Boston: Allyn and Bacon.

Czech, Olaf M., Klaus Podoll, and Frank Schneider. 2018. "Nutzung sozialer Medien durch stationäre Psychotherapie-Patienten." *Der Nervenarzt* 89 (9): 1049–1053. https://doi.org/10.1007/s00115-017-0384-1

Davies, Bronwyn, and Rom Harré. 1990. "Positioning: The Discursive Production of Selves". *Journal for the Theory of Social Behaviour* 20 (1): 43–63. https://doi.org/10.1111/j.1468-5914.1990.tb00174.x

De Choudhury, Munmun, and Sushovan De. 2014. "Mental Health Discourse on Reddit: Self-disclosure, Social Support, and Anonymity. *Proceedings of the International AAAI Conference on Web and Social Media* 8 (1): 71–80.

De Haan Eric, Andrew Grant, Yvonne Burger and Per Olof Eriksson. 2016. "A Large-scale Study of Executive and Workplace Coaching: The Relative Contributions of Relationship, Personality Match, and Self-efficacy." *Consulting Psychology Journal: Practice and Research* 68 (3): 189–207. https://doi.org/10.1037/cpb0000058

Deppermann, Arnulf. 2008. *Gespräche Analysieren: Eine Einführung*. 4th ed. Wiesbaden: VS. https://doi.org/10.1007/978-3-531-91973-7

Dirkse, Dale, Heather Hadjistavropoulos, Hugo Hesser, and Azy Barak. 2015. "Linguistic Analysis of Communication in Therapist-assisted Internet-delivered Cognitive Behavior Therapy for Generalized Anxiety Disorder." *Cognitive Behaviour Therapy* 44 (1): 21–32. https://doi.org/10.1080/16506073.2014.952773

Ekberg, Stuart, Alison Shaw, David Kessler, Alice Malpass, and Rebecca Barnes. 2016. "Orienting to Emotion in Computer-mediated Cognitive Behavioral Therapy." *Research on Language and Social Interaction* 49 (4): 310–324. https://doi.org/10.1080/08351813.2016.1199085

Elvins, Rachel, and Jonathan Green. 2008. "The Conceptualization and Measurement of Therapeutic Alliance: An Empirical Review." *Clinical Psychology Review* 28 (7): 1167–1187. https://doi.org/10.1016/j.cpr.2008.04.002

Enfield, Nick. 2009. "Relationship Thinking and Human Pragmatics." *Journal of Pragmatics* 41: 60–78. https://doi.org/10.1016/j.pragma.2008.09.007

Fietze, Beate. 2011. "Profilbildung und Statuskonkurrenz. Zur Bedeutung der Distinktionsstrategien im Professionalisierungsprozess von Supervision und Coaching." In *Beratung, Coaching, Supervision. Multidisziplinäre Perspektiven vernetzt*, ed. by Eva-Maria Graf, Sabine Rettinger, Ina Pick, and Yasmin Aksu, 23-36. Wiesbaden: VS Verlag für Sozialwissenschaften. https://doi.org/10.1007/978-3-531-93341-2

Fietze, Beate. 2015. "Coaching auf dem Weg zur Profession? Eine professionssoziologische Einordnung." In *Die Professionalisierung von Coaching. Ein Lesebuch für den professionellen Coach*, ed. by Astrid Schreyögg, and Christoph Schmidt-Lellek, 3–23. Wiesbaden: Springer VS. https://doi.org/10.1007/978-3-658-08172-0_1

Freud, Sigmund. 1913. "On the Beginning of Treatment: Further Recommendations on the Technique of Psychoanalysis." In *The Standard Edition of the Complete Psychological Works of Sigmund Freud*, ed. by James Strachey (trans.), 122–144. London: Hogarth Press.

Furedi, Frank. 2004. *Therapy Culture. Cultivating Vulnerability in an Uncertain Age*. London: Routledge.

Giddens, Anthony. 1991. *Modernity and Self-Identity. Self and Society in Late Modern Age*. Stanford: Stanford University Press.

Giesler, Laura. 2019. "Referential Activity in the E-Therapy Program "Look at Your Drinking" – A Text-Mining Approach." Bachelor Thesis, University of Twente.

Ginzburg, Jonathan, and Massimo Poesio. 2016. "Grammar Is a System That Characterizes Talk in Interaction". *Frontiers in Psychology* 7: 1–22. https://doi.org/10.3389/fpsyg.2016.01938

Goffman, Erving. 1967. *Interaction Ritual: Essays on Face-to-Face Behavior*. Chicago: Aldine.

Goffman, Erving. 1971. *The Presentation of Self in Everyday Life*. London: Pelican Books.

Goffman, Erving. 1983. "The Interaction Order." *American Sociological Review* 48 (1): 1–17. https://doi.org/10.2307/2095141

Goodwin, Charles. 1994. "Professional Vision." *American Anthropologist* 96 (3), 606–633. https://doi.org/10.1525/aa.1994.96.3.02a00100

Graf, Eva-Maria. 2012. "'Yes then I Will Tell you maybe a Little bit about the Procedure' – Constructing Professional Identities where there Is not yet a Profession: The Case of Executive Coaching." In *Constructing Identities at Work*, ed. by Jo Angouri and Meredith Marra, 129–151. Basingstoke: Palgrave Macmillan.

Graf, Eva-Maria. 2019. *The Pragmatics of Executive Coaching. Pragmatics & Beyond New Series*. Amsterdam: John Benjamins. https://doi.org/10.1075/pbns.303

Graf, Eva-Maria, Marlene Sator, and Thomas Spranz-Fogasy. 2014. "Discourses of Helping Professions: Concepts and Contextualization." In *Discourses of Helping Professions*, ed. by Eva-Maria Graf, Marlene Sator, and Thomas Spranz-Fogasy, 1–12. Amsterdam/ Philadelphia: John Benjamins. https://doi.org/10.1075/pbns.252.01gra

Graf, Eva-Maria, and Thomas Spranz-Fogasy. 2018. "Helfende Berufe – Helfende Interaktionen." In *Handbuch Text und Gespräch*, ed. by Karin Birkner, and Nina Janich, 418–442. Amsterdam: de Gruyter Mouton. https://doi.org/10.1515/9783110296051-017

Graf, Eva-Maria, and Sabine Jautz. 2019. "Und wie, wie entsteht Veränderung. Und damit habens wir ja auch mit dir zu tun – Einblicke in die inter- und intra-aktivitäts-spezifische Dimension der kommunikativen Basisaktivität "Veränderung ko-konstruieren" im Führungskräfte-Coaching." In *Pragmatik der Veränderung. Problem- und lösungsorientierte Kommunikation in helfenden Berufen. Studien zur Pragmatik*, ed. by Graf, Eva-Maria, Claudio Scarvaglieri, and Thomas Spranz-Fogasy, 209–237. Tübingen: Narr.

Graf, Eva-Maria, Claudio Scarvaglieri, and Thomas Spranz-Fogasy (eds). 2019. *Pragmatik der Veränderung. Problem- und lösungsorientierte Kommunikation in helfenden Berufen*. Studien zur Pragmatik. Tübingen: Narr.

Graßmann, Caroline, Franziska Schölmerich, and Carsten C. Schermuly. 2019. "The Relationship between Working Alliance and Client Outcomes in Coaching: A Meta-analysis." *Human Relations* 73 (1): 35–58. https://doi.org/10.1177/0018726718819725

Greenson, Ralph R. 1965. "The Working Alliance and the Transference Neurosis." *Psychoanalysis Quarterly* 34: 155–181. https://doi.org/10.1080/21674086.1965.11926343

Gülich, Elisabeth. 2003. "Conversational Techniques Used in Transferring Knowledge between Medical Experts and Non-experts." *Discourse Studies* 5 (2): 235–263. https://doi.org/10.1177/1461445603005002005

Habscheid, Stephan. 2011. "Gesprächsberatung in Organisationen und Institutionen." In *Angewandte Linguistik. Ein Lehrbuch*, ed. by. Karlfried Knapp et al., 334–354. Tübingen/Basel: UTB GmbH.

Hall, Christopher, Srikant Sarangi, and Stefan Slembrouck. 1999. "The Legitimation of the Client and the Profession: Identities and Roles in Social Work Discourse." In *Talk, Work and Institutional Order. Discourse in Medical, Mediation and Management Settings*, ed. by Srikant Sarangi, and Celia Roberts, 293–322. Berlin: De Gruyter Mouton. https://doi.org/10.1515/9783110208375.3.293

Hausendorf, Heiko. 2011. *Therapeutisierung durch Sprache*. Gießen: Psychosozial-Verlag.

Heritage, John. 2013. "Epistemics in Conversation." In *The Handbook of Conversation Analysis*, ed. by Jack Sidnell, and Tanya Stivers, 370–394. Oxford: Wiley-Blackwell.

Hochschild, Arlie. 1983. *The Managed Heart: Commercialization of Human Feeling*. Berkeley: University of California Press.

Holly, Werner. 1979. *Imagearbeit in Gesprächen. Zur linguistischen Beschreibung des Beziehungsaspekts*. Tübingen: Narr. https://doi.org/10.1515/9783111378473

Holly, Werner. 2001. "Beziehungsmanagement und Imagearbeit." In *Text- und Gesprächslinguistik. Handbücher zur Sprach- und Kommunikationswissenschaft*, ed. by Klaus Brinker, Gerd Antos, Wolfgang Heinemann, and Sven F. Sager, 1382–1393. Berlin/New York: de Gruyter. https://doi.org/10.1515/9783110169188.2.19.1382

Horvath, Adam O. 2006. "The Alliance in Context: Accomplishments, Challenges, and Future Directions." *Psychotherapy* 43 (3): 258–263. https://doi.org/10.1037/0033-3204.43.3.258

Horvath, Adam, and Lester Luborsky. 1993. "The Role of the Therapeutic Alliance in Psychotherapy." *Journal of Consulting and Clinical Psychology* 61 (4): 561–57. https://doi.org/10.1037/0022-006X.61.4.561

Horvath, Adam, and Leslie S. Greenberg (eds). 1994. *The Working Alliance: Theory, Research, and Practice*. Oxford: Wiley-Blackwell.

Horvath Adam, and Peter Muntigl. 2018. "The Alliance as a Discursive Achievement: A Conversation Analytical Perspective." In *Therapy as Discourse. The Language of Mental Health*, ed. by Olga Smoliak, and Tom Strong, 71–93. Basingstoke: Palgrave Macmillan, Cham. https://doi.org/10.1007/978-3-319-93067-1_4

Hünniger, Julia. 2019. *Selbsthilfeforen als Ressource sozialer Unterstützung. Eine qualitative Studie sozialer Unterstützungsprozesse in Liebeskummerforen*. Wiesbaden: Springer. https://doi.org/10.1007/978-3-658-25166-6

Illouz, Eva. 2008. *Saving the Modern Soul: Therapy, Emotions, and the Culture of Self-Help*. Berkeley: California University Press. https://doi.org/10.1525/9780520941311

Juhila, Kirsi, Tarja Pöso, Christopher Hall, and Nigel Parton. 2003. "Introduction: Beyond a Universal Client." In *Constructing Clienthood in Social Work and Human Services*, ed. by Christopher Hall, Kirsi Juhila, Nigel Parton and Tarja Pöso, 11–24. London: Jessica Kingsley Publishers.

Kysely, Andrea, Brian Bishop, Robert T. Kane, Maryanne McDevitt, and Rosanna Rooney. 2022. "Couples Therapy Delivered through Videoconferencing: Effects on Relationship Outcomes, Mental Health and the Therapeutic Alliance." *Frontiers in Psychology*. https://doi.org/10.3389/fpsyg.2021.773030

Lambert, Michael J. (ed). 2013. *Bergin and Garfield's Handbook of Psychotherapy and Behavior Change*. 6th edition. New York: Wiley-Blackwell.

Lindholm, Loukia. 2017. ""So now I'm Panic Attack Free!": Response Stories in a Peer-to-peer Online Advice Forum on Pregnancy and Parenting. *Linguistik Online* 87 (8): 25–41. https://doi.org/10.13092/lo.87.4171.

Linke, Angelika, and Juliane Schröter. 2017. "Sprache in Beziehungen – Beziehungen in Sprache: Überlegungen zur Konstitution eines linguistischen Forschungsfeldes." In *Sprache und Beziehung*, ed. by Angelika Linke, and Juliane Schröter, 1–32. Berlin/Boston: de Gruyter. https://doi.org/10.1515/9783110496918-002

Linke, Angelika, and Juliane Schröter (eds). 2017. *Sprache und Beziehung*. Berlin: de Gruyter. https://doi.org/10.1515/9783110496918

Locher, Miriam A. 2006. *Advice Online: Advice-giving in an American Internet Health Column*. Amsterdam/Philadelphia: John Benjamins. https://doi.org/10.1075/pbns.149

Locher, Miriam. 2012. "Politeness Research from Past to Future, with a Special Focus on the Discursive Approach." In *New Perspectives on (Im)Politeness and Interpersonal Communication*, ed. by Lucia Fernandez Amaya, Maria de la O Hernandez Lopez, Reyes Gómez Morón, Manuel Padilla Cruz, Manuel Mejias Borrero and Mariana Relinque Barranca, 36–60. Cambridge Scholars Press.

Locher, Miriam A., and Sage L. Graham (eds). 2010. *Interpersonal Pragmatics*. Berlin: De Gruyter Mouton. https://doi.org/10.1515/9783110214338

Locher, Miriam, and Richard J. Watts. 2005. "Politeness Theory and Relational Work." *Journal of Politeness Research* 1 (1): 9–33. https://doi.org/10.1515/jplr.2005.1.1.9

Locher, Miriam A., and Richard J. Watts. 2008. "Relational Work and Impoliteness: Negotiating Norms of Linguistic Behaviour." In *Impoliteness in Language. Studies on its Interplay with Power in Theory and Practice*, ed. by Derek Bousfield, and Miriam A. Locher, 77–99. Berlin: Mouton de Gruyter.

Locher, Miriam A., and Franziska Thurnherr. 2017. "Typing Yourself Healthy: Introduction to the Special Issue on Language and Health Online." *Linguistik Online* 87 (8): 3–24. https://doi.org/10.13092/lo.87.4170.

Locher, Miriam, and Stephanie Schnurr. 2017. "(Im)Politeness in Health Settings." In *The Palgrave Handbook of Linguistic (Im)politeness*, ed. by Jonathan Culpeper, Michael Haugh, and Dániel Z. Kádár, 689–711. London: Palgrave Macmillan. https://doi.org/10.1057/978-1-137-37508-7_26

Luborsky, Lester. 1976. "Helping Alliances in Psychotherapy: the Groundwork for a Study of their Relationship to its Outcome." In *Successful Psychotherapy*, ed. by James L. Cleghorn, 92–116. New York: Brunner/Mazel.

Luhmann, Niklas. 1973. "Formen des Helfens im Wandel gesellschaftlicher Bedingungen." In *Gesellschaftliche Perspektiven der Sozialarbeit*. Band 1, ed. by Hans-Uwe Otto and Siegfried Schneider, 21–43. Neuwied: Luchterhand.

MacIntyre, Alasdair. 1987. *After Virtue: A Study in Moral Theory*. 2nd ed. London: Duckworth.
Marx, Konstanze. 2019. "Von #Gänsehaut bis #esreicht – Wie lässt sich ein Territorium neuer Sagbarkeit konturieren? Ein phänomenologischer Zugang." In *Neues vom heutigen Deutsch. Empirisch – methodisch- theoretisch. Jahrbuch 2018*, ed. by Ludwig Eichinger, and Albrecht Plewnia, 245–264. Berlin/New York: de Gruyter. https://doi.org/10.1515/9783110622591-012
Miller, Katherine, and Jennifer Considine. 2009. "Communication in the Helping Professions." In *The Routledge Handbook of Applied Communication Research*, ed. by Lawrence Frey and Kenneth Cissna, 405–428. Routledge: New York.
Muntigl, Peter, Naomi Knight, Adam O. Horvath, and Ashley Watkins. 2012. "Client Attitudinal Stance and Therapist-client Affiliation. A View from Grammar and Social Interaction." *Research in Psychotherapy: Psychopathology, Process and Outcome* 15 (2): 117–130.
Muntigl, Peter, Naomi Knight, Ashley Watkins, Adam O. Horvath, and Lynne Angus. 2013. "Active Retreating. Person-centered Practices to Repair Disaffiliation in Therapy." *Journal of Pragmatics* 53: 1–20. https://doi.org/10.1016/j.pragma.2013.03.019
Muntigl, Peter, and Adam Horvath. 2014. "The Therapeutic Relationship in Action: How Therapists and Clients Co-manage Relational Disaffiliation." *Psychotherapy Research* 24 (3): 327–345. https://doi.org/10.1080/10503307.2013.807525
Norcross, John C., and Michael J. Lambert. 2018. "Psychotherapy Relationships that Work III." *Psychotherapy* 55 (4): 303–315. https://doi.org/10.1037/pst0000193
Pawelczyk, Joanna and Eva-Maria Graf (eds). 2019. "Understanding Change in Helping Professions." Special Issue for *Communication & Medicine* 16 (2): 1–195.
Peräkylä, Anssi. 2019. "Conversation Analysis and Psychotherapy: Identifying Transformative Sequences." *Research on Language and Social Interaction* 52 (3): 257–280. https://doi.org/10.1080/08351813.2019.1631044
Pick, Ina and Claudio Scarvaglieri. 2019. "Helfendes Handeln. Zum Begriff sprachlichen Helfens und seinen Implikationen für Veränderung." In *Pragmatik der Veränderung. Problem- und lösungsorientierte Kommunikation in helfenden Berufen*, ed. by Eva-Maria Graf, Claudio Scarvaglieri, and Thomas Spranz-Fogasy, 25–64. Tübingen: Narr Francke Attempto.
Pick, Ina and Claudio Scarvaglieri. 2022. "Helfen Im Gespräch: Empirischer Vergleich Der Hilfe in Rechtsberatung Und Psychotherapie." In *Helfen: Situative Und Organisationale Ausprägungen Einer Unterbestimmten Praxis*, ed. by Daniela Böhringer, Sarah Hitzler, and Martina Richter, 163–92. Bielefeld: transcript. https://doi.org/10.1515/9783839454992-008.
Ribbers, Anne, and Alexander Waringa. 2015. *E-Coaching: Theory and Practice for a New Online Approach to Coaching*. London: Routledge. https://doi.org/10.4324/9781315771670
Ribeiro, Eugenia, Antonio P. Ribeiro, Miguel M. Goncalves, Adam O. Horvath, and William B. Stiles. 2013. "How Collaboration in Therapy Becomes Therapeutic: The Therapeutic Collaboration Coding System." *Psychology and Psychotherapy* 86 (3): 294–314. https://doi.org/10.1111/j.2044-8341.2012.02066.x
Rogers, Carl R. 1951. *Client-Centred Therapy*. London: Constable & Robinson.
Sarangi, Srikant. 2002. "Discourse Practitioners as a Community of Interprofessional Practice: Some Insights from Health Communication Research." In *Research and Practice in Professional Discourse*, ed. by Christopher Candlin, 95–135. Hong Kong: City of University of Hong Kong Press.
Scarvaglieri, Claudio. 2013. *›Nichts anderes als ein Austausch von Worten‹. Sprachliches Handeln in der Psychotherapie*. Berlin/Boston: de Gruyter. https://doi.org/10.1515/9783110319033

Scarvaglieri, Claudio. 2017. "Beraten und Psychotherapie: Zur Differenzierung zweier Formate helfenden Handelns." In *Beraten in Interaktion. Eine gesprächslinguistische Typologie des Beratens*, ed. by Ina Pick, 53–76. Frankfurt am Main: Lang.

Scarvaglieri, Claudio. 2020. "First Encounters in Psychotherapy: Relationship-Building and the Pursuit of Institutional Goals." *Frontiers in psychology* 11. https://doi.org/10.3389/fpsyg.2020.585038

Scherr, Sebastian, and Marlene Schmitt. 2018. "Passive Facebook-Nutzung, selektive Selbstdarstellung und negative Wahrnehmungen des eigenen Lebens: Mehrgruppen Cross-Lagged Panelanalysen zu differentiellen Effekten im Kontext psychologischen Wohlbefindens." *M&K Medien & Kommunikationswissenschaft* 66 (1): 58–74. https://doi.org/10.5771/1615-634X-2018-1-58

Schmitt, Reinhold. 1997. "Unterstützen Im Gespräch: Zur Analyse Manifester Kooperationsverfahren." *Zeitschrift für Sprachwissenschaft* 16 (1–2): 52–82. https://doi.org/10.1515/zfsw.1997.16.1-2.52

Spencer, Julie, Jonathan Goode, Elizabeth A. Penix, Wilson Trusty, and Joshua K. Swift. 2019. "Developing a Collaborative Relationship with Clients during the Initial Sessions of Psychotherapy." *Psychotherapy* 56 (1): 7–10. https://doi.org/10.1037/pst0000208

Spencer-Oatey, Helen. 2000. "Rapport Management: A Framework for Analysis." In *Culturally Speaking: Culture, Communication and Politeness Theory*, ed. by Helen Spencer-Oatey, 11–46. London: Continuum.

Spencer-Oatey, Helen. 2002. "Managing Rapport in Talk: Using Rapport Sensitive Incidents to Explore the Motivational Concerns Underlying the Management of Relations." *Journal of Pragmatics* 34 (5): 529–545. https://doi.org/10.1016/S0378-2166(01)00039-X

Spencer-Oatey, Helen, and Peter Franklin. 2009. *Intercultural Interaction: A Multidiscipinary Approach to Intercultural Communication*. Basingstoke: Palgrave-Macmillan. https://doi.org/10.1057/9780230244511

Spencer-Oatey, Helen, Dániel Z. Kádár. 2021. *Intercultural Politeness: Managing Relations Across Cultures*. Cambridge: Cambridge University Press.

Spranz-Fogasy, Thomas. 1992. "Ärztliche Gesprächsführung – Inhalte und Erfahrungen gesprächsanalytisch fundierter Weiterbildung." In *Kommunikationsberatung und Kommunikationstraining*, ed. by Reinhard Fiehler, and Wolfgang Sucharowski, 68–78. Opladen: Westdeutscher Verlag. https://doi.org/10.1007/978-3-322-85086-7_5

Stivers, Tanya. 2015. "Coding Social Interaction: A Heretical Approach in Conversation Analysis?" *Research on Language & Social Interaction* 48 (1): 1–19. https://doi.org/10.1080/08351813.2015.993837.

Stokoe, Elizabeth. 2014. "The Conversation Analytic Role-play Method (CARM): A Method for Training Communication Skills as an Alternative to Simulated Role-play." *Research on Language and Social Interaction* 47 (3): 255–265. https://doi.org/10.1080/08351813.2014.925663.

Stommel, Wyke. 2012. "Salutations, Closings and Pronouns: Some Aspects of Recipient Design in Online Counselling." *Communication & Medicine* 9 (2): 145–158. https://doi.org/10.1558/cam.v9i2.145.

Stommel, Wyke, and Hedwig te Molder. 2015. "Counseling Online and over the Phone: When Preclosing Questions Fail as a Closing Device." *Research on Language and Social Interaction* 48 (3): 281–300. https://doi.org/10.1080/08351813.2015.1058605.

Stommel, Wyke, and Fleur van der Houwen. 2015. "Counseling and New Media Technologies: A Comparison of Problem Presentations in E-mail and in Chat." *Communication & Medicine* 12 (2–3): 243–256. https://doi.org/10.1558/cam.18298.

Thurnherr, Franziska. 2019. "Interpersonal Pragmatics and the Therapeutic Alliance: The Collaborative Work in Email Counseling." Dissertation, University of Basel.

Thurnherr, Franziska. 2022. *Interpersonal Pragmatics and the Therapeutic Alliance: The Collaborative Work in Email Counseling*. NIHIN Studies: Freiburg.

Trasmundi, Sarah B., and Johanne S. Philipsen. 2020. "Embodiments and Co-actions: The Function of Trust and Re-enactment in the Practice of Psychotherapy." *Cognitive Semiotics* 13 (2): 1–29. https://doi.org/10.1515/cogsem-2020-2032

Van Daele, Tom, Maria Karekla, Angelos Kassianos, Angelo Compare, Lise Haddouk, João Salgado, David Ebert, Glauco Trebbi, Sylvie Bernaerts, Eva van Assche, and Nele Witte. 2020. "Recommendations for Policy and Practice of Telepsychotherapy and E-mental Health in Europe and Beyond." *Journal of Psychotherapy Integration* 30: 160–173. https://doi.org/10.1037/int0000218.

Voutilainen, Liisa, Anssi Peräkylä, and Joanna Ruusuvuori. 2011. "Therapeutic Change in Interaction: Conversation Analysis of a Transforming Sequence." *Psychotherapy Research* 21 (3): 348–365. https://doi.org/10.1080/10503307.2011.573509

Voutilainen, Liisa, Federic Rossano, and Anssi Peräkylä. 2018. "Conversation Analysis and Psychotherapeutic Change." In *Longitudinal Studies on the Organization of Social Interaction*, ed. by Simona Pekarek Doehler, Johannes Wagner, and Esther González-Martínez, 225–254. London: Palgrave Macmillan. https://doi.org/10.1057/978-1-137-57007-9_8

Wakke, Denise and Vivien Heller. 2022. "Helping as a Concurrent Activity. How Students Engage in Smalls Groups while Pursuing Classroom Tasks." *Frontiers in Psychology*. https://doi.org/10.3389/fpsyg.2021.784906

Weinzinger, Carolin. 2016. "„genau darum gez doch "–(Nicht-) Wissenszuschreibungen als vertrauensbildende Maßnahmen im Online-Coaching." In *Wissen in institutioneller Interaktion*. Forum Angewandte Linguistik 55, ed. by Alexandra Groß, and Inga Harren, 113–144. Frankfurt a. M.: Lang

Weiste, Elina, Liisa Voutilainen, and Anssi Peräkylä. 2016. "Epistemic Asymmetries in Psychotherapy Interaction. Therapists 'Practices for Displaying Access to Clients' Inner Experiences." *Sociology of Health & Illness* 38 (4): 645–661. https://doi.org/10.1111/1467-9566.12384

Zayts, Olga, and Stephanie Schnurr. 2014. "More than Information Provider and Counselor: Constructing and Negotiating Roles and Identities of Nurses in Genetic Counseling Sessions". *Journal of Sociolinguistics* 18 (3): 345–369. https://doi.org/10.1111/josl.12083

Zetzel, Elizabeth R. 1956. "Current Concepts of Transference." *International Journal of Psychoanalysis* 37: 369–376.

Zayts, Olga, and Stephanie Schnurr. 2011. "Laughter as Medical Providers' Resource: Negotiating Informed Choice in Prenatal Genetic Counseling". *Research on Language and Social Interaction* 44 (1): 1–20. https://doi.org/10.1080/08351813.2011.544221

Forging relationships in psychotherapeutic interaction

Peter Muntigl
Ghent University

Creating and maintaining a positive therapist-client relationship is considered to be essential in achieving therapeutic success, whereas damage to this relationship and the inability to repair disaffiliative episodes may have detrimental effects. So far, very little research has focused on how the relationship between therapists and clients is accomplished and negotiated through talk. Drawing from research in conversation analysis/ CA, I examine a diverse corpus of video-taped psychotherapy sessions to explore the interactional practices that may be 'typically' used to forge and create potential shifts in relationships and affiliation. In this paper, I not only set out to illustrate the central role that talk and conduct plays in therapist-client relationship-building, but also how the relationship is an ongoing interactional achievement.

Keywords: affiliation, conversation analysis, disaffiliation, disagreement, person references, relationship, social networks, troubles-telling, weak-tie support

1. Introduction

In psychotherapy research, the therapeutic relationship is considered to play an essential role in making therapy effective and in facilitating a healing context between the client and therapist (Norcross 2011). Current conceptualizations of the relationship are often given in affectual terms (Norcross and Lambert, 2018), drawing on Gelso and Carter's (1985: 159) earlier definition as "the feelings and attitudes that counseling participants have toward one another, and the manner in which these are expressed". From a process-experiential/ emotion-focused standpoint, a slightly more elaborate picture is given, borrowing elements from Rogerian relationship conditions that involve the components or principles of empathic attunement, therapeutic bonds and task collaboration (Greenberg 2014). But whatever the conceptualization, there seems to be agreement in the psychotherapeutic research

https://doi.org/10.1075/pbns.331.02mun

community that the relationship consists of various elements that correlate with varying degrees of 'effectiveness'. This list of elements includes the alliance, collaboration, goal consensus, empathy, positive regard and affirmation, congruence/ genuineness, repairing alliance ruptures, among others (see Norcross and Lambert 2018 for the full list of elements).

For the most part, these relationship elements speak to some aspect of the 'feelings' or 'attitudes' between therapist-client, but if we look again to Gelso and Carter's definition, that last part "…and the manner in which these are expressed" does not seem to receive much attention.[1] This may be because, as Strong and Smoliak (2018: 7) have claimed, "in today's era of evidence-based therapy … , the focus has largely been on "what works" and less on how what works (namely, interventions) can be shown to work through careful discursive analysis". Further, relationship elements are often assessed in terms of subjective measures, feedback questionnaires or participant (or researchers') observations rather than in terms of being a social construction between people (McNamee and Gergen 1992) or even as an accomplishment arising from (and being transformed through) speakers' sequentially connected social actions (Buttny 1993; Peräkylä 2019). In this chapter, I place emphasis on exploring "how" relationships are built and ongoingly negotiated through talk. Drawing mainly from a corpus of my own (already published) extracts of psychotherapy interactions, I illustrate the following:

1. By what interactional means are relationships actually displayed and oriented to?
2. How therapists may display a 'closer' or more 'distant' relationship with the client and vice versa?
3. How clients actually show that the therapist is or is not being empathic or particularly caring?

My main approach to relationships and to exploring the afore-mentioned questions is grounded in the tenets of conversation analysis (Sidnell and Stivers 2013) and is particularly informed by Pomerantz and Mandelbaum's (2005) work on relationship categories. I also draw from Enfield's (2009) *approach to relationships*, in order to examine the connections between relationship-grounded social behavior, relationship ties and the communicative interactions through which social structure may be accomplished.

1. According to Norcross and Lambert (2018: 304), this part "potentially opens the relationship to include everything under the therapeutic sun."

2. Relationships: A social/ interactional view

Enfield (2009) makes the general point that, when making efforts to study and understand social interaction, analysts should adopt a *relationship thinking* approach. I will not try to summarize all of Enfield's points here, but only those that I think bear relevance to the aims of this chapter. First, relationships are built up, forged through interactions involving co-present participants. Second, the social world implies living in a social system that is characterized through reciprocal role/ identity (e.g., father-son; brother-sister) and polar (e.g., intimacy: close vs. distant) relations. Third, relationship grounded social behavior emerges from competing interests, an interplay between positively and negatively valenced forces. On the one hand, people may act with respect to positive pro-social tendencies associated with trust, compassion and affiliation and, on the other hand, they may also be acting in accordance with so-called Machiavellian tendencies, which license deception and competition. The main point here is that persons are not always wanting to act pro-socially to save or reduce damage to face, affiliate or promote social bonding. Instead, they may work to create boundaries, establish difference, build coalitions and even hurt others (see also Goodwin, 1990). Although a central tendency in most therapies is to offer consistent support of the client's position, therapists are sometimes called upon to challenge the client's self-defeating, pathological perspective (Weiste 2015; Muntigl, Horvath, Bänninger-Huber and Angus 2020) or may even, as for example in couples/family therapy, form allegiances with one of the clients while opposing another (see Muntigl 2013). These competing tendencies are reflected in Bänninger-Huber and Widmer's (1999) proposal that psychotherapy conversations are often guided by what they term a *balance hypothesis*; that is, in order to get productive therapeutic work underway, therapists need to find the appropriate balance between offering sufficient emotional support while maintaining an appropriate level of conflictive tension to encourage clients to directly address their problems. Fourth, deciding on a certain social unit of analysis (individual, dyad, triad, family, ethnic group) may influence our understanding of the interaction. For example, in one-on-one therapy, should the client's talk about a certain relationship (e.g., the father) be examined as a dyadic or family relation, or even as one that somehow implicates the therapist? Finally, talk that indexes a certain relationship type can be reciprocally grounded and mutually defining, thus involving rights and responsibilities associated with both speakers' incumbency in that relationship: Thus, if A is B's therapist, then B is A's client.

2.1 Social networks and relationship ties

Not only in psychotherapy but in our social worlds in general, close, empathic relationships have been argued to be instrumental in promoting well-being, happiness and health (Dunbar 2018). Sociological research claims that persons build social networks of varying intensity or closeness and that these networks vary quite dramatically in size. Not all relationships are equal, but may be separated into hierarchically differentiated structured types, based on degree of intensity, frequency of contact and number of possible members. For example, our most intimate 'support group' generally consists of no more than 5 persons and our 'sympathy group' (i.e., best/good friends) is around 15 (Dunbar 2018; Hill and Dunbar 2003). It has been suggested that there is a limit to the number of friendships that people can maintain. This is because relationships require effort (i.e., time and emotional capital) and that there is only so much time available in a day to devote to relationship work (Hill and Dunbar 2003). According to Dunbar (2018), some of the main 'ingredients' for maintaining close relationships are trust and the capacity to inhibit our actions and desires; for the latter, it is the recognition that you cannot always have it your way and that, to maintain a harmonious or balanced relationship, some give and take is required. Maintaining relationships, especially intimate ones, is also costly, given not only the time one needs to invest with each of the members but, as Dunbar (2018) argues, the cognitive work such as 'mentalizing' (i.e., understanding and working with another's mindset) that is required to uphold them. But, as Enfield (2006) has pointed out, frequency of contact is not always a key factor in determining intimacy; what is important is rather the quality of information that is exchanged and the common ground that is established.

The psychotherapy relationship, although it is also based on some general features such as trust, support and understanding, is different in quality from the social networks identified by Dunbar. Like other professional helping professions (doctor-patient; lawyer-client), the therapist-client 'bond' may more fruitfully be described as a 'working relationship' that is asymmetrical and serves a purpose. For instance, contact and duration of visit between therapist and client is highly regulated, the nature of the social exchange is in many ways non-reciprocating (e.g., clients tell about their troubles but not the other way around) and the therapist's role is generally restricted to offering emotional support. Another way to view the psychotherapy relationship is in terms of *strong* vs. *weak* ties (Granovetter 1983). Although it is generally assumed that relationships comprised of *strong ties* (persons who are interpersonally close) are important in times of great need, when support is required for our security and welfare, research has suggested that people often prefer to turn to weak-tie relationships when seeking assistance or advice. This is because individuals from this network will often be able to tailor their help in less emotional and more objective ways than individuals (i.e., close friends and family) from strong-tie relationships (Adelman, Parks and Albrecht 1987). Wright et al. (2010) propose four dimensions of weak-tie support preference, illustrating how they may indeed be an advantage in contexts of offering professional, emotional support and help:

i. (therapists) *having access to different viewpoints*;
ii. *receiving objective feedback from others* (therapists);
iii. *having a reduced risk of being judged by others* [e.g., the therapist];
iv. (providing professionals with) *reduced social obligations leading to discomfort, stress and conflict.*

These dimensions seem to characterize most professional helping contexts and relationships and would explain at least some of the main benefits in seeking out therapists in times of trouble.

2.2 Affiliation: A conversational building block of social relationships

Relationships are talked into being; that is, to have an intimate/ strong or distant/ weak tie, people need to interact with each other. It has been argued that talk tends to be organized so as to promote social solidarity and avoid conflict and that speakers tend to design their utterances so as to receive affiliative uptake from others and avoid face-threatening situations through a range of linguistic practices (Brown and Levinson 1987; Davidson 1984; Goffman 1967; Heritage 1984). This kind of (pro-social) organization, according to Enfield (2006: 399–400), translates into an *affiliation imperative* that "compels interlocutors to maintain a common degree of interpersonal affiliation (trust, commitment, intimacy), proper to the status of the relationship, and again mutually calibrated at each step of an interaction's progression." In this way, we tend to observe an overwhelming tendency for speakers to produce pro-social actions such as agreement and compliance. But even in the face of speaker disagreement (e.g., with others' opinions, claims, assessments) or refusal (e.g., with others' invitations, proposals, requests), the opposing speaker tends to mitigate the threat to the social relationship by softening the disagreement or refusal with various linguistic markers (Heritage 1984; Muntigl and Turnbull 1998; Pomerantz 1984).

Recent conceptualizations of affiliation within conversation analysis/ CA have focused on how a speaker can work affiliatively within sequence; for example, recipients of talk that endorse or match the teller's affectual stance (Stivers 2008) or, more broadly, responsive actions that are empathic or accommodate the preferences implicated in the prior action (Stivers, Mondada, and Steensig 2011). Thus, responding to a person's troubles telling with, for example, emotional heightening will be deemed affiliative, indexing a more intimate position (Jefferson and Lee 1980), as will responding with the preferred-type 2nd action of an adjacency pair, such as providing an (upgraded) second assessment after a first assessment (Pomerantz 1984; Goodwin and Goodwin 1987). CA studies of psychotherapy interaction – stemming from my research group's focus on (dis)affiliation in psychotherapy – have so far shown how affiliation is accomplished in storytelling and in formulation, noticing and proposal sequences (Muntigl and Horvath 2014; Muntigl, Knight and Angus 2014; Muntigl, Knight and Watkins 2012; Muntigl, Horvath, Chubak and Angus 2020) and also how therapists manage disaffiliation or relational stresses through various interactional practices (Muntigl 2013, 2020; Muntigl, Knight, Watkins, Horvath and Angus 2013).[2]

2.3 Accomplishing relationships in interaction

Whereas affiliative actions may be viewed as basic conversational building blocks through which speakers may uphold social relationships and even maintain or create stronger ties between them, other more relationship specific practices have been identified in the literature. In developing a CA approach to studying relationship categories, Pomerantz and Mandelbaum (2005: 150) identify two areas of investigation by asking the following questions: (1) "How does invoking a relationship category operate with respect to accomplishing a locally relevant conversational action?" and (2) "How does performing certain conversational actions relate to enacting incumbency in specific relationship categories?" These questions draw from Sacks' (1992) work on membership categorization. According to Sacks, categories are "inference-rich" and representative. For a given category term (e.g., stranger, friend, relative) there is an assumption that speakers will draw representative, category-appropriate inferences about the person in question. Further, activities can be "category-bound" and appropriately seen in terms of a given category of person or relationship.

Pomerantz and Mandelbaum (2005) argue that, to be seen as visibly belonging to (or being an incumbent of) a certain relationship category, speakers must produce the sort of conduct that may be demonstrably and accountably linked to that category. Thus, constructing a specific relationship category between persons is a joint accomplishment in which a speaker displays relationship appropriate conduct (for that category) followed by the other party's ratification of the conduct. Drawing from a range of past studies in CA (e.g., Drew and Chilton 2000; Jefferson

2. For a discussion of affiliation in psychotherapy talk, see also Pain (2009)

1974; Lerner 1992; Mandelbaum 1987), Pomerantz and Mandelbaum (2005) list four sequence types that are highly relationship implicative. They are exemplary in showing how certain conversational actions relate to enacting incumbency in specific relationship categories pertaining to 'intimacy', 'involvement' and 'closeness': (1) *Inquiring about tracked events + Providing more details on one's own activities*; (2) *Discussing one's own problems + Displaying interest in the other's problems*; (3) *Making oblique references to shared experiences + Forwarding the talk about shared experiences*; (4) *Using improprieties + Taking up the other's improprieties by using additional improprieties and/or laughter*.

These sequential patterns outlined by Pomerantz and Mandelbaum (2005) constitute some of the typical resources for how persons may enact 'close relationships' in everyday contexts. They also point out that the type of response in each of these sequences plays a key role in showing the quality of relationship that is being enacted. Thus, whereas responses that comply with the requirements of the prior action in each of these sequences will generally result in doing closeness in the relationship (i.e., providing details of personal events, displaying empathy as a recipient to a prior telling, displaying knowledge of a shared event, responding with additional improprieties or laughter), non-complying responses will instead place intimacy at risk and may create a momentary distance in the relationship. Further, having a close or intimate relationship will place expectations on the production of initiating actions for some of these sequences; for instance, not inquiring about tracked events and not telling about one's own problems may involve a breach of intimacy, thus holding those who have made the breach accountable. In a similar vein, affiliation may also place stress on a relationship if it is not appropriately matched to one's interlocutor. For example, inquiring too deeply into someone's life or providing too many details of one's own life may not be deemed suitable if the relationship is distant.

Pomerantz and Mandelbaum (2005) also claim that two of the activities rely on a history of shared experiences together and seem to be necessary for enacting *enduring* close relationships: updating each other concerning past events and creating contexts for displaying mutual shared knowledge and experiences. The other two activities – troubles telling and producing and taking up improprieties – rather, do not presuppose that the persons have a history of shared experiences and, thus, "are not limited to ongoing intimate relationships, yet constitute moments of intimacy and strong affiliation" (Pomerantz and Mandelbaum 2005: 169).[3] Although all these sequence types have been shown to occur in some form that will be tailored to the

3. There are, of course, other activities that have social-affiliative payoffs in forging relationships. Displaying immediate recognition of a caller during telephone call openings, based simply on a greeting such as "hi", is another way to display closeness (Enfield 2006; Schegloff 2007).

therapeutic context, troubles telling sequences will be, for most therapies, by far the most common. This sequence type provides a powerful means for therapists to provide empathy and support (moments of strong affiliation) to the client's distress without having to assume a close relationship. From my analyses of psychotherapy sessions, inquiries about tracked events tend to occur at the very beginning of the session, before the 'actual' therapeutic business gets underway. Making oblique references to shared experiences – e.g., therapists offering a second story that conveys a similar experience – seem to appear only rarely (but see Leudar, Antaki and Barnes 2006), as do occurrences of therapist laughter following client' humorous depictions of situations or individuals. But in general, sequences are built up such that it is therapists who are responsive to clients' personal experience and conduct, rather than the other way around, and so the opportunities to form emotional connections, bilaterally, seem to be more limited than, say, between persons in a sympathy or support group.

Drawing from my own corpora of (mainly) published psychotherapy conversations involving Structural Family, Gestalt, Emotion-focused and Client-centered approaches, I show in the next section how the two basic practices – invoking relationship categories and performing actions that enact incumbency – are accomplished in psychotherapy during various episodes of troubles telling.

3. Using explicit relationship categories: Person and role references

One of the earliest accounts of membership category use in the helping professions comes from Sacks' (1992) work on call-taking in an emergency psychiatric clinic, in which the caller's utterance "it sounds like a real professional" is taken as a criticism directed at the call taker's lack of attentiveness. In this section, I show how person and role references may be used in an affiliative and disaffiliative manner. Most extracts have been selected from my previously published work to illustrate practices of relationship management. The psychotherapy data were derived from 3 sources: (i) The York I depression study involving emotion-focused therapy/EFT and client-centered therapy/CCT (see Greenberg and Watson 1998); (ii) Structural Family Therapy (Muntigl and Horvath 2016); (iii) Gestalt Therapy (Muntigl and Horvath 2014). All sessions were video-taped and conducted in English.

3.1 Person references

Extract (1), taken from Muntigl and Horvath (2016: 111), shows a brief interaction of Structural Family Therapy/ SFT (Minuchin 1974) that involves the therapists Minuchin and Jenny, Suzanne (mother), Marcy (daughter) and Travis (son, not present during therapy). Prior to this extract, Suzanne gives an extended self-deprecating account of her uncertainty and unease about not having brought her son Travis to the family therapy session – person references are shown in bold.

Extract 1.
[Muntigl and Horvath 2016: 111]

```
01   Suzanne:   I was really (0.3) baffed out yesterday after leaving
02              ((name of Travis' school)).
03              (3.4)
04   Jenny:     Marcy,
05              (0.5)
06   Minuchin: you ↑know Jenny, s-something. (0.6) I think that (0.4)
07              actually, (0.3) may I call you by your first name?
08              =wou[ld you m-]
09   Suzanne:       [Suzanne. ]
10              (0.3)
11   Minuchin: Suzanne, .hh (.) >I ↑think< (0.9) actually Suzanne,
     m                                          gaze @ Jenny
12              (.) did something very nice.
13              (1.2)
14   Minuchin: ↑she decided, (1.5) that Travis (0.7) was, (1.2) >↑she
     m          continues talking towards Jenny
15              decided< what is, (0.7) good for Travis.
```

This extract begins with Suzanne completing her self-deprecating account in which she blames herself for Travis' absence. We know from work on self-deprecating actions that the 'preferred' next action is disagreement and/or praise (Pomerantz 1984). We see that praise coming from Minuchin occurs in lines 11–15. Suzanne's decision not to bring Travis is recast as having done "`something very nice`" and, thereafter, he accounts for this positive assessment by stating that "`>↑she decided< what is, (0.7) good for Travis.`". Minuchin's response is strongly affiliative, but even before offering praise he performs some important relationship work. In line 6, Minuchin begins to address the other therapist by her first name, Jenny, but then in line 7, he briefly switches addressees by requesting permission to use Suzanne's first name (`may I call you by your first name?`). Suzanne grants him his request in line 09 and then in line 11, he first acknowledges the granting by repeating her name and then proceeds to praise Suzanne's actions to Jenny. Requesting permission to use the mother's first name works to establish a closer relation with Suzanne. But also, along a scale of 'closeness' or 'intimacy', the use of the first name personal reference puts Suzanne on par with Jenny; that is, Minuchin displays that he is on a first name basis with both of them.

3.2 Role references

References to role relations may also be used to affiliate and to illustrate a positive relationship, as can be seen in another instance of SFT occurring soon after the prior conversation (Extract (2), taken from Muntigl and Horvath (2016: 114)).

Extract 2.

[Muntigl and Horvath 2016: 114]

```
Suzanne:   =well see that's been my problem since I've been
           sobering up. (.) I respond to everybody else↑ (.)
           listen te everybody else an I don't [listen te]
Minuchin:                                      [↑yea:h.  ]
Suzanne:   myself.
Minuchin:  but no: ↑no. I ↑feel that, (0.6) euh ↑I:- [I don't ↑s]ee
Jenny:                                               [ mm hm     ]
           it like that.
           (0.3)
Minuchin:  .hh I think you took (0.5) a ↓ mother's decision, (.)
           <what↑ is good> for my ↑child.
           (1.2)
Minuchin:  >I think< in that↑ (0.4) you listened to ↑you.
           (0.4)
Suzanne:   °uh- (.)↑yeah.y°
           (1.0)
Minuchin:  uh don't you [see?       ]
Jenny:                  [yes. yes I] think so [too:?    ]
Minuchin:                                     [well tha]t's- that's
           very good?
```

Suzanne's turn in lines 1–3 makes a couple of self-deprecatory remarks. The first is that 'she listens to everyone else, but not to herself' and the second is '`since I've been sobering up`'. These remarks invoke the inference-rich category (Sacks 1992) of 'recovering alcoholic' and highlight negative attributes of helplessness and lack of personal agency commonly found in clients' self-critical utterances (Muntigl, Horvath, Bänninger-Huber and Angus 2020). Minuchin affiliates in line 6 by immediately disagreeing with Suzanne's self-critical interpretation ('`↑yea:h.` ... `but no: ↑no.` ... `↑I:- I don't ↑see it like that.`).[4] He then invokes the categories of 'mother' vs. 'child' to empathize the role relation between them – i.e., mothers make (good) decisions for their children. Further, taking up the role of 'mother' is praiseworthy because in doing so he casts her as not displaying helplessness, but decisiveness (`you took (0.5) a ↓mother's decision`; line 10).

4. Although the disagreement could also constitute a direct challenge of Susan's authority – that she is the expert of her own experiences – and thus has the potential to create stress in the alliance between her and Minuchin, this potential negative impact is counter-balanced by the strong affiliative import of his action.

Her mother role, therefore, is tied to authoritative action because, contrary to what she had believed, she is able to listen to herself (line 13).

Invoking role references may also work disaffiliatively, to create distance between speakers. Extract (3) is an example of Gestalt therapy involving the Gestalt therapist Fritz Perls and his client Gloria (Shostrum 1966).[5]

Extract 3.

Perls and Gloria [15:44–16:20]

```
Perls:    good. now play Fritz passing judgement (°on you°)
Gloria:   =YOU ARE. you're sitting up there in
          [your <big ol chair.>]
Perls:    [play Fritz.        ] I am Fritz. I pass judgement.
          (4.5)
Perls:    pass judgement on me now.
          (3.4)
Gloria:   I don't feel close to you at a:ll doctor Perls.
          (1.2)
Gloria:   I feel that's phoney=I feel like you're playing
          <one big game.>
Perls:    right.
          (1.3)
Perls:    sure we're playing ↓games, but- .hhh in spite of the
          games .h I think I've touched you now en then. .hh
          I think I've hurt you when I called you a phoney.
Gloria:   =well of COURSE you DID.
Perls:    en I think I have hit a bull's eye. that's why you
          feel hurt.
```

Prior to this extract, Perls has criticized his client through various disparaging actions (e.g., calling Gloria "a phoney") and noticings that point out discrepancies between her verbal and non-verbal conduct (for this practice, see Muntigl and Horvath 2014). In line 1, Perls proposes that Gloria engage in a form of role-play in which she acts out how Perls "passes judgement" on her. Perls offers up his own name, Fritz, possibly as a bid for achieving more intimacy. If Gloria accepts his bid, she could address Perls by his first name and display less distance between them. Gloria, however, rejects this offer in lines 2–3, leading Perls to re-do his proposal. But, following a silence in line 5, he then 'turns the tables' by requesting that Gloria now pass judgement (i.e., criticize) on him. Following a 3.4-s pause in line 7, Gloria complies by first topicalizing the (negative) relationship between them (`I don't feel close to you at a:ll`). She then appends the role/person category (doctor Perls) turn-finally, which emphasizes the distance between them; that is, she clearly rejects calling him "Fritz" and instead chooses to refer to him by his professional title. She then, in line 10, continues by implying that his interventions

5. I have transcribed this segment from this publically available video (Shostrum 1966).

(i.e., proposals of passing judgement) are phoney and "`one big game.`" The reference term "doctor Perls" thus helps to build distance between her and Perls and also disaffiliates with Perls' attempts to create more intimacy, e.g., by getting her to use his first name.

4. Practices associated with incumbency of relationship categories: Troubles-telling activities

Troubles-telling is an activity that plays a central role in psychotherapy. Clients come to therapy to talk about and narrate distressing episodes of their personal life experiences (Angus and Greenberg 2011; Pennebaker and Seagal 1999). These tellings and narrations convey an affectual stance, commonly indexing a form of complaint about others (Drew 1998; Muntigl, Knight and Angus 2014) or self-criticism (Muntigl et al. 2020). These stances allow for next-turn affiliative responses and displays of empathy (Muntigl, Knight and Watkins 2014), which can convey caring and understanding, thus forging a closer tie between the speakers. This sequence of moves, however, can be a delicate operation. In Goffman's (2010) sense, clients enter this activity with certain *informational preserves* associated with the clients specialized entitlements/ ownership of experience. Or, from a CA perspective, clients have greater epistemic status (i.e., what they know and what they experienced) over their biographies (Heritage 2012) and so responding to these tellings with a specific claim to understanding the client's trouble may be seen as infringing on these epistemic entitlements (Heritage 2011). In the next section, I show how affiliating with the trouble does relationship work, how client opposing moves create relationship stresses and how therapists may work to re-affiliate by directly topicalizing the relationship.

4.1 Affiliating with the trouble

Client talk about their troubles implicates a next, affiliative action from the therapist. In Extract (4), taken from Muntigl et al., 2013: 10), the client Kristina is undergoing emotion-focused therapy for depression (Greenberg and Watson 2006).

Extract 4.
014.18–2b (Muntigl et al. 2013: 10)

```
01  Kris:  and uh. of course my husband doesn't (.) help(h) me in(h) .hhh
    t                                                                 nod
02         .snih many of my uh. (1.3) doesn=make me happy at all(h).
03         (        5.3        )
    k      gazes down
    t      nod
04  Ther:  .hhh so you're wanting him to be supporti:ve and. he['s not.].
```

```
05  Kris:                                                  [↑mm hm.]
    k      looks at T                                       nods
06  Kris:  yes or at [least be int'rested,]
07  Ther:            [feelin    supporte:d] an
08         (0.9)
    t      nod
    k      nod
09  Kris:  yeah.
10         (0.7)
```

In lines 1–2, Kristina complains that her husband neither helps her nor makes her happy. The therapist's response in line 4 is a *gist formulation* – `wanting him to be supporti:ve and. he's not.` – that captures the essence of Kristina's prior turn (Heritage and Watson 1979). By summarizing the client's talk, the therapist displays an understanding of her difficult situation and thus works to empathize with her position and create less relational distance between them. Kristina's strong acknowledgement and nod (line 5), mutual nodding between the therapist and Kristina (line 8) and Kristina's agreement (line 9) create mutual affiliation and show that their viewpoints are in sync.

4.2 Client displays of opposition

As mentioned before, respondents' displays of understanding may place them in a certain dilemma. Although the display does offer support and thus works pro-socially, it also may be viewed as potentially violating the client's informational preserves or greater epistemic status (Goffman 2010; Heritage 2012). In this section, I show how clients and therapists are not always in agreement and these oppositional contexts can produce relational stresses because it may create more relational distance between them. Two kinds of opposition are shown in this section. One involving disagreement followed by resolution and another in which a client criticizes the therapist.

4.2.1 *Disagreement – Resolution*

Extract (5) is a continuation of the Extract (4) and shows, in contrast to the former, how the client voices disagreement with the therapist's affiliative attempt.

Extract 5.

014.18–2b Continued (Muntigl et al. 2013: 10)

```
11  Kris:  y-I would exp[ect at least]
12  Ther:                [very  ↑alone] it sounds like in (a hare)=
13  Kris:  =I ↑was thinking about=it-is- I ↑don't know if it is:
           feeling alone I,
14         (1.0)
15  Kris:  .hhh it's more betrayed den alone.
    k                    looks at T
    t                       slow multiple nods→
```

```
16             (        5.7          )
     t         ----------------->
     k         shifts gaze away
17   Ther:     .hhh betrayed. yeah.
18             (2.2)
19   Ther:     >so he's [let you<] down.
20   Kris:              [mm hm.   ]
     t         shallow multiple nods→
21   Kris:     mm hm.
     t         ----------->
22   Ther:     °°mm hm,°°
     t         --------------->
23             (  6.8  )
     t         ------->
     k         gazes towards T
24   Ther:     he's not there for you when he, (1.0) he should be.
     t                                                fast double nod
25             (       0.7          )
     k         fast shallow nod
26             (       1.6       )
     t         double nod→
27   Kris:     yeah.
```

In line 12, the therapist produces another formulation, but this time it does not do summary work and instead draws an implication about the husband's lack of interest and not being supportive; that is, she must feel "`very ↑alone`". Kristina, in lines 13–15, disagrees with this reading and claims that "`it's more betrayed den alone`". Following this is a lengthy 5.7-s silence in which Kristina shifts her gaze away from the therapist, thus signaling disengagement and momentary distance between them (line 16). The therapist, however, then works to re-affiliate with Kristina in the following ways: (1) retreating from her initial position by withholding a response; (2) doing a series of nods that stretch over the silence; (3) mirroring Kristina's prior talk by repeating the word "`betrayed`" followed by a confirmation (line 17); and (4) producing another formulation that elaborates on Kristina's feelings of betrayal (`>so he's let you< down.`). Through these actions, the therapist demonstrates her readiness to work with Kristina's claimed feeling of betrayal, by minimizing the gap resulting from prior differences in perspective. In the remainder of this extract, lines 21–27, affiliative sequences prevail and are realized in sequences with agreement as response and nodding from both speakers. Re-affiliative practices following formulation-disagreement sequences are taken up in Muntigl et al. (2013).

4.2.2 *Criticizing therapist interventions*

Client opposition may sometimes extend beyond a difference in viewpoints over the client's experience. The opposition, for example, may instead be challenging the appropriateness of a given therapist intervention and may work to criticize the therapist's talk. In Extract (6) involving client-centered therapy, the client Eve has been exhibiting distress over her brother's death occurring a few years back. I will limit my analysis to the critical actions voiced by the client and how this may be impacting on the therapeutic relationship. A full analysis of this extract is found in Muntigl (2020).

Extract 6.
(Muntigl 2020) [05:31–07:42]

```
01   Ther:   somehow it <s::ounds> perhaps as if, (2.2) you're
02           saying you didn't s:top enough to kinda- (1.5) process
03           it, an (.) integrate *it °an-° ( 0.4)* change course?
        e                         *drops arms to lap, looks away*
04           (0.3)
05   Eve:    well. n:- no I never ha:ve. (.) but, =
06   Ther:   = mm hm:[:,]
07   Eve:            [I ] mean-
08           (0.4)
09   Ther:   °does that° sound important?
        e      looks at T
10           (1.6)
        e     looks away
11   Ther:   [to do:?]
12   Eve:    [  hx:. ]
13           (2.1)
14   Eve:    ↑gee when you put it like °tha:t.°
        e    mocking tone
15           (0.8)
16   Eve:    uhm.
17           (1.1)
18   Ther:   >°d'you feel I'm twisting your arm,°<
19           (0.4)
20   Eve:    pardon?
21   Ther:   >°d'you feel I'm twisting your arm,°<
22           (0.6)
23   Eve:    hehheh hehheh heh .hhh .hhh .hh n(h)o it's just so:
24           O:bvious what you're saying. that of course it's tru:e.
25           .hhh uhm.
26           (0.8)
27   Ther:   °°but=chu may not want to. °°
28           (0.7)
29   Ther:   °°doesn't°° matter >whether it's< true° °°or not.°°
30           (0.7)
31   Eve:    ((lip smack)) °ooh I don't know.° .hh *.hhh HX:::.*
        e                                  *heaving shoulders and chest*
32           (3.5)
33   Eve:    like it- it n- (0.3)*~I mean the thing is is is* that,~
        e    choked voice         *rubs hand over eyes*
34           (2.4)
35   Eve:    °.snih°
36           (2.9)
37   Eve:    ~(y'know),~
```

Following the therapist's formulation that explicitly points out the possible consequences of not having sufficiently reflected on the brother's death (`process it, an (.) integrate it`) in lines 1–3 and her subsequent confirmation seeking question (`°does that° sound important?`), the client in line 14 mocks the therapist by conveying her annoyance with what the therapist has said (`↑gee when you put it like °tha:t.°`). The next client criticism occurs in lines 23–24 when she treats the therapist's prior intervention as being incongruous and inappropriate and thus challenges its relevance (`it's just so: O:bvious what you're saying. that of course it's tru:e.`). The client's responses may also be indexing a breach in an important relationship element, which concerns the therapist's degree of *genuineness* or *authenticity* (Rogers 1957); that is, in stating the "obvious," the therapist may be running the risk of appearing as simply supplying formulaic expressions as a response to the client's troubles, thus generating the inference that the therapist lacks an adequate professional commitment. But also, in not appearing 'authentic' the therapist's responses may not be taken up by Eve as empathic, as not fully understanding her personal situation.[6] Eve's criticisms, in this regard, would be conveying an affectual stance of continued anger or frustration at the therapist's response.

4.3 Topicalizing the relationship

Heightened opposition to the therapist's talk (i.e., interventions), especially in the form of outright criticism as seen in Extract (6), may cause what psychotherapy researchers have referred to as alliance ruptures and therefore bring about strains in the therapist–client relationship (Safran and Muran 1996). One of the suggested ways in dealing with these ruptures is to *explore relational themes associated with the rupture* (Safran et al. 2011). For instance, the relationship may be topicalized or made a topic of talk. This kind of practice, but from the client, was already seen in Extract (3). When Gloria said "`I don't feel close to you at a:ll`", she made their increasingly distant relationship (i.e., the lack of affiliation and warmth between them) an interpersonal issue. In Extract (7), taken from Muntigl (2020), relationship topicalization is done by the therapist. This extract, again involving the client Eve, occurs some minutes after Extract (6).

---

6. Some past studies on empathic practices in helping profession contexts may be found in Hepburn and Potter (2012), Muntigl et al. (2014), Ruusuvuri (2005) and Weiste and Peräkylä (2014).

Extract 7.
(Muntigl 2020) [10:51–12:20]

```
01  Eve:    I- I >don't °know what I'm saying.°<
        e             covers eyes with fingers
02          (1.7)
        e   rubs eyes
03  Ther:   [(this is sa-) so <bi:g,>] that (1.1) >that it< (.)
04  Eve:    [  *.hhh          hx:*    ]
        e   *heaving chest*
05  Ther:   kin've=jus seeps into everything? an it's (2.8) °hard° to be
06          r- (0.3) rational? or.
07          (0.3)
08  Ther:   whether you're fee:ling very emotional? and very?
09          (1.4)
10  Eve:    ((lip smack)) >°I dunno.°<
11          (4.6)
        e   rubs eyes
12  Eve:    *.hhh hx:.*
        e   *heaving chest*
13          (               13.5                 )
        e   gazes down, holding fingers at temples
        t   gazes at C
14  Ther:   ((lip smack)) °are you angry, that (we made you) watch
15          the video.°
16          (1.0)
17  Eve:    .hhh no:.
18  Ther:   >°are you angry with°< u:s:.
19  Eve:    no: no no.
20          (1.2)
        t   nod
21  Eve:    hx: .hhh
22          (0.7)
23  Eve:    ↑it- >no it was< ih <was: hard> uhm. (1.0)
24  Eve:    no >it ↑wasn't that it was< hard it was jus .hh wa:y more
25          °intense.°
26  Ther:   <mm: hm::.:>
        t   shallow nod
```

In lines 1–4, Eve displays many features of upset such as covering and rubbing her eyes, aspiration, sighing and whispered talk (Hepburn and Potter 2012). The therapist, in lines 3–8, responds with a formulation that orients to the intensity of her experience ("so <bi:g"; "kin've = jus seeps into everything") and how her emotions may be making it difficult for her to stay in a 'rational' frame of mind. Eve's response in line 10 is disaffiliative (>°I dunno.°<), working to resist the therapist's line of exploration (Hutchby 2002). This is then followed by further displays of upset such as rubbing her eyes, sighing, and holding her fingers at her temples while gazing downwards. Faced with Eve's distress and her resistance to engage with the therapist's understanding of Eve's personal experience, the therapist re-aligns the topic of conversation to what this interactional dynamic and Eve's distress might be conveying at the relationship level; that is, Eve may be feeling resentment toward the therapist and research group because she had to watch the video the previous week (lines 14–18). Anger is not only offered up as defining the present emotional component of their relationship, but it also potentially explains the interactional distance and disconnection between therapist and client, such as why Eve is having difficulty in engaging with and endorsing the therapist's responses. Eve in line 19 strongly contradicts the therapists via repeated *no*-negation, but we also see that she is displaying considerable distress, as evidenced by her pronounced sigh (line 21) and by the difficulty she seems to be having in trying to account for her upset (lines 23–24).

5. Conclusions

As Enfield (2006) has argued, just as there is 'no escape or time out' from the requirements arising from the sequential organization of talk, so is there no time out from the affiliation imperative that guides social interaction. This means that communicative acts will maintain, forge or make adjustments to the relationships within our social networks and to our many working relationships, however subtle. Using examples mainly from my own published research, I have illustrated some of the practices in psychotherapy that do relationship work. Drawing from Pomerantz and Mandelbaum's (2005) approach to relationship categories, I have shown how therapists and clients may use personal/role references to accomplish closer or more distant relationships and also how client troubles telling is an activity that tells us much about how psychotherapeutic relationships may be strengthened through affiliation or become stressed via opposition. For the most part, therapists and clients orient to the affiliative imperative through mutually accomplished pro-social actions, but we have also seen that more oppositional tendencies can come to the fore. Therapists, as Bänninger-Huber and Widmer (1999) have claimed, often must work within the framework of the 'Balance Hypothesis', which translates into both offering support and introducing interventions that may challenge the client's own *territorial preserves* involving, for example, possession, information, conversational rights, and so on (Goffman 2010). For this reason, therapist formulations or interpretations of client's prior descriptions of personal experience may be viewed by clients as deviating too much from their ownership/ entitlement to own experience and, thus, as a violation of their *informational* preserve (Goffman 2010). Such perceived violations may, in turn, lead clients to work at marking differences in their viewpoint with the therapist via disagreement or even censure the therapist for not appearing authentic. We have also seen in the extract involving Gestalt therapy how, when support is absent and thus no 'balance' is achieved, a conflict sequence constituted mainly through reprimanding and defensive actions resulted.

It may also be the case that the 'weak tie' characterization of the therapist-client relationship helps considerably to uphold these conflicting therapeutic aims elucidated in the balance hypothesis; that is, the regular provision of alternate viewpoints (e.g., via formulations or interpretations), the low emotional attachment (e.g., not matching the client's distress) and the therapist's non-judgemental, prizing attitude – all typical features of weak-tie relationships (Wright et al. 2010) – provide a distinct context for creating an empathic relationship in which to engage with the client's troubles while minimizing any perceived violation to the client's informational preserve. In particular, by focusing on the *client's* personal situation, and by refraining from sharing emotionally in the client's experience as might be typical of everyday talk among friends, the therapist is able to maintain a certain amount of relationship distance – and thus keep the tie on the weaker side – while still accomplishing *moments of strong intimacy* through continuous appreciation and understanding of the client's trouble. In this way, therapists may display their understanding and make affective connections with clients' affective stances, without appearing to appropriate clients' ownership/ entitlements to personal experiences. Although this chapter has not supplied an exhaustive list of relationship building (or damaging) practices, indeed this was not my aim, I have made some initial steps in showing how an extremely important aspect of psychotherapy, the relationship, is forged through therapists' and clients' moment-by-moment conduct.

Bibliography

Adelman, M. B., Parks, M. R., and Albrecht, T. L. 1987. "Beyond Close Relationships: Support in Weak Ties." In *Communicating Social Support*, edited by T. L. Albrecht, M. B. Adelman and Associates, 126–147. Newbury Park, CA: Sage.

Angus, Lynne E., and Leslie S. Greenberg. 2011. *Working with Narrative in Emotion-Focused Therapy: Changing Stories, Healing Lives.* Washington, DC: American Psychological Association. https://doi.org/10.1037/12325-000

Bänninger-Huber, Eva, and Christine Widmer. 1999. "Affective Relationship Patterns and Psychotherapeutic Change." *Psychotherapy Research* 9 (1): 74–87. https://doi.org/10.1093/ptr/9.1.74

Brown, Penelope, and Stephen C. Levinson. 1987. *Politeness: Some Universals in Language Usage.* Cambridge University Press. https://doi.org/10.1017/CBO9780511813085

Buttny, Richard. 1993. *Social Accountability in Communication.* London: Sage.

Davidson, Judy. 1984. "Subsequent Versions of Invitations, Offers, Requests, and Proposals Dealing with Potential or Actual Rejection." In *Structures of Social Action: Studies in Conversation Analysis*, edited by J. Maxwell Atkinson and John Heritage, 102–28. Cambridge: Cambridge University Press.

Drew, Paul. 1998. "Complaints About Transgressions and Misconduct." *Research on Language and Social Interaction* 31 (3–4): 295–325. https://doi.org/10.1080/08351813.1998.9683595
Drew, Paul, and Kathy Chilton. 2000. "Calling Just to Keep in Touch: Regular and Habitualised Telephone Calls as an Environment for Small Talk." In *Small talk*, edited by J. Coupland, 137–162. Harlow: Pearson Education.
Dunbar, R. I. M. 2018. "The Anatomy of Friendship." *Trends in Cognitive Sciences* 22 (1): 32–51. https://doi.org/10.1016/j.tics.2017.10.004
Enfield, N. J. 2006. "Social Consequences of Common Ground." In *Roots of human sociality: Culture, Cognition and Interaction*, edited by N. J. Enfield and S. C. Levinson, 399–430. Oxford: Berg Publishers.
Enfield, N. J. 2009. "Relationship Thinking and Human Pragmatics." *Journal of Pragmatics* 41 (1): 60–78. https://doi.org/10.1016/j.pragma.2008.09.007
Gelso, Charles J., and Jean A. Carter. 1985. "The Relationship in Counseling and Psychotherapy: Components, Consequences, and Theoretical Antecedents." *The Counseling Psychologist* 13 (2): 155–243. https://doi.org/10.1177/0011000085132001
Goffman, Erving. 1967. *Interaction Ritual: Essays on Face-to-Face Interaction*. Oxford, England: Aldine.
Goffman, Erving. 2010. *Relations in Public: Microstudies of the Public Order* (with a new introduction by Philip Manning). London: Transaction Publishers.
Goodwin, Charles, and Marjorie Harness Goodwin. 1987. "Concurrent Operations on Talk: Notes on the Interactive Organization of Assessments." *IPrA Papers in Pragmatics* 1 (1): 1–54. https://doi.org/10.1075/iprapip.1.1.01goo
Goodwin, Marjorie Harness. 1990. *He-said-she-said: Talk as Social Organization Among Black Children*. Indiana University Press.
Granovetter, Mark. 1983. "The Strength of Weak Ties: A Network Theory Revisited." *Sociological Theory* 1: 201. https://doi.org/10.2307/202051
Greenberg, L. S. 2014. "The Therapeutic Relationship in Emotion-Focused Therapy." *Psychotherapy* 51 (3): 350–57. https://doi.org/10.1037/a0037336
Greenberg, Leslie, and Jeanne Watson. 1998. "Experiential Therapy of Depression: Differential Effects of Client-Centered Relationship Conditions and Process Experiential Interventions." *Psychotherapy Research* 8 (2): 210–24. https://doi.org/10.1093/ptr/8.2.210
Greenberg, Leslie S., and Jeanne C. Watson. 2006. *Emotion-Focused Therapy for Depression*. Emotion-Focused Therapy for Depression. Washington, DC, US: American Psychological Association. https://doi.org/10.1037/11286-000.
Hepburn, Alexa, and Jonathan Potter. 2012. "Crying and Crying Responses." In *Emotion in Interaction*, edited by Anssi Perakyla and Marja-Leena Sorjonen, 1–32. Oxford: Oxford University Press. https://doi.org/10.1093/acprof:oso/9780199730735.003.0009
Heritage, John. 1984. *Garfinkel and Ethnomethodology*. John Wiley and Sons.
Heritage, John. 2011. "Territories of Knowledge, Territories of Experience: Empathic Moments in Interaction." In *The Morality of Knowledge in Conversation*, edited by Tanya Stivers, Lorenza Mondada, and Jakob Steensig, 159–83. Cambridge: Cambridge University Press. https://doi.org/10.1017/CBO9780511921674.008
Heritage, John. 2012. "The Epistemic Engine: Sequence Organization and Territories of Knowledge." *Research on Language and Social Interaction* 45 (1): 30–52. https://doi.org/10.1080/08351813.2012.646685

Heritage, John, and D. Rodney Watson. 1979. "Formulations as Conversational Objects." In *Everyday Language: Studies in Ethnomethodology*, edited by George Psathas, 123–62. New York: Irvington Publishers.

Hill, R. A., and R. I. M. Dunbar. 2003. "Social Network Size in Humans." *Human Nature* 14 (1): 53–72. https://doi.org/10.1007/s12110-003-1016-y

Hutchby, Ian. 2002. "Resisting the Incitement to Talk in Child Counselling: Aspects of the Utterance `I Don't Know'." *Discourse Studies* 4 (2): 147–68. https://doi.org/10.1177/14614456020040020201

Jefferson, Gail. 1974. "Error Correction as an Interactional Resource." *Language in society* 3, (2): 181–199. https://doi.org/10.1017/S0047404500004334

Jefferson, Gail, and John Lee. 1980. "On the Sequential Organization of Troubles-Talk in Ordinary Conversation." End of grant report to the (British) Social Science Research Council on the analysis of conversations in which "troubles" and "anxieties" are expressed. University of Manchester.

Lerner, Gene H. 1992. "Assisted Storytelling: Deploying Shared Knowledge as a Practical Matter." *Qualitative sociology* 15 (3): 247–271. https://doi.org/10.1007/BF00990328

Leudar, Ivan, Charles Antaki, and Rebecca Barnes. 2006. "When Psychotherapists Disclose Personal Information about Themselves to Clients." *Communication and Medicine* 3 (1): 27–41. https://doi.org/10.1515/CAM.2006.004.

Mandelbaum, Jennifer. 1987. "Couples Sharing Stories." *Communication Quarterly* 35, (2): 144–170. https://doi.org/10.1080/01463378709369678

McNamee, Sheila, and Kenneth J. Gergen, eds. 1992. *Therapy as Social Construction*. Therapy as Social Construction. Thousand Oaks, CA: Sage.

Minuchin, Salvador. 1974. *Families and Family Therapy*. Harvard University Press. https://doi.org/10.4159/9780674041127

Muntigl, Peter. 2013. "Resistance in Couples Counselling: Sequences of Talk That Disrupt Progressivity and Promote Disaffiliation." *Journal of Pragmatics* 49 (1): 18–37. https://doi.org/10.1016/j.pragma.2013.01.003

Muntigl, Peter. 2020. "Managing Distress Over Time in Psychotherapy: Guiding the Client in and Through Intense Emotional Work." *Frontiers in Psychology* 10:3052. https://doi.org/10.3389/fpsyg.2019.03052

Muntigl, Peter, and Adam O. Horvath. 2014. "'I Can See Some Sadness in Your Eyes': When Experiential Therapists Notice a Client's Affectual Display." *Research on Language and Social Interaction* 47 (2): 89–108. https://doi.org/10.1080/08351813.2014.900212

Muntigl, Peter, and Adam O. Horvath. 2016. "A Conversation Analytic Study of Building and Repairing the Alliance in Family Therapy." *Journal of Family Therapy* 38 (1): 102–119. https://doi.org/10.1111/1467-6427.12109

Muntigl, Peter, Adam O. Horvath, Eva Bänninger-Huber, and Lynne Angus. 2020. "Responding to Self-Criticism in Psychotherapy." *Psychotherapy Research* 30 (6): 800–814. https://doi.org/10.1080/10503307.2019.1686191.

Muntigl, Peter, Adam O. Horvath, Lynda Chubak, and Lynne Angus. 2020. "Getting to 'Yes': Overcoming Client Reluctance to Engage in Chair Work." *Frontiers in Psychology* 11 (October): 582856. https://doi.org/10.3389/fpsyg.2020.582856

Muntigl, Peter, Naomi K Knight, and Lynne Angus. 2014. "Targeting Emotional Impact in Storytelling: Working with Client Affect in Emotion-Focused Psychotherapy." *Discourse Studies* 16 (6): 753–75. https://doi.org/10.1177/1461445614546255

Muntigl, Peter, Naomi Knight, and Ashley Watkins. 2012. "Working to Keep Aligned in Psychotherapy: Using Nods as a Dialogic Resource to Display Affiliation." *Language and Dialogue* 2 (1): 9–27. https://doi.org/10.1075/ld.2.1.01mun

Muntigl, Peter, Naomi Knight, and Ashley Watkins. 2014. "Empathic Practices in Client-Centred Psychotherapies: Displaying Understanding and Affiliation with Clients." In *Discourses of Helping Professions*, edited by Eva-Maria Graf, Marlene Sator, and Thomas Spranz-Fogasy, 33–57. Amsterdam: John Benjamins. https://doi.org/10.1075/pbns.252.03mun

Muntigl, Peter, Naomi Knight, Ashley Watkins, Adam O. Horvath, and Lynne Angus. 2013. "Active Retreating: Person-Centered Practices to Repair Disaffiliation in Therapy." *Journal of Pragmatics* 53: 1–20. https://doi.org/10.1016/j.pragma.2013.03.019

Muntigl, Peter, and William Turnbull. 1998. "Conversational Structure and Facework in Arguing." *Journal of Pragmatics* 29 (3): 225–56. https://doi.org/10.1016/S0378-2166(97)00048-9

Norcross, John C., ed. 2011. *Psychotherapy Relationships that Work: Evidence-based Responsiveness* (2nd ed.). Oxford University Press.

Norcross, John C., and Michael J. Lambert. 2018. "Psychotherapy Relationships That Work III." *Psychotherapy* 55 (4): 303–15. https://doi.org/10.1037/pst0000193

Pain, Jean. 2009. *Not Just Talking: Conversational Analysis, Harvey Sacks' Gift to Therapy*. Routledge.

Pennebaker, James W, and Janel D Seagal. 1999. "Forming a Story: The Health Benefits of Narrative." *Journal of Clinical Psychology*, 12. https://doi.org/10.1002/(SICI)1097-4679(199910)55:10<1243::AID-JCLP6>3.0.CO;2-N

Peräkylä, Anssi. 2019. "Conversation Analysis and Psychotherapy: Identifying Transformative Sequences." *Research on Language and Social Interaction* 52 (3): 257–280. https://doi.org/10.1080/08351813.2019.1631044

Pomerantz, Anita. 1984. "Agreeing and Disagreeing with Assessments: Some Features of Preferred/Dispreferred Turn Shaped." In *Structures of Social Action: Studies in Conversation Analysis*, edited by J. Maxwell Atkinson and John Heritage, 57–101. Cambridge, United Kingdom: Cambridge University Press.

Pomerantz, Anita, and Jenny Mandelbaum. 2005. "Conversation Analytic Approaches to the Relevance and Uses of Relationship Categories in Interaction." In *Handbook of Language and Social Interaction*, edited by Kristine Fitch and Robert Sanders, 149–71. Mahwah, N.J: Lawrence Erlbaum Associates.

Rogers, Carl R. 1957. "The Necessary and Sufficient Conditions of Therapeutic Personality Change." *Journal of Consulting Psychology* 21 (2): 95–103. https://doi.org/10.1037/h0045357

Ruusuvuori, Johanna. 2005. "'Empathy' and 'Sympathy' in Action: Attending to Patients' Troubles in Finnish Homeopathic and General Practice Consultations." *Social Psychology Quarterly* 68 (3): 204–22. https://doi.org/10.1177/019027250506800302

Sacks, Harvey. 1992. *Lectures on Conversation*. Edited by Gail Jefferson. Oxford, UK: Wiley-Blackwell.

Safran, Jeremy D, and J Christopher Muran. 1996. "The Resolution of Ruptures in the Therapeutic Alliance." *Journal of Consulting and Clinical Psychology* 64, 447–458. https://doi.org/10.1037/0022-006X.64.3.447

Safran, Jeremy D., J. Christopher Muran, and Catherine Eubanks-Carter. 2011. "Repairing Alliance Ruptures." *Psychotherapy* 48 (1): 80–87. https://doi.org/10.1037/a0022140

Schegloff, Emanuel A. 2007. *Sequence Organization in Interaction: A Primer in Conversation Analysis*. Cambridge; New York: Cambridge University Press. https://doi.org/10.1017/CBO9780511791208

Shostrum, E. L. (Producer). 1966. "*Three Approaches to Psychotherapy*" [Motion picture]. Santa Ana, CA: Psychological Films.

Sidnell, Jack, and Tanya Stivers, eds. 2013. *The Handbook of Conversation Analysis*. Chichester, West Sussex, UK: Wiley-Blackwell.

Stivers, Tanya. 2008. "Stance, Alignment, and Affiliation During Storytelling: When Nodding Is a Token of Affiliation." *Research on Language and Social Interaction* 41 (1): 31–57. https://doi.org/10.1080/08351810701691123

Stivers, Tanya, Lorenza Mondada, and Jakob Steensig. 2011. "Knowledge, Morality and Affiliation in Social Interaction." In *The Morality of Knowledge in Conversation*, edited by Tanya Stivers, Lorenza Mondada and Jakob Steensig. Cambridge University Press, Cambridge, pp. 3–24. https://doi.org/10.1017/CBO9780511921674.002

Strong, Tom, and Olga Smoliak. 2018. "Introduction to Discursive Research and Discursive Therapies." In *Therapy as Discourse: Practice and Research*, edited by Olga Smoliak and Tom Strong, 1–18. The Language of Mental Health. Cham: Springer International Publishing. https://doi.org/10.1007/978-3-319-93067-1_1

Weiste, Elina. 2015. "Describing Therapeutic Projects across Sequences: Balancing between Supportive and Disagreeing Interventions." *Journal of Pragmatics* 80 (April): 22–43. https://doi.org/10.1016/j.pragma.2015.02.001.

Weiste, Elina, and Anssi Peräkylä. 2014. "Prosody and Empathic Communication in Psychotherapy Interaction." *Psychotherapy Research* 24 (6): 687–701. https://doi.org/10.1080/10503307.2013.879619

Wright, Kevin B., Steve Rains, and John Banas. 2010. "Weak-Tie Support Network Preference and Perceived Life Stress Among Participants in Health-Related, Computer-Mediated Support Groups." *Journal of Computer-Mediated Communication* 15 (4): 606–24. https://doi.org/10.1111/j.1083-6101.2009.01505.x

Doing We – Working alliance in psychotherapeutic relationships

A recursive model

Michael B. Buchholz
IPU Berlin

Larger chunks from psychotherapeutic cooperations are presented. Cooperation is studied in empirical psychotherapeutic process research as "working alliance" of which conceptual conflicts are outlined.

I follow a proposal by Ginzburg and Poesio (2016) to micro-analyze hesitation markers as conversational equivalents to embodied pointing gestures. Several stories by patients are told in order to "point" to comparisons *between* the stories. The concept of "tacit comparisons" is, thus, introduced. Then, a recursive model of common ground is proposed with reference to cognitive-linguistic theory of metaphor (Cienki und Müller 2010; Lakoff 1987). The conversation creates in describable steps new metaphors indicating important change.

Keywords: psychotherapy, conversation analysis, larger chunks, meaning making in therapeutic relationships, interactional metaphors, tacit comparison, common ground, psychoanalysis

> In that the separate perceptual frameworks of each participant must be integrated into a common task … the task of translating the view from one perspective into the frame of reference of another is posed.
> (Goodwin 2018b, 295)

1. Introduction

Psychoanalysis in its early years conceptualized the "We" in psychotherapeutic cooperation in a fashion that reminds us of or even pre-announces today's conversation analysis. Unfortunately, all these efforts vanished for reasons not to be discussed here. However, it is fair to remember some of this early and forgotten

https://doi.org/10.1075/pbns.331.03buc

reasoning in the beginning of this chapter. Then, I will quickly cover how leading psychotherapy process researchers conceptualize what is termed the "working alliance". I thereby hope to prepare the floor to better document the actual contribution of conversation analysis for the study of working together in psychotherapeutic contexts. I propose to talk of "Doing We". I will use two somewhat extended case examples presented in transcripts to illustrate my argument.

2. Early psychoanalytic efforts and empirical research

Here is how a first-generation follower of Freud conceptualized what today is called the "working alliance".

> From the beginning the patient is asked to 'work together' against something. Every single hour of analysis gives the analyst the opportunity to apply the word "we" to himself and the realistic part of the patient's ego. [...] One could say that "we" is the instrument for the therapeutic splitting of the ego (translation MBB).
> (Sterba 1934, 69)

The "therapeutic splitting" is a spatial description of doing and feeling and at the same time observing one's doing and feeling. Philosophers termed it "self-observation" or "ex-centric position" (Plessner 1928). Research interests turned to what later was called the "rupture" of a therapeutic working alliance; ruptures should be given special attention, to work on it was found to contribute to success in treatment. "Working together" became the one end-point of a continuum with the other end point of "transference". In clinical profession it was clearly stated: "The transference neurosis is indeed a creature of the analytic situation" (Loewald 1971, 62). Here I do not want to go deeply into the topic of transference neurosis and the like; it suffices to point out that there was a clear formulation of a situational and interactive approach in those early writings.

Many lines of thinking could not build a tradition, they were torn apart by WW II. In the 1990s the reasoning about "working alliance" was taken up by empirically working psychoanalysts (Safran und Muran 2000) who initiated an enormous amount of research on what was now called "working alliance" (WA). WA was determined to be the most influential factor in psychotherapy of every kind (Bordin 1979; Falkenström, Granström und Holmqvist 2014; Kanninen, Salo und Punamäki 2000). Now it was "alliance" and "rupture" to be conceptualized as the two ends of a continuum in therapeutic cooperation.

When empirical researchers measured WA by questionnaires (Falkenström et al. 2019; Hatcher, Lindqvist und Falkenström 2019) a new problem emerged: WA became an *individual* patient variable measured in order to evaluate its predictive power for the overall therapeutic outcome. This had an unintended side effect: what was conceptualized as a cooperation between *two* participants in therapeutic conversation became a kind of quality attributable to one person, the patient, only. The new continuum, then, extended between the pole of individual inability and cooperative readiness or ability. One wavered back and forth between two poles, frankly admitted by one of the early founders of this research tradition in a recent paper titled as "confessions of a rupture researcher":

> We have also found it useful to define ruptures by specific patient communications or behaviors – even though, we have always considered a rupture as something co-constructed by patient and therapist, as an interaction between their respective personality configurations and immediate needs.
>
> (Safran and Muran 2000) (Muran 2019, 3)

Either a rupture is defined as "co-constructed" or it is a kind of "specific patient communications or behavior". Can one maintain both? No, one cannot. There is a deep *conceptual* problem in how "Doing We" is studied in empirical psychotherapy process research.

Former editors of the leading journal "Psychotherapy Research", William Stiles, Clara Hill and Robert Elliott in a common paper were concerned about the "equivalent paradox": all so-called "bona-fide"-therapies produced comparable outcome although therapists adhered to highly divergent theories. They concluded that using qualitative coding systems would not heal this paradox, better be to walk on

> ...four paths for future research: case study approaches, conversation analyses, comprehensive process analyses, and more sophisticated process analyses.
>
> (Stiles, Hill und Elliott 2015, 288)

This is an opportunity for conversation analysis to propose how the interactional approach can be sustained and combined with psychotherapy process research (PPR). CA can "heal" this critical gap in psychotherapeutic cooperation research by studying observables of interaction. If "mind" is part of what we do, then, relating through meaning making and making meaning through relating are two sides of the same coin.

My first example will show how the therapeutic "handling" of a typical problematic situation (TPS) (Buchholz 2016) can distort or deepen the process of "Doing We". The following Examples (2)–(4) show how a patient's suicidal threat runs through many sessions and threatens the therapeutic "Doing We", if the therapist does not handle it as skilful as the therapist here does. Examples (5)–(7) show other dimensions of Doing-We; the therapeutic use of metaphor (by patient and therapist) creates something like a recursive spiral indicating how therapist and patient mutually observe each other's "Doing We".

3. First example: A "failed" we-construction

My examples are taken from our CEMPP-Project which used conversation analysis to compare the processes in five psychodynamic, five psychoanalytic and five cognitive behavioral therapies. From these 3 therapeutic orientations we had a session from the beginning, from the middle phase and from the end, taken from the Munich Psychotherapy Study,[1] amounting to a corpus of 15 sessions in every orientation. The whole corpus were 45 sessions. Our German transcripts use GAT II (Selting et al. 2011).[2] Here is the beginning of a fourth session of a cognitive behavioral therapy.

Excerpt 1. Cognitive-behavioral therapy (CBT)

```
 1  P: so those questionnaires they indeed are always very hard to
       fail in (1.3)
 2  P: ah fill in
 3  T: what äh how do you feel about
 4  P: I always find it so exh- so stressful
 5     ((5 lines omitted))
 6  P: I always have so many questionnaires to fill in a[gain
 7  T:                                                  [yes
 8  P: this interview, I think dear my god so (1.3) that's so difficult
 9  T: then we could go through it
10     (1.0)
11  P: we would be more professional then <<laughingly>>. I gonna go
       to get the questionnaires?
```

This CBT-session starts with a Freudian slip and its self-initiated self-repair (Albert und Ruiter 2018). To fill in the questionnaire is required by the therapist in the session before – and if the patient does not return with the questionnaire filled it this indicates some "trouble" in "Doing We". The female patient states in a self-comment and excuse, roughly translated, not to have "failed, em filled in" the therapist's questionnaire. This is a slip with relevance for cooperation. Schegloff 2000) predicts that the repressed idea, if ignored, will reappear within approximately one minute. And it is what happens (line 4). A second slip, quickly self-repaired, goes again unnoticed by the therapist who sticks to her interventionist program. Unnoticed – it might be that the therapist did notice. However, in CA there is a strong methodological assumption that noticing should come in the interactional domain, not only as a mindful registration. (Muntigl und Horvath 2014) These authors mean

1. Thanks to my colleague Prof. Dr. Dorothea Huber for granting access to the audio tapes of the Munich-Study ((Huber und Klug 2016).

2. If readers want to have the German transcripts turn to the author.

by "noticing" a pointing to something the patient displays. This is omitted here and one can assume that CBT does not have a theory for what slips are. This is freely admitted by CBT-therapists for dreams:

> Whenever a patient reports a dream to a CBT therapist, the latter can only politely mention that s/he does not know what to do with it. (Montangero 2009, 240)

Now, there is a remarkable difference between the two slips. (Schegloff 2013) assumed that in pauses following self-initiated self-repairs speakers might resonate about how their utterance might sound in the recipient's ear. Slips are self-observed. The first slip ("to fail in"), then, might evoke in the recipient's ear the idea that the speaker is unwilling to "fail/fill in" the questionnaire delivered by the therapist. The slip is relevant for "Doing-We", a correction is required, a "cognitive load" requiring time.

Neurologically, a delay in response following a slip (line 1 here, 1.3 sec) discard would make sense (Bögels, Magyari und Levinson 2015). To re-listen to one's own utterance takes about 0.6 seconds, to plan a repair-utterance takes another 0.6 second. Thus, the pause (1.3 sec) in line 1. This pause could be understood as an example of what Harvey Sacks called the "My mind is with you"-dimension of conversation (MMWY), to have the listener's mind in mind.

> Now, in the middle of a conversation, we know well, in some ways, who it is we're talking to. And there are enormously elaborated ways in which we bring off that 'my mind is with you' – I use that rather loose sounding phrase and you might figure that it could get shot down, but we'll see in due course that people really can achieve showing that 'my mind is with you.' And the question is, at the beginning of a conversation, how rapidly can parties achieve that sort of a thing?
> (Sacks und Jefferson 1992/1995, 166 ff.)

Sacks assumes this "my-mind-is-with-you"-dimension (MMWY) to be a global but tacit dimension of every human relationship that steps beyond simple exchange of adjacency pairs. A self-initiated self-repair followed by a pause of 1.2 seconds can be considered as a slip with relevance for Doing-We. Following Schegloff's prediction (2000) the next slip follows (line 4: "exh(austing)- stressful"). The German word repaired means "anstrengend" (of which only the first syllable is uttered) and the meaning is defused by a normalizing adjective: stressful. As the patient's first slip was responded by a kind of standard therapeutic question (line 3) one can conclude that she observed the therapist as not attentive to slips (Montangero 2009).

The patient demonstrates to participate carefully. She clearly voices her idea about what she thinks drives a therapist, quickly she responds to power play or non-affiliation and she voices her displeasure by commenting on the therapist's project to get the questionnaire filled in. As this is a very empathic display of the patient's empathic competence, we can discard the idea that patients lack empathy in general. PPRS supports such a view:

> „Clients contribute to both the experience of empathy and its effects in psychotherapy in several ways. Empathy may be at least as much a client variable as it is a therapist variable. Who the client is almost certainly influences therapist empathy."
> (Elliott et al. 2018, 406)

Empathy is co-constructed, however, it is displayed in different versions. The We-construction by the patient (line 11) has a "vertical" dimension. This cooperation by conformity is self-commented and acknowledges the therapist's need for professionalism in a kind of empathy which people in an inferior position often display recognizably by a "we" commented by some irony (her laughter) based on empathy and compliance. She interprets the therapist's insistence on filling-in questionnaires as motivated: to give the interaction the flair of professionalism. Alluding to the hierarchy the patient is doing "interpretive work". This observation has a long *clinical* tradition. Sandor Ferenczi, a psychoanalyst of the first generation

> ...was among the first to suggest that the patient may have unique insight into therapist's countertransference problems and that for the benefit of the treatment, patients should be encouraged to point out the ways in which the analyst is affecting the process. (Miller-Bottome und Safran 2018, 230)

Patients have unique insights into how therapists think. This observation was met in CA, too.

> ...there are enormously elaborated ways in which we bring off that 'my mind is with you' ... we'll see in due course that people really can achieve showing that 'my mind is with you.' And the question is, at the beginning of a conversation, how rapidly can parties achieve that sort of a thing?
> (Sacks und Jefferson 1992/1995, 166 ff.)

4. "My-mind-is-with-you" (MMWY): A silent dimension

MMWY encompasses co-operation outside the treatment room, too. It opens a way for CA to observe how a couple mutually observes doing-we. One can use the MMWY-dimension in order to analyze larger chunks of talk. There is a surprising closeness between clinical theorizing and some traditions in social sciences. A psychoanalyst used the term "meeting of minds" for what Ferenczi had described:

> Understanding would seem to be an act that involves some sort of mutual engagement, a particular form of the meeting of minds. (Loewald 1979, 165)

Later, in 1995, social scientist Jerome Bruner introduced this term more precisely:

> What I want to offer here is a sketch of some relevant points. At its most sophisticated level, joint attention is, in effect, a 'meeting of minds.' It depends not only on a shared or joint focus, but on shared context and shared presuppositions.
> (Bruner 1995/2014)

Later, a book by a relational psychoanalyst was titled "A meeting of minds" (Aron 1996). It is, as if this term shifted from the hands of psychotherapists to social scientists and back to psychoanalysts indicating some usefulness in all these fields. As "resonating minds" the topic has found interest in empirical psychotherapy process studies (Mergenthaler 2008). But its cognitive naming ("mind") made it distasteful for most conversation analysts while psychoanalysts did not know how to study the "meeting"-dimension. The cognitive, the psychodynamic and the conversational areas were believed to be mutually separated by unsurmountable walls. Enfield's (2013) linguistic book "Relationship Thinking" breaks through these walls:

> „So when we study human interaction, we are studying the mind, in the real sense of that word: an interpretative system that is distributed through and across people, places, and times". (N. J. Enfield 2013, XVIII)

Here are some further examples how this breakthrough is set in motion. An illustrative example ((Brockmeier 2017): A husband before leaving the house in the morning cannot find the car-key. He calls for his wife: "Do you know where…" and before ending his question he hears her response: "in the right pocket of your trousers yesterday". Asked with surprise, wherefrom she knows, she responds laughingly, from yesterday coming home and observing what he did in some absent-mindedness. Brockmeier documents the paradigmatic shift from a memory-as-archive conception to remembering-by-conversation (Wooffitt 2005). There is a longer way (Edwards und Middleton 1987) to a new paradigm. It was used by (Edwards und Potter 1992) who analyzed the "forgetfulness" of the German Chancellor Helmut Kohl. Others (Mahr und Csibra 2018) coming from neuro-cognitive research turn the question: What is an episodic memory and which is its conversational function? The little example of the car-key is a cooperative "episodic memory". Its function "serves to justify a belief about the occurrence of this event" (Mahr und Csibra 2018: 6). In conversation an episodic memory makes claims in *negotiating epistemic authority* (remembering for others with good or bad reasons; it is selective and displays motivated forgetfulness in presenting reasons; it documents and supports epistemic vigilance and a more precise interpersonal monitoring (Wagner Cook 2014) and, finally, can deliver past events as reasons for actual utterances). People share experience with others and sometimes speculate what others think and can install procedures to mutually check these speculations. This is the epistemic dimension. They treat and meet each other as people thinking about thinking people.

The deontic dimension is touched as you are not always entitled to communicate your speculations or share it with third persons. There are more, e.g. embodied (as dancers know) and affiliative dimensions as people who were in love will easily confirm. And people, who commonly survived great danger.[3]

Thus, "meeting of minds" is an umbrella term for the interplay of emotional-cognitive and conversational features, and it will be useful to respect both aspects when studying therapeutic conversation that is extended over several sessions. Participants somehow keep in mind what was spoken and use it (selectively) for next opportunities.

A therapeutic session is a complex situation. Every kind of analysis must be conceptually prepared to how participants do next doings with reference to past sessions, a week or a month ago. Without the assumption of a shared interactional memory no concatenations of interactive turns beyond the sheer presence of sequentiality could be done.

5. From sequentiality to larger chunks: Tacit comparisons

The study of larger chunks of talk concatenating inter-session events (Buchholz und Kächele 2017) is a challenge. Here, I analyse three excerpts of a psychotherapeutic treatment included in our CEMPP-project. The excerpts derive from various sessions in this treatment of a suicidal patient. In this psychoanalytic treatment, the male patient is lying on the couch for the first time in treatment. It is a patient who – in a serious crisis of his professional life – attempted to commit suicide in a hotel room abroad. He survived, but all his relatives were not informed about the incident, he says that they were unclear about his state, would not understand him and he did not want to put too much burden on their shoulders. Talking about all this with his therapist and not with his wife is inferred by the therapist as a conflict of loyalty. In the following excerpt he explains why it is difficult for him to tell her of his suicide attempt.

Excerpt 2. Psychodynamic therapy (sitting vis-à-vis)

1 P: *because I always have the feeling that she's a completely (1.4) ((clicks tongue))*
2 *well how shall I say .h such a controlled person who hmhm*
3 *who is quite not ve:ry or quite quite hard (.) has hardly any feelings then*
4 *I believe that she wouldn't understand it .h that she would find it ridiculous .h*

3. This distinction between epistemic, deontic and affiliative dimension is taken from (Stevanovic und Peräkylä 2014).

5 (1.0)
6 T: hm
7 (10.3)
8 P: an=well for it's always like that when I (-) .h have or sEE someone in my circle of friends when I notice he is a bit (1.2) hhh yes how shall I put it?
9 hhwh=wh=who is a bit weaker (---) I trEAt them the same way (---) do you understand?
10 .hh and then I think th=that they perhaps do exactly the same thing (.) I don't want that so
11 (2.7)

My first analysis uses a term by Goodwin (2015: 201) who spoke of the "visible cognitive life of the hearer" (Goodwin 2015). His analysis of the interplay between hearer and speaker is based on Goffman's distinction between the analytic roles of *author* (who created the text), *animator* ("sounding box", the speaker quoting another author's text), *principal* (who is responsible for the selection of a quotation), *figure* (a character in a described scene) and *tokens* (utterances by which the listener comments on what is heard) (Goffman 1983).

The patient in Excerpt (2) addresses the therapist as a helping person *and* as a complice in a betrayal of his wife who is kept uninformed although he acknowledges that she should know about his state. She is a *figure* in his marital scenario. Talking as *author* with the therapist includes a second scenario with the patient as *animator* describing his wife in the service to justify him why he talks with the therapist and not with her. She is said to be "quite quite hard" (line 3). His wife's inaccessibility is a person-*description* for which he is the author. In line 4 he begins his utterance prefaced with "I believe" and adds a quasi-quotation that she would find it "ridiculous". He *animates* her voice.

The therapist cannot decide about the truth of this "scenario within the talk-in-interaction", a silence arises followed by the therapist's "hm"-token, bringing him into the second-position as a listener followed by a 10-sec pause. Then, the patient's "it's always like that" (line 8) sounds like a conclusive summary of what was said. At the same time, it is used as *opening* a new self-positioning. While he seems to suffer from his wife's inaccessibility, he begins to describe himself as somebody who treats others "the same way".

Sliding into an active position is interrupted by "how shall I put it?" What might be heard as a hesitation marker indicates a positional shift (a) from "victim" to "culprit" within the told story and (b) within the talk-in-interaction. Within the story it is a kind of "turning-the-table"-operation: he changes to more activity of a kind from which he claims to suffer when the same activity is executed by his wife. Within the talk-in-interaction he loses the self-ascribed justification (his wife would not understand him) to talk to the therapist. These positional shifts can be analyzed with Goffmanian concepts.

Further analysis is required in order to analyze phrases like "well how shall I say" (line 2), "how shall I put it?" (line 8). Who is addressed with the personal pronoun "you" in "do you understand?" (line 9)? As long as the patient presents himself in a victim-position of being excluded from his wife's inaccessibility the therapist is positioned as a "partner substitute". But who is the therapist after the patient changes his self-positioning into someone who does what he accuses others to do to him? My second analysis pays more attention to phrases like self-commenting, delays and self-repairs. Some pauses indicate conflicts in the speaker's speech-project: the clicking of the tongue, hesitation markers like "how shall I put it"? (line 2) can be heard as indicating some difficulties to realize his speech-project.

Such phrases are sometimes conceptualized simply as "fillers" in everyday thinking. Conversation analysts (Chafe 1985; Lerner 2013) have studied them more precisely as "hesitation markers" paving the way to the observation that some cognitive-emotional "load" (Peräkylä et al. 2015) is indicated by the delay. Recently, an interesting proposal was made (Ginzburg und Poesio 2016) to view such remarks in analogy to the pointing gesture.

> In all but the simplest situations, the identification of the demonstratum among the objects in the **pointing cone** identified by a pointing gesture is a complex reasoning process involving consideration of a number of additional aspects of the Interaction situation.
>
> Beyond this, Clark (2003) showed that pointing is neither the only nor the prototypical way to carry out a demonstration. For instance, a customer can felicitously demonstrate to the teller in a supermarket the referents of a demonstrative like *These two things over here* by **placing** the two objects on the counter rather than merely pointing at them."
>
> (Ginzburg und Poesio 2016, 10) emphasis in the original)

There is not only an "origo", as (Bühler 2011 (1934)) termed what psychoanalysts would call the "ego" and CA studies address as "agency" (Barnes 2000; Deppermann 2015; Emirbayer und Mische 1998; Nicholas J. Enfield und Kockelman 2017). Pointing gestures refer to selected things in a commonly shared environment. Geologists, archaeologist or expert witnesses in the courtroom (Goodwin 2018a) use certain practices (e.g. telling narratives, stimulating imagination) to make the listener "see" what can be seen in a handful of earth or dirt or in a video record. Trained experts use observable practices to make newcomers see what can be seen by the professional:

> Learning to see and construe the world in the ways that make possible the accomplishment of relevant activities... (Goodwin 2018a, 426)

In archaeology an expert instructs a student by pointing to certain details in a handful of dust, shards and different colours the beginner found. Expert "invent" narratives to make things visible for the beginner. “Instead of listening to a description of a past event, participants systematically reconstruct the *now invisible processes* that created what can be seen in the present.” (Goodwin 2015: 213, italics MBB). A narrative is used as a kind of “instructing” the other’s ability to “see-in-depth” (Goodwin).

In psychotherapy the “instruction” goes in both ways. A patient is *expert* for his life instructing the therapist about important and relevant stories, details and relationships; the patient uses practices of “pointing” to things which are “now invisible” (Goodwin) or phantasmatic (as Bühler named it). They are “things” in a conversational reality, achieve meaning in narratives and as details of a “scenario”. On the other hand, the therapist is *expert* for how to “see” these things in a more coherent way in order to achieve higher levels of personal integration. It has been shown that therapists often use reformulations to point to the same detail. Reframing sometimes makes details of meaning visible (Antaki 2008; Deppermann 2011; Weiste und Peräkylä 2013).

Extending Goodwin’s analyses of co-operation between experts and learners into a two-way direction *and* the analysis of practices of pointing (to “details” and “scenarios”) can be used to observe what’s going on in the treatment room. In psychotherapy it is often enough the patient who “instructs” the therapist in order to make him/her “see” (Buchholz 2015, 2019a, 2020). While Goodwin’s protagonists can point to a *perceptual* world with many objects and details, a patient does not have this possibility. There is no perceptual thing to point to. Patients can only point to *conversational* objects like topics, experiences or (reported) events. Some of them cannot be directly shared, like e.g. dreams. They must be told (Peräkylä und J. R. Bergmann 2020) but do not have a reference in an external world. The aim of this effort is to arrange a commonly shared imagination which remains always insecure, instable and fragile. These qualities evoke emotions the patient-as-teller experiences as vulnerability; he never can be completely sure that what s/he tells equals a *full* copy of one’s own imagination (Buchholz 2015).

The commonly shared environment is, thus, not a visible one but audible only. It is a cognitive-emotional scenario referred to by the speaker who tries to make sure that the recipient imagines something *sufficiently equivalent* (Birkner und Ehmer 2013; Deppermann und Schmidt 2016; Ehmer 2011; Sinha und Rodriguez 2008). MMWY-dimension is at risk as the patient is on the way to tell something morally objectionable: he complains of his wife being so inaccessibly “hard” and now (line 8) projects to complain of his friends as “weak” – but before he uses this word inserts a break and asks “how shall I put (say) it?” By juxtaposing the first episodic memory with a second, he notices that both generate a strong contrast in need of explanation. *He* notices? Or does he imagine how such a contrast between two episodic memories is heard by the therapist? Such a question cannot be securely answered.

However, if MMWY is a silent dimension in every conversation as Sacks assumed, we cannot ignore such a possibility. A patient is not only a teller, s/he listens to her-/himself in an attempt to catch how the therapist listens.

Hesitation markers as pointing to tacit comparisons

The signs of complex reasoning (see box 1), of repetition or self-repairs indicate, first, a *structural* insecurity: a teller can never be fully secure that a recipient imagines "the same world". This is why telling a narrative generally is accompanied by the listener's "change-of-state-tokens". If they are delivered, the "emotional load" can be (physiologically) shown to be shared (Peräkylä et al. 2015). Second, presenting contrasting elements which point to the teller's self (disliking inaccessible hardness *and* disliking weak friends) is not a structural insecurity. It is specific. It is a way of tacitly informing the therapist that the patient situates himself between Scylla and Charybdis: neither weakness nor hardness helps. The therapist's task for installing a helpful "Doing We" must be to find another solution.

To ask "do you understand?" (line 9) in such a context of high emotional contrast is not only a polite phrase; the question is if the therapist "sees" (Goodwin) the contrast between the two selected episodic memories. With an "emotional load" on the teller's shoulders: Not realizing the contrast would make the therapist "weak" or insufficient; realizing the contrast would expose the patient to some incoherence in himself.

Box 1. Phrases pointing to complex reasoning

Practices

"well should I say",
"person who hmhm who is quite not ve:ry or quite quite hard",
"she would find it ridiculous",
"someone in my circle of friends when I notice he is a bit (1.2) hhh yes how should I put it .hh wh=wh=who is a bit weaker (---)"
"and then I think"
"do you understand?"

Bühler (2011/1934: 140) called such a comparison an "imagination-oriented deixis". The patient does not point to his friends or to himself. He points to an operation of "turning-the-table", changing the positions of receiving and doing. I propose to call this conversational manoeuvre a "tacit comparison" (Buchholz et al. 2021). He shows how difficult he considers the therapist's task to understand him. Using a tacit comparison, the patient points to the tasks of a cooperation needed which he could not describe nor define. I propose to conceptualize tacit comparisons as functional equivalents to gestural pointings (Deppermann und Blühdorn 2013). By presenting two contrastive episodic memories the patient indicates that only a therapist comparing both can deliver a solution – the patient is in need of the therapist's mind. Excerpt (3) shows how both interact later in the same session (11 min omitted):

Excerpt 3. Continuation of the same session

```
86  T:  .h and the other thing I strongly feel .h °°w:°° again and
        again >>when we talk so together<< is .h mh; how far you have
        shyly withdrawn a little bit because here sOMething happened
        .h what not only you know and the Sheriff (.) but (.) I think
        so (.) too (.) other people (.)
87  P:  Yea=ah,=
88  T:  =with whom you deal (.) professionally=
89  P:       =Yea=ah,=
90  T:  =people who know it now .hh and if that's perhaps still a
        question that
91  T:  depresses or moves you or still is=is a [problem for you
92  P:                                           [errm
93  P:  Most people do not know concretely well [this= this situation
        about my suicide attempt .h
94  T:                                           [Mhmh
95  P:  (.) only those really inaugurated err::m        [.h who
96  T:                                                  [Oh=yeah
97  P:  needed to know and very good friends [I really did not
98  T:                                       [Mhmh
99  P:  go out and have err::m .h I must say have err::m .h have told
        many lies (..) in quotation marks
```

The therapist changes the patient's assumption that nobody knew (line 86). He introduces something like: others know. He introduces this claim as counterpart to the patient's shy withdrawal, opposed to "when we talk so together". This is a therapist-generated double practice: introducing reality *and* cultural knowledge (Scarvaglieri 2020) and a "we". That "other people" know can be exemplified by that he, the therapist, "knows".

The therapist embeds his contribution in a "We-frame" (line 86: "When we talk so together"), addressing the tacit comparison activity by the patient in an indirect manner. The therapist tailors his question as if he were just formulating the patient's perspective (line 90) as a "question", which people to inform, and then just this is reformulated (Antaki 2008) as "a problem for you" (line 91). Thus, a self-restricted focus *how much* other people knew is reformulated into *how many* other people knew – a rarely described reformulation activity. The distinction between "weak" and "hard" is replaced by a more fitting one "initiated" people and "very good friends" – a silent agreement that the therapist is a "knower", too. The moral problem which we found in Excerpt (3) can be articulated as "lies in quotation marks" (line 99). Here the hesitations indicate the tacit comparison of various listeners.

This reformulation is a confession bringing a new solution: that he told lies to his friends. In the following excerpt, 29 sessions later (approximately half a year), this problem is treated again:

Excerpt 4. Same psychodynamic therapy, 29 sessions later:

```
100  P:  right now [the question arises again
101  T:               [Mhmh;
102  P:  in me .h (--) can you understand that; because you have a lot
         to do with suicide suspects err::m .h (1.2) candidates in
         your life and and ..h can you put yourself in=in=i:n such a
         situation? .hh
103      (1.1)
104  P:  How or °mh::° whAt can really happen in a man thAt he is
         capable to such a step (.)
105  T:  Mhmh; mhmh
106  P:  and that does not need to be answered (.) it is li:::ke a:
         again the situation only .h to say how can my wife then (-)
107  T:  Mhmh; mhmh; (.)
108  P:  if I were to [put the question err:m to you can YOU do that;
109  T:                  [Mhmh;
110  P:  [.hhh and anywhere I have
111  T:     [Mhmh;
112  P:  I err::m probably expected that otherwise I would have .h (-)
         asked (.)
113  T:  Tha:t I wanted to say, too
114      (3.0)
115  T:  No matter how hard (--) °but probably you did expect that°=
116  P:  =yes
117      (7.8)
118  P:  But even then I .hh (--) did not say anything
119  T:  Mhmh;
120      (1.8)
121  T:  .hh that's a kind of silencing that would have cost you your
         life
122      (2.2)
123  P:  °Really (--) that's right°.
```

The phrase "suicide suspects" is "Selbstmordverdächtige" in German. This is a creative pun which the patient self-repairs after a short break of 1.2 seconds (line 102). Again, we find this pause of 1.2 sec after a self-initiated self-repair. The speaker listens to his slip as if *he* were the listener. Here the suicide suspects are repaired into "candidates". In German the link from "…mord" in "Selbstmord" (suicide) to "Mord-Verdächtige" is unusual, but possible. "Self", "murder", "suspect/candidate" – can be combined in ways which affect the role of the listener. This is what motivates the patient's repair. The German phrase "Mord-Verdächtige" positions the therapist in a role as a kind of detective. Detectives usually deal with murder-suspects – what creates emotional complexity:

a. to *implicitly* name the therapist a "detective" is a variant of tacit comparison which might offend him; further utterances by the patient may be hearable as offence which could downgrade the therapist's competence, e.g. to doubt if the therapist can put himself into the patient's situation (line 102). The therapist does not need to answer the question (line 106). He formulates an excuse by a new comparison: to have posed the question only explain that, if not even the expert can empathize with him – how could he expect it from his wife?
b. to *implicitly* have named himself a "murderer" might have scared the patient. Indeed, committing suicide is an act in which someone dies. It is the agentive part. All his attempts to hide if he were really dead would be pointless. He realizes to have fought the wrong fight. What he thought to be of help (his policy of silencing) shows up as a contribution to what he is fighting against.

The therapist (line 121) directly changes the frame of the patient's silencing strategy. To hide the suicide attempt from others was projected as a kind of support to continue the masquerade of his normal social life. The opposition of his "inaccessible hard" wife and "weak" friends disappears; however, a self-construction to hide from others commits a kind of social suicide; to hide oneself creates the fear of being discovered, against which one must then fight by meeting other people who are assessed as "too weak" or "too strong". And the self-suspicion to be a murderer cannot be dismissed.

In the therapist-created new frame it turns out that just the hiding was of high risk: "that would have cost you your life" (line 121), because if nobody knew, then, nobody would have been able to help. The patient responds in surprise and dismay, as if he had never before thought about that possibility. The rotation of the hiding-frame into a deadly agency-frame enforces a new "We-Doing" in order to deliver substantial support to such a patient's vital crisis. A shift of self-perception and perception of relevant others is the result of confessing a fundamental "error" in his problem-construction. It can be considered a therapeutic pinnacle if it succeeds. Actual Doing-We aims to create a longer-term "We-constellation", which becomes, then, the base of further work. Therapeutic change, if it is meant to endure, requires connection. Such forms of connections are not yet fully under study (Buchholz 2019c). They are important to influence how a patient thinks about her/himself outside the treatment room. To establish long-term "We-constellations" requires therapeutic skills including mind and memory (theories). Goodwin points into this direction:

> „What one is dealing with is not a linguistic text, but cognitively sophisticated actors using language to build the consequential events that make up their life world."
> (Goodwin 2015, 208)

After observing how a patient uses tacit comparisons in order to point to what he could not say otherwise, I turn to another example of "Doing We". "Pointing to" takes a path to metaphor.

6. From pointing to metaphor: A recursive model

Elsewhere I presented a model of "common ground" (Buchholz 2016). I referred to linguistic and psychological theories of common ground. The model is based on everyday observation and inspired by Sacks:

> The fact that there is a job that any person could clearly do by themselves (sic), provides a resource for members for permitting them to show each other that whatever it is they're doing together, they're just doing together to do together. That is to say, if one wants to find a way of showing somebody that what you want is to be with them, the best way to do it is to find some way of dividing a task which is not easily dividable, and which clearly can be done by either one alone.
> (Sacks und Jefferson 1992/1995, 147)

In a first step, people in everyday interaction who do not know each other begin "Doing-We" by pointing to something in their environment ("nice weather today"); the pointing can be a gesture (pointing to the clouds), a gaze mutually observed or a listening to a sound as e.g. in a concert. CA contributed the analysis of "tags" by which speaker X challenges speaker Y to agree. If speaker X can guide attentiveness of Y (e.g. by a pointing gesture) to the *perceptual* object, step 2 follows. Y will look at the *perceptual object* or listen attentively; both realize *epistemologically* the same element as "commonly perceived" and they realize *affiliatively* that this "common perception" alters their relationship towards each other (which they can then approve or disapprove). Both cannot avoid to have realized a "common ground".

They perceive not only the object, but more what Sacks named "doing together to do together".[4] In this second step the *perceptual object* is somewhat addressed with words – it changes into a *conversational object*. This alteration opens the possibility to a third step: to *link* other *topics* using *conversational* contributions with the common realization that the common ground is stronger *established*.

In step 1 objects in a perceptual environment challenge "joint attention" (Kidwell und Zimmerman 2007) of both; step 2 into a conversational world is realized by using some fusion of perception, memory and cognitive inference

4. "A comparable contrast surfaces in ... what might be called 'mentation' on the one hand and 'action' or 'practices' on the other hand. ... But *the* central question is whether human sociality is a matter of *knowing* together or of *doing* together." ((Schegloff 2006, 73).

(Tomasello 1995/2014); in step 3 another cognitive ability is required which is named "analogical reasoning" (Korner 2015; Vosniadou 1995). This ability is observed even in embodied gestures (Calbris 2013). If this cycle starts with pointing to an *interactional* event in a common world, then a fourth step can be observed.

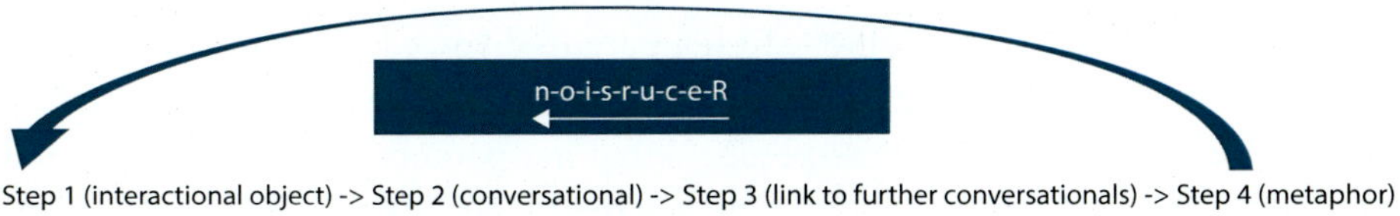

Figure 1. Recursion from metaphor-delivering-a-shared-view on the interactional object, recurring to level 1 (pointing to an interactional object)

Here, a metaphor-for-interaction is proposed. If the metaphor "fits" both participants "share attention (and emotion)" for a moment; although, of course, from complementary point of views. The metaphor articulates a momentary truth – for both. This is of special relevance for Doing-We in therapeutic interactions. What is pointed to are *interactional* events treated *as if* they were *perceptual objects*. The interactional event is highlighted by the metaphor and gives the "Doing We" a special twist. It emerges from the participants' observation of doing-we, resulting from a creative mind of one of the participants. If the metaphor is felt to fit both participants share a "meeting of minds". Thus, the interactively ratified metaphor can be treated *as* "perceptual object" again, which participants point to and use it. The whole 4-step procedure can re-start on a higher level. Such recursion (Corballis 2011), using the same operational procedures of mental and conversational "stuff" to achieve higher levels, was in psychoanalysis erroneously confused with "repetition" or even "repetition compulsion" (Buchholz 2019b; Kirsch und Buchholz 2020). By recursion however, the process is spiralling to higher levels of shared experience. It is the sheer amount of what therapist and patient went through. But not only this. This amount of shared experience is mutually observed and the mutual observation is observed. Such a process requires some reduction of complexity and one of the most important "tools" here is the use of metaphors, as cognitive linguistics teach us. If a metaphor fits for an interaction element as a description, both participants share this experience and at the same time are on different sides. One is teacher, the other pupil, one is "up" the other "down" – as metaphorical descriptions for an experienced interaction it cannot be denied (if it is felt to be a fitting metaphor).

7. We-Constellation: To overcome emotional deafness

What follows is an example for such a recursive process. I give some introduction to this treatment. A female patient during her twenties comes to treatment because she never had sexual fulfilment with men and because she starts crying for inexplicable reasons. When she was nine years her parents divorced. She remembers being informed; she left the kitchen in order to curb her aroused feelings. Unfortunately, she was successful in this. She remembers that her parents tried to reconcile and planned a common family holiday. One day before departure she discovered that her father had a new girlfriend meanwhile. Asked in the session, which feelings she then had, she answers: None. She also denies having felt "disappointment". But she remembers how awful it was when her mother drank too much when she was still in kindergarten. She cried and fled into her father's arms, while her mother scolded, screamed and threw porcelain, which broke and injured her father.

She remembers to have mentally fled to observe everything from a "fly-on-the-wall-perspective", as if she were not part of the scenario. Therapists name this response a "dissociation". The first time she realizes that most of what she had thought about her "wonderful childhood" resulted from tellings by her mother. It is gradually becoming clearer that she speaks with a "borrowed voice", silencing her own voice to easier adapt to her mother. She had to pay a price for that:

Excerpt 5. A psychoanalytic session, patient lying on the couch

1	*T:*	*Your voice (1.3) comes=second place (-) First place come (1) mo- come Mama's words=*
2	*P:*	*=yeah 'cause=again=I have the feeling that I again don't (-) don't think or not hmn don't know what I shall say what I feel or think or what's my sentiment (1) and that I=don't=feel=and =sometimes=still so DEAf! (.) and have the feeling that I have always done it this way*
3	*T:*	*°yeah°*
4	*P:*	*so emotion-deaf (.) not (1) so not really deaf ears (12)*
5	*T:*	*This would be (1) well here you have found a word now (1) which (.) is good and so important*
6	*P:*	*emotion-deaf?*
7	*T:*	*°emotion-deaf°*
9		*(6)*
10	*P:*	*Ya - anyhow=really=and=if=I (.) if a little μ of=feeling comes up then=it=irritates=me or I want it gone quickly*
11	*T:*	*°ya°*

The patient silenced her own "voice", her memories and her thinking, her taking stance – and points to (step 1) how agentively she flattens waves of emotional arousal (a "μ" as she says for "a minimum") to make feelings disappear. The result of this flattening operation was "not thinking" and "emotional deafness". The therapist values (step 2) her new metaphor (line 7) and she links (step 3) to be deaf not for words, but for emotions. This newly created word can become the object of cooperation and in line 10 she further elaborates on it.

"Emotional deafness" is a metaphor resulting from the tacit comparison of several episodic memories: To have chosen a "fly-on-the-wall"-perspective as escape; to replace her own voice by her mother's voice, and the observation to flatten her feelings. In speaking very fast in the session, she tells that she and her boyfriend plan a holiday week. She wonders if she must inform her friends, her sister, her mother? The metaphor of emotional deafness is now treated as a recursive uptake. The excerpt starts in the following session with her reasoning whom to inform of her new "honeymoon" to travel with her boyfriend.

Excerpt 6. Same session (cont.)

46 P: *an=then I said nope! Not for now an=then I thought whether*
I tell anyone at all because nobody will notice where I-
well=clear >Anita and Larissa ((two girlfriends of her)) know
this=that I am not at Home (1.6) and erm Petra ((girlfriend))
knows it, too. But nobody really knows where I am
47 *(0.3)*
48 T: *I do! I know it too*
49 P: *YES! YOU know it too, but=*
50 T: *°(h) (h) ((silent laughter)*
51 P: *=Yes right You know that (.) I forget this anyhow sometimes*
(.) for me >its so natural that you know that (-) that (.) as
if I have incorporated this (2) as if you=you were my second
HEAD °although (.) this would be beautiful then I would think
more°
52 *(7)*
53 P: *or as if I have four EARs (.) so to speak*
54 *(6)*
55 T: *which is (.) °a beautiful metaphor°*
56 P: *Four EARs?*
57 T: *((laughing softly))*
58 *(2)*
59 T: *°ya°*
60 T: *(4)*
61 T: *Well then these are ears*
62 *(0.4)*
63 P: *°h:m°*
64 *(0.3)*
65 T: *which would listen to your own listening again*
66 *(1)*
67 P: *Yea:hh*
68 T: *°can I put it that (.) [way?°*
69 P: *[Yeah (.) so (-) an=then I also thought*
about (-) and a mouth quasi (.) an auxiliary mouth
70 T: *HM::!*
71 *(7)*
72 P: *°Ya!°*
73 *(1)*
74 P: *°so I would understand that°*

```
      (6)
T:    the auxiliary mouth (.) that's [me
P:                                   [oh yeah (.) of course
T:    °hmhm°
```

She reasons whom to inform and concludes that nobody knew where she is (line 46). Now, the therapist points to the *interactional* event (step 1, line 48) that he indeed knows her plans. This is prompted by a confirmation (line 49). The "fact" to be just informed is an epistemologically undeniable "truth" which she confirms a second time after the therapist's silent laughter. The epistemological contradiction to which the therapist pointed (she maintains: "nobody knows", while he is informed [5]) is now taken up by her as resulting from her forgetting and, affiliatively, ignoring his presence as "so natural" followed by her observation as if she had "incorporated" the therapist's presence. Step 1 (pointing to an interactional event of observation) + step 2 (changing the interactional event into a conversational topic) + step 3 (linking with other conversational topics) is walked through and a metaphor of incorporation (line 51) is created which could explain her ignorance of the therapist's outer presence; metaphorically, he is located *as if* "in corpore" by her. This metaphor is extended, to the therapist being a "second head", which would make her "more thinking". Two heads "Doing We" were endowed with 4 ears, adding a "so to speak" which indicates her distinction between the literal and the metaphoric.

After the pause in line 54 the therapist qualifies this metaphorical expressiveness as "beautiful", she asks for assurance which he confirms and after two pauses (line 58 and 60) the therapist treats the metaphor again *as if* it were an observation, restarting the recursive process on step 1 (but on a higher level). The "4 ears" are pointed to (step 1) as if the metaphorical objects were *perceptual objects*. Then ratification (step 2) follows again and then step 3 with a new link is added (line 65). After agreement about this step (line 68) it is now the patient who extends the metaphor using it for a completely new description of the relationship: she be a "mouth" and the therapist an "auxiliary mouth" (line 69). Both cooperate now on a level of "listening to listening" (Faimberg 1996).

It is a metaphoric image ad hoc created as her *description* of the therapeutic cooperation – while *doing*-the cooperation. The therapist joins the metaphor by ratification and so a higher level of "Doing-We" is achieved. Creativity comes into conversation from both participants; the resulting metaphoric play continues:

5. This is comparable to Sacks example of a caller at the LA emergency department who complains: "There is nobody to talk to" in a moment where he finds somebody to talk to.

Excerpt 7. (continued)

79	P:	*Yes I believe because I do not perceive you in that sense as an individual human being, which you are of course, but always within this framework of analysis here and also in this room I think*
80	T:	*°hm°*
81		*(4)*
82	P:	*and I do not even have to say that (.) so when I for example anyhow (1.3) if=I (.) I have said to Petra ((a girlfriend)) (1) or I have sometimes Petra told things I say- then which even Mama doesn't know (.) does nobody know and I've told her that and there she said (.) Yes and (.) and Mr. A ((name of the therapist)) knows it and then I yes=yes of course! (1) so (-) this is (.) I don't mention this anymore because for me it's clear that you know*
83		*(3)*
84	P:	*at least that what I say here*
85		*(4)*
86	T:	*°hm!°*
87		*(2)*
88	T:	*and there's still maybe one or the other thing you do not tell then (-) if it became hearable*
89	P:	*Ya::!*
90	T:	*then, by my auxiliary mouth it would again become hearable to your ears*
91	P:	*Yes, probably I should talk out exactly the things I do not say here*
92	T:	*°hm°*

After the metaphor of four ears or of mouth and auxiliary mouth is mutually acknowledged the recursion starts again, taking this metaphor as starting point (step 1) again from a higher level of describing the "Doing We".

In line 79 she points (step 1) to knowing the therapist as a person all to himself and makes this a conversational object for her own reasoning (step 2) executed by comparisons (step 3) how she handles her information policies to let others know (or not know) about her projects. A new narrative element is added: One of her girlfriends reminded her that her therapist surely knows. In line 84 the patient adds: he, the therapist, knows, "at least what I am saying here" which is attentively appreciated by the therapist in line 86. Here she does not step through the full recursive cycle, step 4 is omitted.

The therapist (line 88) returns to level 1 and points (using "and there" as one of the *pointing words*, following Bühler) to a new *interactional* object (not-telling), which now appears in the common world (step 2). The therapist *links* (step 3) this with a reason (line 90): that things would not be silenced for his ears but for her own and the patients responds with the formulation of a new task for herself (line 91).

8. Conclusion

Not every cycle 1–4 ends with a creative metaphor; often enough step 3 is achieved and no step to level 4 follows. I conclude that to reach level 4 is the little miracle which cannot be predicted.

In psychotherapeutic sessions work is done under paradoxical conditions of "cooperation in insecure circumstances" that requires a high level of complex and often implicit reasoning in both participants. The rules of cooperation cannot be *defined in advance* as both participants do not know each other in advance. In more technical cooperations (as in bureaucracies or engineering) rules often can be dealt with in prescriptions. This level of cooperation is based on other mental equipment for cooperatively negotiating rules of cooperation (Tomasello und Vaish 2013; Trevarthen 1979). To conceptualize therapeutic tasks in a way that separates people and brings them together as "individualized agents" in a second step produces conceptual confusion as shown in the psychotherapeutic process research studies on "rupture-and-repair". However, we are more or less socially wired for a "meeting of minds" (Kirsch und Buchholz 2020). My first example shows how the patient documents empathy for her therapist.

Seriously disturbed people need a therapist ready for unusual conversation, different from everyday talk in many aspects. However, often enough they are treated by beginners who respond to the first story told and do not yet know that people sometimes use storytelling for "tacit comparisons" which makes things hearable for the therapeutic ear which sometimes cannot be communicated otherwise. Patients do not appreciate to be treated as "a case of…". Such a mindset violates the expectation to be treated as individual expert with a long history of maltreatment, lack of support and wrong decisions in life. So, psychotherapists deal with high levels of human complexity and variants of cooperation. I have proposed a 4-step model of how cooperation might evolve, but I do not claim that this is the one-and-only model. I am curious for other CA-derived models of cooperation in psychotherapy.

CA paid attention to micro-analytically observable details of interaction often overlooked even by experienced clinicians. The non-face-to-face situation in psychoanalysis might make "hesitation markers" hearable as indicators of cognitive complexity to be dealt with before a more resilient cooperation can be established. Studying therapeutic cooperation it might become urgent for CA to cast an eye onto larger chunks of talk and how they unfold.

The therapeutic task is not only cooperation rules on "problems" that can be named from the start. Very often the first task is to invite patients deliver fuller descriptions of problems. This is a dimension of "Doing-We". While technical cooperation can focus on unnamed aspects of known things, "Doing-We" in therapy must assume that there are unknown aspects of unknown experiences. Pointing to interactive events is an attempt to focus joined attention to unknown aspects of unknown things. If Doing-We succeeds not only a "problem" is solved, but new objects of conversation are also created. Doing-We appears in a new light shed by a freshly created metaphor creating a new way of Being-We for both participants. Both participants do not only cooperate by sharing attention and pointing to common objects, but for moments they share a common form of being which to make talkable, then, is the next task.

References

Albert, Saul und J. P. de Ruiter. 2018. "Repair: The Interface Between Interaction and Cognition." *Topics in Cognitive Science* 10 (2): 279–313. https://doi.org/10.1111/tops.12339.

Antaki, Charles. 2008. „Formulations in psychotherapy." In *Conversation Analysis and Psychotherapy*, hrsg. von Anssi Peräkylä, Charles Antaki, Sanna Vehviläinen und Ivan Leudar, 26–43. Cambridge/New York: Cambridge University Press. https://doi.org/10.1017/CBO9780511490002.003

Aron, Lewis. 1996. *A Meeting of Minds – Mutuality in Psychoanalysis*. Hillsdale, NJ: The Analytic Press.

Barnes, B. 2000. *Understanding agency. Social theory and responsible action*. London: SAGE Publications Ltd.

Birkner, Karin und Oliver Ehmer, Hrsg. 2013. *Veranschaulichungsverfahren im Gespräch*. Mannheim: Verl. für Gesprächsforschung.

Bögels, Sara, Lilla Magyari und Stephen C. Levinson. 2015. „Neural Signatures of Response Planning Occur Midway Through an Incoming Question in Conversation." *Scientific reports* 5:12881. https://doi.org/10.1038/srep12881.

Bordin, Edward S. 1979. "The Generalizability of the Psychoanalytic Concept of the Working Alliance." *Psychotherapy: Theory, Research, Practice, Training* 16: 252–60. https://doi.org/10.1037/h0085885

Brockmeier, Jens. 2017. „From Memory as Archive to Remembering as Conversation." In *Handbook of Culture and Memory*, hrsg. von Brady Wagoner, 39–72 1: Oxford University Press. https://doi.org/10.1093/oso/9780190230814.003.0003

Bruner, Jerome S. 1995/2014. „From Joint Attention to the Meeting of Minds (1995)." In Moore, Dunham, and Dunham 1995/2014, 1–14.

Buchholz, Michael B. 2015. „Listening to Words, Seeing Images – Metaphors of emotional involvement and the movement of the metaphor." *Psychoanalytic Discourse* 5 (1): 20–38.

Buchholz, Michael B. 2016. "Conversational Errors and Common Ground Activities in Psychotherapy – Insights from Conversation Analysis." *IJPS* 8 (3): 134–53. https://doi.org/10.5539/ijps.v8n3p134.

Buchholz, Michael B. 2019a. „Commentary I: Clinically rethinking CA studies to improve therapeutic conversation." *Communication and Medicine* 16 (2): 184–90. https://doi.org/10.1558/cam.41910

Buchholz, Michael B. 2019b. „Re-Petition in (Therapeutic) Conversation: A Psychoanalyst's Perspective Using Conversation Analysis." In *Repetition, Recurrence, Returns: How Cultural Renewal Works*, hrsg. von Joan R. Resina und Christoph Wulf, 85–108. Lanham, Boulder, New York, London: Lexington Books.

Buchholz, Michael B. 2019c. „Veränderung braucht Verbindung.“ In *Pragmatik der Veränderung – Problem- und lösungsorientierte Kommunikation in helfenden Berufen*, hrsg. von Eva-Maria Graf, Claudio Scarvaglieri und Thomas Spranz-Fogasy, 75–95. Berlin: Springer.

Buchholz, Michael B. 2020. "Seeing the Situational Gestalt – Movement in Therapeutic Spaces." *Gestalt Theory* 42 (2): 1–31. https://doi.org/10.2478/gth-2020-0011.

Buchholz, Michael B., Oliver Ehmer, Christopher Mahlstedt, Stefan Pfänder und Elke Schumann. 2021. „Speaking that silences. A single case multi-method analysis of a couple's interview.“ In *Silence and silencing in psychoanalysis. Cultural, clinical, and research aspects*, hrsg. von Aleksandar Dimitrijević und Michael B. Buchholz, 333–97. Abingdon, Oxon, New York, NY: Routledge.

Buchholz, Michael B. und Horst Kächele. 2017. „From turn-by-turn to larger chunks of talk: An exploratory study in psychotherapeutic micro-processes using conversation analysis." *Research in Psychotherapy: Psychopathology, Process and Outcome* 20:161–78. https://doi.org/10.4081/ripppo.2017.257.

Bühler, Karl. 2011 (1934). *Theory of language. The representational function of language. (transl. by Donald Fraser Goodwin and Achim Eschbach)*. Amsterdam, Philadelphia: John Benjamins. https://doi.org/10.1075/z.164

Calbris, Genevieve. 2013. „Elements of meaning in gesture: The analogical links.“ In *Body – Language – Communication. An International Handbook on Multimodality in Human Interaction*, vol. 1, hrsg. von Cornelia Müller, Alan Cienki, Ellen Fricke, Ladewig, H. Silva und David McNeill, 658–77. Berlin [u.a.]: De Gruyter Mouton. https://doi.org/10.1515/9783110261318.658

Chafe, Wallce. 1985. „Some Reasons for Hesitating.“ In *Perspectives on Silence*, hrsg. von Deborah Tannen und Muriel Saville-Troike, 77–89. Norwood, NJ: Ablex Publishing Corp.

Cienki, Alan und Cornelia Müller, (Hrsg.). 2010. *Metaphor and Gesture*. Paperback. Gesture studies 3. Amsterdam: Benjamins. https://doi.org/10.1075/gs.3

Clark, H. 2003. "Pointing and placing," In *Pointing: Where Language, Culture, and Cognition Meet*, ed. by Sotaro Kita, 243–268, Hillsdale, NJ: Erlbaum.

Corballis, Michael C. 2011. *The Recursive Mind: The Origins of Human Language, Thought, and Civilization*. Princeton: Princeton University Press.

Deppermann, Arnulf. 2011. "The Study of Formulations as a Key to an Interactional Semantics." *Human Studies* 34 (2): 115–28. https://doi.org/10.1007/s10746-011-9187-8.

Deppermann, Arnulf. 2015. „Agency in Erzählungen über Gewalterfahrungen in Kindheit und Jugend.“ In *Narrative Bewältigung von Trauma und Verlust.*, hrsg. von Eduard C. Scheidt, Gabriele Lucius-Hoene, Anja Stukenbrock und Elisabeth Waller. 1. Aufl, 64–75. Stuttgart: Schattauer.

Deppermann, Arnulf und H. Blühdorn. 2013. „Negation als Verfahren des Adressatenzuschnitts: Verstehenssteuerung durch Interpretationsrestriktionen." *Deutsche Sprache* 13 (1): 6–30. https://doi.org/10.37307/j.1868-775X.2013.01.03

Deppermann, Arnulf und Axel Schmidt. 2016. "Partnerorientierung zwischen Realität und Imagination: Anmerkungen zu einem zentralen Konzept der Dialogtheorie." *Zeitschrift für germanistische Linguistik* 44 (3). https://doi.org/10.1515/zgl-2016-0021.

Edwards, Derek und David Middleton. 1987. "Conversation and Remembering: Bartlett Revisited." *Appl. Cognit. Psychol.* 1 (2): 77–92. https://doi.org/10.1002/acp.2350010202.

Edwards, Derek und Jonathan Potter. 1992. "The Chancellor's Memory: Rhetoric and Truth in Discursive Remembering." *Appl. Cognit. Psychol.* 6 (3): 187–215. https://doi.org/10.1002/acp.2350060303.

Ehmer, Oliver. 2011. *Imagination und Animation. Die Herstellung mentaler Räume durch animierte Rede*. Linguae & litterae 7. Berlin, New York: de Gruyter. https://doi.org/10.1515/9783110237801

Elliott, Robert, Arthur C. Bohart, Jeanne C. Watson und David Murphy. 2018. "Therapist Empathy and Client Outcome: An Updated Meta-Analysis." *Psychotherapy (Chicago, Ill.)* 55 (4): 399–410. https://doi.org/10.1037/pst0000175.

Emirbayer, Mustafa und Ann Mische. 1998. "What is Agency?". *The American Journal of Sociology* 103 (4): 962–1023. https://doi.org/10.1086/231294

Enfield, N. J. 2013. *Relationship thinking – Agency, enchrony, and human sociality*. Foundations of Human Interaction. New York: Oxford University Press. https://doi.org/10.1093/acprof:oso/9780199338733.001.0001

Enfield, Nicholas J. und Paul Kockelman, Hrsg. 2017. *Distributed Agency*. Oxford, New York: Oxford University Press. https://doi.org/10.1093/acprof:oso/9780190457204.001.0001

Faimberg, Haydée. 1996. "'Listening to Listening'." *Intern. J. Psychoanal.* 77: 667–77.

Falkenström, Fredrik, Fredrik Granström und Rolf Holmqvist. 2014. "Working Alliance Predicts Psychotherapy Outcome Even While Controlling for Prior Symptom Improvement." *Psychotherapy Research* 24 (2): 146–59. https://doi.org/10.1080/10503307.2013.847985.

Falkenström, Fredrik, Mary Kuria, Caleb Othieno und Manasi Kumar. 2019. "Working Alliance Predicts Symptomatic Improvement in Public Hospital-Delivered Psychotherapy in Nairobi, Kenya." *Journal of Consulting and Clinical Psychology* 87 (1): 46–55. https://doi.org/10.1037/ccp0000363.

Ginzburg, Jonathan und Massimo Poesio. 2016. „Grammar Is a System That Characterizes Talk in Interaction." *Front. Psychol.* 7:1–22. https://doi.org/10.3389/fpsyg.2016.01938.

Goffman, Erving. 1983. "The Interaction Order." *Amer. Sociol. Rev.* 48: 1–17. https://doi.org/10.2307/2095141

Goodwin, Charles. 2015. „Narrative as Talk-in-Interaction." In *the Handbook of Narrative Analysis*, hrsg. von Anna de Fina und Alexandra Georgakopoulou, 197–218. Blackwell handbooks in linguistics. Chichester, West Sussex, UK: Wiley Blackwell. https://doi.org/10.1002/9781118458204.ch10

Goodwin, Charles. 2018a. *Co-Operative Action. Learning in doing*. New York, NY: Cambridge University Press.

Goodwin, Charles. 2018b. „Seeing in Depth." In *Co-Operative Action*, hrsg. von Charles Goodwin, 275–306. Learning in doing. New York: Cambridge University Press.

Hatcher, Robert L., Karin Lindqvist und Fredrik Falkenström. 2019. "Psychometric Evaluation of the Working Alliance Inventory-Therapist Version: Current and New Short Forms." *Psychotherapy research : journal of the Society for Psychotherapy Research*, 1–12. https://doi.org/10.1080/10503307.2019.1677964.

Huber, Dorothea und Günther Klug. 2016. "Münchner Psychotherapiestudie." *Psychotherapeut*, 1–6. https://doi.org/10.1007/s00278-016-0139-7.

Kanninen, K., J. Salo und R. -L Punamäki. 2000. „Attachment Patterns and Working Alliance in Trauma Therapy for Victims of Political Violence." *Psychotherapy Research* 10 (4): 435. https://doi.org/10.1093/ptr/10.4.435

Kidwell, Mardi und Don H. Zimmerman. 2007. „Joint attention as action." *Journal of Pragmatics* 39: 592–611. https://doi.org/10.1016/j.pragma.2006.07.012

Kirsch, Michael und Michael B. Buchholz. 2020. „On the Nature of the Mother-Infant Tie and Its Interaction With Freudian Drives." *Front. Psychol.* 11:596. https://doi.org/10.3389/fpsyg.2020.00317.

Korner, Anthony. 2015. „Analogical Fit: dynamic relatedness in the psychotherapeutic setting with reference to language, autonomic response, and change in self-state." Dissertation, Department of Linguistics, Macquarie University.

Lakoff, George. 1987. *Women, Fire, and Dangerous Things. What Categories Reveal About the Mind.* Chicago/London: The University of Chicago Press. https://doi.org/10.7208/chicago/9780226471013.001.0001

Lerner, Gene H. 2013. „On the Place of Hesitating in Delicate Formulations: A Turn-Constructional Infrastructure for Collaborative Indiscretion." In *Hayashi, Raymond, and Sidnell 2013*, 95–134.

Loewald, Hans W. 1971. "The Transference Neurosis: Comments on the Concept and the Phenomenon." *J. Amer. Psychoanal. Assoc.* 19: 54–66. https://doi.org/10.1177/000306517101900105

Loewald, Hans W. 1979. "Reflections on the Psychoanalytic Process and Its Therapeutic Potential." *Psychoanal. Study Child* 34: 155–68. https://doi.org/10.1080/00797308.1979.11823004

Mahr, Johannes und Gergely Csibra. 2018. "Why Do We Remember? The Communicative Function of Episodic Memory." *The Behavioral and brain sciences* 42 (1): 1–93. https://doi.org/10.1017/S0140525X17000012.

Mergenthaler, Erhard. 2008. „Resonating Minds: A School-Independent Theoretical Conception and Its Empirical Application to Psychotherapeutic Processes." *Psychotherapy Research* 18: 109–27. https://doi.org/10.1080/10503300701883741

Miller-Bottome, Madeleine und Jeremy D. Safran. 2018. „Ferenczi's Contributions to Relational Psychoanalysis: The Pursuit of Mutuality." In *Ferenczi's Influence on Contemporary Psychoanalytic Traditions. Lines of Development---Evolution of Theory and Practice over the Decades*, hrsg. von Aleksandar Dimitrijevic, Gabriele Cassullo und Jay Frankel, 227–31. Milton: Routledge.

Montangero, J. 2009. „Using dreams in cognitive behavioral therapy." *Dreaming* 19: 239–54. https://doi.org/10.1037/a0017613

Muntigl, Peter und Adam O. Horvath. 2014. „"I Can See Some Sadness in Your Eyes": When Experiential Therapists Notice a Client's Affectual Display." *Research on Language and Social Interaction* 47 (2): 89–108. https://doi.org/10.1080/08351813.2014.900212

Muran, J. Christopher. 2019. „Confessions of a New York rupture researcher: An Insider's guide and critique." *Psychotherapy Research* 29 (1–2): 1–14. https://doi.org/10.1080/10503307.2017.1413261

Peräkylä, Anssi und Jörg R. Bergmann. 2020. "Practices of joint meaning creation. Dreams in psychoanalytic discussion." *The International journal of psycho-analysis*, 1–28. https://doi.org/10.1080/00207578.2020.1775088.

Peräkylä, Anssi, Pentti Henttonen, Liisa Voutilainen, Mikko Kahri, Melisa Stevanovic, M. Sams und Niklas Ravaja. 2015. "Sharing the Emotional Load. Recipient Affiliation Calms Down the Storyteller." *Social Psychology Quarterly* 78 (4): 301–23. https://doi.org/10.1177/0190272515611054.

Plessner, Hellmuth. 1928. *Die Stufen des Organischen und der Mensch (3. Auflage 1975).* Berlin/New York: de Gruyter. https://doi.org/10.1515/9783111537429

Sacks, Harvey und Gail Jefferson. 1992/1995. *Lectures on Conversation.* Edited by Gail Jefferson, with an Introduction by Emanuel A. Schegloff. 2 Bände. Oxford: Basil Blackwell.

Safran, Jeremy D. und J. Christopher Muran. 2000. *Negotiating the Therapeutic Alliance – a Relational Treatment Guide.* New York: The Guilford Press.

Scarvaglieri, Claudio. 2020. "Starting points for therapeutic change." *CAM* 16 (2): 117–28. https://doi.org/10.1558/cam.33827.

Schegloff, Emanuel A. 2000. "Das Wiederauftauchen des Unterdrückten." *Psychother. Soz.* 2 (1): 3–29.
Schegloff, Emanuel A. 2006. „Interaction: The Infrastructure for Social Institutions, the Natural Ecological Niche for Language, and the Arena in Which Culture Is Enacted." In *Roots of Human Sociality. Culture, Cognition and Interaction*, hrsg. von Stephen C. Levinson und Nicholas J. Enfield, 70–96. Oxford: Berg Publishers.
Schegloff, Emanuel A. 2013. „Ten operations in self-initiated, same-turn repair." In *Hayashi, Raymond, and Sidnell 2013*, 41–70.
Selting, Margret, Peter Auer, Dagmar Barth-Weingarten, Jörg R. Bergmann, Pia Bergmann, Karin Birkner, Elisabeth Couper-Kuhlen et al. 2011. "A system for transcribing talk-in-interaction: GAT 2 translated and adapted for English by Elizabeth Couper-Kuhlen and Dagmar Barth-Weingarten." *Gesprächsforschung – Online-Zeitschrift zur verbalen Interaktion* 12: 1–51. www.gespraechsforschung-ozs.de.
Sinha, Chris und Cintia Rodriguez. 2008. „Language and signifying objects: From convention to imagination." In *The Shared Mind. Perspectives on Intersubjectivity*, hrsg. von Jordan Zlatev, Racine, Timothy, P., Chris Sinha und Esa Itkonen, 357–78. Amsterdam / Philadelphia: John Benjamins Publishing Company. https://doi.org/10.1075/celcr.12.19sin
Sterba, Richard F. 1934. "Das Schicksal des Ich im therapeutischen Verfahren." *Intern. Zeitschrift für Psychoanalyse* 20: 66–73.
Stevanovic, Melisa und Anssi Peräkylä. 2014. "Three Orders in the Organization of Human Action: On the Interface Between Knowledge, Power, and Emotion in Interaction and Social Relations." *Language in Society* 43 (02): 185–207. https://doi.org/10.1017/S0047404514000037.
Stiles, William B., Clara E. Hill und Robert Elliott. 2015. "Looking Both Ways." *Psychotherapy Research* 25 (3): 282–93. https://doi.org/10.1080/10503307.2014.981681.
Tomasello, Michael. 1995/2014. „Joint Attention as Social Cognition." In Moore, Dunham, and Dunham 1995/2014, 103–30.
Tomasello, Michael und Amrisha Vaish. 2013. "Origins of Human Cooperation and Morality." *Annu. Rev. Psychol.* 64 (1): 231–55. https://doi.org/10.1146/annurev-psych-113011-143812.
Trevarthen, Colwyn. 1979. „Communication and Cooperation in Early Infancy: A Description of Primary Intersubjectivity." In *Before Speech: The Beginning of Interpersonal Communication*, hrsg. von Margaret Bullowa, 321–48. Cambridge: Cambridge University Press.
Vosniadou, S. 1995. „Analogical Reasoning in Cognitive Development." *Metaphor and Symbolic Activity* 10: 297–308. https://doi.org/10.1207/s15327868ms1004_4
Wagner Cook, Susan. 2014. „Gesture and working memory." In *Body – Language – Communication: An international handbook on multimodality in human interaction*, vol. 2, hrsg. von Cornelia Müller, Alan Cienki, Ellen Fricke, Silva H. Ladewig, David McNeill und Jana Bressem, 1936–42. Handbücher zur Sprach- und Kommunikationswissenschaft 38,2. Berlin [u.a.]: de Gruyter.
Weiste, Elina und Anssi Peräkylä. 2013. "A Comparative Conversation Analytic Study of Formulations in Psychoanalysis and Cognitive Psychotherapy." *Research on Language & Social Interaction* 46 (4): 299–321. https://doi.org/10.1080/08351813.2013.839093.
Wooffitt, Robin. 2005. „From Process to Practice: Language, Interaction and 'Flashbulb' Memories." In *Conversation and Cognition*, hrsg. von Hedwig t. Molder und Jonathan Potter, 203–25. Cambridge/New York: Cambridge University Press. https://doi.org/10.1017/CBO9780511489990.010

What about you?

Responding to a face-threatening question in psychotherapy

Aurora Guxholli, Liisa Voutilainen and Anssi Peräkylä
University of Helsinki

In psychotherapy, the envisioned change in patient's feelings, thoughts and behaviour often targets their self-experience. This threatens simultaneously the patient's face and the therapeutic relation. We focus on face-threats in transformative question-answer sequences where therapists question the patient's face by shifting the focus of talk on patient's self and in response patients confront the dilemma of having to choose between saving their face or the relation with the therapist. Data come from 47 video recorded psychotherapy sessions conducted in Albanian language. Analysis shows that patients resist the transformation but only after making considerable efforts to save both their face and the therapeutic relation. We conclude that challenging the patient's self-experience is a delicate task in terms of the therapeutic relation.

Keywords: psychotherapy, change, face-threat, therapeutic relation, transformative sequence, self-experience

> Between stimulus and response there is a space. In that space is our power to choose our response. In our response lies our growth and our freedom.
> Viktor E. Frankl

Introduction

Concerns and questions about self are the very reason patients seek psychotherapy. Talking about oneself, however, is a complicated matter also in the context of psychotherapy, invoking in a particular way questions about the social value of the self that patients present to therapists. According to Goffman (1955), people hold a certain idea about who they are, an image of self which they reveal in interaction

https://doi.org/10.1075/pbns.331.04gux

with others. Goffman referred to this image as *face*: a line of action through which the person expresses their view of self and, by attributing positive social values to it, expects the co-interactants to ratify it in return. Moreover, the person experiences an immediate emotional response to the face they bring forth in interaction, "he cathects his face; his feelings become attached to it" (Goffman 1955, 213). One feels good when their face is ratified or even praised, and bad or hurt when this is not the case.

Following Goffman's notion of face as omnirelevant in social interaction, Brown and Levinson's (1987) work on politeness has demonstrated how virtually all conversational actions involve an intrinsic face-threat to the recipient or the speaker (O'Driscoll 2017, 98). Actions performed to minimise face-threats have been the focus of research in linguistic pragmatics (see e.g., Ruiz de Zarobe & Ruiz de Zarobe 2012), offering a structural model of finite repertoires of realisation strategies (Kasper 1996). Other research has focused on depiction of face in interaction. For example, in a recent study on narrative interaction in psychodynamic therapy, Deppermann and colleagues (2020) showed how patients draw on two lines of action to depict a face for themselves: they *represent* it, for example by recounting memories of past events (the autobiographical, told self) and *perform* it in the moment by moment unfolding of the therapeutic talk (the interactive and emotional self). In this study, we examine patients' responses to face-threats in psychotherapeutic interaction.

To facilitate change in the patient's overall psychological functioning, therapists target the patient's contact with parts of the self. They focus primarily on problematic emotional experiences, therefore chiefly working with the interactive (emotional) self as displayed in the here and now of the therapeutic interaction. They do so by interpreting the patient's inner experiences – pointing to something implicit in the patient's talk and challenging the description of it – while inviting self-reflection from the patient (Vehviläinen 2003; Peräkylä 2004; Antaki 2008; Bercelli, Rossano and Viaro 2008; Rae 2008; Voutilainen 2012; Deppermann, Scheidt and Stukenbrock 2020). In a single-session study of client-centred therapy, Muntigl (2020) found that creating a secure space for the client to experience intense emotions as presently felt enhances the self-exploration process. Patients, on their part, rely on self-reflexive abilities to alter the way they see their self in the world (Fonagy et al. 2002) starting from the therapeutic relationship.

Throughout this process, in any psychotherapeutic approach, the patient's (but not only) experience gets transformed. Peräkylä (2019) has demonstrated how the transformation is carried out in the sequence of adjacent turns, where the therapist and patient display understanding of and respond to each other's actions targeting three overlapping realms of the patient's experience: *referents*, *emotions*, and *relation*. In this study, we investigate moments in which therapists, by making a shift in referents, focus the talk on the patient's self. We analyse transformative question-answer sequences in which (a) therapists use a question to shift the patient's focus of talk on self, taking an issue with the face they have presented so far in the interaction and, in response (b) patients, confronted with the dilemma of saving either their face or the relation with the therapist, do considerable interactional work to save both. We show how, by not ratifying the presented self, the shift threatens both the patient's face and the therapeutic relation.

Ratifying the patient's face often goes against the therapeutic goal of conceiving the self in new, more functional ways, presenting a dilemma for the therapist (Deppermann Scheidt and Stukenbrock 2020). It is in such moments that tension arises between two aspects of the therapeutic work, change in patient's self-experience and preservation of the therapeutic relationship where new experiences of emotional expression and response can take place (Voutilainen 2012). Conversation analytic (CA) studies on affiliation, emotions and empathy have shown how in and through talk, therapists – despite the psychotherapeutic modality – display an ever-present orientation toward building and maintaining the therapeutic relationship (see also Muntigl, this volume). They utilise a variety of interactional practices to prepare a ground of affiliation (Voutilainen, Peräkylä and Ruusuvuori 2010a; Voutilainen 2012), or mend disaffiliation resulting from disagreement (Muntigl 2013; Muntigl and Horvath 2014; Weiste 2015; Guxholli, Peräkylä and Voutilainen 2021) or therapist's misaligning and/or challenging utterances (Voutilainen, Peräkylä and Ruusuvuori 2010b; Scarvaglieri 2020; Muntigl 2020), including prosody (Weiste and Peräkylä 2014). The present study builds on this prior CA research and sheds light on the not-so-talked about co-participant's contribution in safeguarding the therapeutic relation – the patient.

Ratification of patient's face entails affiliation by merit of being a responsive action designed as preferred (Heritage 1984) and supportive of the expressed positive affect (Stivers 2008). Lack of ratification, on the other hand, projects disaffiliation therefore posing a double threat to the therapeutic relation and the patient's experience of self. Questioning the patient's self-image goes against the fundamental assumption in the Western culture that subjects have privileged access to their own self (Heritage 2011). Heritage (2011) has shown how, in everyday interaction, participants find it difficult to respond to reported subjective experiences due to lack of access to that experience, the preferred response being restricted to displays of affiliation and empathy. He called this phenomenon the "problem of experience".

In psychotherapy, however, it is the institutional task of the therapist to understand, but also alter the patient's experience of self. A number of CA studies focusing on management of epistemic asymmetry have shown how therapists make use of *formulations* to transform the clients' talk in such a way that it fosters a new understanding of the experience (Fitzgerald 2013) or to co-describe the clients' inner experience, demonstrating that this experience is somewhat similarly available to both therapist and patient (Weiste, Voutilainen and Peräkylä 2015). Providing evidential foundation for their *interpretations* by summarising the patient's talk and using their same descriptive terms is another practice that therapists rely on to manage the epistemic asymmetry (Weiste, Voutilainen and Peräkylä 2015).

Other than lack of direct access to patient's experience, the therapeutic relationship is also asymmetrical in that the therapist, guided in his hearing by clinical curiosity, is primarily the inquirer, whereas the patient the inquired. In other words, the therapist's task to help the patient bear the emotional pain and guide them towards change in self-experience is not reciprocated by the patient doing the same in return. In our analysis, we used the Psychotherapy Interaction Sequential Organization Model (Peräkylä 2019) shown in Figure 1 below, where the "third position" action reveals how therapists take the epistemic asymmetry into account and make their clinical hearing available to the patient. We investigate how the therapist's question as "target action" initiates the transformation of all the three overlapping realms of experience: *referents*, *emotions*, and *relation*, and show how this transformation is facilitated in and through the interaction (Peräkylä 2019). Figure 2 below illustrates a simplified version of the action sequence shown in Extract I.

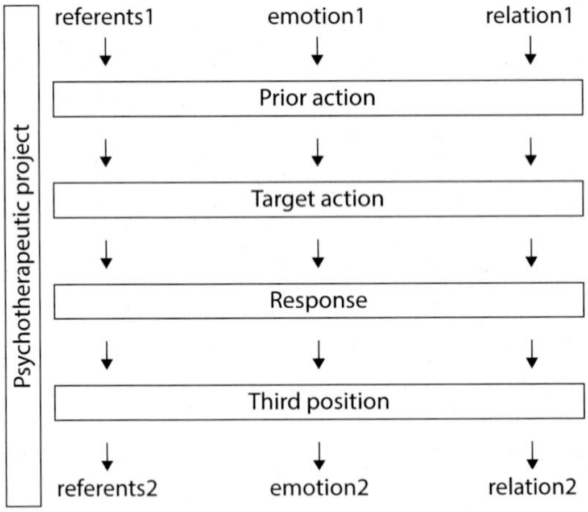

Figure 1. Transformation of experience through action sequences (Peräkylä 2019)

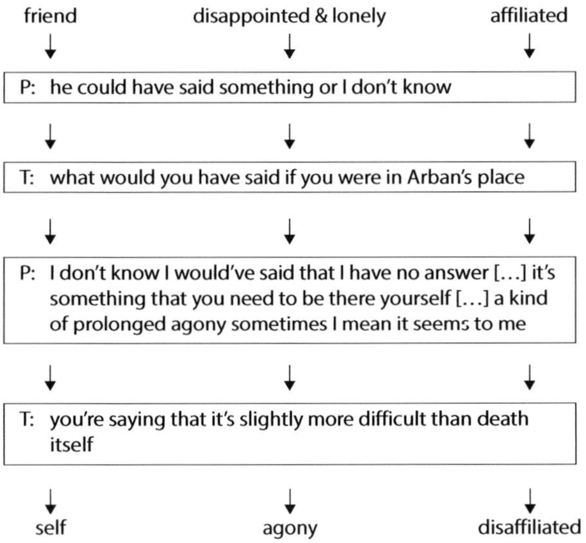

Figure 2. Illustration of transformation of experience through action sequences taking place in Extract I

Data and method

Data come from a total of 47 sessions of psychoanalytic psychotherapy[1] (18), psychodynamic psychotherapy (10), and cognitive-behavioural psychotherapy (19) in Albanian language. Five dyads participated in the study. All participants consented in writing to the video recording of the sessions. Approximately 10 sessions from each dyad were video recorded, each session lasting 50 minutes. A total of 24 instances in which the therapist shifts the patient's focus of talk from other/s or talk at abstract/generic level to patient's self were identified. Only 2 instances were found in cognitive-behavioural psychotherapy, the phenomenon predominantly occurring in psychoanalytic psychotherapy and psychodynamic psychotherapy. Each action sequence was transcribed following CA transcription conventions (Jefferson 2004). All names and other identification potential details in the data extracts were altered. Data was analysed with conversation analysis.

1. In Albania, it is common practice that, in psychoanalysis, the patient sits (instead of lying down) in a 45-degree angle with the therapist. Another difference with the traditional psychoanalytic practice regards the frequency of the sessions, with the therapist and patient meeting once a week or every other week. To distinguish between conventional psychoanalysis and this adjusted format, we refer to the practice in our data as *psychoanalytic psychotherapy*.

Patient's dilemma in response to therapist's focus-of-talk shifting question

In the corpus under examination, therapists deployed a question to shift the focus of talk from other/s or talk at abstract/generic level to patient's self. These focus-of-talk shifting questions posed a threat to the patient by not ratifying the face they had presented so far in the talk and, as such, carried the risk of disaffiliation. In what follows, we show three instances in which the degree of face-threat posed by the therapist's question varies from carefully mitigated (Extract I), mitigated to some extent (Extract II) to upfront challenging (Extract III). We found that, despite the therapists' interactional work to acknowledge the patients' epistemic right to their subjective experience of self, patients chose to save their face but not without doing considerable interactional work to save both their face and the affiliation with the therapist.

Patient's responses to carefully mitigated face-threats

We found that therapists carefully mitigated the disaffiliative nature of the face-threatening question by acknowledging more epistemic rights to the patient regarding their subjective experience of self. To this end, they relied on a number of interactional resources such as question design, prosody and efforts to establish shared understanding. In carefully mitigated face-threats, therapists designed their utterance as open format question, produced it with empathic prosody, and displayed explicit orientation to intersubjectivity. The following extract (I) is an example of a carefully mitigated face-threat.

The stretch of talk is extracted from a psychoanalytic psychotherapy session. The session takes place towards the end of the second year of the therapeutic process. The therapist is a woman in her early forties and the patient a man in his late twenties. The patient is talking about his father who has been ill lately. He expresses concern about his father's health and repeatedly claims to have been pondering on death related thoughts. While his talk remains mainly descriptive (i.e., describing his father's most recent hospitalisation episode), emotional states (i.e., anxiety and fear) can be inferred particularly from his choice of words, amounting to an overall state of helplessness (i.e., "it must be accepted that death is for everyone so we can't deny it"). Following the therapist's unsuccessful attempt at exploring the patient's death related fantasies, the patient shifts the focus of talk from his father to himself, disclosing that he feels lonely and needs to talk to someone. He complains about being single and, in response to the therapist's query about his friends, he first says that they are busy with "their own things", then moves on to tell the following story.

Extract I. What would you have said? [22:08–23:30]

Prior action

01 P >s'e di< ku:r: (4.6) >nuk e di< ka nja ca nja një
>I don't know< whe:n: (4.6) >I don't know< there's been a while some one
02 muj e gjys diçka e tillë domethënë edhe që:: (1.4)
month and a half something like this I mean and tha::t (1.4)
03 °ku di un° me Arbanin po flisja në *Facebook* ((e paqartë))
°I don't know° I was talking to Arban on Facebook ((not clear))
04 >po që< po i tho:sha: (0.7) si? mund të jetohet me një prind
>but well< I was te:lli:ng him (0.7) how? can one live with a sick
05 të sëmurë °domethënë° [e më thoshte] që:: (1.6) ji aty për atë.
parent °I mean° [and he was telling me] tha::t (1.6) be there for him.
06 T [Mhm,]
07 P atë e di un, po si ta përballoj?
I know that, but how do I cope with it?
08 (1.2)
09 P nuk është puna [se] (0.5) se ç'duhet të b(h)ëj domethënë
it's not [that] (0.5) what I should d(h)o I mean
10 T [Mhm,]
11 P unë e di shumë mirë °po,° (1.0) s:'ktheu përgjigje,
I know it very well °but,° (1.0) he d:idn't answer,
12 s'ka:: (1.0) ku di un (1.0) normalisht nuk ësht
there's no:: (1.0) I don't know (1.0) normally it's not
13 se ësht (.) shumë retorike si pyetje domethënë po,
that it's (.) very rhetorical as a question I mean but,
14 ku di un,
I don't know,
15 (2.2)
16 P mund të kishte thënë diçka:, heh [ose] nuk e di se
he could have said somethi:ng, heh [or] I don't know
17 T [MHM,]
18 (5.0)

Target action

19 T °çfarë do kishe thënë ti.(0.4) nëse do ishe në:: .hh
°what would you have said. (0.4) if you were in:: .hh
20 vend të Arbanit.°
Arban's place.°
21 (4.5)

Response

22 P s'e di do kisha thënë që s'kam përgjigj(h)e domethënë
I don't know I would've said that I have no answ(h)er I mean
23 P [ësht] (1.3) °nuk° (0.3) me vërte nuk ká: përgjigje
[it's] (1.3) °there's no° (0.3) there's really no answer
24 T [MHM,]
25 P [domethënë] ësh::=shu:m:,
[I mean] it's::=ver:y:,
26 T [°Mhm,°]
27 (3.7)
28 P s'e di është gjë që duhet të jesh vetë [aty që]
I don't know it's something that you need to be there yourself

(*continued*)

Extract I. (*continued*)

29	T	[((krruan zërin))]
		[((clears throat))]
30	P	ta:: (1.5) kshu po prapë domethënë (0.2) °di un° (2.3) mcht
		in order to:: (1.5) like yet I mean (0.2) °I don't know° (2.3) mcht
31		(1.0) kshu si nji- nji lloj (1.2) agonie e zgjatur °ndonjëherë
		(1.0) like a- a kind of (1.2) prolonged agony °sometimes
32		do të thotë° kshu më duket,
		I mean° it seems to me,
33		(3.8)

Third position

34	T	po thua që është pak më e vështirë sesa vetë (0.5) vdekja,
		you're saying that it's slightly more difficult than (0.5) death itself,

In the action prior to the sequence under scrutiny here, the patient tells a story (lines 1–16) to illustrate his need to talk to someone. In his telling, he complains about his best friend, Arban, who could not answer his question about "how to live with a sick parent" (lines 4–5). The friend's answer was not satisfactory, and the patient's follow up question (line 7) received no answer at all. Despite reproaching his friend for not giving an answer (lines 7, 9 & 11), the patient's overall complaint is directed towards the situation he finds himself in; he defines his question as rhetorical (line 13), acknowledging thus that by asking it, he was trying to make a point – that he finds himself in a very difficult situation – rather than get an answer. Yet soon after having displayed understanding for his friend's inability to help him out with a piece of advice, the patient adds that he "could have said something" (line 16). This part of his talk is marked by the contrastive "but" (line 14) and embedded with knowledge disclaimers (see the "I don't know" in lines 14 and 16) and laughter (line 16), acknowledging not only the overall difficulty in producing emotional talk but also the contradictory nature of the claims being made.

The patient's talk displays two main affects: feeling lonely and being disappointed in his friend. In his story, he tells how by talking to his friend, he was trying not only to overcome his loneliness but also receive advice on how to "cope with it" (line 7). At a transition relevance place, the therapist affiliates with the patient by endorsing his stance quite strongly (line 17), producing a high-volume minimal response token, not characteristic neither of the therapist's volume nor of such response tokens. Despite this strong display of affiliation, the patient does not complete his turn (see the long silence in line 18). One possible grammatical continuation of the turn in Albanian could have been "ose nuk e di se *çfarë mund të kishte thënë*" (in English: 'or I don't know *what he could have said*'); another possibility, a repetition of what he said before: "ose nuk e di se *kjo nuk ka përgjigje*" (in English: "or I don't know cause *there is no answer to this*"). Following the contradictory nature of his claims, the patient steps back and abandons the turn altogether.

In the target action (lines 19–20), the therapist invites the patient to further elaborate on his current emotional state and the corresponding needs. First, she orients to the patient's turn as incomplete (see the long gap on line 18). Next, she asks him to put himself in his friend's position to explicate possible things that his friend could have told him (for a detailed discussion on how therapists deal with implicit content of patients' talk see Koivisto and Voutilainen 2016). By means of a content question, the therapist shifts the focus of talk from the patient's friend to the patient (him)self (notice the emphasis on the second-person pronoun "you"), and the emotional need/s he was trying to fulfil by talking to him. The question is produced in low volume and accompanied by a wide smile, and an extension clarifying the hypothetical situation is added following a short 0.4 s pause. The question's recipient-tilted epistemic asymmetry addresses the patient as the subject of the hypothetical self-experience that it invokes. It is by means of such interactional work that the therapist, on the one hand, acknowledges the patient's previously displayed difficulties in producing emotional talk and elaborating on his momentary need/s whilst, on the other hand, pressures him for an answer by gazing at him intensely.

Though most of the constraints for an answer are carefully mitigated by interactional work, the therapist's invitation bypasses the patient's previous claim that the question is rhetorical thus unanswerable. In pressing for an answer, the therapist's question sets the ground for two competing interactional scenarios: (a) if the patient comes up with a preferred answer response, he would be complying with the question's topical (emotional needs) and action (elaboration of his needs) agendas, in this way preserving the affiliation with the therapist at the cost of losing face by contradicting his previous claim that this is an unanswerable question; or (b) if the patient comes up with a dispreferred non-answer response, he would remain faithful to his claim and consequently to the line he has been drawing for himself as a person who understands and accepts others' inability to help him out, at the cost of disaffiliating with the therapist.

Faced with the difficult choice between saving his face or the affiliation with the therapist, in his response the patient forgoes the latter but not without doing some interactional work to mitigate the relational harm. First, a long silence (line 21) ensues, possibly indicating the cognitive work that the proposed shift necessitates and the upcoming of a dispreferred non-answer response (notice also the knowledge disclaimer at turn-initial position). The patient formats the rest of the turn as an answer response (lines 22–23). While partially complying with the question's topical agenda, namely the shift in focus of talk on self (in line 22, he responds from a first-person position "I"), the patient declines its action agenda as he neither explicates possible answers that would fulfil his momentary need/s nor elaborates on them. His talk is interpolated with laughter (line 22), fillers (see the repeated use of "I mean" in lines 22 and 25), word searching pauses (line 23), and prolonged vowels (lines 23 and 25), indicating the patient's difficulties in coming up with an answer.

Following the therapist's minimal responses (lines 24 and 26) and withdrawal from taking a turn (line 27), the patient expands his answer with an account for his friend's difficulties with coming up with an answer (lines 28 and 30). By doing so, he steps out of the hypothetical self-frame he was supposed to be responding from, coming back to the actual situation where "he is there himself" (line 28). He does, however, preserve the focus of talk on self, qualifying the situation he finds himself in as "prolonged agony" (lines 31–32). In the third position turn (line 34), by means of a rephrasing formulation (Weiste and Peräkylä 2013), the therapist accepts the patient's non-answer response maintaining the focus of talk on (him) self and his emotions. She invites the patient to further continue reflecting on his emotional state and the corresponding needs, hence pursuing the interactional project initiated in lines 19–20.

To sum up, in Extract I, the therapist's focus-of-talk shifting question took an issue with the patient's represented self, posing a threat to the patient's face and the therapeutic relation. As such, it presented a dilemma for the patient, to save his face or the affiliation with the therapist. After trying to save both, the patient chose to preserve the line he had been drawing for himself at the cost of disaffiliating with the therapist.

Patient's responses to mitigated face-threats

In our data corpus, therapists did not always carefully mitigate the disaffiliative nature of the face-threatening question. We found that, at times, therapists acknowledged more epistemic rights to themselves than to the patient when questioning the latter's subjective experience of self, prioritizing their professional authority. As we will see in the following Extract (II), deploying an open format question is not sufficient in mitigating the threat posed to the patient's face and the therapeutic relation.

The stretch of talk below is extracted from the 10th encounter in a psychodynamic psychotherapy. The therapist is a woman in her early forties and the patient is a woman in her early twenties. The patient is complaining about others seeing her as an object of their sexual fantasies. To illustrate this, she describes two recent events where she felt sexually harassed: an encounter with an acquaintance and a workplace episode with her boss. The therapist attempts at eliciting elaboration of such experiences, inviting the patient to reflect upon her own experience of the events. The patient's focus of talk remains primarily on others, explicating what they do and attributing blame on them. On the few occasions when she shifts the focus of talk on herself, she depicts a very positive portrait of an independent, open minded, and honest person. Following several failed attempts at inviting the patient to see her own behaviour (open and honest) from the others' perspective (too close and intimate), the talk shifts to the patient's ex-boyfriends. Right before Extract II, following the patient's claim to being perhaps "very picky", the therapist inquires about Blendi, a former boyfriend, asking what she found special about him.

Extract II. What about you? [35:50–37:35]

Prior action

01	P	mcht më pëlqejnë kta- kta çunat e mir, kta si të urtë, pak si kshu, **mcht I like these- these good guys, these like amiable, a little like,**
02		që janë ((rregullon pantallonat)) [edhe ky] ishte **who are ((straightens her trousers)) [and this] was**
03	T	[£vërte::t?£] **[£really::?£]**
04	P	po::(h) [heh] **ye::s(h) [heh]**
05	T	[£ua:u] kisha [mendim komplet] tjetër për ty£ **[£wo:w] I had [a totally different] idea about you£**
06	P	**[heh heh]**
07	P	£jo::(h). >jo jo jo<£= **£no::(h). >no no no<£=**
08	T	=domethën për <u>çfarë</u> mund të pëlqeje <u>ti</u>.= **=I mean about <u>what you</u> might like.=**
09	P	=>jo jo fare më pëlqejn shumë- (.) edhe Eri prandaj më pëlqente se **=>no no not at all I like them very much- (.) and Eri that's why I liked him cause**
10		ishte shumë< (.) çun i mir. **he was a very< (.) good guy.**
11	T	**[°ëhë::,°]**

12	P	[i kam] shum qef kta:: mcht (.) #e-# atë iden e *bad boy*-it e kam **[I very] much like these:: mcht (.) #e-# the bad boy idea I really**
13		((tund kokën në formë refuzimi)) °e kam kshu::° **((head gesture indicating refusal)) °I really like::°**
14		((lëviz duart në formë refuzimi)) nuk= **((hand gesture indicating refusal)) it doesn't/I don't**
15	T	=*<u>exc</u>luded* **=<u>exc</u>luded**
16	P	((vazhdon lëvizja e duarve)) fare= **((hand gesture continues)) totally=**
17	T	**=m::?**
18		(1.4)
19	P	dua nji- nji çun shum t mir, një kshu si:: (.) si çun <u>ma</u>:mi pak nji:: **I want a- a very good guy, one like:: (.) like <u>mama</u>'s boy somehow a::**
20		((ngre shpatullat)) .hh nji person të mir ((rrotullon duart)) [të but] **((raises her shoulders)) .hh a good person ((rotates her hands)) [soft]**
21	T	[të u:rt?] **[a:miable?]**
22	P	Po::. **Yes::.**
23	T	**[Mhm,]**

(continued)

Extract II. *(continued)*

24	P	[Blendi] nuk ishte i urt, >medemek< ishte:: ((rrotullon duart)) .hh >ajo që **[Blendi] was not amiable, >I mean< he was:: ((rotates her hands)) .hh >what I**
25		më pëlqente te ai ishte që ishte pak si si fëmijë në ca::< në ca **liked about him was that he was a little like like a child in some::< in some**
26		[pjesë .hh entu-] **[aspects .hh enthu-]**
27	T	[sesi për m-] qa:nte:? **[how] he would cry::?**
28	P	entuziazmi i vet ishte si si fmi::j, **his enthusiasm was like like a chi::ld,**
29	T	Ëhë, **Mhm,**
30	P	e kur fliste >për shembull për gjërat< ësht shum:: ashu edhe- (.) mcht **and when he talked >for example about things< it's very:: like and- (.) mcht**
31		>edhe ishte shum i mir,< shum:: (2.0) ktë kishte. edhe Eri £ëf Eri **>and he was very good,< very:: (2.0) that's how he was. and Eri £um£ Eri**
32		atë që më pëlqente ishte shum i mir, (1.0) **what I liked about him was that he was very good, (1.0)**
33		[shum çun i mir, (0.5) shum njeri i mir,] (0.5) ktë vlersoj shum, **[a very good guy, (0.5) a very good person,] (0.5) this is what I appreciate a lot,**
34	T	[.hhhh ((mbështet shpinën)) hhhh] **[.hhhh ((sits backwards)) hhhh]**
35		(0.5)
36	T	që të jet njeri i mir?= **that he is a good person?=**
37	P	=po::.= **=yes::.=**

Target action

38	T	=po ti si je? **=what about you?**
39		(1.0)

Response

40	P	çar? **what?**
41	T	ti si je. **how are you.**
42	P	((buzëqesh; ngre shpatullat)) **((smiles; rasies her shoulders))**
43	T	në ktë parametrin e mirsis që ti i vendos ata, **in this goodness parameter where you place them,**
44		(2.4)
45	P	<£un jam e mi::r:: (.) kur du:a:£> **<£I am goo::d:: (.) when I wa:nt: to£>**
46		(1.0)

Extract II. (*continued*)

```
47  T  Ëhë,
       Mhm,
48     (1.0)
49  P  jam e mir po- (.) po kam:: (1.0) >ta kam thënë dhe njëherë unë
       mund të bëhem
       I am good but- (.) but I have:: (1.0) >I've told you once before I
       would do everything
50     copa për personat< që i kam shumë përzemër.
       for the persons< that I love very much.
51  T  ((tund kokën))
       ((nods))
52  P  që po vendosa që u:n:: të kam qef ((lëviz dorën në mënyrë të
       prerë))(2.0)
       that if I made up my mind that I:: like you ((hand gesture
       indicating decisiveness))(2.0)
53  e  bëj gjithçka::, (.) gjithçka: m: jam atje::,
       I do everything::, (.) everything: m: I am there::,
```

Third position

```
54  T  Ëhë, okej, që i mbështet edhe:[::  ] m: jepesh për ta::,
       Mhm, okay, that you support them a::[::]nd m: devote yourself to them::,
55  P                                [po:,]
                                     [yes:,]
56  T  [dhe sa]krifikon po thua për kta,
       [and ma]ke sacrifices you're saying for these,
57  P  [ po:,]
       [yes:,]
58  P  po.
       yes.
59  T  .hh e- e kupto:j ktë gjënë po:: .hh pse i kërkon ti (.)
       .hh I- I understa:nd this bu::t .hh why are you after (.)
60     >duket sikur i kërkon më të mirë se veten,<
       >it seems like you are after men [who are] better than yourself,<
61     (1.7)
62  T  më të u:rt, të:: >që jan< (0.4) [prapë ësht te pushteti të::nd]
       quieter, >who are< (0.4) [again it's about you::r power]
```

```
63  P                                  [po dhe un jam shumë e u::rt]
                                       [but I am very a::miable too]
64     .hh >jo nuk ësht atje, edhe unë jam shumë e u:rt,< (0.5) jam
       shumë e qetë, si njeri
       .hh >no it's not that, I am very a:miable too,< (0.5) I am very
       quiet, as a person
```

In the action prior to the sequence of analytic interest here, the patient claims to like "good guys" (lines 1–2). By means of a news marking "really" (Jefferson 2015) the therapist expresses surprise (line 3), the post-expansion soon unfolding into an account (lines 5 and 8). Despite the disagreement-implicating nature of the therapist's repair (Schegloff 2007), the talk ensues in an atmosphere of shared amusement (notice the shared laughter and smiley voices in lines 3–7). In what follows, the therapist does a lot of interactional work to mitigate the face-threatening potency of her abrupt uptake: she aligns with the patient's talk, continuously displaying understanding of what she is saying; invites further talk from the patient (see the continuer in line 11 and the minimal acknowledgment tokens in lines 23 and 29); displays attentiveness and understanding of what the patient is saying at present (see the highlighting formulations (Weiste and Peräkylä 2013) signposting beyond mere receipt of the patient's talk) and has been saying before (see the declarative question in line 27, suppling a detail the patient has shared with her in a previous session).

The patient, on the other hand, does not orient to the therapist's turn as a face-threat. She responds to it light-heartedly (see the laughter in lines 4 and 6) and after firmly yet smilingly discarding it (lines 7 and 9), goes on to further expand her turn. In doing so, she reiterates her epistemic primacy on the matter at hand, one which the therapist has been working to acknowledge following the potential infringement. In what follows, she asserts what kind of guys she likes in general and explicates how the two recent boyfriends fit to this preference. When the talk steers back towards Eri, another former boyfriend, the patient repeats how he was "very good" (lines 31–33). She enhances this part of her talk with two alterations (line 33), first inserting the word "guy", next replacing it with "person" (for more on self-initiated same-turn repairs, see Schegloff 2013), modifying her preference to target the referents as "persons" and not just "boyfriends".

Not long after the epistemic gradient (Heritage 2010) has been re-calibrated, in a second post-expansion (line 36) the therapist takes issue with the patient's claim, deploying a disagreement-implicated other initiated repair (Schegloff 2007). Sticking to her epistemic primacy on the matter at hand, the patient orients to it as an understanding problem, confirming quickly and without making any further adjustments (line 37). What happens next is the target action under investigation in this study.

In line 38, the therapist invites the patient to talk about how she sees herself. By means of a content question, the therapist shifts the focus of talk from others to patient's self. Though the question's open format respects the patient's epistemic primacy (for more on design of questions and epistemic gradient, see Heritage and Raymond 2012), the shift is morally loaded in that it questions how the patient sees herself, suggesting a possibility that she might see herself as not so good or even a bad person. The question constrains the patient to choose between two options, each giving rise to a different interactional scenario: (a) if she answers saying that she sees herself as a good person, in attempting to save face, she would be not-so-modestly asserting what must have been regarded as self-evident knowledge, in this way rejecting the suggested possibility of being otherwise; or (b) if, on the other hand, she says that she sees herself as not that good, or that she thinks of herself as being a bad person, in giving in to the suggested possibility, she would be endorsing what seems to be the therapist's epistemic stance at the cost of admitting something negative about herself.

The patient faces the difficult choice between saving her face or the relation with the therapist. Responding to an ostensibly face-threat embedded in a focus-of-talk shifting question seems to warrant cognitive work, as indicated in the delays in patient's response (lines 39 and 44). The patient first deploys an understanding check (line 40), orienting to the problematic nature of the therapist's question. The therapist refrains from reworking her question, instead merely repeating it (line 41), this time highlighting the shift to (patient's) self (notice how she emphasizes the second-person pronoun "you" and deploys a closing intonation to underline the topical nature of the shift). Following another non answer response accompanied by smiling (line 42), the patient refrains from embracing either scenario. The therapist, however, firmly treats the patient's non answer response as no more than an understanding problem and, by means of an increment (Schegloff 2007), clarifies what she means.

Finding herself in a difficult position, with the therapist declining to meet her halfway, the patient proceeds to save as much as she can of both her face and the therapeutic relation. In her response, she downplays a face-saving answer by specifying that being good is conditional upon her will (line 45). The turn is produced in slow pace, with prolonged vowels and consonants, and the patient is smiling all the way through, revealing thus her uneasiness at coming up with what she considers to be a dispreferred answer, and perhaps some uncertainty regarding whether the answer gratifies the therapist's question. By conditioning her being good, hence implying that she is not always so, she partially ratifies the therapist's right to question the way she sees herself, accepting to some degree her implicit suggestion. While working to avoid disaffiliating with the therapist, the patient tries to compensate for the face loss by deploying one extreme case formulation after another (lines 49–50, 52–53).

In the third position turn, the therapist strongly endorses the patient's stance: she produces a strong affiliative nodding (line 51); accepts the patient's answer (see the sequence closing "okay" (Schegloff 2007) in the beginning of line 54); and formulates the patient's talk in such a way that it sheds very positive light on the patient (lines 54 and 56). Only after having reassured the patient that she endorses her answer and their relation is now at a safe place, the therapist comes back to her question, this time designing it as an interpretation (lines 59–60, 62). She clarifies the interactional project ("your power") she embarked on previously in the talk and reveals the links that guided her to such an interpretation ("seems like you are after men [who are] better than yourself"). By orienting to the patient's response as not fully answering her question, the therapist invites her once more to focus the talk on her subjective experience of herself, in explicit pursuit of the interactional project at hand.

In brief, in Extract II, the therapist's shift in the focus of talk questioned the patient's overall conceptualisation of the self, posing a threat to both the patient's face and the therapeutic relation. As such, it placed the patient in the difficult position of choosing between saving her face or the affiliation with the therapist. The patient made considerable efforts to preserve the affiliation with the therapist. Ultimately, the patient chose to save her face, strategically modifying it in such a way that while partially accepting the therapist's implicit suggestion, she added more positive social attributes to it.

Patient's responses to upfront challenging face-threats

In the corpus under investigation here, we found that, at times, the face-threat embedded in a focus-of-talk shifting question was plainly challenging. In terms of turn design, these questions were formatted as declaratives, setting high constraints to the patients' response while acknowledging more epistemic rights to the therapists with regards to the patient's subjective experience of self. Moreover, the interactional environment amidst which they were deployed – ongoing disaffiliation – intensified relational impasse instead of remedy. By challenging the patient, the therapists put the therapeutic relation at a strong test. The following Extract (III) is an example of an upfront challenging face-threat.

The talk below is extracted from mid-session of a psychoanalytic psychotherapy encounter. The therapeutic process is still at the very beginning, this stretch of talk taking place during the 9th encounter. The therapist is a woman in her late twenties and the patient is a woman in her mid-thirties. Since the beginning of the session, the patient has been talking about how she relates to her family members and other close relations, portraying herself in very positive tones: caring, considerate, respectful, highly responsible towards others. She also claims to be the favourite, most loved family member. Her talk is produced at a generic level, not referring to any concrete person or situation. To illustrate her self-related claims, she makes use of hypothetical situations or figures of speech (i.e., she is the engine, and her close relations are the train cars). The therapist's responses are designed to elicit talk on concrete and emotional subjective experiences, with a particular focus on the patient's present moment in life. Following such recurrent attempts, the patient describes a recent conflict with one of her sisters, revolving around the sister interfering with how the patient is raising her child. The therapist inquires into the siblings' relationship during the patient's childhood. The patient says that they "have always been there for each other" and mentions that, at present, each of them has a child. She goes on to talk about her siblings' children, as shown in the extract III below.

Extract III. This is what it was for you? [32:03–34:59]

```
01  P  .hh unë kam marrë p- (0.2) pjesë shum në rritjen £e::£ të dyve
       .hh I have p- (0.2) participated a lot in the upbringing £o::f££
       both
02     atyre ↑por për- për ktë arsye↑ jam trajnuar herët heh heh=
       of them ↑but for- for this reason↑ I was trained early on heh heh=
03  T  =°Mhm,°=
04  P  dh::e:: kur ka ardhur puna te djali im nuk i kam lënë
       a::nd:: when it came to my son I didn't let
05     asnjërin [se:: m]
       anyone [cau::se m]
06  T           [ pak e] padrejt↑
                [a bit un]fair↑
07  P  ë:(h)?
       uh(h)?
08  T  pak e padrejt
       a bit unfair
09     (2.0)
```

Prior action

```
10  P  [HH kam pasur ktë fiksim] sikur nëse::
       [HH I've had this fixed idea] that i::f
11  T  [ndoshta? (0.4) ndoshta.]
       [maybe? (0.4) maybe.]
12  P  [          ndoshta £m nuk .hh n::£          ] më është
       dukur (.) ëphh .hh
       [maybe £m I don't .hh n::£] it seemed to me (.) uphh .hh
13  T  [°po° (.) po them se çfarë mund të mendojë motrat ë?]
       [°yes° (.) I'm saying what the sisters might think no?]
14  P  °pse p-° (2.0) PSE? PO IA LE KTË SI BARRË NA MBAJE TI
       °why am I° (2.0) WHY? AM I LEAVING THIS LIKE A BURDEN HERE YOU KEEP IT
15     SE DO PUSHOJ UNË KTË:: KJO ËSHTË PËRGJEGJËSIA IME.
       CAUSE I'LL REST THI::S THIS IS MY RESPONSIBILITY.
16  E  KAM BËRË UNË, E KAM MENDUAR [MIRË,] E KAM DËSHIRUAR,
       I DID IT, I THOUGHT IT [THROUGH,] I WANTED IT,
17  T                             [ °po°]
                                  [°yes°]
18  P  (2.0) PRANDAJ DHE E KAM BËRË. TANI KJO ËSHT (0.5) e imja.
       (2.0) AND THAT IS WHY I DID IT. NOW THIS IS (0.5) mine.
19     .hh më dukeshe (.) gjithmonë sikur po t'ia le dikujt
       .hh it always seemed to me (.) that if I leave him to someone
20     është lo:dhje për tjetrin, (0.2) dhe kjo është vetëm
       it's ti::redness for the other, (0.2) and this is only
21     e [imja,]
         [mine,]
```

Target action

```
22  T  [ për  ] ty kshu ishte? lodh[je:? dikur?]
       [this] is what it was for you? tired[ne:ss? at the time?]
```

(*continued*)

Extract III. (*continued*)

Response

```
23  P                                   [    .hhth    ] ë:::: në #në::::#
                                        [.hhth] uhm:::: in #in::::#
24       gjat:ë: llojit të martesës që kisha u:në ishte një lloj
         du:ring: the kind of marriage that I: had it was a kind of
25       lodhje se kërkonte mcht nerva dhe durim, ti nuk mund t'ia
         tiredness cause it required mcht nerves and patience, you can't
26       .hh shkarkosh .hh [ë:: nervat ë::] dhe Atë
         .hh discharge .hh [uhm:: your anger uhm::] and That
27  T                      [ mcht.hh ]
28  P    çfarë të b:: bën me tjetrin të humbasësh durimin
         what m:: makes you lose patience with the other
29       t'ia shkarkosh fëmijës .hh pra nuk kisha tch(t) .hh
         to discharge that to the child .hh so I didn't have tch(t) .hh
30       (0.2) kisha dëshir të m- >mos ISHA E LODHUR< që dhe
         (0.2) I wanted to n- >not BE TIRED< so that I (could) also
31       TA GËZOJA në të njëjtën kohë=
         ENJOY IT at the same time=
32  T    =Mhm,
33       (1.0)
34  T    [Mm,]
35  P    [.hh] po::r e kisha marrë si përgjegjësi, (1.5)
         [.hh] bu::t I had undertaken it as a responsibility, (1.5)
36  T    Mm,
37  P    .hh që:: (.) unë e bëra ktë↑ (0.2) ky fëmijë nuk zgjodhi
         .hh that:: (.) I did this↑ (0.2) this child did not choose
38       që të lindi↑
         to be born↑
39  T    °Mhm,°
40  P    atëhere (2.0) [ un ] do t'i sh- shkoj ↑deri në fund çdo gjëje.
         so now (2.0) [I] will en- endure everything.
41  T                  [Mm,]
42  T    Mm,
43       (1.0)
44  P    dhe kjo është përgjegjësi vetëm e imja. e askujt tjetër.
         and this responsibility is only mine. no one else's.
```

```
45  T    °po,°
         °yes,°
         [38 lines omitted]
```

Third position

```
83  T    mcht .hh >po duket siku::r< ndoshta:: mcht mcht kur-
         mcht .hh >well it seems li::ke< maybe:: mcht mcht when-
84       kur ke qenë ti ë? në krye të:: të detyrës për t'u
         when you were no? in charge of:: of things looking
85       kujdesur për fëmijën e motrës tënde:,=
         after your sister's child:,=
86  P    =M,=
87  T    =duket siku::r (0.5) ndoshta:: (1.5) ka qenë një lodhje për ty.
         =it seems li::ke (0.5) maybe (1.5) it was a tiredness for you.
```

```
88       (1.0)
89  P    .hhhh=
90  T    =ë?
         =m?
```

Extract II. *(continued)*

```
91   P   edhe ishte po unë e shikoja si::[ :: ] phu >nuk e di<
         might have been but I saw it as::[::] phu >I don't know<
92   T                                  [Ëhë,]
                                        [Mhm,]
93   P   e shikoja dhe si detyrën time
         I saw it as my duty as well
94   T   detyrë
         duty
```

In the beginning of the extract, the patient repeats [first mentioning not shown here] how she has not allowed her family members to babysit her child (lines 4–5). Prior to the target action, the patient responds (lines 7, 10–21) to the therapist's challenge (lines 6 and 8), assessing her behaviour as "unfair". The assessment is produced in overlap, interrupting the patient's talk. The therapist downplays the challenging potency of her face-threatening assessment by wearing a playful smile, using "a bit" to lessen its accusatory power, and deploying questioning intonation (notice the rise in intonation at the end of the turn). Despite all this interactional work, the patient disaffiliates by first delaying her response (see the repair sequence in lines 7–8, followed by a long silence in line 9), next exiting the good-humoured frame of talk she herself initiated in line 2 to continue with her account.

To soothe the disaffiliation, the therapist tries to further downplay the challenge. She adds some more epistemic uncertainty to her stance (notice the repeated "maybe" in line 11, the first one granting epistemic primacy to the patient, while the second revealing the therapist's own epistemic uncertainty). The patient asserts her epistemic right regarding the matter by deploying, in line 12, a repetitional response (Stivers 2005; Heritage and Raymond 2005) and goes on to pursue her interactional project. The therapist, on the other hand, also pursues her self-repairing interactional project, this time attributing the assessment's authorship to the patient's sisters (line 13). Moreover, by accompanying her turn with an "air quotes" gesture, she highlights the challenge's euphemistic aspect, yet another attempt at reaffiliating with the patient back in the good-humoured frame of talk.

The patient, however, declines from reaffiliating with the therapist, hence maintaining an orientation to the challenge as a face-threat. In what follows, she strengthens her account in defence of her decision by providing the therapist with direct access to her past experience when her child was a baby (notice the use of reported thought when describing how "it seemed to [her]" in line 12). At the same time, she displays a strong irritation in the present situation, as indicated by the raised volume and emphasised parts of her talk. The therapist withdraws from pursuing her interactional project any further. She gives the floor to the patient, in this way aligning with her project (line 17).

In response to the patient's shifting of the focus of talk from her sisters to a generic "someone" (line 19), the therapist makes another referential shift, this time to the patient's self. In the target action (line 22), abruptly and in overlap with the patient's turn, she deploys a declarative question, also shifting the focus of talk from rights and responsibilities to emotional states (being tired). The therapist links the patient's previously mentioned baby-sitting experiences of her sister's children to her recent saying that "if [she] leaves him to someone, it's tiredness for the other" (lines 19–20), suggesting that the patient's baby-sitting experience was tiresome for her "at the time" (line 22). In inviting the patient to elaborate on the suggestion, the therapist utilises empathic prosody to tune down the epistemic certainty embodied in the declarative design of her turn and to elicit talk on emotions associated with the experience (notice the question-like rise in intonation at the first possible end of the turn, also at the end of the first and second extensions).

The interactional consequences projected by the shift pose a threat to the therapeutic relation. Firstly, the question's constraints are very high in that it not only proposes a limited number (two) of possible answer responses, but it also projects a preference for confirmation. Secondly, the question's preference constrains the patient to both align with the therapist's interactional project (to focus the patient's talk on concrete, emotional subjective experiences) and affiliate with the latter by endorsing her epistemic stance, at the cost of losing face as a result of contradicting the line she has been drawing for herself throughout the session: a caring and highly responsible person, a favourite among family members. Lastly, deployed amidst ongoing disaffiliation, a dispreferred disconfirming response would result in the patient saving her face, but further escalating the relational impasse.

In her response, the patient carries out the occasioned cognitive work to make the suggested shift, while keeping the floor to herself. Despite not having the answer just yet (notice the word searching in line 23), the patient takes the turn rather quickly, projecting the upcoming of a preferred confirming response. She does not, however, respond to the question as put to her but adjusts it so that it retrospectively transforms into "babysitting your own child was tiresome for you". The agenda modifying transformative answer (Stivers and Hayashi 2010), allows the patient to save face while endorsing the therapist's stance. Attributing tiredness to an external factor (her marriage) relieves her from the responsibility of having mispresented herself so far in her account of the family memories. What is more, admitting to having raised a child in a difficult marriage allows her to continue scoring points for herself. She aligns with the transformed question's shift of focus on self by talking about a concrete emotional subjective experience and, ostensibly, affiliates with the therapist by endorsing her epistemic stance.

The patient's attempt at partial collaboration does not however succeed. In a third position action (lines 83–85 and 87) the therapist comes back to her suggestion, this time designing it as an interpretation. The interpretation is mitigated (notice the use of the uncertainty markers such as "maybe" and the question tag "no"/"right"; the hesitation markers such as the long pauses in line 87, the prolonged vowels, and the self-initiated repair), carefully downgrading the epistemic asymmetry. By going back to her suggestion, the therapist does not accept the patient's transformative answer. Instead, she once more invites her to focus her talk on herself and elaborate on her own subjective emotional experience, assiduously pursuing her therapeutic project.

To summarise, in Extract III, the therapist's abrupt and overlapping shift in the focus of talk questioned the patient's autobiographical self as represented in her account of past family events. The patient resisted the challenge by retroactively transforming the question's agenda in such a way that it allowed her to save her face and, at the same time, affiliate with the therapist.

Discussion

In his book, *The Presentation of Self in Everyday Life*, Goffman (1959, 13) stated that in interaction, an individual makes implicit or explicit claims to be a person of a particular kind, obliging co-interactants to value and treat them accordingly. At the same time, they implicitly forgo all claims to be things they do not appear to be and hence forgo the treatment that would be appropriate for such individuals. Making such a claim inflicts a moral obligation upon others – they are now informed as to what the individual is and how they ought to see them. In this study, we showed how, in psychotherapeutic interaction, the therapists' questioning of the patient's self-presentation led to defensive moves by the latter. Moreover, both therapists and patients oriented to the patient's self as a delicate object, with the former deploying interactional work to mitigate the face-threat and the latter choosing to save face at any cost.

Psychotherapy aims to bring about change in a patient's relation to their experiences (Peräkylä et al. 2008). We investigated moments in psychoanalytic psychotherapy and psychodynamic psychotherapy when ratifying the patient's face was incongruent with the therapeutic goal of altering the experience of self. In psychotherapy, self is both subject to and object of the psychotherapeutic work. As such, it is an overarching yet delicate topic. In our data, patients took great care to attribute positive social values to themselves. This is not surprising given the vulnerability inherent in being a patient. Psychotherapy research has revealed how most people experience negative feelings such as embarrassment or shame in revealing private, uncomfortable experiences (Greenberg, Rice and Elliot 1997). The therapists in our data oriented to the difficulty of not ratifying the patient's face by mitigating (though to varying degrees) the face-threatening nature of their move. Likewise, the patients, confronted with the dilemma of saving either their face or the affiliation with the therapist, prioritised their face but not without doing considerable interactional work to save both.

We found that therapists rely on interactional work to mitigate face-threats. They do so primarily by acknowledging the patient's epistemic authority to their experience of self. To this end, they design their turn as questions and, when carefully mitigating the potential threat, rely on empathic prosody and display orientation to intersubjectivity. Less mitigated face-threats were formatted as declaratives, acknowledging less epistemic authority to the patient and more to the therapist. How therapists handle the sensitive task of altering a patient's experience without undermining their epistemic authority has been a topic of interest for a number of CA studies. Findings show that therapists first ratify the client's perspective and only next introduce a competing perspective by using lengthy multi-unit turns (Deppermann, Scheidt and Stukenbrock 2020). They present the evidential basis for their interpretations and speak from a shared perspective (co-describing) which involves emotional attunement and empathy (Weiste, Voutilainen and Peräkylä 2015). Also, they display supportive disagreement – work to find congruence between their perspectives and that of the client, validate the client's emotional experience and respect their epistemic rights – which prompts clients to confirm and elaborate on their experiences (Weiste 2015). Similar findings by Voutilainen (2012) and Voutilainen, Peräkylä and Ruusuvuori (2010a) indicate that therapists first recognise the patient's emotional experience by displaying understanding of and validating it, next suggest alternative views to the experience in question.

Failure to handle with care the fine balance between self-exploration and relational work may prompt irritation and anger in the client, with relational ruptures arising as the therapeutic relationship becomes the focus of ensuing talk (Weiste 2015). Similarly, the client may call into question the therapist's right to know their inner experience (Weiste, Voutilainen and Peräkylä 2015). Of all the experiences investigated in these studies, self-experience seems to be the most difficult to work with. As our analysis revealed, even in carefully mitigated face-threats, patients chose to save their face at the cost of disaffiliating with the therapist. Similarly, Deppermann, Scheidt and Stukenbrock (2020) found that, in response to mitigated threats, patients may resist or confirm only partially or in passing, not elaborating in detail the therapist's perspective. These findings indicate that, in psychotherapy, similar to everyday social interaction, the experience of self is connected to the sociality of the situation and treated by all participants as a sacred object (Goffman 1959).

Patients, on the other hand, found it difficult to shift the focus of talk on self and come up with an answer which saves either their face or the affiliation with the therapist. Such difficulties were displayed in their partial compliance with the question's agendas (Extract I), initial non-answer responses followed by partial acceptance of face-threat (Extract II) and agenda-modifying transformative answer

(Extract III). The dispreferred nature of their responses halted the progressivity of interaction (Stivers and Robinson 2006), putting at risk the accomplishment of the therapist's invited action of self-exploration, initiated by the focus-of-talk shifting question. By taking an issue with the patient's face, the therapist's question destroyed the cathexis, with shame and anxiety replacing the pleasure (Goffman 1955). Not ratifying the patient's face also brought forth the risk of disaffiliation or furthering disaffiliation when occurring amidst it. As such, the therapist's question was found to be a heavily loaded vehicle, initiating transformation of all the three realms of experiences: *referents*, *emotion* and *relation* (Peräkylä 2019).

These findings are in line with other CA studies on patient resistance. For example, in a study of couple counselling, Muntigl (2013) found that client resistance resulted in unproductive trajectories of talk that furthered the disaffiliation and impeded the therapeutic work. Likewise, Ekberg and LeCouteur (2015) investigated client resistance in cognitive-behavioural therapy and found that, though therapists' proposals suggesting behavioural change were designed in ways that were contingent on the client's approval, clients typically responded with active resistance, drawing upon an aspect of their experience that allowed them to assert the inability to accept the proposal. These findings show how even in psychotherapy, where the patient's experiences are foregrounded, this privileged position does not relieve them from the need to have their face valued and treated as they think they should be treated, nor does it protect them from feeling threatened when the therapist proposes otherwise.

Resistance, though often discussed as something that the patient does (for more on cooperation in psychotherapeutic process, see Buchholtz, this volume), is collaboratively managed (Muntigl 2013). As early as 1954, joining the ongoing debate on the patient's resistance and analyst's counter resistance, Anna Freud suggested that:

> With due respect for the necessary strictest handling and interpretation of the transference, I feel still that we should leave room somewhere for the realization that analyst and patient are also two real people, of equal adult status, in a real personal relationship to each other. I wonder whether our – at times complete – neglect of this side of the matter is not responsible for some of the hostile reactions which we get from our patients and which are apt to ascribe to 'true transference' only.

In our data, we showed how therapists first questioned the patient's face and only following patient resistance, endorsed it. This order of work is reverse in comparison to the findings discussed here and might account in part for the patient resistance to self-explore. We conclude that foregrounding transformative work with displays of empathy first might be the preferred order of work in the psychotherapeutic setting.

Future research can expand the analytical focus to include longitudinal work towards change in patients' self-experience and examine how the therapeutic relation evolves to support patients in achieving that change. Furthermore, investigation of strategies to collaboratively manage the face-threatening dimension of the therapeutic work can contribute to a better understanding of how both patients and therapists orient to the therapeutic relation as part of the overall therapeutic work. On a last note, since the data in this study comes from not a typical Western society, further research in similar social and cultural contexts will broaden our understanding of the dynamics of face and face-threats in psychotherapeutic or other types of encounters.

Bibliography

Antaki, C. 2008. "Formulations in Psychotherapy." In *Conversation Analysis and Psychotherapy*, ed. by Anssi Peräkylä, Charles Antaki, Sanna Vehviläinen and Ivan Leudar, 43–61. Cambridge: Cambridge University Press. https://doi.org/10.1017/CBO9780511490002.003

Bercelli, Fabrizio, Federico Rossano and Maurizio Viaro. 2008. "Clients' Responses to Therapists' Reinterpretations." In *Conversation Analysis and Psychotherapy*, ed. By Anssi Peräkylä, Charles Antaki, Sanna Vehviläinen and Ivan Leudar, 43–61. Cambridge: Cambridge University Press. https://doi.org/10.1017/CBO9780511490002.004

Brown, Penelope and Stephen C. Levinson. 1987. *Politeness. Some Universals in Language Usage*. Cambridge: Cambridge University Press. https://doi.org/10.1017/CBO9780511813085

Deppermann, Arnulf, Carl E. Scheidt and Anja Stukenbrock. 2020. "Positioning Shifts from Told Self to Performative Self in Psychotherapy." *Frontiers in Psychology* 40–57. https://doi.org/10.3389/fpsyg.2020.572436.

Ekberg, Katie and Amanda LeCouteur. 2015. "Clients' Resistance to Therapists' Proposals: Managing Epistemic and Deontic Status." *Journal of Pragmatics* 90: 12–25. https://doi.org/10.1016/j.pragma.2015.10.004.

Fitzgerald, Pamela. 2013. *Therapy Talk: Conversation Analysis in Practice*. Hampshire: Palgrave Macmillan. https://doi.org/10.1057/9781137329530

Fonagy, Peter, György Gergely, Elliot Jurist and Mary Target. 2002. *Affect Regulation, Mentalization, and the Development of the Self*. New York: Other Press.

Freud, Anna. 1954. "The Widening Scope of Indications for Psychoanalysis: Discussion." *Journal of the American Psychoanalytic Association* 2 (4): 607–620. https://doi.org/10.1177/000306515400200404.

Goffman, Erving. 1959. *The Presentation of Self in Everyday Life*. New York: Anchor Books.

Goffman, Erving. 1955. "On Face-work. An Analysis of Ritual Elements in Social Interaction." *Psychiatry* 18 (3): 213–231. https://doi.org/10.1080/00332747.1955.11023008.

Greenberg, Leslie S., Laura N. Rice and Robert Elliot. 1997. *Facilitating Emotional Change: The Moment-by-Moment Process*. New York: The Guildford Press.

Guxholli, Aurora, Liisa Voutilainen and Anssi Peräkylä. 2021. "Safeguarding the Therapeutic Alliance: Managing Disaffiliation in the Course of Work with Psychotherapeutic Projects." *Frontiers in Psychology* 139–157. https://doi.org/10.3389/fpsyg.2020.596972.

Heritage, John. 2011. "Territories of Knowledge, Territories of Experience: Empathic Moments in Interaction." In *The Morality of Knowledge in Conversation*, ed. by Tanya Stivers, Lorenza Mondada and Jakob Steensig, 159–183. Cambridge: Cambridge University Press. https://doi.org/10.1017/CBO9780511921674.008

Heritage, John. 2010. "Questioning in medicine." In *Why Do You Ask? The Function of Questions in Institutional Discourse*, ed. by Susan Ehrlich and Alice F. Freed, 42–68. Oxford: Oxford University Press.

Heritage, John. 1984. *Garfinkel and Ethnomethodology*. Cambridge: Polity Press.

Heritage, John and Geoffrey Raymond. 2012. "Navigating Epistemic Landscapes: Acquiescence, Agency and Resistance in Responses to Polar Questions." In *Questions: Formal, Functional and Interactional Perspectives*, ed. by Jan-Peter de Ruiter, 179–192. Cambridge: Cambridge University Press. https://doi.org/10.1017/CBO9781139045414.013

Heritage, John and Geoffrey Raymond. 2005. "The Terms of Agreement: Indexing Epistemic Authority and Subordination in Talk-in-Interaction." *Social Psychology Quarterly* 68 (1): 15–38. https://doi.org/10.1177/019027250506800103.

Jefferson, Gail. 2015. "On the Sequential Organization of Troubles-talk in Ordinary Conversation." In *Talking about Troubles in Conversation*, ed. by Paul Drew, John Heritage, Gene Lerner and Anita Pomerantz, 27–61. Oxford: Oxford University Press.

Jefferson, Gail. 2004. "Glossary of Transcript Symbols with an Introduction." In *Conversation Analysis: Studies from the First Generation*, ed. by Gene H. Lerner. 13–31. Amsterdam: John Benjamins Publishing. https://doi.org/10.1075/pbns.125.02jef

Kasper, Gabriele. 1996. "Politeness." In *Handbook of Pragmatics Online*. Edited by Jan-Ola Östman and Jef Verschueren. Amsterdam: John Benjamins Publishing. https://doi.org/10.1075/hop.2.pol1.

Koivisto, Aino L. and, Liisa Voutilainen. 2016. "Responding to What is Left Implicit: Psychotherapists' Formulations and Understanding Checks after Clients' Turn-final *että* ('that/so)." *Research on Language and Social Interaction* 49 (3): 238–257. https://doi.org/10.1080/08351813.2016.1198195.

Muntigl, Peter. 2020. "Managing Distress over Time in Psychotherapy: Guiding the Client in and through Intense Emotional Work." *Frontiers in Psychology* 6–23. https://doi.org/10.3389/fpsyg.2019.03052.

Muntigl, Peter. 2013. "Resistance in Couples Counselling: Sequences of Talk that Disrupt Progressivity and Promote Disaffiliation." *Journal of Pragmatics* 49 (1): 18–37. https://doi.org/10.1016/j.pragma.2013.01.003.

Muntigl, Peter and Adam O. Horvath. 2014. "The Therapeutic Relationship in Action: How Therapists and Clients Co-manage Relational Disaffiliation." *Psychotherapy Research* 24 (3): 327–345. https://doi.org/10.1080/10503307.2013.807525

O'Driscoll, Jim. 2017. "Face and (Im)politeness." In *The Palgrave Handbook of Linguistic (Im) politeness*, ed. by Jonathan Culpeper, Michael Haugh and Daniel Z. Kádár, 89–118. London: Palgrave Macmillan. https://doi.org/10.1057/978-1-137-37508-7_5

Peräkylä, Anssi. 2019. "Conversation Analysis and Psychotherapy: Identifying Transformative Sequences." *Research on Language and Social Interaction* 52 (3): 257–280. https://doi.org/10.1080/08351813.2019.1631044.

Peräkylä, Anssi. 2004. "Making Links in Psychoanalytic Interpretations: A Conversation Analytical Perspective." *Psychotherapy Research* 14 (3): 289–307. https://doi.org/10.1093/ptr/kph026.

Peräkylä, Anssi, Charles Antaki, Sanna Vehviläinen and Ivan Leudar. 2008. *Conversation Analysis and Psychotherapy*. Cambridge: Cambridge University Press. https://doi.org/10.1017/CBO9780511490002

Rae, John. 2008. "Lexical Substitution as a Therapeutic Resource." In *Conversation Analysis and Psychotherapy*, ed. by Anssi Peräkylä, Charles Antaki, Sanna Vehviläinen and Ivan Leudar, 62–79. Cambridge: Cambridge University Press. https://doi.org/10.1017/CBO9780511490002.005

Ruiz de Zarobe, Leyre and Yolanda Ruiz de Zarobe. 2012. *Speech Acts and Politeness Across Languages and Cultures*. Peter Lang. https://doi.org/10.3726/978-3-0351-0438-7

Scarvaglieri, Claudio. 2020. "First Encounters in Psychotherapy: Relationship-building and the Pursuit of Institutional Goals." *Frontiers in Psychology* 92–105. https://doi.org/10.3389/fpsyg.2020.585038.

Schegloff, Emanuel A. 2013. "Ten operations in Self-initiated, Same-turn Repair." In *Conversational Repair and Human Understanding*, ed. by Jack Sidnell, Geoffrey Raymond and Makoto Hayashi, 41–70. Cambridge: Cambridge University Press.

Schegloff, Emanuel A. 2007. *Sequence Organization in Interaction: A Primer in Conversation Analysis*. Cambridge: Cambridge University Press. https://doi.org/10.1017/CBO9780511791208

Stivers, Tanya. 2008. "Stance, Alignment, and Affiliation during Storytelling: When Nodding is a Token of Affiliation." *Research on Language and Social Interaction* 41 (1): 31–57. https://doi.org/10.1080/08351810701691123.

Stivers, Tanya. 2005. "Modified Repeats: One Method for Asserting Primary Rights from Second Position." *Research on Language and Social Interaction* 38 (2): 131–158. https://doi.org/10.1207/s15327973rlsi3802_1.

Stivers, Tanya and Makoto Hayashi. 2010. "Transformative Answers: One Way to Resist a Question's Constraints." *Language in Society* 39 (1): 1–25. https://doi.org/10.1017/S0047404509990637.

Stivers, Tanya and Jeffrey D. Robinson. 2006. "A Preference for Progressivity in Interaction." *Language in Society* 35 (3): 367–392. https://doi.org/10.1017/S0047404506060179.

Vehviläinen, Sanna. 2003. "Preparing and Delivering Interpretations in Psychoanalytic Interaction." *Text* 23 (4): 573–606. https://doi.org/10.1515/text.2003.022.

Voutilainen, Liisa. 2012. "Responding to Emotion in Cognitive Psychotherapy," in *Emotion in Interaction*, ed. by Anssi Peräkylä and Marja-Leena Sorjonen, 235–255, Oxford: Oxford University Press. https://doi.org/10.1093/acprof:oso/9780199730735.003.0011

Voutilainen, Liisa, Anssi Peräkylä and Johanna E. Ruusuvuori. 2010a. "Recognition and Interpretation: Responding to Emotional Experience in Psychotherapy." *Research on Language and Social Interaction* 43 (1): 85–107. https://doi.org/10.1080/08351810903474799.

Voutilainen, Liisa, Anssi Peräkylä and Johanna E. Ruusuvuori. 2010b. "Misalignment as a Therapeutic Resource." *Qualitative Research in Psychology* 7 (4): 299–315. https://doi.org/10.1080/14780880902846411.

Weiste, Elina. 2015. "Describing Therapeutic Projects across Sequences: Balancing between Supportive and Disagreeing Interventions." *Journal of Pragmatics* 80: 22–43. https://doi.org/10.1016/j.pragma.2015.02.001.

Weiste, Elina, Liisa Voutilainen and Anssi Peräkylä. 2015. "Epistemic Asymmetries in Psychotherapy Interaction: Therapists' Practices for Displaying Access to Clients' Inner Experiences." *Sociology of Health & Illness* 38 (4): 645–661. https://doi.org/10.1111/1467-9566.12384.

Weiste, Elina and Anssi Peräkylä. 2014. "Prosody and Empathic Communication in Psychotherapy Interaction." *Psychotherapy Research* 24 (6): 687–701. https://doi.org/10.1080/10503307.2013.879619.

Weiste, Elina and Anssi Peräkylä. 2013. "A Comparative Conversation Analytic Study of Formulations in Psychoanalysis and Cognitive Psychotherapy." *Research on Language and Social Interaction* 46 (4): 299–321. https://doi.org/10.1080/08351813.2013.839093.

So let's say men can't understand that much

Gender and relational practices in psychotherapy with women suffering from eating disorders

Joanna Pawelczyk and Elena Faccio
Adam Mickiewicz University Poznań / University of Padua

In this paper we look at three extracts of two psychotherapy sessions between a female therapist and a woman patient suffering from bulimia and depression. We use conversation analysis and membership categorization analysis to examine how gender, indexing the quality of the emotional bond between participants, is interactionally managed in view of the session's goals.

The findings show the patient relying on gender as category-sharing to account for her actions and seek understanding. The therapist, however, tends to resist the category-sharing and engages the patient in extensive work around gender categories. Women psychotherapists should be particularly attuned to women patients' invoking of category-sharing and critically consider its relevance and application in the situated context of therapy work.

Keywords: gender, psychotherapy, eating disorders, alignment, affiliation, conversation analysis, membership categorization analysis

1. Introduction

Therapeutic relationship comprises an agreement between the psychotherapist and the patient to work toward the same goals, as well as an agreement as to how these goals will be accomplished. Importantly, it also reflects the emotional connection between the therapist and the patient (Bordin 1979, 1994). Its role and significance for treatment outcome has been recognized independently of the types of problems clients bring to psychotherapy as well as the various types of treatment approaches (Muntigl and Horvath 2015: 41; Wampold 2001; Norcross 2011; see also Buchholz this volume). As summarized by Voutilainen and Peräkylä (2016), following Wampold (2001), the therapeutic relationship is an essential element of

https://doi.org/10.1075/pbns.331.05paw

the so-called common factors of psychotherapy. It is discursively enacted by a range of interactional practices that the patient and the therapist rely on in pursuing the therapy goals (see also Muntigl this volume). Buchholz (this volume) highlights the highly co-constructed character of the therapeutic relationship as performed by the therapist and the client with the reference "Doing We". An important aspect of the therapeutic relationship is gender, greatly impacting the quality of the bond between the therapist and the patient (Ackerman and Hilsenroth 2003).

In this paper, we are interested in how gender emerges in the conversation between a woman patient suffering from eating disorders (EDs) and her woman therapist and how it is further sequentially managed as an important aspect of the collaborative working relationship, i.e., therapeutic alliance. The working relationship involves various interactional practices indexing the social relation between the therapist and the patient in the here-and-now (see Muntigl this volume). We aim to demonstrate how gender is implicated and intertwined in these practices, as well as what and how gendered assumptions are invoked in therapy work.

In the analysis, we draw on the ethnomethodological conceptualization of gender as participants' category (Speer and Stokoe 2011; Schegloff 2007). Thus we look at what the participants, i.e., the therapist and the patient, do and say in interaction, including what assumptions about men and women they bring to and invoke in the conversation. The relevance of gender must therefore be identified in the therapist's and patient's explicit and/or implicit interactional orientation to that category. In other words, gender must matter to the interacting participants, and the analyst's task is to demonstrate that relevance in the fine-grained details of the interaction. The relevance can manifest itself in invoking the category in and through the micro-details of local social action, but also in sustaining and/or resisting it. By adopting the 'gender-as-members'-category' perspective, we are explicitly moving away from gender as an essentialist characteristic of therapist and patient (Gerhart and Lyle 2001).

Various dominant cultural assumptions about being a woman (and being a man) as well as femininity (and masculinity) are deeply embedded in the daily functioning of women (and men) suffering from EDs (see Pawelczyk et al. 2021). Gender ideologies are both culture- and time- dependent. In this paper we are focusing on the *dominant/hegemonic* gender ideologies that continue to be prevalent in the western societies in the twenty-first century. According to the dominant hegemonic view, women are expected to be polite, docile, sexually available, emotional and take care of the house and family (Carlson 2018: 36; Fitzsimons 2002: 152) while men are expected to be rational, able to restrain their emotions, competitive, powerful and independent (Fitzsimons 2002: 103). These opposing and mutually exclusive norms and expectations toward women and men, also constitute a benchmark or a "rigid regulatory frame" (Butler 1990: 33) against which women's and men's behaviors are socially evaluated and judged. These gendered propositions and ideas of what men and women are supposed to be like tend to be extensively internalized by women patients. As demonstrated by critical feminist research (see Malson and Burns 2009; Holmes 2016), there is a need to unpack and work with women patients' understanding and relevance of these propositions in their daily functioning as part of psychotherapeutic work. In the process of therapy work with a woman therapist, women patients might orient to gender as a resource, a common ground between them and their therapist, to be relied and drawn upon in constructing and maintaining the therapeutic relationship. This is to say that gender can facilitate some women patients' therapy work by helping them narrate their experiences with the hope of being (better) understood due to category-sharing with the therapist. For example, Gerhart and Lyle (2001: 450–451) argue that "client constructions of gender may be one of the primary discourses clients draw from when deciding how to interact with therapists." It is interesting, then, to examine how women therapists as experts and professionals orient to that invoking and its further interactional trajectories in view of the specific goals of the therapy session and the therapy process in general.

In this paper, we examine sequences of interaction between a woman patient and a woman psychotherapist in which gender is invoked explicitly and/or implicitly to demonstrate how it is further interactionally managed in view of the therapy goals and intertwined in relational practices of (dis)affiliation, (dis)alignment, work around epistemic primacy to experience, and co-construction of utterances and turns. We also examine the content and function of gendered propositions in the local context of specific therapy moments.

The next section gives an overview of relational practices in psychotherapy. This is followed in Section 3 by a presentation of the data and methods of analysis. An analysis of the relevant extended excerpts of two psychotherapy sessions is offered in Section 4, followed by concluding remarks in Section 5.

2. Psychotherapy and relational practices

Psychotherapeutic conversation, as any other human interaction, strives for harmony and solidarity as evidenced in its organization (e.g., Levinson 1983; Enfield 2006). However, episodes of conflict occur which impact the quality of the relationship, and as such they need to be interactionally managed in the local here-and-now (Muntigl and Horvath 2015; see Muntigl this volume). This becomes of particular relevance in psychotherapy, as a type of goal-oriented institutional interaction where patients seek help and thus should feel supported and validated in their relationship with the therapist.

As discussed by Peräkylä (2019), every psychotherapeutic session between the therapist and the patient offers a new opportunity to work on and/or modify the social relations between the participants. In other words, similarly to ordinary conversations, the relationship between the therapist and the patient is not predetermined, nor does it ever remain fixed. Rather, it is an ever-changing phenomenon both over the course of the therapy process itself as well as in the course of a single session, and as such it requires continuous attendance (explicit or implicit) on the part of the psychotherapist and often also the patient (see also Muntigl this volume).

The shifting interactional trajectory of the ongoing conversation between the therapist and the patient and the accompanying socioemotional relations can be identified and accounted for by applying the concepts of (dis)affiliation and (dis) alignment. Following Stivers (2008; Stivers et al. 2011: 20; Muntigl et al. 2013), affiliation describes the level of affect in an interaction. Thus, utterances are regarded as affiliative when they show preference in orienting to the prior utterance, for instance "agreeing with statements, complying with requests and offering empathy" (Muntigl et al. 2013: 5). Alignment (and disalignment) relate to how interactants orient to other participants' interactional behavior, i.e., whether they follow the expected (normative) structure by cooperating in accomplishing the interactional tasks. Importantly, "dis/affiliation does not imply dis/alignment or vice versa" (Muntigl et al. 2013: 5, following Stivers et al. 2011). The moments of disaffiliation may moreover be mobilized by the therapist to accomplish "affective therapeutic exploration of the client's problem" (Muntigl and Horvath 2015: 47). This is to say that the therapeutic relationship is built out of moments not just of affiliation, but also of disaffiliation. The CA-oriented research – as discussed by Guxholli et al. (2021) – has demonstrated how both patients and therapists can jeopardize the therapeutic relationship with their various interactional practices. Such therapeutic ruptures, however, can be interactionally resolved (see also Guxholli et al. this volume).

The relational practices in the psychotherapy interaction also include (dis) agreement and resistance, and relate to the epistemic relation between the psychotherapist and the patient (Peräkylä 2019). The issue of the right to one's experience becomes particularly salient in the context of psychotherapy work (see Pawelczyk and Talarczyk 2017). Patients have epistemic primacy in their experience (see Pomerantz 1980; Sacks 1984), yet they are in the therapy process with the aim to understand that very experience anew and ultimately modify it with the help of the expert, i.e., the therapist (Weiste et al. 2015; Ekberg and LeCouteur 2015). The interactional dynamics of the right to know have implications for the evolving therapeutic relationship. For instance, the therapist's formulation of the patient's problem or his/her emotive extension of the client's account (Pawelczyk 2011; Voutilainen and Peräkylä 2016) may be oriented to by the patient with a disaffiliative action and followed by the patient's disaligning moves (see e.g., Muntigl et al. 2013: 5). Following the research of Muntigl et al.'s (2013), the current paper examines whether the woman patient's experience as formulated by the woman therapist tends to be contested by the patient and, if so, how the therapist responds to that disagreement.

Although every interaction is premised on co-construction between the interacting parties (Jacoby and Ochs 1995; Johnson 2007), the co-construction "as transpiring in the psychotherapeutic interaction involves therapist's *greater* interactional involvement" (Pawelczyk and Sokalska-Bennett 2019: 219). Co-construction is another practice that builds the relationship between the psychotherapist and the patient. It includes joint production of utterances (Muntigl et al. 2013), whereby one speaker begins a turn and another completes or extends it. Here the second speaker must be "able to project when turn-constructional units (TCUs: Sacks et al. 1974) are nearing completion" (Muntigl et al. 2013: 11) and concurrently complete them in a grammatically and semantically appropriate manner. Such "collaborative completion" (Lerner 2013) allows the interacting parties to speak as if with a single voice. The practices of co-construction go beyond the joint production of utterances, however. For example, 'no-gap-no-overlap' transitions between the participants' utterances (Sacks et al. 1974) or the use of the other speaker's vocabulary items (Pawelczyk 2011; Muntigl and Horvath 2015) create interactional alignment and index cooperation and involvement between the interacting parties.

As recently summarized by Peräkylä (2019; see also Muntigl et al. 2013), the therapist's orienting to the patient's answers or statements in the three-action structure is fundamental to the therapy process. The action undertaken by the therapist in the third turn is also consequential for the socioemotional relation between the participants. Third-position practice determines to a great extent how the session progresses. It also constitutes one of the greatest challenges for practitioners themselves, as it evidences how the therapist makes sense of what the patient just proffered (Peräkylä 2019). For example, it may act as a "sequence closing third" (Schegloff 2007) and miss or even close off an opportunity to pursue an issue of great clinical relevance. On the other hand, third-position action may also work toward bringing about reaffiliation between the therapist and the patient (Muntigl et al. 2013). Methodologically, the salience of third-position action for the ensuing therapeutic project (and the therapy process in general) calls for an in-depth analysis and a thorough consideration (Peräkylä 2019).

Doing therapy work is concurrently doing socioemotional relations as the transactional and the relational aspects of an interaction are always accomplished jointly.

3. Data and methods

Three extended extracts of two audio-recorded psychotherapy sessions between a woman patient suffering from depression and EDs (bulimia and anorexia), aged 56, and a woman psychotherapist are analyzed below with the methods of conversation analysis (CA) and membership categorization analysis (MCA). The woman psychotherapist has been in practice since 2002 and works within the interactionist and socio-constructionist approach.

The woman patient was informed about the study, its aims and methods. She agreed to participate in the study and completed the informed consent. The sessions were originally conducted in Italian.

Extract (1) comes from a session held in May 2019, while Extracts (2) and (3) are taken from a session conducted in November of the same year (2019). The patient resumed psychotherapy work with the same psychotherapist after a 12-year break, and is also working with a psychologist and a dietician. In these sessions, the psychotherapist and the woman patient explore the patient's ways of relating to other people, in particular her husband and sons, and the potential influence of gender differences on the construction of the patient's role as a wife and mother.

The analyzed extracts are English translations of the Italian originals. The translation was made by the second author. The analysis is based on the original Italian recorded data and the corresponding transcripts (Thomassen 2009: 86). In the process of data translation, we remained cognizant of Schegloff's (2002) remark that translation is already part of the analysis of the original data set (see also Hepburn and Bolden 2017). All identification details have been removed or changed in data extracts to ensure participants' anonymity.

The analytical apparatus of CA, affording a detailed description of relations between adjacent turns, has revealed a number of sequential patterns that comprise therapy talk (for a summary see Peräkylä 2013, Peräkylä 2019; Voutilainen and Peräkylä 2016). The adjacent turns demonstrate how participants make sense of and process what has been said and done in the prior turn and then across sequences of turns. The turns, and the actions they perform, enable the participants to concurrently project their social relations in the here-and-now of the interaction (Muntigl and Horvath 2015) and thus the (changing) interactive trajectory of therapeutic relationship. As evidenced by robust CA-oriented research, "momentary relation[s] get transformed through sequentially organized actions" (Peräkylä 2019: 271).

The interest of MCA lies in its use of categorial aspects and category work as performed by interaction participants to accomplish various actions (Hester and Eglin 1997; Stokoe 2010, Stokoe 2012). This method allows us to examine – once again, at the micro-level of interactional detail – how commonsensical assumptions are drawn upon "as part of the local construction of social meaning" (Smithson and

Stokoe 2005: 153). In using MCA, the analytical focus falls on participants' invoking of categories and their explicit or implicit categorization work as evident in the use of category-bound activities and predicates (Stokoe 2012). As applied to the data extracts analyzed below, MCA allows us to access and unpack the patient's commonsensical assumptions attributed to men (and masculinity) and women (and femininity) in the interactional here-and-now. This is of particular importance, as certain dominant assumptions about women/men and femininity/masculinity, i.e., gendered propositions are deeply internalized by patients suffering from EDs (Pawelczyk et al. 2021), and the context of psychotherapy constitutes the appropriate professional space to work with them.

4. Data analysis

The data analysis section is divided into two parts. In part 1, one extended data extract from a session conducted in May 2019 is qualitatively analyzed, while part 2 offers an analysis of two data extracts from a session conducted in November of the same year.

In the exchange presented below, the patient orients to the therapist's question around difficulties in following the prescribed diet as part of the therapy. We join the extract when the patient is elaborating on the theme from the previous session, i.e., the difficulties in continuing with the therapy work and sustaining the proper diet. The extract (lines 01–12) begins with the patient's elaborating on her views concerning the importance of the 'proper' body.

Extract 1.

16.50
01 P: I understand what is right and what is wrong (.)
02 but in any case:: on an:: emotional level on an
03 (.) irrational level I do not:: accept this thing
04 I still think that the body must be made in a certain
05 way >otherwise you cannot go out because otherwise
06 you cannot (.) move as you want I can't move a leg move
07 a foot when I go around I am quite static I stay still<
08 because I am afraid that every (.) movement of my body
09 could arouse attention from people ↑which (2.0) I don't
10 want that's it (.) but I know that I don't have to give
11 all this great importance to the body but in any case
12 I give it to it anyway (.) ↓<I give it to it anyway>
37.49
13 […] maybe I how can I say (have been) burned by life
14 yes ↓but maybe it's my fault in large part(.) but
15 surely:: in relationships:: I have difficulties in the
16 sense that even in the family I don't (.) relate much
17 >even with my husband< nothing has changed compared

```
        to the past I am always let's say >the mother the wife<
        but I am (.)nobody actually knows what I think in
        my heart that's it (4.0) ↓nobody really knows me that's
        why I've always (.) left the relationship with others
        (.) fairly superficial (.) because I'm a little
        ashamed a little:: these things here so maybe
        relationships [yes
T:                    [in your case it seems to me so
        (.) strange that:: (2.0) that you have difficulties
        in relationships (.) you are <so welcoming in your
        room> (.) is so warm it is so:: it is also so honest
        so:: that (.) and I had the impression (.) talking to
        the colleagues that also >all of them have perceived
        this thing< about you >it's not just my impression< (.)
        and it's not just a chemistry between me and you you
        generate this kind of effect (.) who knows if you are
        aware of this=
P:      =↓no
T:      no
P:      ↓no
T:      there are so many people who love you:: >WHEN YOU LET THEM
        ENTER INTO THAT ROOM< people feel a feeling of:: affection
        for you >without any difficulty< (2.0) and it seems to me
        a waste that this magic has not activated:: at home I
        understand that for you it is hard living (.) in the family
        where you experience those roles(.)
        pierced by feelings of guilt::=
P:      =↓yes
T:      so it's obvious that if you feel guilty (.) you have
        to play the part of the mother who tries to be
        perfect and who doesn't
P:                                //↓yes I try to be perfect
T:      but it's like, this is a mask
P:      ↓yes (.) I know (.) sometimes it's hard sometimes yes
```

In lines 01–12 the woman patient self-discloses how she – being overweight – feels about going outside and going out. She begins and closes that part of her contribution with a morally implicative statement of being aware of right and wrong (line 01). This is in reference to the difference between her cognition and feelings concerning why an overweight person should or should not go out.

The patient accounts for her lack of acceptance for overweight people going out in emotional terms, as evident in the use of such items as 'emotional level' (line 02), 'irrational level' (line 03) as well as a micropause (line 03) and a pattern of stretching the final sounds. This is followed by justifying claims (lines 04–07) which bolster the patient's view that only individuals with a certain body image can go out. In line 06 the patient shifts the perspective from general to personal by using the pronoun 'I' and drawing on her own subjective experience (Pawelczyk and Talarczyk 2017). We learn from that contribution about her internalized fear of being (negatively) judged and evaluated by others ('movement of my body could arouse attention from people'). In closing this part of her contribution, the patient extensively underlines her internalization of the fear of being judged by others by twice repeating 'I give it to it anyway'.

In line 13 the patient resumes accounting for the importance of body image and shifts the (topical) focus to herself as being responsible for projecting such a stance. She downgrades her contribution with the items 'maybe' (twice, lines 13 and 14) and 'in large part' (line 14). In line 15 the patient invokes 'relationships', a potentially troubling aspect for her, and the category 'husband' (line 17) to demonstrate her difficulties in relating even to her intimate partner. The item 'even' preceding the reference 'husband' ("nemmeno con mio marito") implicitly positions the husband as the person with whom the patient is expected to share her issues and worries.

In line 18 the patient invokes the categories 'the mother' and 'the wife' to give a sense of her proper functioning in these roles. Her invoking of the two categories in the interactional here-and-now implies her meeting the social expectations of what it means to be a wife/mother yet immediately removes the emotional aspects from them. In line 19, following an incomplete statement, the patient refocuses her turn on the emotional aspect by stating 'nobody actually knows what I think in my heart'. Following a 4-second pause (line 20) the patient upgrades her claim to 'nobody really knows me'. In this way she casts herself as an individual who is not emotionally involved in her relationships, even the most intimate ones. In lines 21–24 the patient is interactionally struggling to convey a sense of her trouble, yet she again invokes 'relationships' (line 24) as the source of her discomfort. It can be claimed that the patient in lines 13–24 offered the therapist an affectual stance (Stivers 2008; see also Muntigl et al. 2014) to be further interactionally worked with.

The therapist begins her contribution in line 25 in the patient's turn-constructional unit (TCU). In her affiliative yet disaligning response, the therapist rejects and overall disagrees with the patient's proffered view of her problems, i.e., relationships. Thus the therapist's perception of the patient is starkly different, being much more positive in comparison to the patient's view. This can be identified, among others, in lines 27–28 where the therapist relies on the intensifier 'so' (four times) to contest the patient's grim assessment of her relationships. Additionally, the therapist invokes the opinions of other experts to affirm her case (lines 29–32) and uses the item 'all of them' (line 30) and 'not just my impression' to upgrade her account. The therapist's contribution ends with a statement taking on the function of a question (lines 33–34) whether the patient is aware of her positive effect on people, thereby challenging the patient's view of difficulty in her relationships.

The patient immediately orients to the therapist's question in line 35 with the 'no-gap-no-overlap' by providing a strong disagreement token (Pomerantz 1984) indexing lack of affiliation. The patient's 'no' (line 35) is mirrored by the therapist (Ferrara 1994) in third position action (line 36) with its interactional function of asking for elaboration (Pawelczyk 2011). The patient's 'no' in lines 35 and 37 projects her epistemic primacy as the epistemic rights related to her own experience are jeopardized (Muntigl et al. 2013: 5), and she reasserts her right to know it. The patient does not proffer any extension, however, and thus rejects the therapist's appeal for elaboration with another disaligning item 'no' (line 37). Building on the question posed by Muntigl et al. (2013), it is interesting to examine what is going to happen next, i.e., how the therapist realigns herself with the patient and resumes (effective) therapeutic work.

The therapist in lines 38–44 continues her interactional project of asserting the patient's ability to function well in relationships once she lets herself do so. This time, however, the therapist invokes and draws on the assumptions and categories brought up by the patient herself (lines 18–24). Thus the therapist invokes the family context (line 42) and the categories of mother and wife (line 43) as well as the patient's previous experiences ('feelings of guilt'). Returning to the question posed by Muntigl et al. (2013), the therapist manages to re-establish affiliative ties with the patient (see the patient's 'yes', line 45) by extensively relying on the items and categories introduced by the patient herself and adding a highly personal aspect of the 'feelings of guilt' (line 44).

Continuing the interactional work of re-affiliation, the therapist strongly aligns with the patient's position ('so it's obvious that if you feel', line 46) by doing categorial work around the 'mother' initially invoked by the patient (line 18). In line 47 the therapist begins to build her utterance by ascribing the category-bound characteristic 'perfect' to being a mother. The patient, however, interrupts the therapist's turn under construction by echoing (Ferrara 1994) the therapist's item 'yes I try to be perfect' (line 49). The interruption signals a strong alignment with what the therapist was in the midst of producing. The interacting parties have accomplished interactive unity.

In lines 49–51 the therapist and the patient are involved in the co-construction of the patient's experience. The therapist (line 50) builds her turn on what the patient produced in line 49 by adding a potentially disaffiliative element, i.e., the patient's ideal acting is actually a cover ('this is a mask'). With this statement, the therapist is making a claim to the patient's subjective experience. The patient, however, proffers an acknowledgment token, thereby agreeing with the therapist's view. This is followed by further manifestations of re-established affiliation, demonstrated by the patient's 'I know' and a comment signaling upcoming reflective talk ('sometimes it's hard sometimes yes').

Extract (2) below is from an exchange that took place in the November session. We join the extract when the patient reflects on her therapy work and in particular on her work with the psychiatrist whom she met eight years ago when she was admitted to an eating disorder treatment center.

Extract 2.

```
10.56
P:   I have embarked on a path let's say that certainly helps me (.)
     and the psychiatrist told me to continue on this path
     he talks more nowadays it's true but (.) sometimes::
     when I'm there (.) >maybe because he's a man?
     I don't know< maybe I don't want (.) to get
     into certain subjects certain dynamics=
T:   =>what difference does< (.) a man or a woman
     make(.) for you?
P:   well I'm::(.)probably wrong when I think this (.)
     but I've always thought that:: maybe it's a mistake
     (.) I thought that (.) a woman anyway is more::
     let's say:: (.) sensitive she can catch more (.)
     details let's say:: nuanced things she is more
     able to:: (.) understand the signals of diseases and
     (.) she is more:: able to read let's say about the
     person than a man let's say she is more:: sensitive
     so to speak she has this greater sensitivity she has
     this extra:: capacity so I have always thought so
     maybe I'm wrong=
T:   =but:: are you speaking in reference to your problems
     or in general?
P:   in general in general
T:   so let's say men can't understand that much
P:   yes:: in my opinion (.) they have less sensitivity
     >they are colder yes< (.) they are colder (.)
     in my opinion
T:   but does it concern (.) life in general? (.)
     beyond the psychiatric or psychological ↑roles
P:   yes in my opinion (.) they are more:: they do
     not notice so:: many things in a woman (.) so many
     changes even small ones even those nuances as well::
     even the ones in the mood they don't notice these
     things >surely my husband does not notice them< he
     does not have this:: great sensitivity or this great
     let's say:: he does not notice the moods of people
     (.) he has always been like that in short (.) and
     even after telling him what he didn't realize,
     sometimes he says >no, it didn't seem to me he
     never noticed things like this here it is<
T:   and what can you do ↓when
P:                                  //I think that nothing can
     be done in the sense that my husband is like that he
     is very practical he is very:: (2.0) what could one say
     empirical I don't know
```

In line 03 the patient refocuses her contribution on the psychiatrist she is working with to emphasize the practitioner being more talkative now compared to her previous experience of working with him. She invokes gender (line 04) by making a claim in the form of a question that the psychiatrist's seeming resistance to discussing certain topics is linked to being a man. In other words, the category 'man' is invoked to account for the psychiatrist's potential unwillingness to enter into certain topics. The claim is mitigated with the items 'maybe' and 'I don't know'. It is also produced more quickly compared to the surrounding talk, thereby constructing its taken-for-granted character. At the end of her turn, however, the patient topicalizes herself as potentially not willing to discuss certain issues in her conversations with the psychiatrist.

The therapist, then, has been offered two options as to why certain topics are not brought up in the patient's work with the psychiatrist. This is also indicative of the need and interest of the patient to be engaged in discussing certain issues apparently not brought up in her psychiatric sessions. The therapist orients to the patient's claims with a question which sustains the relevance of gender in the ongoing exchange (lines 07–08). The therapist does not pursue the thematic thread (Voutilainen et al. 2018) of 'topics not raised' with the psychiatrist, but rather topicalizes the significance of the practitioner's gender for the patient. The therapist, by not endorsing the patient's view of men (lines 20–21), does not draw on the category-sharing with the patient as an affiliation practice.

In lines 11–18 the patient is going categorial by attributing a number of characteristics bound to being a woman. Her accounting sequence is considerably hedged by various items and particles which occur close to one another ('well', micropauses, 'maybe', 'let'say'). In fact, the very beginning of her turn (lines 09–10) is framed as potentially distancing from what she is about to produce.

In the rest of her turn, the patient, still relying on hedging and mitigation devices, produces a gender-based categorization as to what women are like. The patient attributes a number of characteristics to being a woman such as 'sensitive' (line 12, 16), 'she can catch more details, nuanced things' (lines 12–13), 'more able to understand' (lines 14), 'more able to read about the person' (lines 15–16), 'has this greater sensitivity' (line 17) as well as 'this extra capacity' (line 18). These category-bound characteristics concurrently define a good practitioner (a psychotherapist and a psychiatrist) in the patient's view. The patient is thus accounting for women as making better mental health practitioners.

It may be assumed that the patient's turn (lines 10–19) constitutes a highly affiliative opportunity for the therapist – a woman herself – to align with the patient, as "when speakers produce such phrases, they invite recipients to display recognition of, or collaboratively develop, the construction of a culture's categories, as the basis for moving through courses of action" (Stokoe 2010: 428). The therapist, however, with the 'no-gap-no-overlap' transition in lines 20–21 asks the patient to specify whether her gender-related claims refer to her own personal experience or rather describe a non-specific context. The therapist does not, at this point, build on the patient's categorial work produced in lines 10–19. The therapist (line 23) uses the item previously used by the patient (line 14) to offer a formulation (Antaki 2008) that summarizes what the patient proffered in lines 10–19. However, the formulation puts the category 'men' rather than 'women' in the subject position. In this way the therapist resumes the gender-related talk initiated by the patient and creates an opportunity for the patient to unpack her commonsensical understandings around the category 'men'.

The patient orients to the formulation with an agreement token (line 24) and attributes immense lack of sensitivity to 'men', as demonstrated by echoing the phrase 'they are colder' (line 25). The first time, the phrase is produced faster compared to the surrounding speech and receives an item 'yes' at the end. It is then repeated at a regular pace, thus indexing the patient's confidence in the proffered claim followed by 'in my opinion' (line 25). The therapist, however, pursues a specification of what the patient's descriptions refer to in the form of a question (lines 27–28). This time, the patient is asked to make a distinction between her experiences in therapy treatment as opposed to her subjective life experiences. The patient does not orient directly to the therapist's question, i.e., she does not provide a clear answer. Rather, she continues to produce gender-based categorial phrases in the first part of her turn. She does not specify whether she is describing her personal experiences or her experiences in the therapy room. Men are described as not being able to observe any changes happening 'in a woman' (lines 31–32). The patient has built the case of women and men as starkly different relational categories.

Yet in line 33 the patient–unprompted by the therapist–switches her account from general to personal (Pawelczyk and Talarczyk 2017). The new thread is introduced with 'surely my husband does not notice them'. The patient does not directly accuse or blame her husband for acting in a certain way, but rather frames it as a consequence of belonging to the category 'men' (Pawelczyk et al. 2021). This becomes evident in the items preceding 'sensitivity' (line 34). The use of 'this' and the elongation of the final sound point to the element that has already been referred to and discussed by the patient (see line 24) and used in reference to the all-encompassing category 'men'. According to the patient, her husband – similarly to the category 'men' (see line 35) – is not attentive to how people feel (line 37). The husband's behavior as being reflective of belonging to the category 'men' is further sustained in line 36 and lines 37–39, as despite the patient's interventions the husband's behavior remains unchanged. The patient's concluding phrase 'here it is' (line 39) constructs her claim as non-negotiable.

In line 40 the therapist attempts to align with the topical thread proffered by the patient by asking a question. However, the attempt is interrupted by the patient (line 41), who projects the question by proffering the answer that her husband's behavior cannot be changed. The category-belonging is again echoed with the phrase 'in the sense that my husband is like that' (line 42). In the remaining part of her turn, the patient is involved in producing other characteristics of her husband ('practical', line 43), then interactionally struggles to come up with other characteristics, as demonstrated by the elongation of the last sound on 'very' and a two-second pause as well as the phrase 'what could one say' (line 43). She then offers the adjective 'empirical' to upgrade her account of why her husband's behavior cannot be changed. She finishes her turn with the utterance 'I don't know', marking the end of the question-answer sequence.

Extract (3) is a continuation of the conversation presented in Extract (2).

Extract 3.

```
15.23
01    T:  And:: in reference to your children do you have
02        the same impression that one can't
03    P:                                     //yes:: yes::=
04    T:  =yes=
05    P:  =yes I have the same impression yes=
06    T:  =so did you come across the conclusion that it
07        is >a question of gender<
08    P:  of gender (.) yes (.) I think that (.) men are
09        missing something:: in their
10    T:                              // what do men miss?
11    P:  sensitivity foresight and:: um:: (4.0) understanding
12        (2.0) um::
13    T:  but can I ask you (.) you've also met Dr Y ↑do you
14        think the same about him too? or::
15    P:  (3.0) eh maybe he is:: a person who:: (.) the exception
16        that confirms the rule I think he (.) is so inside
17        in these things that:: he actually
18        comprehends all things:: how can I say:: he
19        has such an open vision in these things that he
20        understands everything (2.0) he has spent a lifetime
21        in an eating disorder center and then:: he succeeds
22        where so many others would never:: succeed (.) he has
23        something that makes a difference
24    T:  but can you tell me (.) >do you think that this sensitivity<
25        (.) is somehow related (2.0) to:: food or bodily problems is
26        it involved somehow?
27    P:  this missing sensitivity?=
28    T:  =>that you define as typically feminine<
29    P:  ↓yes (.)↓yes (.)
30    T:  is it related:: to the food problem:: and therefore
31        to the desire for a certain type of bo::dy? is it linked
32        to this question or not?
33    P:  (.) yes (.) in my opinion yes because:: >everything about
34        me::< in my opinion is closely linked to >this eating
35        problem here< (.) in my opinion yes
36    T:  in what sense?
37    P:  that:: (2.0) in my opinion sensitivity is also suffering
```

```
(.) in the sense that:: the person who is sensitive
suffers so much (.) from anything (.) so:: he or she
feels this (.) suffering in a greater:: way because he is
sensitive not superficial (.) so uhm:: (.) well I::
I can say that these eating disorders
have probably ↑caused this sensitivity they are precisely
↑the cause and I I:: suffer all my life it is all my life
that I have been affected by this
```

In lines 01–02 the therapist is attempting to find out whether the patient's thoughts concerning men in general and her husband in particular also apply to her male adult children. The therapist's question in progress is interrupted by the patient (line 03), who produces an upgraded agreement to an unfinished utterance. This is mirrored by the therapist (line 04) in a highly collaborative moment between the interacting parties as they produce their turns (lines 03–06) in a 'no-gap-no-overlap' manner. The patient further echoes her agreement in line 05.

The therapist (lines 06–07) formulates the patient's view, which constitutes a potentially disaffiliative move as the therapist is entering the patient's territory of knowledge (Heritage 2011). What is interesting though is that it is not clear at this point what the pronoun 'it' (line 06) refers to. The therapist's reference 'it is a question of gender' invokes the previous discussion on men and the patient's claim that her husband belongs to that category, which is contrasted with the category 'women'.

The patient affiliates with the therapist's formulation by recycling the therapist's phrase with an extra emphasis followed by a micropause and an agreement token. In the second part of her turn (lines 07–08), the patient – beginning her utterance with an epistemic hedge 'I think' (line 08) – introduces another category-tied predicate in her categorial work on men. She refers to men as 'missing something' (line 09). Her turn and thus the utterance is incomplete, however, as it is interrupted by the therapist (line 10). The therapist with her interruption projects some kind of urgency to find out the answer, as the patient was only completing her TCU and about to proffer that information.

The patient produces the answer as a three-part list (Jefferson 1990). While the first two parts are provided immediately, i.e., 'sensitivity' and 'foresight' (line 11), the third part, i.e., 'understanding', follows a hesitation marker and a prolonged pause. The third aspect is followed by another, this time shorter pause and another hesitation marker (line 12). The therapist's question (lines 13–14) constitutes a potentially disaligning move, as one of the patient's male doctors–who is liked and respected by the patient–is invoked. To stave off the possible disalignment, the therapist modifies the utterance with the phrase 'but can I ask you', a micropause and an explicit mention of the doctor (line 13). Additionally, the therapist ends her TCU with the item 'or', thus opening up space for the patient's extension.

In her account (lines 15–23) the patient interactionally addresses the potential disalignment and attempts to sustain her view with a number of items and practices used in her account. She delays her turn with a three-second pause, signaling that what is about to be produced might be troubling to the other interacting party. The patient also relies on such items as 'maybe' (line 15), the phrase 'the exception that confirms the rule' (lines 15–16) that is produced louder compared to the surrounding talk, the epistemic hedge 'I think' (line 16), and a number of pauses and micropauses. At the end of her turn, having built her case for the doctor as an exception to the category 'man', she closes her account by stating that her male doctor possesses some extra abilities. What the patient is attempting to convey in her turn is that her doctor's lacking the commonsensical characteristics of being a man is linked to his experience of dealing with and treating EDs.

In lines 24–26 the therapist, on the basis of the patient's account (lines 15–23), formulates a question linking the patient's mentionable 'sensitivity' to issues around EDs. In lines 27–29 both interacting parties are involved in a 'no-gap-no-overlap' exchange that focuses on repairing the scope of the therapist's question. The therapist then draws on the patient's earlier linking of the category 'woman' to the category-bound characteristic 'sensitivity' (line 28). The patient proffers an upgraded agreement (line 29), yet it remains unclear what the agreement refers to. The therapist then poses the question again (lines 30–32). Following a micropause, the patient proffers an agreement followed by another pause, but the answer does not adhere to the question posed by the therapist. Rather, the patient invokes her own position by stating that EDs to a great extent define her life (lines 33–34).

The patient's voice is strongly preferred in the therapy work thus the therapist with her question in line 36 attempts to sustain and advance the patient's agency in orienting to the question. In her turn (lines 37–45) the patient embarks on the project of linking a greater sense of suffering and EDs as contributing to a person's greater sensitivity. The latter part is extensively hedged, as demonstrated by the micropauses (line 41), the hesitation marker 'uhm', and the discourse marker 'well'. In the last part of her answer, the patient again invokes her own position (lines 44–45). An important point can be drawn from that account. Since sensitivity was previously invoked as a category-bound characteristic of women and sensitivity is the result of suffering from EDs, it can be claimed that in the patient's view there is a close connection between being a woman and suffering from EDs.

5. Concluding remarks

Our close qualitative analysis has demonstrated the interactional trajectory of the therapeutic relationship between the woman suffering from EDs and her woman therapist. It has been shown that the relationship between the patient and the practitioner is re-established and re-newed not only between the sessions, but also at every moment of a single therapeutic encounter.

The methods of CA enabled us to showcase how the therapeutic relationship changes, as observed in the micro-level detail of the interaction and the subsequent turns between the participants. Applying the analytical gaze of CA, we were able to identify how the woman patient and the female therapist affiliate and align in their exchanges, but also re-establish affiliative ties following an episode of disaffiliation. Their therapeutic relationship was also maintained and further shaped by the practices of co-constructing their utterances indexing cooperation as well as in their interactional work around the issue of ownership of experience. In particular, we have shown how re-affiliation was accomplished by the therapist not by retreating from her position, but rather reformulating it to incorporate the patient's mentionables. Therapeutic relationship is thus an ongoing accomplishment interactionally crafted out of moments of affiliation and disaffiliation.

CA combined with MCA allowed us to examine how gender – as participants' category – was invoked in the interaction and further sequentially managed. The therapist to a great extent relied on gender categories and gendered propositions invoked by the patient. Such reliance enabled the therapist to work toward the patient's unpacking the commonsensical assumptions concerning the categories 'men' and 'women' that play a significant role in the patient's cognition and behavior, not only in the therapy room but also in her daily functioning.

Gender was both explicitly and implicitly involved in the relational work. The patient extensively relied in her accounts on gender as category-sharing. The therapist, on the other hand, tended to resist this and aimed for the patient to unveil her gendered propositions leading at points to relational ruptures followed by episodes of re-affiliation. The patient and the therapist's engagement in local negotiation of gender categories foregrounded the patient's voice and her ways of managing her daily struggle with the illness. As the analysis has shown the usefulness of working with gender as invoked by the patient, it is recommended that psychotherapists working with people suffering from EDs draw on that invoking in accessing the patient's internalized gendered assumptions that greatly affect their daily functioning.

Transcription conventions (see Jefferson 2004)

P	patient
T	therapist
.?	punctuation for intonation
↑	rising intonation
↓	falling intonation
::	elongation of the sound
(3)	timing in seconds
(.)	a pause of less than a second
HERE	increase in volume
Here	increase in emphasis
>here<	faster speech
<here>	slower speech
[ ]	the start and end of the overlapping speech
//	interruption
=	neither gap nor overlap in talk; *latch*

References

Ackerman, Steven, and Mark Hilsenroth. 2003. "A Review of Therapist Characteristics and Techniques Positively Impacting the Therapeutic Alliance." *Clinical Psychology Review*, 23 (1): 1–33. https://doi.org/10.1016/S0272-7358(02)00146-0

Antaki, Charles. 2008. "Formulations in Psychotherapy." *Discourse Studies* 7 (6): 627–647 https://doi.org/10.1177/1461445605055420

Bordin, Edward S. 1979. "The Generalizability of the Psychoanalytic Concept of the Working Alliance." *Psychotherapy: Theory, Research & Practice* 16 (3): 252–260. https://doi.org/10.1037/h0085885

Bordin, Edward S. 1994. *Theory and Research on the Therapeutic Working Alliance: New Directions*. In *Wiley series on personality processes. The working alliance: Theory, research, and practice* ed. by Adam O. Horvath, and Leslie S. Greenberg, 13–37. John Wiley & Sons.

Buchholz, Michael, B. This volume. "Doing We – Working alliance in psychotherapeutic relationships. A recursive model."

Butler, Judith. 1990. *Gender Trouble: Feminism and the Subversion of Gender Identity*. New York: Routledge.

Carlson, Jennifer. 2018. "Representation." In *The Social Life of Gender*, ed. by Raka Ray, Jennifer Carlson, and Abigail Andrews, 33–55. Los Angeles: Sage. https://doi.org/10.4135/9781506300054.n6

Ekberg, Katie, and Amanda LeCouteur. 2015. "Clients' Resistance to Therapists' Proposals: Managing Epistemic and Deontic Status." *Journal of Pragmatics* 90: 12–25. https://doi.org/10.1016/j.pragma.2015.10.004

Enfield, N. J. 2006. "Social Consequences of Common Ground." In *Roots of Human Sociality: Culture, Cognition and Interaction*, ed. by N. J. Enfield, and Stephen C. Levinson, 399–430. Oxford: Berg.

Ferrara, Kathleen. 1994. *Therapeutic Ways with Words*. New York: Oxford University Press.

Fitzsimons, Annette. 2002. *Gender as a Verb. Gender Segregation at Work*. Aldershot: Ashgate.

Gerhart, Diane R., and Randall Lyle. 2001. "Client Experience of Gender in Therapeutic Relationships: An Interpretive Ethnography." *Family Process* 40 (4): 443–58. https://doi.org/10.1111/j.1545-5300.2001.4040100443.x

Guxholli, Aurora, Liisa Voutilainen, and Anssi Peräkylä. This volume. "What about you? Responding to face-threats in psychotherapy."

Guxholli, Aurora, Liisa Voutilainen, and Anssi Peräkylä. 2021. "Safeguarding the therapeutic alliance: Managing disaffiliation in the course of work with psychotherapeutic projects." *Frontiers in Psychology* 11:596972. https://doi.org/10.3389/fpsyg.2020.596972.

Hepburn, Alexa, and Galina B. Bolden. 2017. *Transcribing for Social Research*. London: Sage. https://doi.org/10.4135/9781473920460

Heritage, John. 2011. "Territories of Knowledge, Territories of Experience: Empathic Moments in Interaction". In *The Morality of Knowledge in Conversation* (Studies in Interactional Sociolinguistics), ed. by Tanya Stivers, Lorenza Mondada, and Jakob Steensig, 159–183. Cambridge: Cambridge University Press. https://doi.org/10.1017/CBO9780511921674.008

Hester, Stephen, and Peter Eglin. 1997. "Membership Categorization Analysis: An Introduction." In *Culture in Action. Studies in Membership Categorization Analysis*, ed. by Stephen Hester, and Peter Eglin, 1–23. Washington, D.C.: International Institute for Ethnomethodology and Conversation Analysis & University of America Press.

Holmes Sue. 2016. "'Blindness to the Obvious?': Treatment Experiences and Feminist Approaches to Eating Disorders." *Feminism and Psychology* 26 (4): 464–486. https://doi.org/10.1177/0959353516654503.

Jacoby, Sally, and Elinor Ochs. 1995. "Co-construction: An Introduction." *Research on Language and Social Interaction* 28: 171–183. https://doi.org/10.1207/s15327973rlsi2803_1

Jefferson, Gail. 1990. "List Construction as a Task and Resource." In *Interaction Competence*, ed. by George Psathas, 63–92. Lanham, MD: University Press of America.

Jefferson, Gail. 2004. "Glossary of Transcript Symbols with an Introduction." In *Conversation Analysis: Studies From the First Generation*, ed. by Gene H. Lerner, 13–23. Amsterdam: John Benjamins. https://doi.org/10.1075/pbns.125.02jef

Johnson, Rebekah. 2007. "The Co-Construction of Roles and Patterns of Interaction in Family Discourse." *Working Papers in TESOL & Applied Linguistics* 7 (2): 1–26.

Lerner, Gene. 2004. *Conversation Analysis. Studies from the First Generation*. Amsterdam: John Benjamins. https://doi.org/10.1075/PBNS.125

Levinson, Stephen. 1983. *Pragmatics*. Cambridge: Cambridge University Press. https://doi.org/10.1017/CBO9780511813313

Malson, Helen, and Maree Burns (eds). 2009. *Critical Feminist Approaches to Eating Dis/orders*. London – New York: Routledge. https://doi.org/10.4324/9780203876442

Muntigl, Peter. This volume. "Forging relationships in psychotherapeutic interaction."

Muntigl, Peter, Naomi Knight, Ashley Watkins, Adam O. Horvath, and Lynne Angus. 2013. "Active Retreating: Person-Centered Practices to Repair Disaffiliation in Therapy." *Journal of Pragmatics* 53: 1–20. https://doi.org/10.1016/j.pragma.2013.03.019

Muntigl, Peter, Naomi Knight, and Ashley Watkins. 2014. "Empathic Practices in Client-Centered Psychotherapies: Displaying Understanding and Affiliation with Clients." In *Discourses of Helping Professions*, ed. by Eva-Maria Graf, Marlene Sator, and Thomas Spranz-Fogasy, 33–57. Amsterdam: John Benjamins. https://doi.org/10.1075/pbns.252.03mun

Muntigl, Peter and Adam O. Horvath. 2015. "The Therapeutic Relationship in Action: How Therapists and Clients Co-manage Relational Disaffiliation." In *The Therapeutic Relationship. Innovative Investigations*, ed. by Hadas Wiseman, and Orya Tishby, 41–59. New York: Routledge.

Norcross, John C. (ed). 2011. *Psychotherapy Relationships that Work: Evidence-Based Responsiveness* (2nd ed.). New York, NY: Oxford University Press. https://doi.org/10.1093/acprof:oso/9780199737208.001.0001

Pawelczyk, Joanna. 2011. *Talk as Therapy. Psychotherapy in a Linguistic Perspective*. Berlin – Boston: Mouton. https://doi.org/10.1515/9781934078679

Pawelczyk, Joanna, and Małgorzata Talarczyk. 2017. "'What should a woman think and imagine to have bulimia?': Co-Constructing Patient Expertise in Psychotherapy with Bulimia Patients." *Communication & Medicine* 14 (2): 135–149. https://doi.org/10.1558/cam.30380

Pawelczyk, Joanna, and Aleksandra Sokalska-Bennett. 2019. "Co-Constructing and Re-Constructing Self: Client Change in Psychotherapy." In *Pragmatik der Veränderung: Problem- und lösungsorientierte Kommunikation in helfenden Berufen*, ed. by Eva-Maria Graf, Claudio Scarvaglieri, and Thomas Spranz-Fogasy, 65–88. Tübingen: Narr.

Pawelczyk, Joanna, Elena Faccio, and Małgorzata Talarczyk. 2021. "Working with Gender in Psychotherapy: A Discursive Analysis of Psychotherapy Sessions with Women Suffering from Bulimia." *Text & Talk* 41 (2): 187–210. https://doi.org/10.1515/text-2019-0132

Peräkylä, Anssi. 2013. "Conversation Analysis in Psychotherapy." In *The Handbook of Conversation Analysis*, ed. by Jack Sidnell, and Tanya Stivers, 551–574. Oxford: Blackwell Publishing.

Peräkylä, Anssi. 2019. "Conversation Analysis and Psychotherapy: Identifying Transformative Sequences." *Research on Language and Social Interaction* 52 (3): 257–280. https://doi.org/10.1080/08351813.2019.1631044

Pomerantz, Anita. 1980. "Telling my Side: 'Limited Access' as a Fishing Device." *Sociological Inquiry* 50 (3–4): 186–198. https://doi.org/10.1111/j.1475-682X.1980.tb00020.x

Pomerantz, Anita. 1984. "Agreeing and Disagreeing with Assessments: Some Features of Preferred/Dispreferred Turn-Shapes." In *Structures of Social Action: Studies in Conversation Analysis*, ed. by John M. Atkinson, and John Heritage, 57–101. Cambridge: Cambridge University Press.

Sacks, Harvey. 1984. "On Doing 'Being Ordinary'." In *Structures of Social Action: Studies in Conversation Analysis*, ed. by Maxwell Atkinson and John Heritage, 413–429. Cambridge: Cambridge University Press.

Sacks, Harvey, Schegloff Emanuel A., and Gail Jefferson. 1974. "A Simplest Systematics for the Organization of Turn-Taking for Conversation." *Language* 50: 696–735. https://doi.org/10.1353/lan.1974.0010

Schegloff, Emanuel. 2002. Reflection on Research on Telephone Conversation: Issues of Cross-cultural Scope and Scholarly Exchange, Interactional Import and Consequences. In *Telephone Calls: Unity and Diversity in Conversational Structure Across Languages and Cultures*, ed. by K. K. Luke, and Theodossia Soula Pavlidou, 249–281. Amsterdam: John Benjamins. https://doi.org/10.1075/pbns.101.16sch

Schegloff, Emanuel A. 2007. *Sequence Organization in Interaction: A Primer in Conversation Analysis*. Cambridge: Cambridge University Press. https://doi.org/10.1017/CBO9780511791208

Smithson, Janet, and Elizabeth Stokoe. 2005. "Discourses of Work-Life Balance: Negotiating 'Genderblind' Terms in Organizations." *Gender, Work and Organization* 12: 147–168. https://doi.org/10.1111/j.1468-0432.2005.00267.x

Speer, Susan, and Elizabeth Stokoe. 2011. "An Introduction to Conversation and Gender." In *Conversation and Gender*, ed. by Susan Speer, and Elizabeth Stokoe, 1–27. Cambridge: Cambridge University Press. https://doi.org/10.1017/CBO9780511781032.002

Stivers, Tanya. 2008. "Stance, Alignment, and Affiliation During Storytelling: When Nodding Is a Token of Affiliation." *Research on Language and Social Interaction* 41 (1): 31–57. https://doi.org/10.1080/08351810701691123

Stivers, Tanya, Lorenza Mondada, and Jakob Steensig (eds.). 2011. *The Morality of Knowledge in Conversation* (Studies in Interactional Sociolinguistics). Cambridge: Cambridge University Press. https://doi.org/10.1017/CBO9780511921674

Stokoe. Elizabeth. 2010. "Gender, Conversation Analysis, and the Anatomy of Membership Categorization Practices." *Social and Personality Psychology Compass* 4 (7): 428–505. https://doi.org/10.1111/j.1751-9004.2010.00261.x

Stokoe, Elizabeth. 2012. "Moving Forward with Membership Categorization Analysis: Methods for Systematic Analysis." *Discourse Studies* 14 (3): 277–303. https://doi.org/10.1177/1461445612441534

Thomassen, Gøril. 2009. "The Role of Role-Play in Medical Education: Managing Activity Ambiguities in Simulated Consultations Between Medical Students and Patients." *Communication & Medicine* 6 (1): 83–93. https://doi.org/10.1558/cam.v6i1.83

Voutilainen, Liisa, and Anssi Peräkylä. 2016. "Interactional Practices of Psychotherapy." In *The Palgrave Handbook of Adult Mental Health*, ed. by Michelle O'Reilly, and Jessica Nina Lester, 540–557. Basingstoke: Palgrave. https://doi.org/10.1057/9781137496850_28

Voutilainen, Liisa, Federico Rossano, and Anssi Peräkylä. 2018. "Conversation Analysis and Psychotherapeutic Change." In *Documenting Change Across Time: Longitudinal Studies on the Organization of Social Interaction*, ed. by Simona Pekarek Doehler, Johannes Wagner, and Esther González-Martínez, 225–254. London: Palgrave Macmillan. https://doi.org/10.1057/978-1-137-57007-9_8

Wampold, Bruce E. 2001. *The Great Psychotherapy Debate: Models, Methods and Findings*. Mahwah, NJ: Lawrence Erlbaum.

Weiste, Elina, Voutilainen Liisa, and Anssi Peräkylä. 2015. "Epistemic Asymmetries in Psychotherapy Interaction: Therapists' Practices for Displaying Access to Clients' Inner Experiences." *Sociology of Health & Illness* 38 (4): 645–661. https://doi.org/10.1111/1467-9566.12384

Relationship management by means of solution-oriented questions in German psychodiagnostic interviews

Susanne Kabatnik, Christoph Nikendei, Johannes C. Ehrenthal and Thomas Spranz-Fogasy
University of Greifswald / University of Heidelberg / University of Cologne / Leibniz-Institute for the German Language Mannheim

The article addresses *Solution-Oriented Questions (SOQs)* as an interactional practice for relationship management in psychodiagnostic interviews. Therapeutic alliance results from the concordance of alignment, as willingness to cooperate regarding common goals, and of affiliation, as relationship based upon trust. SOQs particularly allow for both: They are situated at the end of a troublesome topic area, which is linked to low agency on the patient's side, and they reveal understanding of and interest in the patient. Following the paradigm of Conversation Analysis and German *Gesprächsanalyse* this paper analyzes the design and functions of SOQs as a means for securing and enhancing the relationship in the process of therapy. Our data comprise 15 videotaped first interviews following the manual of the Operationalized Psychodynamic Diagnostics. The analyses refer to all SOQs found but will be illustrated by means of a single conversation.

Keywords: relationship, therapeutic alliance, solution-oriented questions, psychodiagnostic interview, psychotherapy

1. Introduction

Psychotherapy is to a large extent shaped and supported by the relationship between the participants, which is fundamental for common interactional work as well as for obtaining the institutional goals. The establishment and maintenance of the therapeutic relationship or alliance is crucial for the success of therapy (Muntigl and Horvath 2018). As many researchers have argued, the working alliance is the most effective success factor in therapeutic interaction: "The strength of the alliance is arguably the

https://doi.org/10.1075/pbns.331.06kab

best and most reliable predictor of outcomes [...] and is generally considered one of the most important common factors in therapy" (Ribeiro et al. 2013: 295; see also Horvath and Greenberg 1994; Horvath 2006; Ardito and Rabellino 2011; Lambert 2013; Flückiger et al. 2012). Psychotherapy as a co-constructed treatment format primarily relies on structural characteristics of communication: the fundamental sequentiality of verbal interaction (Deppermann 2008), i.e., the sequence of utterances of at least two speakers provides and guarantees the production of intersubjectivity and thus forms the basis of therapeutic effectiveness (Peräkylä et al. 2008) – also in terms of relationship management. However, it is difficult to investigate relationships because they are usually not explicitly addressed (cf. Mandelbaum 2003) and can often only be analyzed on the basis of how interactants communicate with each other (for online communication cf. Kabatnik in this volume).

The topic of interpersonal relationship has a long tradition in pragmatics research. In language theoretical approaches from Humboldt via Schütz, Mead, Bakhtin to Linell, dialogicity is emphasized as central (Mandelbaum 2003). Bühler's (1934) functions of expression and appeal are relationally indicative and constitutive as well as Jakobson's (1960) phatic function or the functions of illocution and perlocution in speech act theory. Watzlawick et al. (1967) emphasize the relational aspect in addition to informative content. Special impulses for linguistics, however, have come primarily from the sociology of interaction, for example with Goffman's concepts of role and face, or from the politeness-theory of Brown and Levinson. Davies and Harré (1990) developed the concept of positioning, which focusses on the dynamic aspects of interpersonal encounters. Based on these concepts, Holly (2001) characterizes relationship in interaction as elementary, ubiquitous, and common, but also as potentially superficial, delicate, and explosive, and therefore mostly implicit. Bucholtz and Hall (2005) outline a framework for the construction of identity generated in linguistic interaction. Locher and Watts (2008) highlight that relational work includes the whole spectrum of the interpersonal aspects of social practices, i.e., both politeness and impoliteness. Arundale (2010) extends the face concept to a cross-cultural and culture-specific dimension and conceptualizes face as a relational phenomenon. The ethnomethodologically-based Conversation Analysis (Sidnell and Stivers 2013) highlights the construction character of interaction and thus also of relationships-in-interaction. Participants in the conversation themselves, with their interrelated actions, constitute what they are doing at the moment, which action goals are being pursued, and the relationship between them. Mandelbaum (2003: 217) in her study "Interactive Methods for Constructing Relationships" describes relationships from this perspective "as collections of communicative practices, or things that we do through communication, in contrast to thinking of them as social structural things that we *have*" (emphasis by Mandelbaum).

While psychological and psychotherapeutic research usually conducts extensive studies on the topic of relationship within and outside the therapeutic setting, systematic linguistic analyses remain rare (Linke and Schröter 2017), although many relationship-relevant phenomena such as theme setting, variation of expression, intonation or lexical modification are of a linguistic nature. On the interactional micro-level, Conversation Analysis distinguishes two central practices of micro-managing the interpersonal relationship or the alliance between patient and therapist: alignment and affiliation (e.g., Muntigl and Horvath 2014; Muntigl et al. 2012). Alignment and affiliation are two key qualities of interactional interpersonal relationship that form "an infrastructure of therapy" (Peräkylä 2019: 273), which enables patient and therapist to attach to each other. Alignment characterizes the mutual willingness and intention to cooperate, to pursue a common goal willingly, and to work together in a cooperative process. Affiliation, on the other hand, characterizes a more fundamental quality: the emotional agreement and the relationship and bond based on trust between patient and therapist (Lindström and Sorjonen 2013; Steensig 2019). While alignment refers to the more structural characteristics of the sequential organization, e.g., the observance of the right to speak or the fulfillment of conditional relevance, affiliation is associated with the factual and substantive agreement of the epistemic attitude of the interlocutors and their emotional-empathic support.

Psychotherapeutic conversations are characterized by narratives of the patient and interventions of the therapist, which are intended to guide the patient's explanations. In addition to the therapists' supporting actions, challenging actions promote the therapeutic process, too (Marciniak et al. 2016). Conversational analysis has identified four key types of therapeutic speech actions: questions, formulations, extensions, and interpretations (Weiste and Peräkylä 2015). In this paper we focus on formulations and questions. Weiste and Peräkylä (2013) differentiate four types of formulations: *highlighting, rephrasing, relocating,* and *exaggerating formulations*. All of these action formats aim to promote awareness and expand and restructure the patient's knowledge and thus ultimately bring about change (see Peräkylä 2019).

In addition to their cognitive content, verbal actions also imply different attitudes towards the patient, relationship offers, and support (see Watzlawick et al. 1967: 4; Konerding 2015: 234). It is about gaining trust and establishing a relationship based on trust, getting patients to cooperate, and establishing common goals. Therapeutic issues are also strongly relationship-implicative in this respect. However, in terms of relationship management, questions have often been viewed critically; they are considered to be too invasive in such a sensitive relationship context due to sequential constraints and therefore lead to patients being blocked in their willingness to talk about their emotional needs. Nevertheless, questions in psychotherapeutic conversations are endemic, and many formulations are treated as (declarative) *questions* too by both therapists and patients (see Marciniak 2016: 6; Spranz-Fogasy 2010). In a study by Mack et al. (2016) on questions, all functions identified for formulations could also be determined for questions. In addition, the following other question types were identified: *Requesting Example* (cf. Spranz-Fogasy et al. 2020), *Questions for Collaborative Explanation Finding* (cf. Mack et al. 2016) and *Solution-Oriented Questions* (cf. Kabatnik et al. 2019; Spranz-Fogasy et al. 2018; Läpple et al. 2021). While the first type requires a broader, content-related presentation of the patient by asking for examples (= clarification of problem issues), the second aims at causes for symptoms or mental disorders (= explanation), the latter type – on which we focus here – aims at patients' treatment expectations, wishes or life perspectives (= solution). These subjects of *Solution-Oriented Questions* (SOQs) imply possible changes or therapeutic goals and can therefore be analyzed as a specific change-enabling interactional and therapeutic practice (see Kabatnik et al. 2019; Spranz-Fogasy et al. 2018). The desire for change is the central motivation of any form of psychotherapy (Weiste and Peräkylä 2015: 8) and thus also for the change of relationship and relationship behavior. In the following we therefore analyze relationship implications of SOQs in their immediate sequential context and across the course of the conversation. First, however, we will present the data on which the analyses are based.

2. Data and method

The data of the research comprise 15 videotaped psychodiagnostic interviews with 15 patients (8 female / 7 male) with diagnoses of depressive disorders, and five psychotherapists (1 female / 4 male). The interviews follow the concept and manual of the OPD system (OPD Task Force 2009). On average, the interviews last for about 75 min (a total of 18 hours 43 minutes). Data was collected at the Department for General Internal Medicine and Psychosomatic at the Heidelberg University Clinic (2008 to 2015). The study was approved by the ethics committee of the University of Heidelberg (S-195/2014) and all participants gave their written informed consent in accordance with the Declaration of Helsinki. The original data is in German.[1]

The OPD system was first developed in 1992 by psychoanalysts and experts in psychosomatic medicine and in psychiatry. The central idea is that a psychic problem is not sufficiently operationalized by its categorization within a descriptive classification system for symptoms. To understand all dimensions, the symptoms must be enriched by a psychodynamic dimension, and understood in relation to a

1. We only present the English translation; the original German data are placed on the book's web page.

patient's individual biographical background and psychodynamic characteristics. Thus, OPD represents a diagnostic method that helps to assess the patients' psychodynamics via conversation in terms of a specifically designed interview. The interview thereby functions as a manualized instrument that allows for drawing a precise and individualized pattern of the patients' suffering and specific underlying problems. OPD allows therapists to classify patients' problems according to a manual and applies categories and scales to assess the findings; this guarantees the comparability of the diagnostic results (cf. Sachse 1999). Psychotherapists thereby diagnose patients' conditions and their underlying psychodynamic constraints along five axes (cf. Ehrenthal and Benecke 2019), which allow the therapist to define a therapeutic focus in respect to underlying psychodynamic conflicts, patients' personality function, and particular dysfunctional relationship patterns (Schauenburg et al. 2020).

As the data were derived from a time-limited diagnostic interview session, it does not allow us to draw any conclusions about psychodynamic psychotherapy as a whole. Nevertheless, the data is valuable for investigating the context of certain question types and their sequential organization as well as their relationship conditions and relationship building implications.

The 'target action' (Peräkylä 2019: 7) of our analysis are *Solution-Oriented Questions* (SOQs). In our corpus we found 27 SOQs in twelve interviews. Other question types not discussed here were 33 explicit *Requesting Examples* and 57 *Questions for Collaborative Explanation Finding* (Spranz-Fogasy et al. 2020). The SOQs were analyzed by means of Conversation Analysis (Sidnell and Stivers 2013) and German *Gesprächsanalyse*[2] (Deppermann 2008).

3. Analyses

Solution-Oriented Questions (SOQs) are verbal interventions by therapists to find solutions for patients' problems that have been discussed or to determine patients' expectations for their future life or for therapy (Mack et al. 2016). The problems addressed always refer to the patients' reduced agency (Deppermann 2015; Kook 2015; Marciniak 2017). SOQs play a key role in psychodiagnostic interviews, especially for depressive patients with limited agency and prospects. The primary goal of this question format is to discuss and work out a solution for the problem discussed (see Mack 2016; Spranz-Fogasy et al. 2018). Solutions that are negotiated as a result of such questions are always hypothetical; in the protected space of the

2. *Gesprächsanalyse* is a German research paradigm based on CA that also draws on pragmatics, discourse analysis, and linguistic text analysis.

psychotherapeutic setting, patients can experiment with different ideas of possible solutions without fear of consequences.

The following analyses refer to the investigation of all 27 SOQs. To make the analyses easier to understand, we will first illustrate SOQs by means of a single conversation in which the therapist articulates a total of five SOQs and a development in the search for a solution as well as in the therapeutic relationship becomes clear. We also refer to this interview regularly in subsequent property- and structure-related descriptions which will apply to all occurrences of SOQs in our corpus. Thereby we analyze the design of SOQs, describe the position of SOQs within the overall interaction, and analyze their sequential processing locally and also within the whole interview with respect to the formation of relationship during the interaction. The patient in our reference interview suffers from depression and has already made several attempts for therapy. Her main problem of accepting help is addressed right at the beginning of the interview. The patient shows a skeptical and resistant attitude towards the therapeutic agenda. The aim of the interview is to build a trust-based relationship with the patient, to get her to cooperate and to work out common (therapeutic) goals. Because SOQs ask about the patient's goals, solutions, wishes, and hopes, and offer support in the search for them, they seem to be predestined for the purpose of building a trustful relationship (further practices of relationship cf. Muntigl in this volume and Graf and Jautz in this volume).

In interview T3_2 we identified the following five SOQs, presented here with their content reference points and thematic context:[3]

Extract 1. SOQ 1: Therapy hopes/desires (00:34:11)

```
T:  i mean (.) what do you hope for or what (0.5) would you wish for
    (.) if you allowed yourself to wish for anything
```

Extract 2. SOQ 2: Balance between own needs and the needs of others (00:42:16)

```
T:  how could you create a balance where you don't feel that others
    (0.28) ehm come off badly but where your own needs could also be
    considered
```

Extract 3. SOQ 3: Good quarreling 1 (00:56:16)

```
T:  could you imagine that (.) how that [i.e., good quarreling; the
    authors] (.) could look like or how you want it
```

Extract 4. SOQ 4: Good quarreling 2 (00:56:23)

```
T:  and if you'd fantasized a little bit [i.e., about good quarreling;
    the authors]
```

Extract 5. SOQ 5: Accepting help (01:19:33)

```
T:  could that be a topic for you (0.56) which you would like to deal
    with here
```

3. Transcription conventions follow Selting et al. 2011.

SOQs offer support for collaborative reflection and planning (cf. Thurnherr in this volume also sees clients as active participants in the therapeutic alliance). Thematically, SOQs refer either to the therapy (see Extracts (1), (5) above) or to the patients' lives (Extracts (2), (3), (4)) and address the patients' wishes (Extract (1)), ideas (Extracts (3), (4)), concrete perspectives (Extract (2)), or goals (Extract (5)) (see Spranz-Fogasy et al. 2018; Kabatnik et al. 2019). SOQs can also contain explicit relationship topics, such as the balance of needs (Extract (2)) and the patients' conflict behavior in relationships (Extracts (3), (4)). For patients, answering such questions means to distance themselves from familiar, albeit dysfunctional, interpersonal regulatory patterns and correspondingly stressful intrapsychic affects, and to explore solutions that aim at gaining freedom of action and overcoming patterns of dysfunctional self- and relationship regulation. SOQs thus aim at the epistemic-emotional state of consciousness of the patient and exert high interactive pressure on the patient to act.

Design

SOQs have several common features regarding their formulation design, often associated with delays (Extracts (1), (3), (5)) or terminations and repairs (Extract (2)) (19 of 27). This suggests that SOQs are not an easy undertaking for therapists either:[4] Concerning the patient's problem, their emotional and mental state and the potential sensitivity of the therapeutic relationship, these interventions must be treated with caution. In addition, subjunctive forms (see Extracts (1)–(5); 16/27) with reference to the future are usually used (see Extract (5); 23/27), which opens the space for speculation and at the same time marks the tentativity of the issues to be negotiated. The therapist thus places him-/herself on the same epistemic level as the patient, as he does not know the solution to the problem either but is prepared to accompany the patient in developing solutions (cf. Džanko in this volume points out that the demonstration of epistemic equivalence ensures stronger commitment).

Regarding the semantic-grammatical question type, *wh*-questions are significantly more frequent (Extracts (1), (2); 20/27). *Yes/no* questions are also possible but occur almost exclusively as integrated *wh*-questions (see Extract (3)). Thus, basal categorical information is asked, such as person, time, and place, and the patient's problem is at the center of the therapeutic intervention. The presuppositions of the questions, i.e., the existence of hope and wishes (Extract (1)), the balance between

4. In the remaining 8/27 SOQs the questions are prepared by the therapist; see also Extract (4), which follows Extract (3) almost immediately.

needs (Extract (2)), the possibility of good conflict (Extract (3) and (4)), and the acceptance of help as a possible therapy topic (Extract (5)) suggest thinkable solutions and thus also define a framework for answers. These presuppositions make such questions interactionally delicate and at the same time challenging for establishing relationship between the participants. The patient's problems discussed above can be expected to lead to deficits in the patient's ideas and strategies for solutions and face-threatening repair initiatives on the part of the therapist (Brown and Levinson 1987) – which is also reflected in our data (cf. Kabatnik et al. 2019; Spranz-Fogasy et al. 2018).

Another striking feature is the dominant, sometimes multiple, direct addressing (24/27) of patients despite individual therapy (cf. Günthner in this volume for addressing as a relationship-building instrument). On the one hand, this direct addressing activates patients' personal knowledge (cf. Spranz-Fogasy et al. 2018). On the other hand, despite clear identification, such person references indicate patient-centeredness and can thus be interpreted as an expression of affiliative activities (cf. Schwitalla 2010: 192). Thus, not only is the patient in the focus of the therapist's attention, but also his or her problem, ideas, wishes and conceptions on emotional and interpersonal issues. SOQs allow for both cognitive and emotive-volitional projections, which are also expressed in the cognitive (Extract (3)), emotional (Extract (1)) and volitional (Extract (5)) lexicon of the predicates of the questions (see Extracts (1)–(5)). By querying wishes, hopes, and concrete ideas, the patient's entire spectrum of experience is covered and thus acts as a precursor to the negotiation of common goals in terms of alignment. The use of the respective verb type also indicates which reactions therapists assume to elicit through their questions. Cognitive verbs such as "to imagine, think, believe" already aim at concrete solutions, while emotional verbs such as "to hope, wish, want" trigger a solution orientation in the first place (Reinicke 2018). From a clinical perspective, cognitive verbs operate simultaneously at a greater emotional distance, while emotional verbs tend to be closer to the delicate and "painful", similar to Wachtel's (2011) description of effects of rational vs. experiential strategies and wordings.

Regarding the requirements for contextualization, SOQs show different degrees of complexity – from short initiatives, previously prepared utterances (see Extract (4), prepared by Extract (3) and the patient's following answer) to increasingly complex utterances with inserted and/or deferred clarifications of the framework conditions as well as an often long lead time as in the following extract:

Extract 2′. SOQ 2 with presequences (00:41:49)

```
T:  and I believe that this is also happened to you (0.25) is (0.21)
    has also happened to you in all these years (0.31) that you
    actually °h (0.45) the area of needs and desires and the °h (0.21)
    feelings ((incomprehensible)) (0.64) for really (0.28) yes for
    good (0.64) very good reasons (.) to have deposited or deposited
    somewhere (.) °hh (1.0) and which of course (.) is under pressure
    as a steam boiler and and you just h° (0.29) probably have little
    (.) handling for how can one (0.2) how can you achieve balance
    where both °h you don't have the feeling that other °hh (0.28) um
    ((clicks)) come off badly but where your own needs are seen
```

The frequent high complexity of SOQs with long lead times, insertions as well as the intermediate and subsequent clarification of framework conditions also point to the delicate nature of these questions. Therapists thus document their awareness of the patient's difficult mental state, which is addressed in the preceding interactional negotiation of low agency in the reference interview in connection with the patient's relationships. In addition, this way of formulating documents that therapists consider the psychological state of patients when formulating the intervention and tailor their statements to suit the addressee (cf. Clark 1992), so that the patient's understanding of the intervention can be made easier and possible misunderstandings can be avoided from the outset.

Beyond that, SOQs can also be used to implicitly criticize the patient's previous behavior (Bröcher 2017), as for example in Extract (4), which shows the connection to the insufficient response to SOQ in Extract (3) and calls on the patient to undertake further solution-finding activities. This type of criticism can also represent an activity that endangers the relationship due to its potentially face-violating character.

In the context of OPD interviews, however, SOQs are primarily a diagnostic tool, as the therapist implicitly asks whether or where the patient already sees possibilities for action and shows willingness to cooperate. Thus, an important function of SOQs is to test (cf. Bröcher 2017; Oelschläger 2017) whether the patient is ready for developing common goals or projections for them. In addition, responsibility can be transferred and its handling by the patient can be observed (Oelschläger 2017). Transfer of responsibility with simultaneous support then also documents confidence in the patient's ability to find solutions and at the same time presupposes a secure basis of trust between patient and therapist.

Positioning and context

SOQs usually appear in the last third of the interviews (18/27). However, they can also – as in our reference interview – appear in the first (3/27) and second third (6/27) of the interview, but then always at the end of a complex problem negotiation (9/27). This specific position of SOQs at the end of the conversation and/or of complex topics indicates on the one hand that SOQs require a basis of trust and relationship, due to their invasive character in terms of content and interaction with which they address the patients' level of experience and demand a reaction. On the other hand, they can also create a relieving change of perspective from problem elaboration and the past to the alignment of goals and the future. Due to the preceding problem elaboration, a patient's low agency is documented and addressed in all 27 SOQs of our corpus (cf. Marciniak 2017). A problem or conflict is indicated retrospectively, for which possible solutions are sought. In the way it is formulated, the offer of support is expressed by asking for possible solutions, but these are marked as hypothetical so that patients can carry out thought experiments in the protected space without fear of real consequences. This is explicitly formulated in SOQs 3 and 4, in which the therapist addresses the patient's imagination and fantasy, but also in all other cases, e.g., through the subjunctive (cf. Mack et al. 2016). The therapist can thus initiate ideas for solutions, develop them together with the patient, but also correct them if necessary.

By addressing low agency in the forefield of SOQs, in our reference interview interpersonal relationships of the patient were discussed before each SOQ. Prior to SOQ 1, the patient's recurring suicidal thoughts are discussed, where she claims not to commit suicide because of her mother. The therapist calls this behavior a *dangerous deal* because the patient makes herself dependent on another person. After his observation of the great inner distress of the patient and the question of her attitude towards therapy, with SOQ1 follows a question concerning therapy hopes and wishes, with which the therapist addresses the subjective dimension and implicitly asks how he can help her.

Prior to the second SOQ, the focus is on earlier therapy attempts of the patient. She admits that she has not always been honest with her therapists. On the one hand, this may mean that the patient has not been able to build up enough trust with her therapists to confide her feelings, thoughts, and experiences in them. On the other hand, it may indicate a behavior that endangers the relationship,[5] which is also criticized by the patient as *false honesty*. Nevertheless, the therapist deals

5. In the case of malicious deception, exposure can have far-reaching consequences for the relationship. Certain contexts, such as therapy situations or relationships, can encourage such deception (Goffman 1977: 98).

with these self-reproaches of the patient understandingly, that she had neglected the emotional sphere for years for good reason, which is a face-saving activity of the therapist.

This is followed by the second SOQ for establishing balance, in which the therapist implicitly asks how the patient can trust him without neglecting her need for protection (see Extract (2)' with presequences). SOQ 1 and 2 are interlinked, because both questions deal with the subjective dimension of the patient, marked in SOQ 2 by *feel*, so that the second SOQ is not a general question about establishing balance. Given the contextualization with past therapeutic behavior, this SOQ can also be related to the patient's behavior in the current therapy, which is marked by the very general subject *others*, with whom both therapeutic and non-therapeutic relationships are addressed.

The third and fourth SOQ follow almost immediately after each other and deal with the previous topic of the patient, her father and her parents' dispute behavior. She then describes her own argumentative behavior as *I am one of them (.) I can (.) nothing can discuss (.) nothing can't argue if I have a fight I am gone* (00:55:14). The self-attribution of this quarrelling behavior by *I am also such a one* points to a manifest conflict behavior of the patient. After the question of the therapist, if the patient does not know *other disputes […], where people have argued well*, the negation of the patient and the rephrasing formulation of the therapist *that means that you do not know how to argue well*, the therapist asks in SOQ 3 for good arguing. With this he asks whether the patient has any ideas about good arguing behavior, and furthermore, how she would like to shape arguing situations in the future. With the volitional lexicon of the question (*want*) the subjective dimension is also addressed here. Due to the lack of a with-whom-addition, the patient's general conflict behavior is addressed, including that in therapy, which is essential for the ability to argue because patients are also confronted in therapy with unpleasant contents and assessments to which they must respond (cf. Marciniak et al. 2016: 4).

Before SOQ 5, the relationship with a former partner of the patient is discussed. The patient reports the escalation of a dispute at a party, for which border violations by a guest are cited as the trigger. As the dispute escalates, the patient wants to flee. After the therapist praises the patient for her strength and the patient continues with her self-reproaches, the therapist interrupts her self-deprecation by means of an *exaggerating formulation* and takes up the initial topic of accepting help again with SOQ 5. Topically, the previous SOQs are continued here, because the balance between the patient's own and other people's needs from SOQ 2 is dealt with, as well as the conflict behavior from SOQ 3 and 4 and the therapy wishes from SOQ 1.

In the context of the SOQs, different relationships of the patient, e.g., with her parents, partner or other therapists, are negotiated with regard to reduced agency of the patient, on the one hand, and relationship-relevant behavior, e.g., honesty, the expression of feelings or argumentative behavior, on the other. The context analysis shows that each SOQ in our reference interview has relationship implications and thus also deals with relationship-relevant aspects, not only between the patient and her family members and friends, but also between the therapist and the patient.

Sequential organization and global development of relationship

Positions 0–2

Based on the data of the 15 OPD interviews, we have created a step-by-step model of the sequential organization of SOQ, which we would like to demonstrate using the five SOQs in our reference interview. The model comprises five sequence positions of therapist- and patient-side utterances. With respect to the SOQs throughout the interview, the sequence varies in the second, third, and fourth position. Nevertheless, it is possible to derive a pattern for the sequence organization of solution negotiation, summarized schematically here:

0-Position	P/T:	discussion of relationship
1-Position	T:	SOQ with relationship implications
2-Position	P:	dispreferred answer/disalignment *non-answer/answer-like/partial conform response*
3-Position	T:	expansion initiation/repair initiation *or: topic change and subsequent therapeutic action*
4-Position	P:	preferred answer/(improved) alignment/repeated resistance
5-Position	T:	ratification; subsequent therapeutic action

Figure 1. Sequence pattern of Patient (P)/Therapist (T) with SOQ as target action

In the following we discuss in parallel the sequential development of all five SOQs in our reference interview. In the **0-position** the first SOQ is preceded by the topic of the patient's repeated suicidal thoughts and the role of her mother, the second SOQ is preceded by discussions about years of suppression of the patient's feelings, the third and fourth SOQs are preceded by the topic of deficient argumentative behavior and before the fifth SOQ, low agency is shown in the patient's deficit to accept help (Extracts (1)–(5), see Table 1 below).

In the **1-position** the therapist utters a SOQ with a concrete offer of help. Due to the strong interactive pressure to react to the question, the patient's individual resources are activated to find a solution and an interactive negotiation phase is initiated. Since SOQs set a certain answer conditionally relevant, which aligns with the question in terms of form and content, we were able to establish a typology based on MacMartin (2008) and Voutilainen et al. (2011) according to different degrees of (dis)preference of patient answers in the **2-position**: With *answer-like responses*, patients shift the focus of the questions (cf. Winkler in this volume sees "semi-response" answers as a source of information and a challenge). In *non-answer-like responses*, patients show their resistance in a more open way, e.g., by complaining about the question (= not wanting to) or expressing their inability to answer (= not being able to). *Partially conforming responses* are responses that are partially consistent with the question, but still contain characteristics of dispreferred responses, such as delay signals or explanations (see Spranz-Fogasy et al. 2018, Kabatnik et al. 2019; on preference organization in general see Pomerantz and Heritage 2013). Thus, dispreferred answers may indicate disalignment and deviating positions. All SOQs in our corpus and thus also in our reference interview are followed by dispreferred answers:

Table 1. Sequence position 0–2 in case T3_2

Sequence position // Timeline of extracts	0-low Agency	1-SOQ T	2-Response P	P response type
1:00:32:37–00:34:26	Suicidal thoughts, mother, great need of P	**Therapy hopes/wishes**	uhm that (0.26) does not work at all because it was taken from me ((laughs)) hh° i actually came with the wish or things (.) in my brain (1.08) uhm (0.26) that I can forget (0.32)	answer-like refocusing & non-answer, sarcasm
2:00:39:37–00:42:26	Shaking attack, earlier therapy tries, suppression of feelings for years	**Creating a balance between your own needs and those of others**	i have tried sports (0.47) but (0.25)	answer-like refocusing
3:00:55:14–00:56:21	Deficits in dispute behavior	**Desired image about good quarrelling**	uhmuhm (0.31) i wouldn't know	non-answer
4:00:56:23–00:56:40	Deficits in dispute behavior	**Desired fantasy for good quarrelling**	(2.15) uh argue well (0.25) uhm_uhm (2.24) yes i think arguing well is simply uh (.) °h (0.24) to stay objective just (.) uh to stay in a certain tone and not to step out there and simply (.) °h discussing (0.46) and then of course to find a common denominator	optimized answer, partly refocusing
5:01:16:58–01:19:42	Dispute with partner, inability to accept help	**Therapy topic/ desire**	(2.33) yes (0.29) somehow +++ yeah but somehow i do not know how to edit it	Partially conforming response

In our reference interview, the patient responds to the first SOQ on therapy hopes or wishes as a change of topic and positive reorientation with a *non-answer response* by denying the wish qua *extreme case formulation* (*not at all*; cf. Pomerantz 1986) and shifting the focus via *answer-like refocusing response* to an unrealistic wish, thereby expressing that she is not yet ready for common therapy goals.

The patient responds to the second SOQ for establishing a balance between her own and other people's needs – also in therapy – by shifting the focus to solution attempts that have already failed, thus rejecting the therapist's attempt to support her in developing balance.

The third and fourth SOQs follow each other and are related to each other as well as to their answers: At first, the patient is resistant to the SOQ on good arguing behavior. After feedback signals and long pauses, the patient then globally rejects knowledge about good conflict behavior via an *extreme case formulation* (*I wouldn't know*), to which the therapist reacts with a fourth and insistent SOQ to fantasize about constructive conflict behavior. On the one hand, the therapist thereby indicates that the patient's previous answer was insufficient, i.e., the therapist criticizes the first answer to the question. On the other hand, the therapist asks the patient for more willingness to cooperate by *if you'd fantasized a little bit* and asks the patient to think beyond any responsibility or duty to act. This is a specific support of the psychotherapeutic setting, in which the patient is encouraged to experiment. The insistent SOQ is highly successful here because the patient reformulates and optimizes her first response: After a short hesitation and a repetition of the question, the patient develops a concise and reasonable concept of good arguing, which enables the therapist to go deeper into the emotional level of quarreling. She answers the question in detail and responds with an – at this point surprisingly – elaborate conceptualization of good conflict behavior. By answering the therapist's question in this way, the patient shows an increased willingness to cooperate, which is elicited by the therapist's sensitive and personalized insistence. The sequences of SOQs 3 and 4 follow the ideal-typical sequence of the local solution negotiation 'low agency – SOQ – disagreed answer – therapeutic intervention – preferred answer'. Thereby, via recursion, changes in knowledge, attitude, ability to act, resistance as well as the willingness to cooperate and joint agreement on objectives can be achieved (cf. Kabatnik et al. 2019; Spranz-Fogasy et al. 2018).

The setting of common goals finally succeeds – at least partially – at the end of the conversation, as shown in the patient's response to SOQ 5 to accept help. The patient's response to the fifth and final SOQ on her initial therapy wishes and acceptance of help is finally partially-conforming. She first follows the therapist's agenda affirmatively, but then openly addresses deficits in the implementation and gives the following reasons: *well, I would like to say yes, I (.) so in the (moment) yes,*

I would really be that one hundred percent without (secondary thoughts I would like the) help and I would like to accept it (01:19:44–01:19:44).

Despite the mentioned deficits in the implementation, a clear increase in the patient's willingness to cooperate can be seen when comparing the initial and final state. The initial manifest(ed) resistance to the therapist's agenda decreases over the course of the conversation and the development of common (therapeutic) goals in terms of alignment is thus prepared for.

Positions 3 and 4

The patients' answers, which are always dispreferred in our entire data, form a starting point for further therapeutic treatment. The patients have not yet developed a solution concept for their own problems and are not (yet) prepared to follow the therapist's agenda. Thus, the patients' dispreferred answers represent a critical moment in and for the interaction. Alignment must therefore first be accomplished in the third and fourth sequence position. Therapeutic responses to the patients' resistance are insistence to expand, repair initiation or change of topic (see Figure 2; cf. Läpple et al. 2021.).[6] While repair initiation addresses the patient's dispreferred answer as a problem of alignment and change of topic even ignores the lack of alignment, insistence marks the patient's lack of affiliation with the implications of a SOQ. In any case, at this sequential position the current status of the relationship becomes virulent and assessable for the therapist. This also helps us to observe changes in the relationship in the course of the interaction.

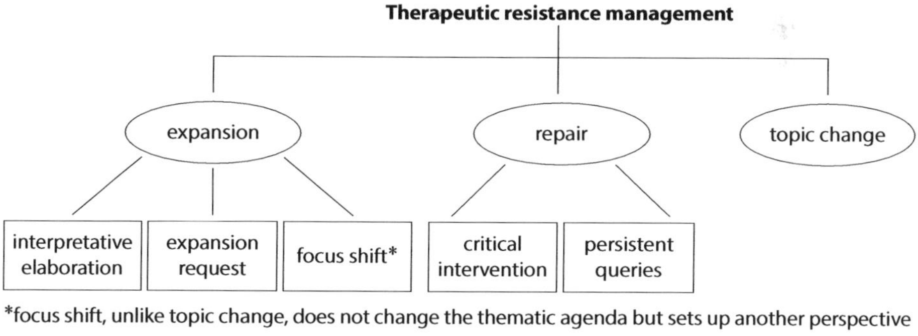

Figure 2. Therapeutic resistance management

6. In recent analyses of psychotherapy sessions, we found a further type of resistance management: topicalization of resistance. We assume that this type does not occur in OPD interviews, because this is not necessary for the rationale of these interviews (i.e., assessment) and could be counterproductive in this context due to time constraints and the depth of intervention. Explicit topicalization of resistance is discussed in Vehviläinen 2008.

In the following we discuss the sequential development of all five SOQs in our reference interview for positions 3 and 4 in parallel as above (continuation of Table 1 with positions 3 and 4).

Table 2. Sequence position 0–4 in case T3–2

Sequence position // Timeline of extracts	**0-low Agency**	**1-SOQ T**	**2-Response P**	**3-Reaction T**	**4-Response P**
1:00:32:37–00:34:34	Suicidal thoughts, mother, great need of P	Therapy hopes/ wishes	does not work, wish was taken away immediately, being able to forget	**Expansion with interpretative elaboration**	`h° yes I just don't know (really) how to deal with it (.) um I don't know how I could build it up`
2:00:39:37–00:42:40	Shaking attack, earlier therapy tries, suppression of feelings for years	Creating a balance between your own needs and those of others	trying to solve the problem with sport	**Topic change**	`yes (.) ((laughs)) ((incompre-hensible)) ((laughs)) yes (.) she was quite funny`
3:00:55:14–00:56:21	Deficits in dispute behavior	Desired image about good quarrelling	Rejection	**SOQ4**	Response 4
4:00:56:23–00:56:52	Deficits in dispute behavior	Desired fantasy for good quarrelling	stay objective and debate, find a common denominator	**Expansion request**	`don't know(.) ((sniffles)) I have no idea`
5:01:16:58–01:19:44	Dispute with partner, inability to accept help	Therapy topic/ desire	Consent on notification of implementation deficits, side issues	**Focus shift**	`neither do I, but I want to get this ((laughs))`

The therapist responds to the patient's first answer to SOQ 1 about therapy hopes and wishes (2 – Response P: does not work, wish was taken away immediately, being able to forget, see Tables 1 & 2) with understanding and empathy for her unrealistic wish:

Extract 1′. postsequences: 3 – Reaction T – Expansion with interpretative elaboration (00:34:35)

```
T:  ((smacks)) °hh that would be nice if you could just start all over
    again and forget everything(.) again °hh what it is about (.)
    difficult things (.) about (.) insults to to °h
```

In doing so, he follows the patient's idea, but shows through the subjunctive and conditional sentence *that would be nice if one could simply start from the beginning again* that the patient's idea is unrealistic / impossible, while considering the idea to be generally legitimate. In this way, the therapist ratifies the patient's wish, while concurrently criticizing it. The therapist's reaction can be classified as an expansion with interpretative elaboration. In the **4-position**, the patient initially reacts in an affirmative way, but then refers to her ignorance or inability to deal with difficult issues.

The therapist reacts to the patient's answer to SOQ 2 (SOQ 2: creating a balance between your own needs and those of others, 2 – Response P: trying to solve the problem with sport, see also extract SOQ 2) with a critical intervention by pointing out the repeated misbehavior by *this is again the +++ fend for yourself* and then changing the topic: [...] *°hhh you told about your grandma (0.21) where you said (as a child) you were there quite often and °hh.* The patient answers affirmatively, laughs and changes the topic to the positive relationship with her grandmother. The rapid change of topic prevents possible justifications and a loss of face of the patient. Change of topic (with 4/27 occurrences in all SOQs) can indicate that the therapist takes a step back and postpones his/her intervention through SOQs because he does not yet consider the therapeutic alliance to be sufficiently secured.

The therapist reacts to the processing of SOQs 3 and 4 on the patient's dispute behavior with a request for expansion, in which he asks the patient to include the subjective dimension in the discussion. Through the *and* in *and what do you do if then a feeling (comes) (0.97) and you ((incomprehensible)) the discussion (.) (but) no dispute* he ratifies the patient's answer on the one hand, but at the same time marks it as incomplete. The patient evades the call for completion on the subjective dimension by falling back into resistance. This example shows the patient's manifest resistance to the therapist's agenda. The willingness to cooperate, which was gained interactively before, is still fragile and the therapist must proceed in small steps and cautiously in order not to overtax the patient.

In the patient's partially compliant response to SOQ 5, the therapist then addresses the patient's concerns about her secondary thoughts (see above) with a focus shift. He recognizes the patient's secondary thoughts as a marker relevant for therapeutic progress, but characterizes the patient's concerns as unfounded, because he *would not know how to do this (.) that (0.38) can be approached one hundred percent without (zero thoughts).* In this way he legitimizes the patient's secondary thoughts, thereby addressing the reasons for the patient's resistance and trying to eliminate them so that the patient can engage in a relationship of trust and common goals. The patient agrees with the therapist but remains vague in her confession with *but I want to get this*; the reference point of *this* can be both the therapy and a therapy without secondary thoughts.

SOQs are relevant for the alignment of goals between therapist and patient, which are approached in this conversation by comparing the initial and final state. At the end of the interview, the patient's responses show a change towards a higher readiness to cooperate and a lower resistance. Dealing with this resistance also indicates that both the patient and the therapist regard the relationship as stable and that a possible conflict does or must not endanger future therapeutic work. Gradually, the use of SOQs leads to affiliation via alignment and intersubjectivity, thus strengthening and securing the therapeutic alliance.

4. Discussion

In psychotherapy, relationship building is a difficult endeavor even more in psychodiagnostic first interviews. A trustful relationship between people who do not know each other needs to be established, while at the same time a certain distance is required, e.g., patient and therapist will not be on first name terms or the therapist will not tell the patient about his/her own painful experiences. On the one hand then, the participants must maintain asymmetry in the conversation, and on the other hand the patient should feel understood and comfortable enough to be willing to share highly sensitive thoughts, experiences and feelings. SOQs elicit such sensitive thoughts in the form of, e.g., wishes or goals, and always have relational implications by thematizing relationships in the sequential forefield.

SOQs are thus frequently found in the data and appear at specific positions in the negotiation process: towards the end of topic developments and always in connection with depictions of patients' low agency in relation to the current topic or problem. With SOQs, the therapist expresses understanding for this and documents his or her interest in the patient. SOQs have a systematic value in the psychotherapeutic process: they serve to release the patient from his or her attachment to the problem and to open up for a – potentially better – future.

While hesitant formulations indicate that SOQs are interactively sensitive to the current relationship from a therapist's perspective, a conspicuous direct address shows an intense patient-centeredness and invites the patient to reveal her or his goals, wishes or hopes. The protected therapeutic setting and the formulation of SOQs in a hypothetical, speculative manner serve to relieve the patient of actual duties or responsibilities and to stimulate the patient's self-reflection. SOQs thus lead to an expansion of the patient's agency, to the restructuring of knowledge, and thus to potential change.

With SOQs the therapist offers help and him-/herself as a "companion" who is willing to search for solutions together with the patient and to strengthen the willingness to cooperate. The patients' reactions are always primarily dispreferred – which in turn indicates the sensitivity of the issue – and at first sight it seems as if the relationship is endangered by this conflict; yet, the subsequent negotiation leads to overcoming the patients' resistance and to an increased cooperation. This corresponds to the therapeutic concept of challenging the patients, but not overburdening them.

By negotiating possible solutions, the therapist also receives information about the state of the therapeutic alliance and the patient's current therapeutic conditions. Design and sequence organization form the structural basis for the coordinated co-construction of intersubjectivity and the affiliative insight into the perspective and attitude of the respective interaction partner. Even in OPD first-interviews, the use of SOQs requires an already established and relatively stable / safe therapeutic alliance and SOQs can in turn reinforce and strengthen this alliance. SOQs are therefore not only an important practice on the content and thematic level, but also a therapeutically effective instrument on the relationship level.

Albeit the specificity of the underlying data, OPD diagnostic interviews, the limitation to patients with depression disorder, and the small data base greatly limit scope and validity of the analyses, the results of the present study are nevertheless informative for psychotherapeutic action. They provide clues as to which SOQs are relationship related regarding the constitution and maintenance of relationship and trust. In this sense, SOQs are to be seen as one particular communicative practice *doing* relationship in contrast of acting *in* relationship (Mandelbaum 2003).

Acknowledgements

We want to thank William Doehler for proofreading the English. Our thanks also go to the anonymous reviewers for their helpful comments on an earlier version.

References

Ardito, Rita, and Daniela Rabellino. 2011. "Therapeutic alliance and outcome of psychotherapy: historical excursus, measurements, and prospects for research." *Frontiers in Psychology* 270: 1–11. https://doi.org/10.3389/fpsyg.2011.00270.

Arundale, Robert B. 2010. "Constituting face in conversation: Face, facework, and interactional achievement." *Journal of Pragmatics* 42(8): 2078–2105. https://doi.org/10.1016/j.pragma.2009.12.021

Bröcher, Leonie. 2017. *Lösungsorientierte Fragen in psychodiagnostischen Gesprächen: Die Funktionen der Testung, impliziter Kritik und Ermittlung tatsächlicher Lösungsmöglichkeiten*. Universität Mannheim: Master Thesis.

Brown, Penelope, and Stephen Levinson. 1987. *Politeness: Some universals in language use*. Cambridge: University Press. https://doi.org/10.1017/CBO9780511813085

Bühler, Karl. 1934. *Sprachtheorie: Die Darstellungsfunktion der Sprache*. Jena: Gustav Fischer.

Bucholtz, Mary, and Kira Hall. 2005. "Identity and interaction: A sociocultural linguistic approach." *Discourse studies* 7(4–5): 585–614. https://doi.org/10.1177/1461445605054407

Clark, Herbert. 1992. *Arenas of Language Use*. Chicago: University of Chicago Press.

Davies, Bronwyn, and Rom Harré. 1990. "Positioning: The discursive production of selves." *Journal for the Theory of Social Behaviour* 20(1): 43–63. https://doi.org/10.1111/j.1468-5914.1990.tb00174.x

Deppermann, Arnulf. 2008. *Gespräche analysieren: Eine Einführung*. Wiesbaden: Verlag für Sozialwissenschaften. https://doi.org/10.1007/978-3-531-91973-7

Deppermann, Arnulf. 2015. "Agency in Erzählungen über Gewalterfahrungen in Kindheit und Jugend." In *Narrative Bewältigung von Trauma und Verlust*, ed. by Carl Eduard Scheidt, Gabriele Lucius-Hoene, Anja Stukenbrock, and Elisabeth Waller, 64–75. Heidelberg: Schattauer.

Ehrenthal, Johannes C., and Cord Benecke. 2019. "Tailored treatment planning for individuals with personality disorders: The OPD approach." In *Case Formulation for Personality Disorders: Tailoring Psychotherapy to the Individual Client*, ed. by Ueli Kramer, 291–314. Cambridge, MA: Elsevier. https://doi.org/10.1016/B978-0-12-813521-1.00015-1

Flückiger, Christoph, Aaron C. Del Re, Bruce E. Wampold, Dianne Symonds, and Adam Horvath. 2012. "How central is the alliance in psychotherapy? A multilevel longitudinal meta-analysis." *Journal of Counseling Psychology* 59(1): 10–17. https://doi.org/10.1037/a0025749

Goffman, Erving. 1977. "The arrangement between the sexes." *Theory and Society* 4: 301–331. https://doi.org/10.1007/BF00206983

Holly, Werner. 2001. "Beziehungsmanagement und Imagearbeit." In *Text- und Gesprächslinguistik. Handbücher zur Sprach- und Kommunikationswissenschaft*, ed. by Klaus Brinker, Gerd Antos, Wolfgang Heinemann, and Sven Sager, 1382–1393. Berlin/New York: de Gruyter. https://doi.org/10.1515/9783110169188.2.19.1382

Horvath, Adam. 2006. "The alliance in context: Accomplishments, challenges, and future directions." *Psychotherapy* 43(3): 258–263. https://doi.org/10.1037/0033-3204.43.3.258

Horvath, Adam, and Leslie Greenberg (eds.). 1994. *The working alliance: Theory, research, and practice*. Oxford: Wiley.

Jakobson, Roman. 1960: "Linguistics and poetics." In: *Style in language*, ed. by Thomas A. Sebeok A., 350-377, Cambridge, Mass.: Institute of Technology Press.

Kabatnik, Susanne, Thomas Spranz-Fogasy, Christoph Nikendei, and Johannes C. Ehrenthal. 2019. "Lösungsorientierte Fragen im psychotherapeutischen Gespräch." In *Pragmatik der Veränderung*, ed. by Eva-Maria Graf, Claudio Scarvaglieri, and Thomas Spranz-Fogasy, 147–175. Tübingen: Narr.

Konerding, Klaus-Peter. 2015. "Heilung durch Sprache und Sprechen: Linguistik und Psychotherapie." In *Handbuch Sprache in der Medizin*, ed. by Albert Busch and Thomas Spranz-Fogasy, 225–242. Berlin: De Gruyter. https://doi.org/10.1515/9783110296174-013

Kook, Jiyeon. 2015. *Agency in Arzt-Patient-Gesprächen*. Bern: Peter Lang. https://doi.org/10.3726/978-3-0351-0837-8

Lambert, Michael J. (ed.). 2013. *Bergin and Garfield's handbook of psychotherapy and behavior change*. 6th ed. New York: Wiley.

Läpple, Sina, Christoph Nikendei, Johannes C. Ehrenthal, and Thomas Spranz-Fogasy. 2021. *Therapeutische Reaktionen auf Patientenwiderstand in psychodiagnostischen Gesprächen – am Beispiel Lösungsorientierter Fragen*. Göttingen: Verlag für Gesprächsforschung.

Lindström, Anna, and Marja-Leena Sorjonen. 2013. "Affiliation in conversation." In *Handbook on Conversation Analysis*, ed. by Jack Sidnell, and Tanya Stivers, 350–369. Chichester: Blackwell.

Linke, Angelika, and Juliane Schröter. 2017. "Sprache in Beziehungen – Beziehungen in Sprache. Überlegungen zur Konstitution eines linguistischen Forschungsfeldes." In *Sprache und Beziehung*, ed. by Angelika Linke, and Juliane Schröter, 1–32. Berlin: de Gruyter. https://doi.org/10.1515/9783110496918-002

Locher, Miriam A., and Richard J. Watts. 2008. "Chapter 4. Relational work and impoliteness: Negotiating norms of linguistic behaviour". In *Impoliteness in Language: Studies on its Interplay with Power in Theory and Practice*, ed. by Derek Bousfield, and Miriam A. Locher, 77–100. Berlin, New York: De Gruyter Mouton.

Mack, Christina, Christoph Nikendei, Johannes C. Ehrenthal, and Thomas Spranz-Fogasy. 2016. "*[...] hab ich glaub ich die richtigen Fragen gestellt: Therapeutische Fragehandlungen in psychodiagnostischen Gesprächen*." Mannheim: IDS.

MacMartin, Clare. 2008. "Resisting optimistic questions in narrative and solution-focused therapies," In *Conversation Analysis and Psychotherapy*, ed. by Anssi Peräkylä, Charles Antaki, Sanna Vehviläinen, and Ivan Leudar, 80–99. Cambridge: Cambridge University Press. https://doi.org/10.1017/CBO9780511490002.006

Mandelbaum, Jenny. 2003. "Interactive methods for constructing relationships." In *Studies in language and social interaction*, ed. by Phillip J. Glenn, Curtis LeBaron, and Jenny Mandelbaum, 207–220. Mahwah, NJ: Lawrence Erlbaum. https://doi.org/10.4324/9781410606969-18

Marciniak, Agnieszka. 2017. *Agency in lösungsorientierten Fragen im psychodiagnostischen Gespräch. Agency-Implikationen und Reaktionen in Wunschfrage-Sequenzen*. Universität Mannheim: Master Thesis.

Marciniak, Agnieszka, Christoph Nikendei, Johannes C. Ehrenthal, and Thomas Spranz-Fogasy. 2016. "... Durch Worte heilen. Linguistik und Psychotherapie." *Sprachreport* 32/3: 1–11.

Muntigl, Peter, and Adam Horvath. 2018. "The alliance as a discursive achievement: a conversation analytical perspective." In *Therapy as Discourse: Practice and Research*, ed. by Olga Smoliak, and Tom Strong, 71–93. Palgrave Macmillan.

Muntigl, Peter, Naomi Knight, and Ashley Watkins. 2012. "Working to keep aligned in psychotherapy: using nods as a dialogic resource to display affiliation." *Language and Dialogue* 2(1): 9–27. https://doi.org/10.1075/ld.2.1.01mun

Muntigl, Peter, and Adam Horvath. 2014. "'I can see some sadness in your eyes': When experiential therapists notice a client's affectual display." *Research on Language and Social Interaction* 47(2): 89–108. https://doi.org/10.1080/08351813.2014.900212

Oelschläger, Eileen. 2017. *Lösungsorientierte Fragen in psychodiagnostischen Gesprächen: Testen, Übertragen der Verantwortung und implizite Kritik*. Universität Mannheim: Master thesis.

OPD Task Force (eds.). 2009. *Operationalized Psychodynamic Diagnosis OPD-2. Manual of Diagnosis and Treatment Planning*. Bern: Hogrefe.

Peräkylä, Anssi. 2019. "Conversation Analysis and Psychotherapy: Identifying Transformative Sequences." *Research on Language and Social Interaction*, 52(3): 257–280. https://doi.org/10.1080/08351813.2019.1631044.

Peräkylä, Anssi, Charles Antaki, Sanna Vehviläinen, and Ivan Leudar (eds.). 2008. *Conversation Analysis and Psychotherapy*. Cambridge: Cambridge University Press. https://doi.org/10.1017/CBO9780511490002

Pomerantz, Anita. 1986. "Extreme case formulations: A way of legitimizing claims." *Human Studies* 9: 219–30. https://doi.org/10.1007/BF00148128

Pomerantz, Anita, and John Heritage. 2013. "Preference." In *The Handbook of Conversation Analysis*, ed. by Jack Sidnell, and Tanya Stivers, 210–228. Chichester: Wiley Blackwell.

Reinicke, Rebecca. 2018. *Emotive und kognitive Verben in lösungsorientierten Fragen in psychodiagnostischen Gesprächen*. Universität Mannheim: Master Thesis.

Ribeiro, Eugenia, Antonio P. Ribeiro, Miguel M. Goncalves, Adam Horvath, and William Stiles. 2013. "How collaboration in therapy becomes therapeutic: the therapeutic collaboration coding system." *Psychology and Psychotherapy* 86(3): 294–314. https://doi.org/10.1111/j.2044-8341.2012.02066.x

Sachse, Rainer. 1999. *Lehrbuch der Gesprächspsychotherapie*. Göttingen: Hogrefe.

Schauenburg Henning, Jennissen Simona, and Cierpka Manfred (eds.). 2020. *Heidelberger Standards zur psychodynamischen Diagnostik nach OPD-2*. Heidelberg: Medizinische Fakultät Heidelberg.

Schwitalla, Johannes. 2010. "Von sich selbst oder dem direkten Adressaten in der 3. Person sprechen." In *Perspektiven auf Kommunikation*, ed. by Werner Kallmeyer, Ewald Reuter, and Jürgen Schopp, 163–184. Berlin: Saxa.

Selting, Margret, et al. 2011. "A System for Transcribing Talk-in-Interaction: GAT 2." Translated by Elisabeth Couper-Kuhlen, and Dagmar Barth-Weingarten. *Gesprächsforschung* 12: 1–51. http://www.gespraechsforschung-ozs.de/heft2011/px-gat2-englisch.pdf.

Sidnell, Jack, and Tanya Stivers (eds.). 2013. *The Handbook of Conversation Analysis*. Chichester: Wiley-Blackwell.

Spranz-Fogasy, Thomas. 2010. „Verstehensdokumentation in der medizinischen Kommunikation: Fragen und Antworten im Arzt-Patient-Gespräch." In Verstehen in professionellen Handlungsfeldern, ed. by Arnulf Deppermann, Ulrich Reitemeier, Reinhold Schmitt, and Thomas Spranz-Fogasy, 27–116, Tübingen: Gunter Narr Verlag.

Spranz-Fogasy, Thomas, Susanne Kabatnik, and Christoph Nikendei. 2018. "Wissenskonstitution durch Lösungsorientierte Fragen in psychodiagnostischen Gesprächen." In *Rhetorik und Medizin*, ed. by Ernest W. B. Hess-Lüttich, 111–133. Berlin: de Gruyter. https://doi.org/10.1515/rhet.2018.007

Spranz-Fogasy, Thomas, Eva-Maria Graf, Johannes C. Ehrenthal, and Christoph Nikendei 2020. "Requesting examples in psychodiagnostic interviews: Therapists' contribution to the sequential co-construction of clients' change." *Communication & Medicine* 16(2): 129–141. https://doi.org/10.1558/cam.34112

Steensig, Jakob. 2019. "Conversation Analysis and Affiliation and Alignment." *The Encyclopedia of Applied Linguistics:* 944–948. https://doi.org/10.1002/9781405198431.wbeal0196.pub2.
Vehviläinen, Sanna. 2008. "Identifying and managing resistance in psychoanalytic interaction," In *Conversation Analysis and Psychotherapy*, ed. by Anssi Peräkylä, Charles Antaki, Sanna Vehviläinen, and Ivan Leudar, 120–138. Cambridge: Cambridge University Press. https://doi.org/10.1017/CBO9780511490002.008
Voutilainen, Liisa, Anssi Peräkylä, and Johanna Ruusuvuori. 2011. "Therapeutic change in interaction: Conversation analysis of a transforming sequence." *Psychotherapy Research* 21(3): 348–365. https://doi.org/10.1080/10503307.2011.573509
Wachtel, Paul. 2011. *Therapeutic Communication, Second Edition: Knowing What to Say When.* New York: Guilford.
Watzlawick, Paul, Janet Beavin, and Don Jackson. 1967. *Pragmatics of Human Communication. A Study of Interactional Patterns, Pathologies, and Paradoxes.* New York.
Weiste, Elina, and Anssi Peräkylä. 2013. "A comparative conversation analytic study of formulations in psychoanalysis and cognitive psychotherapy." *Research on Language and Social Interaction* 46(4): 299–321. https://doi.org/10.1080/08351813.2013.839093
Weiste, Elina, and Anssi Peräkylä. 2015. "Therapeutic Discourse." In *The International Encyclopedia of Language and Social Interaction*, ed. by Karen Tracy, 1–10. Oxford: Wiley-Blackwell. https://doi.org/10.1002/9781118611463.wbielsi102

The role of semi-responsive answers for relationship building in coaching

Oliver Winkler
ZHAW School of Applied Linguistics

This paper discusses the role of semi-responsive answers of clients for relationship building in coaching. Coaching is a process-oriented type of counseling in which a coach and a coachee collaboratively work on solving a particular worklife or daily life related concern of the coachee. The paper aims at identifying and analyzing semi-responsive answers of coachees (second pair part) as reactions to initiating turns of coaches (first pair part). It is hypothesized that semi-responsive answers are of particular relevance for any coaching process as they reveal ambivalences, (inner) conflicts, uncertainties and/or opposition on the client's side which ought to be noticed and appropriately addressed by the coach. A conversation analysis manual was developed in order to systematically identify and analyze the linguistic characteristics of semi-responsiveness in coachee's answers. First, theoretical and methodological aspects regarding a conversation analysis manual to study structures of social interaction are discussed. Second, a code-system to identify semi-responsive answers is demonstrated. Finally, based on the transcribed data, semi-responsive answers are analyzed with respect to how they are addressed by the coaches in third position. The data consists of 21 face-to-face coaching sessions (64 hours) in Swiss and Standard German. The analysis demonstrates that semi-responsive answers are both a valuable source of information and a challenge as they require the coach to maintain a balance between facilitating the process and maintaining a good relationship with the client.

Keywords: semi-responsiveness, coaching relationship, conversation analysis, coding manual

1. Introduction

Relationship building and coaching alliance are key concepts in both the practical and theoretical field of coaching. There is a consensus that relationship has an impact on the effectiveness of coaching (Mannhardt and De Haan 2018). However,

https://doi.org/10.1075/pbns.331.07win

relationship building remains a challenging research subject due to its multifaceted nature (Haan and Gannon 2016). The focus of this study is based on the notion that relationship is a highly dynamic and fluid phenomena, co-constructed in the moment-by-moment-interaction and subject of constant change over the course of a conversation. Hence, to understand the process of relationship building it is necessary to closely focus on the turn-by-turn interaction and the way how interactants respond to each other.

Coaching is a process-oriented type of counseling in which a coach and a coachee collaboratively work on a particular concern brought in by the coachee. In contrast to psychotherapy, coaches do not work on pathological concerns with their coaches. Instead, concerns in coaching often revolve around worklife or daily life topics whereas the role of the coach is to help the coachee to understand the problem and to find and activate the coachee's personal ressources. Coaching is characterized by its collaborative and equal working relationship in which both coach and coachee bring in their expertise. The coachee is expert on his/her life, the coach is the expert on managing the coaching process (Behn-Taran 2014: 20; Migge 2018: 114).

However, the coaching interaction itself is asymmetrical as it is defined by institutional roles, characterized by a "[…] coach being responsible for the process and the client being responsible for the content […]. (Graf 2019: 128). The main tool for a coach to a lead the coachee through the process is to ask questions. The coachee, on the other hand, is invited to answer these questions in a way that feels appropriate to him or her. However, coachee's answers often show different degrees of responsiveness depending on the position and character of the questions (e.g. questions concerning delicate or difficult issues). A common type of answers are semi-responsive answers, characterized by the fact that they, to some degree, evade or not fulfill the expectations in the prior turn.

In this paper it is hypothesized that such semi-responsive answers of clients play a crucial role regarding relationship building and coaching alliance. I argue that semi-responsive answers provide the coach with important information on the client's stance and state of mind as well as the client's attitude towards the ongoing process. Meanwhile, reacting appropriately to semi-responsive answers is challenging as the coach has to move the process forward and simultaneously maintain a good coach-client-relationship.

This paper first gives a brief overview on the concept of responsiveness, how it is conceptualized within the research area of Conversation Analysis (CA) and how the concepts of relationship and responsiveness are connected. I will then go on to describe the CA-grounded manual as a method used to detect semi-responsive answers in coaching. In the remaining part of the paper three excerpts from authentic coachings are closely analyzed focusing specifically on responsiveness and coaching alliance. In the final part some notions on the challenge of analyzing coachee's reaction to semi-responsive answers of clients are discussed.

2. Theory

2.1 Helping conversation

Societal disruption by technical, environmental, political and socio-economic developments increase the need for individual professional help. Consequently, professional coaching – besides other helping formats – is gaining in importance and represents a rapidly growing global market. Previous psychological research established that coaching can be effective (De Meuse, Dai and Lee 2009; Burn and Talati 2017; Jones, et al., 2015; Sonesh et al. 2010; Theeboom, Beersma and van Vianen 2014). However, little is known about the relative importance of specific aspects (interventions, activities) within the coaching process to its overall positive effects.

In recent years, there has been a number of studies using conversation or discourse analysis to examine therapeutic conversation (Peräkylä et al. 2008; Voutilainen and Peräkylä, 2016; Peräkylä 2013; 2019; Scarvaglieri 2013; Voutilainen, Peräkylä and Ruusuvuori 2010), counselling (Nothdurft, Reitemeier and Schröder 1994; Pick 2017; Sarangi 2002; Vehviläinen 1999) and coaching interaction (Deplazes et al. 2018; Graf 2015; 2018; 2019; Graf and Spranz-Fogasy 2018; Winkler 2017). Regarding the field of coaching, the most extensive work to date is the book "The Pragmatics of Executive Coaching" by Graf (2019) in which she establishes a theoretical and methodological framework to study coaching as a discourse type. According to Graf (2019: 3), 'discourse of coaching' "[...] refers first of all to the concrete communicative interaction in which the participants, i.e. coach and client, engage and through which the very action of coaching is constituted."

Given that coaching is constituted through interaction between client and coach it is evident that the interaction process should be a research subject of its own right. In fact, studying interaction is the only way to gain insight into the process itself. Qualitative methods such as discourse analysis or conversation analysis provide concepts and categories which allow for a deeper insight into the 'how' of coaching (Graf 2019: 6). The 'how' refers to interactional practices, actions, patterns, phrases, words as well as non- and paraverbal behavior which all contribute to what coaching is. Thus, using conversation analysis allows to reveal the interactional and transformative process of coaching and its specific linguistic manifestation.

2.2 Conversation analysis and responsiveness

The concept of responsiveness is a research subject in various scientific contexts such as sociology, political sciences, data science, medicine, pedagogy, linguistics and psychology. While the extension and use of the concept varies across disciplines the core denotation of responsiveness is defined as "the quality of reacting quickly and positively" (Oxford Dictionaries). Responsiveness is a key concept within psychological process research where it is often described as 'therapist responsiveness' or 'appropriate responsiveness' (AR). Kramer and Stiles (2015: 278) define the concept of responsiveness as follows:

> However, therapists generally have benign goals, and they act to advance those goals in ways consistent with their theoretical and personal principles. This can be called appropriate responsiveness. So, appropriate responsiveness means doing the right thing. In general, we suggest therapists and clients try to do the right thing at the right time.

The definition of appropriate responsiveness in process research sets a clear focus on the role of the coach and his/her (successful) interventions. This perspective, however, does not coincide with the perspective of CA where the concept of responsiveness is treated as a fundamental principle of any conversation:

> For there to be the possibility of responsiveness – of one participant being able to show that what they are saying and doing is responsive to what another has said and done – one party needs to talk after the other, and, it turns out, they have to talk singly. (Schegloff 2007: 1)

Thus, in Schegloff's view, the concept of responsiveness is directly linked to the fundamental principle of the organization of turn-taking. Although the concept of responsiveness is regarded as fundamental, it is not explicitly used as a category to analyze talk-in-interaction. Schegloff, for instance, uses the term 'nextness' to describe the connection between turns: "Next turns are understood by co-participants to display their speaker's understanding of the just-prior turn and to embody an action responsive to the just-prior turn so understood [...]" (Schegloff 2007: 15). On a phenomenological level this principle is constituted through 'adjacency pairs'. A first pair part (FPP) of an adjacency pair displays the understanding of the prior turn and opens a position to be filled by a second pair part (SPP). In CA this interdependence between FPP and SPP in adjacency pairs is referred to as "conditional relevance" (Schegloff 2007: 19).

2.3 Semi-responsive answers in coaching

While Schegloff treats responsiveness from a rather formal perspective, the German CA researcher Johannes Schwitalla (1979) is the first to examine responsiveness in SPP with respect to formal and functional aspects (see also Brinker and Sager 2010; Deppermann 2008; Henne and Rehbock 2001; Mroczynski 2014). Schwitalla observes that evasive answers as a type of reacting to initiating turns often occur in natural conversation. To demonstrate how evasive answers are constructed he takes samples from talk-shows and public interviews with politicians. Schwitalla suggests that these answers reveal an underlying basic dialogical rule which he calls the "Annahme der inneren Verbundenheit der Sprecherbeiträge" [the rule of the inner connections of turns] (Schwitalla 1979: 195). From there, he goes on to define three degrees of responsiveness in second position:

> An answer is fully and entirely responsive if it addresses the topic and fulfils one of the intentions expected from the initiating turn. It is semi-responsive if it only addresses one of the levels, and non-responsive if it ignores both levels.
> (Schwitalla 1979: 200, translated OW)

I argue that Schwitalla's distinction of responsiveness is relevant with regard to coaching interaction, too, and I hypothesize that semi-responsive answers are of particular relevance for any coaching process as they reveal ambivalences, (inner) conflicts, uncertainties and/or opposition on the client's side which ought to be noticed by the coach. I assume that, as a coach, being able to perceive and react appropriately to semi-responsive answers ultimately increases the chance of maintaining a good coach-client-relationship and reaching a positive process outcome.

2.4 Third position actions and the coach-client-relationship

Basic principles of sequence organization are used to study processes of therapeutical interaction (Peräkylä 2019; Voutilainen, Peräkylä and Ruusuvuroi 2010; Weiste amd Peräkylä 2013). Based on existing studies Peräkylä (2019: 261) suggests a three-turn structure as a basic model which consists of a first position ("Prior Action", "Target Action"), a second position ("Response") and a "third position action". According to Peräkylä (2019: 261) such a model helps "[...] to depict the existing research on psychotherapy interaction, and to serve as a heuristic aid, helping researcher to identify sequential relations in their psychotherapeutic data." Thus, there seems to be a consensus in CA that three-turn-models are helpful to examine interaction and patterns of transformation in therapeutic as well as other settings (e.g. conflict talk). However, regarding the study of responsiveness it turns out to be complicated: If responsiveness is directly related to the principle of conditional relevance, then, responsiveness in second position and responsiveness in third position do not share the same characteristics. In coaching (and other therapeutic settings), normally the SPP is represented by the answer of a client as a reaction to an FPP of the coach. Thus, responsiveness in a SPP refers to how a client responds to what has been made relevant in the FPP. The third position action (TPA), however, is conducted by the coach as a "response to the response" (Peräkylä 2019: 262). The interdependency between TPA and SPP is different to adjacency pairs (FPP-SPP) as there is no conditional relevance between TPA and SPP. This poses a serious problem for CA research in terms of defining responsiveness in third position and, consequently, analyzing responsiveness in third position. Nevertheless, third position actions of the coach as reactions to semi-responsive answers of a client seem to be particularly relevant with respect to coaching alliance and relationship building (see also Graf and Jautz in this volume). Once the coach has identified a semi-responsive response (e.g. evasion, hesitation, rejection), he/she must decide on whether to respond to the semi-responsiveness or to ignore it. In either way the challenge of the coach is to hold a balance between enhancing the process on the one hand (e.g. by insisting on an initial question instead of going along with the client) and maintaining the coach-client-relationship on the other hand.

2.5 Research question

As previously outlined, semi-responsive answers are particularly important regarding relationship building and process management. Thus, they represent 'trainable moments' in talk and deserve a special focus in coaching training.

In this paper, I argue that a profound understanding of responsiveness in second position is necessary in order to gain a better understanding of third position actions. Therefore, the study is designed to give a special focus to the degree of responsiveness in client answers in second position. A conversation analytic coding manual is used to identify and analyze semi-responsive answers in coaching. The application of a CA-manual to a large collection of coaching conversations provides insight into the specific characteristics of semi-responsive answers of the client. Moreover, the CA-manual is designed to be used as a tool in coaching training and other educational settings.[1]

1. The CA-manual is currently used for coaching training in the MA Applied Psychology at the Zurich University of Applied Sciences.

3. Method

3.1 CA-grounded manual

Most of CA research is committed to qualitative approaches as the focus lies on exploring structures and principles of social interaction and interactional practices in different contexts. However, in the last years there is a shift towards new approaches such as formal coding, mixed methods studies or even quantitative studies (Stivers 2015). In her article, Stivers raises the question "[…] whether or not it is possible to do formal coding in a manner that is […] true to CA principles and thus to the structural organization of social interaction." (Stivers 2015: 9) She argues "[…] that a CA-grounded formal coding approach can be done." (Stivers 2015: 10) However, Stivers points out some aspects of formal coding which seem problematic with respect to analyzing talk-in-interaction and social practices. One reason why formal coding is a disputed method within the CA research community is its reductionistic character. CA researchers criticize that formal coding is neither sensitive to the linguistic complexity of interactional practices nor to their specific position in the interaction. However, Stiver argues that formal coding in CA is possible if the coding is true to certain principles of CA:

> Specifically, formal coding can be done in a way that (a) the behaviors of interest are audio/video recorded, (b) is grounded in the analysis of social interaction more generally and in analyses of behaviors as practices in their own right, and (c) takes into account both composition and position. (Stivers 2015: 10)

These principles set out by Stivers have been taken into consideration when developing a CA-manual to code semi-responsiveness in coaching.

3.2 Sample

The manual draws upon an empirical basis consisting of two data sets with real face-to-face coaching. The first data set comprises 10 face-to-face coaching processes, consisting of approximately 20h of face-to-face-coaching. All coachings were carried out at the IAP Institute of Applied Psychology at ZHAW Zurich University of Applied Sciences. The IAP provides study programs in the sector of continuing education as well as consulting and coaching services for private persons, institutions and companies. All coaches are employees at ZHAW/IAP and senior practitioners with 5–20 years of coaching/counselling experience. All clients are private persons who receive coaching due to various psychological concerns (e.g. fear of driving a car, problems with self-esteem, conflicts at the workplace etc.). The second data set consists of 11 face-to-face career coaching processes of which each process contains 2 sessions with appr. 2 hours of coaching, resulting in a total amount of 44 hours of coaching. All coaches are employees at ZHAW/IAP and senior practitioners with 5–20 years of coaching/counselling experience. Here, the client group consists of both adults and teenagers. All participants (coaches and coachees) gave a written informed consent. They were given the possibility to withdraw their participation at any point during the study. The names of all participants in the transcripts are anonymized.

The language use in the coachings varies between German and Swiss German dialects. Coaches with a German origin speak standard German or German dialect whereas all coachees (except one) speak Swiss German dialect. All video-material is transcribed in reference to the GAT-system (Selting et al. 2009).

3.3 Developing categories (Codes)

The process of developing a CA-grounded coding manual started with a systematic examination of the transcribed material of both data sets regarding semi-responsive answers by clients (SPP) to initiating turns by coaches (FPP). Schwitalla's (1979) rough definition of semi-responsive answers (see paragraph 1) is the theoretical basis to identify semi-responsive answers in the transcribed data. The result of this first coding cycle is a data collection containing a large number of sequences with initiating turns of coaches and semi-responsive answers of clients. The second cycle revolved around distinguishing different categories (codes) of semi-responsiveness based on the analyzed material in the first cycle. An iterative process of recurring and intertwining cycles of data analysis based on data sets ultimately resulted in a coding manual. All codes of the coding system were discussed with and examined by two conversation analysts.[2] In order to further test both intercoder agreement and practicability of the manual the whole dataset was coded by two Psychology students who received a special training on using the CA-grounded manual. Hereafter, some minor final adjustments to the manual were done.

The coding system consists of 3 main categories (Codes: *topic*, *intention*, *linguistic markers*) and respective sub-categories to identify semi-responsiveness in clients' SPP. The categories *intention* and *topic* refer to Schwitalla's (1979) original definition. The category *linguistic markers* encompasses specific linguistic features indicating semi-responsive answers which were identified in the preceding coding cycles.

2. Special thanks to Jevi Sulejmani

Table 1 provides an overview of the codes and illustrates each code with an excerpt from the data set.

Table 1. Coding system

Code	Code description	Excerpts
Topic		
topic shift	*The key topic in the first pair part (FPP) is no longer included in the second pair part (SPP). It is either fully ignored, replaced or transferred into another topic.*	CO: spielt da so diese ANGST auch mit rein? *CO: Does also fear come into play?* CL: aso wenn mir für üsi wert nüme istönd (.) dänn ischs scho passiert *CL: well if we don't stand up for our values (.) then it's over*
topic expansion	*Shift from a concrete topic to a generalization of the initial topic OR adding new topics to the original topic.*	CO: was sind das so für personen die die du im team hast? *CO: What kind of people are in your team?* CL: das ist jetzt eben spannend also (.) geplant war das eigentlich als sone art (.) ich sags jetzt mal provokativ sone elite team (.) also die die wirklich sehr sehr gut sind (.)und sich über monate und jahre wirklich auch bewiesen haben und bewährt haben (.) die sollen in das team kommen (.) jetzt ist KLAR, (.) wenn du son team startest (.) hab ich auch politische constrains das heisst ich muss auch politische personen mitnehmen die schon lange da in dem ähnlichen Bereich arbeiten (.) hab auch personen reingenommen die mir quasi (.) ans herz gelegt worden sind durch mein chef aufgrund von hintergründen (.) die ich langsam versteh (.) momentan sinds also quasi drei personen und ich. *CL: It's interesting well (.) the plan was to put together a kind of (.) provocatively speaking elite team (.) people who are really good (.)who have proven themselves over the past months and years (.) they shall be part of the team (.) of course (.) if you start a team (.) I also have political constraints which means I have to take political persons who were recommended by my boss due to backgrounds which I start to understand (.) right now there are about three persons and myself.*

(continued)

Table 1. (*continued*)

Code	Code description	Excerpts
topic narrowing	*Shift from a generalized topic to a concrete level of the initial topic (i.e. a specific situation or incident)*	CO: isch vilicht au so chli d sinnfrog vilich do? *CO: is it perhaps also the search of meaning perhaps?* CL: für mich isch es käs für was oder so (.) ich ha det (.) aso ich cha alles bruche (.) es goht nur um de grad (.) aso bim für was. *CL: for me it's not about the why (.) I have it (.) I can use it all (.) it is only about the degree (.) when I ask why*
Intention	*Fully or partially ignoring a question, dispreferred answers (e.g. refusal to a request)*	CO: was wür der da gfalle? CL: (10.9) CO: isch ja so usem buch use häsch_s ag[striche] oder. *CO: What would you like to do?* *CL: (10.9)* *CO: you marked it in the book, didn't you?*
Linguistic markers		
perspectivation	*Shift of deictic reference ((e.g. "you" (FPP) → "they" (SPP))*	CO: fühle si sich da au e chli usgnützt? *CO: do you feel exploited* CL: es hät öpis öpis mit usnütze z tue (.) find ich (.) und das und so gahts au vilne andere (.) es hätt öpis mit usnütze z tue und das isch dä teil wo me sehr vil mues investiere °h zum de: eifach de JOB mache (.) und dass das niemert intressiert *CL: it has something to do with exploiting someone(.) I think (.) and many others feel alike (.) it has to do with exploiting someone and it is this part where one has to invest a lot °h to do the job (.) and that that no one cares*
modality	*Expressions, sentences with mitigating functions (hedgings, subjunctives, hesitation markers, long pauses)*	CO: ähm wann findet das statt [das Auftreten des mangelnden Selbstvertrauens] (.) gibts spezielle situatione weisch wo du sagsch hey (.) besonders da oder? *CO: ehm when does it take place [the lack of confidence] (.) are there any special occasions so that you can say(.) right here* CL: mm:? ((2,2s)) jo aso ((2,1s)) es isch scho meischtens wenns sich d stress situation so zuespitzt = aso ich mach no bruefsmatur momentan ja und ähm ((0,7s)) ich mue h allne bereich irgendwie (.) hundert prozent geh und °h ((1,2s)) und ähm: denn sind wider prüefige: ((1,2s)) buechhaltig also es sind halt ganz vil chlini sach wo °h im einzelne kei problem wär aber wenn halt alles zäme chunt °h ähm ((1,1s)).

Table 1. *(continued)*

Code	Code description	Excerpts
		CL: *mm:? ((2,2s)) well ((2,1s)) often it occurs when a stressful situation becomes critical =well I am currently studying yes and ehm ((0.7s)) I have to give my best everywhere and °h (1,2s)) and ehm then there are exams ((1,2s)) bookkeeping so there are many small things which wouldn't be a problem but if they all appear together h° ehm ((1.1s)).*
tense	*Shift of tense ((e.g. present (FPP) → past tense (SPP))*	CO: was können sie ihrer frau in einem solchen moMENT sagen (.) also in einem moment wo sie sagt wir haben das ja schon beSPROCHEN CO: *what can you say to your wife in such a moment (.) so in a moment where she says we have already talked about it* CL: ja ich hab ihr dann gesagt es WAR für mich nicht so klar ich wollte das dann eben noch MAL besprechen CL: *Well I had told her that it wasn't clear to me and that I wanted to talk about it again*

3.4 Applying the codes

The first step of applying the codes is to import the coding system into the software-tool MAXQDA. The software allows for systematically analyzing, coding and visualizing data. Based on the coding-system illustrated in Table 1, each sequence (FPP/SPP) of a coaching process is to be assigned to one of the following binary codes:

a. FPP (Coach), SPP (Client): responsive
b. FPP (Coach), SPP (Client): semi-responsive
c. FPP (Client), SPP (Coach): responsive
d. FPP (Client), SPP (Coach): semi-responsive

In order to follow the basic principles of Conversation Analysis it is crucial to consider the interactional context of each single turn. Coding a SPP as responsive or semi-responsive on the basis of the coding system can only be done by simultaneously analyzing the design of the preceding FPP. For instance, whether there is a topic shift in the SPP can only be determined by examining the topical structure of the corresponding FPP. In this respect, it is also important to note that the criterias developed to identify semi-responsiveness are not mutually exclusive. One and the same string of text can be coded with several codes from the categories defined in the manual (Table 1).

4. Results

In the theoretical chapter I have argued that semi-responsive answers are crucial moments in talk as they provide immediate feedback on how an intervention is received by the client as well as where the client sees herself/himself in the ongoing process. When a semi-responsive answer occurs, a coach has to decide whether and how to react to it. The decision of when and how to respond to a semi-responsive answer is crucial because it can be beneficial for the coaching relationship as well as harming it when done at the wrong time or in the wrong way. Thus, third positions (as reactions to semi-responsive answers) are complex practices as they imply for a coach to both be able to identify and 'analyze' the semi-responsive characteristics of the answer and to adequately respond to it at the right place within the process.

Given the applied character of the approach and the intention to use the manual in coaching training and education I develop a framework for feedback. The focus of the framework is to provide an overview of where semi-responsive answers occur and where and how the coach reacts to it. This framework combines a macro-analytical with a meso- and micro-analytical perspective. With respect to the macro-analytical element the coding of the complete coaching process can be depicted graphically by using a codeline (Figure 1) which is presented to the coach in a feedback session.

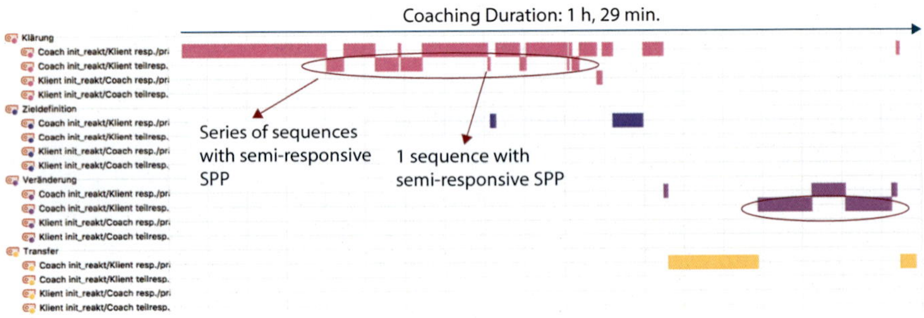

Figure 1. Codeline of a coaching session

The codeline visualizes the coding over the course of coaching. The bars represent the series of two-part-sequences. The red-circled bars show sequences (or series of two-part-sequences) containing semi-responsive answers of the client. The different colors of the bars represent five different phases of the coaching process (Deplazes, Graf and Künzli 2018). The codeline provides an overview of how often and where within the course of coaching responsive and semi-responsive answers occur. Figure 1 shows that semi-responsive answers occur both within the phase of clarification (pink) as well as within the phase of developing change (purple) while the phase of goal definition (blue) and transfer only contain responsive answers of the client. While the macro-analytical perspective of phase is not part of the coding manual as such, it is used as a heuristic tool to give feedback to the coach and to provide him/her with an overview over where – within the course of coaching – semi-responsive answers occur.

The second element of the feedback is to 'zoom in' on a meso- and micro analytic level in order to analyze and discuss, together with the coach, the semi-responsive answers as well as the coachee's reaction to it.

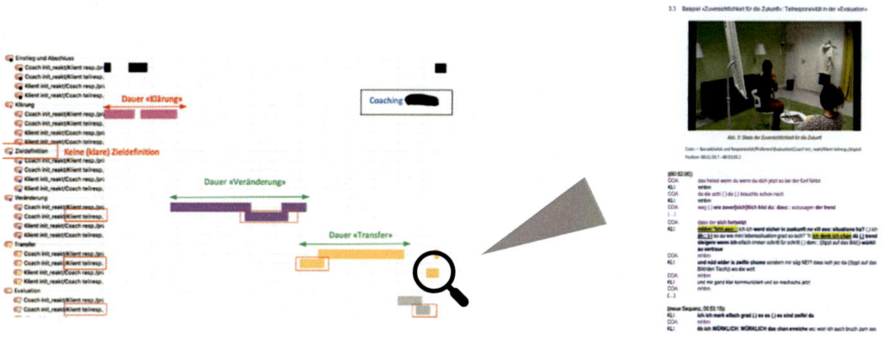

Figure 2. Zooming in on the sequences

To illustrate this process of analysis and feedback, three excerpts from different coaching dyads shall be discussed regarding the construction of semi-responsive SPP and coaches' reaction in third position.

(1)

```
1  CO:  und dann hast du gesagt so jetzt ist es
2       pas[SIE]RT,
        and then you said WELL (.) now it
        hap[pened]
3  CL:     [jo]
           [yep]
4  CO:  und wie hast du dich dann geFÜHLT in dem moment;
        and how did you FEEL at this moment;
5  CL:  jo ich glaub do fühlt sich <<lachend> NIE[mand]
6       hervorragend oder;>
        well i think in such a case <<laughing>
        NO[one] feels good do they>
7  CO:                  [mhm]
                        [mhm]
8  CO:  und wie hast DU dich gefühlt;
        and how did YOU feel at this moment;
```

In the sequence prior to the excerpt, coach and client talk about a certain situation at work in which the client had insulted one of his employees. In line 1–2 the coach rephrases the client's 'inner voice' and then asks the client how he felt in this situation (line 4). The client reacts with a semi-responsive answer. He does not fulfill the expectations expressed in the FPP as he is not answering the question (*intention*). Furthermore, semi-responsiveness is indicated by the change of perspectivation and tense between line 4 and 5 (*you* → *no one*; *did you feel* → *feels*) as well as by hesitation markers (*well I think*) and laughter. In the TPA (line 8) the coach reacts to the semi-responsive answer by conducting a repair turn in which he stresses the pronoun *you*. By doing so he both clarifies and insists on the initial meaning of the FPP.

(2)

1 CO: [weiss] weiss ihre frau dass sie das mittlerweile (.) schon anders sehen?
[does] does your wife realize that you already see it differently?
2 CL: ja: ich weiss (xxx) - es ist jetzt auch schon wieder so (.) das mit diesen bildern
3 dass ist wälzen wir jetzt auch schon zwei drei jahre mit uns rum °hh das hat
4 wahrscheinlich auch schon wieder so ne eigene (-)verfahrene (-) dynamik
5 [erhalten]
well: i know (xxx) - it's like (.) about these pictures we have been carrying around this for
two or three years °hh it turned into a (-) insoluble (-) thing of its own
6 CO: [mhm]
7 CL: aso man könnte es wahrscheinlich (-) versuchen wiedermal (-) völlig
8 vorbehaltlos zu thematisieren und dann nochmal an die sache ranzugehen
Well, maybe one could (-) try again (-) to discuss it without reservation and then tackle it again
9 CO: mhm
10 meine (.) meine frage ist (.) [denken sie] dass ihre frau
My (.) my question is (.) [do you think] that your wife
11 CL: [(xxx) ja]
[(xxx) yes]
12 CO: von IHRER veränderung (.) schon etwas hat wahrnehmen können
has already noticed something about your change

In Excerpt (2), coach and client talk about a conflict between the client and his wife which revolves around the organization of family parties. In sequences prior to this excerpt, the client has mentioned that he recently had become more sympathetic towards his wife's point of view. The coach follows up on this and asks the client in line 1 about the wife's perception of his change. In line 2, the answer of the client shows characteristics of semi-responsiveness in all 3 categories. The coach talks about the wife's perception of change (line 1) while the client takes up the conflict as a general problem and suggests a possible solution (line 2) (*topic expansion*). The client does not answer the question, thus does not fulfill the potential expectation in line 1 (*intention*). Moreover, there is a shift of perspectivation between line 1 and 2 (*your wife* → *we*) as well as features of modality (*maybe, could, well, I know*). Like in Example (1), the coach reacts to the semi-responsive answer with insisting on her initial question in the FPP.

(3)

```
 1 CO:   (.) CH:Önn:t jetz aso i bi jetz wirklich (.) [xxx]
 2       wenn ich so dr I:Druck e <<stotternd> so> au assoziatione ha-
 3       =chönnt (.) e TEIL vo dere tru:r au (.) si: (1.5)- dass (.) si
         sich au-
         (.) Could it well I am really [xxx]
         I have the impression <<stammering>well> also an association-
         = could (.) it be that (1.5) part of this sorrow that (.) you
 4 CL:   ((schnieft))
         ((sniffling))
 5 CO:   dass si sich wie en art d erLÄUBnis gän, dass si sich
 6       U:Snütze lön?
         that you allow yourself to be exploited?
 7 CL:   (3.8) ja: aso VIli händ mir gseit ich söll das planspi:il doch
         ei:fach verweigere.
 8       (aber) ich bi UNsicher gsi ob das guet isch-
 9       (2.0) ich ha irgendwie: (-) me hät: mich scho LANG gfragt,
10       =aber schi:nbar hätt me denn au ANDeri grfagt, aber die händ
         das alli NÖD
         welle,
         (3.8) well many people told me to refuse to develop the
         business game
         (but) I was not sure if that is ok-
         (2.0) somehow I have (-) a long time ago they've asked me to do it
         and apparently they've also asked other peopie, but no one
         wanted to do it
11 CO:   mhm
12 CL:   und ich ha SCHO mol eisgschribe.
         And i have already written one
13 CO:   WOW-
```

In Excerpt (3), the client talks about her current situation at work. The employer requires her to attend a training in order to continue working on the same tasks. In sequences prior to this excerpt, the client has started to cry. In the FPP (line 1–3) the coach initiates the topic *sorrow* and asks the client whether she thinks that there is a connection between her feelings of sorrow and the fact of allowing oneself to be abused by others. What follows in SPP is a semi-responsive answer of the client in which she moves the topical focus away from the personal and emotional topic of sorrow to a description of specific circumstances regarding a special working task (line 7–10). Further elements indicating semi-responsiveness is the change of perspectivation (*many people, they*) as well as the pause in the beginning of the SPP (line 7). Unlike the reactions of the coach in Excerpt (1) and (2), the coach in Excerpt (3) does not insist on her initial question but reacts with an affiliative turn in line 13.

In all three excerpts the questions of the coaches focus on topics regarding the client's feelings or personal attitudes, questions which potentially put the client in discomfort as they invite the client to open up on him/herself. The semi-responsive answers analyzed above are similar in the way that the client shifts the focus away from the personal aspects (feelings, attitudes) which becomes visible in the linguistic analysis. In the following chapter I will address the problem of the third position and discuss the role of relationship building in the coach's reactions to the semi-responsive answers of the clients.

5. Discussion

The analysis of the three excerpts illustrates different ways of how semi-responsive answers are addressed by the coach in third position (TPA). In Excerpt (1) the coach decides to repeat his original question from the FPP in third position. However, FPP and TPA are not identical as the coach modulates the initial question para-linguistically by stressing the personal pronoun *DU* (*you*) (Excerpt (1), line 8). Thus, the coach realizes and localizes the semi-responsive elements in SPP and decides to 'oppose' the client by insisting on his initial question. However, by modulating just a single word of the initial turn the coach insists in both an efficient as well as sensitive way.

The reaction of the coach to the semi-responsive SPP in Excerpt (2) is similar to the reaction in Excerpt (1), as the coach repeats her initial question in TPA. However, the coach decides to conduct a repairing turn consisting of a meta-communicative insertion and a rephrasing of the initial turn (Excerpt (2), lines 10–12). By explicitly initiating a repair through repeating the question of the FPP, the coach in Excerpt (2) acts in a slightly more directive manner than the coach in Excerpt (1). Unlike Excerpt (1) and (2), the coach in Excerpt (3) does not insist on her initial questions and, thus, does not refer to the semi-responsiveness of the client's answer. Instead, the coach 'goes along' and supports the coach with an affiliative action (*wow*) (Excerpt (3), line 13). What can be observed in the three excerpts is that third positions following semi-responsive answers play a crucial role with respect to relationship building as they are sort of a crossroad where it is up to the coach to decide whether to intervene in a directive manner or not. Here, the challenge is to maintain a balance between facilitating the process and maintaining the relationship with the client. What, in the excerpts above, is being described as two options of addressing semi-responsive answers (repair/insisting, Excerpt (1) and (2) vs. 'go along with the client, Excerpt (3)) can be related with the psychological concepts of pacing and leading. While the coach in Excerpts (1) and (2) decide to 'confront' the client, the coach decides not to do so in Excerpt (3) as it might not be beneficial for the relationship at this specific moment, given the emotional state of the client.

However, this brings us back to the problem of responsiveness in third position (paragraph 1). From a practical point of view all three third position actions can be regarded as responsive as coaches appear to be sensitive towards the specific moment of the process and the client-coach-relationship. However, from a research point of view there is a theoretical gap as it remains unclear what responsiveness in third position exactly means and on what basis it is to be defined and systematically analyzed.

6. Conclusions

In the reflections above, I presented a framework to identify semi-responsive answers of clients in second pair part and, based on three excerpts from the data set, analyzed in detail how semi-responsive answers are constructed and addressed by coaches in third position. The analysis showed that semi-responsive answers are both a valuable source of information and a challenge as they require the coach to find a solution of moving the process forward efficiently and maintaining a good coach-client-relationship.

By identifying semi-responsive answers through a conversation analysis manual, my research contributes to a deeper micro-analytical understanding of coaching interactions. I demonstrate that a better understanding of the communicative shape of the client's answers, especially semi-responsive answers, is crucial for a coach to react appropriately and efficiently. I find that CA-grounded coding allows for an exhaustive analysis of semi-responsive answers in coaching sessions. Using a QDA-tool helps to quantify and visualize conversational data and increases the accessibility of CA results for students and professionals. However, the CA-manual presented in this study also comes with limitations. First, the coding itself is still ambivalent and blurred to a certain extent as there is no crystal-clear boundary regarding when to choose a code. To optimize the coding process statistical test to measure intercoder reliability are to be performed. Second, the CA-manual cannot be used to solve the responsiveness problem as it does not describe or even predict what to do in third position following a semi-responsive answer. Third position actions are expected to vary considerably due to different theoretical backgrounds, experiences, styles, attitudes of the coaches and, as demonstrated in the analysis, the specific features of the coach-client-relationship. Therefore, third position actions in coaching as a subject of systematic study is suggested to be worked on by promoting an interdisciplinary and multi-perspective[3] approach, combining conversation analysis and psychological approaches. The starting point is to conduct a profound CA analysis of third position actions based on a large corpus of coaching conversation and to extract interactional patterns. Hereafter, the linguistic manifestations of third position actions could be compared with results from psychological process research (e.g. process factor analysis), which eventually would allow for building clusters of third position actions. Such cluster could give insight into the relation between theories of psychological interventions and linguistic practices. Whether such an approach allowed for making a step beyond a mere phenomenological description towards a prediction of appropriate third position actions in respondence to semi-responsive answers remains unclear. However, the results in the present study suggest that a systematic analysis of third position actions would allow for deeper insights into the mechanisms of process management at the meso and micro levels of interaction and thus provide with valuable insights for coaching education.

References

Behn-Taran, Angelika. 2014. *"I am my own worst enemy." A linguistic analysis of interactive dynamics of relational patterns in business coaching conversations.* https://edoc.ub.uni-muenchen.de/18299/1/Behn-Taran_Angelika.pdf.

Brinker, Karl, and Sven Frederik Sager. 2010. *Linguistische Gesprächsanalyse. Eine Einführung.* Berlin: Schmidt.

Burt, Daniel, and Zenobia Talati. 2017. "The unsolved value of executive coaching: A meta-analyses of outcome using randomized control trial studies." *International Journal of Evidence Based Coaching and Mentoring* 15 (2): 17–24.

De Haan, Erik, and Judie Gannon. 2016. "The Coaching Relationship." In *The SAGE Handbook of Coaching*, ed. by. Tatiana Bachkirova, Gordon Spence, and David Drake, 195–216. London: SAGE Publications Ltd, doi.org/10.4135/9781473983861.n11

De Meuse, Kenneth P., Dai, Guangrong, and Robert J. Lee. 2009. "Evaluating the effectiveness of executive coaching: beyond ROI?" *Coaching*, 2(2): 117–134.

Deplazes, Silvia, Eva-Maria Graf, and Hansjörg Künzli. 2018. "Das TSPP-Modell – Eine Blaupause für die Coaching-Prozessforschung." *Coaching | Theorie & Praxis* 4: 69–82. https://doi.org/10.1365/s40896-018-0025-0.

Deppermann, Arnulf. 2008. *Gespräche analysieren. Eine Einführung* (4. Aufl.). Wiesbaden: VS. https://doi.org/10.1007/978-3-531-91973-7

3. The framework presented in this paper is part of the interdisciplinary project with the title "Entwicklung eines Mehr-Ebenen-Responsivitäts-Modells auf der Basis der Wirkfaktorenanalyse und der Konversationsanalyse (Developing a multi-layer-responsiveness-model based on process factor analysis and conversation analysis)", at the ZHAW School of Applied Linguistic and the ZHAW School of Applied Psychology.

Graf, Eva-Maria. 2015. "Kommunikative Basisaktivitäten im Coaching-Gespräch: Ein linguistischer Beitrag zur Coaching-Prozessforschung." *Coaching | Theorie & Praxis* 1: 5–14. https://doi.org/10.1365/s40896-015-0001-x

Graf, Eva-Maria. 2018. "Äußerung für Äußerung zum Coaching-Prozess: Das Potential einer gesprächsanalytisch fundierten Coaching-Prozessforschung." In *Coaching-Prozessforschung. Forschung und Praxis im Dialog*, ed. by Robert Wegener, Michael Loebbert, Agnes Fritze, and Marianne Hänseler, 141–161. Göttingen: Vandenhoeck & Ruprecht. https://doi.org/10.13109/9783666402920.137

Graf, Eva-Maria, and Thomas Spranz-Fogasy. 2018. "Welche Frage, wann und warum? – Eine qualitativ-linguistische Programmatik zur Erforschung von Frage-Sequenzen als zentrale Veränderungspraktik im Coaching." *Coaching | Theorie & Praxis* 4: 17–32. https://doi.org/10.1365/s40896-018-0021-4.

Graf, Eva-Maria. 2019. *The Pragmatics of Executive Coaching*. Amsterdam/Philadelphia: John Benjamins. https://doi.org/10.1075/pbns.303

Henne, Helmut, and Helmut Rehbock. 2001. *Einführung in die Gesprächsanalyse*. Berlin: De Gruyter. https://doi.org/10.1515/9783110906189

Jones, Rebecca J., Stephen A. Woods, and Yves R. F. Guillaume. 2015. "The effectiveness of workplace coaching: a meta analysis of learning and performance outcomes from coaching." *Journal of Occupational and Organizational Psychology* 89: 249–277. https://doi.org/10.1111/joop.12119.

Kramer, Ueli, and Williams Stiles 2015. "The Responsiveness Problem in Psychotherapy: A Review of Proposed Solutions." *Clincal Psychology Science and Practice* 22(3): 277–295. https://doi.org/10.1111/cpsp.12107.

Mannhardt, Sonja, and Erik De Haan. 2018. "Coaching-Beziehung". In *Handbuch Schlüsselkonzepte im Coaching*, ed. by. Siegfried Greif, Heidi Möller, and Wolfgang Scholl, 85–94. Berlin: Springer. https://doi.org/10.1007/978-3-662-49483-7_6

Migge, B. 2018. *Handbuch Coaching und Beratung*. Weinheim: Beltz.

Mroczynski, Robert. 2014. *Gesprächslinguistik. Eine Einführung*. Tübingen: Narr.

Nothdurft, Werner, Ulrich Reitmeier, and Peter Schröder. 1994. *Beratungsgespräche. Analyse asymmetrischer Dialoge*. Tübingen: Narr.

Oxford Dictionaries. 2022. "Responsiveness." https://premium.oxforddictionaries.com/definition/english/responsiveness

Peräkylä, Anssi, Charles Antaki, Sanna Vehviläinen, and Ivan Leudar (eds). 2008. *Conversation Analysis of Psychotherapy*. Cambridge: Cambridge University Press. https://doi.org/10.1017/CBO9780511490002

Peräkylä, Anssi. 2013. "Conversation Analysis in Psychotherapy." In *The Handbook of Conversation Analysis*, ed. by. Jack Sidnell, and Tanya Stivers, 551–574. Hoboken, NJ: Wiley-Blackwell Publishing.

Peräkylä, Anssi. 2019. "Conversation Analysis and Psychotherapy: Identifying transformative sequences." *Research on Language and Social Interaction* 52:3: 257–280, https://doi.org/10.1080/08351813.2019.1631044.

Pick, Ina (ed.). 2017. *Beraten in Interaktion. Eine gesprächslinguistische Typologie des Beratens*. Frankfurt am M.: Lang.

Sarangi, Srikant. 2002. "The Language of Likelihood in Genetic Counselling Discourse." *Journal for Language and Social Psychology* 21(1): 7–31. https://doi.org/10.1177/0261927X02021001002.

Scarvaglieri, Claudio. 2013. "*Nichts anderes als ein Austausch von Worten. Sprachliches Handeln in der Psychotherapie*." Berlin/Bosten: de Gruyter. https://doi.org/10.1515/9783110319033

Schegloff, Emanuel. 2007. *Sequence Organization in Interaction. A Primer in Conversation Analysis*. Cambridge: Cambridge University Press. https://doi.org/10.1017/CBO9780511791208

Selting, Margret et al. 2009. "Gesprächsanalytisches Transkriptionssystem 2 (GAT 2)." *Gesprächsforschung – Online-Zeitschrift zur verbalen Interaktion* 10: 353–402.

Schwitalla, Johannes (1979). "Nonresponsive Antworten." *Deutsche Sprache, Zeitschrift für Theorie*, Praxis, Dokumentation. 7. Jahrgang. 193–211.

Sonesh, Shirley C., Chris W. Coultas, Christina N. Lacerenza, Shannon L. Marlow, Lauren E. Benishek, and Eduardo Salas. 2015. "The power of coaching: a meta-analytic investigation." *Coaching* 8(2): 73–95. https://doi.org/10.1080/17521882.2015.1071418

Stivers, Tanja. 2015. "Coding Social Interaction: A Heretical Approach in Conversation Analysis?" *Research on Language and Social Interaction* 48:1: 1–19. https://doi.org/10.1080/08351813.2015.993837

Theeboom, Tim, Bianca Beersma, and Annelies van Vianen. 2014. "Does coaching work? A meta-analysis on the effects of coaching on individual level outcomes in an organizational context." *The Journal of Positive Psychology* 9(1): 1–18. https://doi.org/10.1080/17439760.2013.837499

Vehviläinen, Sanna. 1999. *Structures of Counselling Interaction. A Conversation Analytic Study of Counselling Encounters in Career Guidance Training*. Helsinki: University of Helsinki.

Voutilainen Liisa, Anssi Peräkylä, and Johanna Ruusuvuori. 2010. "Recognition and Interpretation: Responding to Emotional Experience in Psychotherapy." *Research on Language & Social Interaction* 43(1): 85–107. https://doi.org/10.1080/08351810903474799

Voutilainen, Liisa, and Anssi Peräkylä. 2016. "Interactional Practices of Psychotherapy." In *The Palgrave Handbook of Adult Mental Health*, ed. by. Michelle O'Reilly, and Jessica Lester, 540–557. Houndmills: Palgrave. https://doi.org/10.1057/9781137496850_28

Winkler, Oliver. 2017. "Anwendung der Gesprächsanalyse als Feedback-Instrument im Chat-Coaching." *Coaching | Theorie & Praxis*: 17–25. https://doi.org/10.1365/s40896-017-0016-6

Working alliance and client design as discursive achievements in first sessions of executive coaching

Eva-Maria Graf and Sabine Jautz
Klagenfurt University / Siegen University

While outcome research has convincingly proven that the working alliance is a key success factor in coaching, qualitative process-oriented insights are so far missing. We strive to fill this gap by shifting the focus from 'the working alliance is crucial' to 'how is the working alliance discursively accomplished in authentic coaching interactions?'. The guiding assumption is that the coaching alliance emerges locally as a joint product of coach and clients' negotiation process. We analyze the first sessions of two different coach-client dyads from the executive coaching protocol *Emotional Intelligentes Coaching* within an integrative discourse analytic framework. Our analyses demonstrate that the coach displays a specific 'client design' in the local discursive management of the working alliance.

Keywords: executive coaching, working alliance, client design, integrative discourse analysis, first sessions

1. The relevance of the working alliance[1] in coaching: An introduction

Modern welfare states are characterized by an increasing number of highly differentiated helping frameworks, in which existing reciprocity rules originating in personal relationships are no longer valid. Instead, help is offered in institutional and organizational frames, within which asymmetrical working relationships are established between a help seeking layperson and a qualified, help offering expert. Such helping interactions are based on complementary relational pairs and pursue a (more or less) clearly defined purpose or goal (Böhringer, Hitzler and Richter 2022).

1. We will use 'coaching alliance' and 'working alliance' interchangeably throughout this contribution.

https://doi.org/10.1075/pbns.331.08gra

Coaching represents one of these frameworks, where the helping is accomplished via professionally and institutionally molded conversations between helper/ coach and helped/ client. Relationship building and communication (focusing on knowledge generation and distribution) are discursive core tasks of helping in coaching (Graf and Spranz-Fogasy 2018). This contribution focuses on executive coaching, the most established and widely practiced form of coaching. Kilburg (2000: 65f.) defines executive coaching as follows:

> [...] a helping relationship formed between a client who has managerial authority and responsibility in an organization and a consultant who uses a wide variety of behavioral techniques and methods to assist the client to achieve a mutually identified set of goals to improve his or her professional performance and personal satisfaction and consequently to improve the effectiveness of the client's organization within a formally defined coaching agreement.

Coaching theory and practice unanimously emphasize the relevance of the coach-client relationship and particularly stress its implication for enabling change in and for the client: "[t]he 'product' of coaching comes from the bond between a coach and a client" (Hudson 1999: 26).

Despite such acclaimed importance, the working relationship between coach and client represents a neglected issue in research and its theoretical and empirical discussion has only recently started to gain momentum. In analogy with psychotherapy research, the construct of the 'working alliance' has been adapted as a theoretical framework for conceptualizing and analyzing the working relationship in coaching (cf. Gessnitzer and Kauffeld 2015; Ianiro et al. 2015; Graßmann et al. 2019). While existing outcome research positively assesses the significance of the coaching alliance as success factor for the effectiveness of coaching, knowing "that" it works is no longer considered sufficient: As Theeboom et al. (2014: 14) argue, "it is the time to shift attention from the question 'does it [the working alliance; EG and SJ] work?' to 'how does it work?'".

A so far missing aspect is the discursive co-construction of the working alliance by coach and client as part of their talk-in-interaction along the coaching process. As argued by Graf and Pawelczyk (2014: 67), a "[...] coaching alliance is not a preordained entity but rather an interactional phenomenon that needs to be performed and accomplished in the actual conversation between [...] coach and client". Qualitative insights into sequentially organized (relational) practices across coaching sessions that embody such coaching alliances are paramount for a true understanding of the relationship between coach and client (and for the effectiveness of coaching at large). The current study is the first to explicitly address the working alliance as interactional and discursive achievement in the context of the helping format executive coaching (but see Behn-Taran 2014 for a more general analysis of relational patterns in coaching and Winkler this volume).

In particular, it investigates how two very different coach-client dyads from the executive coaching protocol *Emotional Intelligentes Coaching* (Graf 2019) establish and manage their coaching alliance during their first session. Although such an alliance bears on the entire coaching process, its establishment and initial management entail specific affordances (see also Neukom et al. 2011): Initiating the coaching alliance is tightly interwoven with initiating the complementary institutional identities/ roles 'coach' and 'client'. In addition, initiating the working alliance encompasses negotiating, framing and defining content and procedure of coaching, i.e., its tasks and goals.

Our contribution is organized as follows: Section 2 summarizes the most relevant theoretical and empirical insights in the coaching alliance gained outside of linguistics. Section 3 discusses the Basic Activity Model of Coaching as a linguistic concept to investigate the local co-construction of the working alliance as part of the participants' talk-in-interaction. Section 4 details methodology and data and Section 5 presents analysis and findings regarding the establishment of the working alliance by two coach-client dyads during their first sessions under the foci "Getting started" (5.1), "Voicing expectations regarding coach, coaching and coaching alliance" (5.2) and "Negotiating the expectations" (5.3). Section 6 interprets the findings with a special emphasis on the coach's 'client design', i.e., how she locally adapts her bonding as well as task and goal negotiations to the respective client's emotional needs and epistemic prerequisites.

2. The coaching alliance: Relevant theoretical and empirical perspectives

Four overarching characteristics have emerged across the numerous definitions and readings of the helping format coaching (Graf 2019: 25ff.) that frame and mold this interaction type: Coaching is conceptualized as a person-centered, process-oriented, solution-focused and co-active form of organizational intervention that aims to support clients' strife towards self-awareness, self-reflexivity and self-regulation to improve their (professional) performance and satisfaction. Co-activity is the most far-reaching of these characteristics: Unlike classic asymmetrical and hierarchically organized relationships found in, e.g., management consulting, coaching transpires in and through a (communicative) collaboration between egalitarian partners who each bring their respective expertise to the process and who engage in collaborative goal setting, constructing solutions, and fostering clients' self-directed learning and professional (and personal) growth (Jautz 2017).

Quantitative outcome research considers the working alliance a key success factor in coaching and thus an important variable for its effectiveness (for an overview see Graßmann et al.'s (2019) recent meta-analysis). The attested positive impact of the coaching alliance thereby replicates findings in earlier psychotherapy research, the original setting for investigating the relationship between professional and client/ patient: Edward Bordin not only termed the special relationship between therapist and client the 'working alliance',[2] he was also the first to stress that the positive function of the working alliance is generalizable across all helping relationships (Bordin 1979).

Against the backdrop of the pan-theoretical character of the originally psychotherapeutic concept 'working alliance', coaching research adopted the notion and also accentuates the affective bond between coach and client with a strong focus on tasks and goals. Authors thereby agree that such a coaching-specific working alliance and its positive influence on the coaching outcome emerges from and is based on a collaborative, non-hierarchical, egalitarian coaching relationship molded by trust, respect and empathy (Ianiro et al. 2015; Gessnitzer and Kauffeld 2015; Graßmann et al. 2019; Will et al. 2019). While existing (quantitative outcome) research on the working alliance focuses primarily on its positive contribution to the overall effectiveness of coaching, theoretical discussions also address set-up, character and quality of the coaching relationship. Most recently Sills (2021: 69) raises the issue of flexibility on the side of the coach and their ability to respond to clients: "Coaching approaches are not 'one size fits all' […]. [W]hile the coach needs to whole-heartedly believe in their approach, she also needs to be willing to flexibly respond to the client where the client is and in the way they find most useful" (Sills 2021: 73f.). In what follows, we will refer to such flexibility on the coach's side from an interactional perspective as 'client design'.

3. The coaching alliance: A linguistic approximation via the Basic Activity Model

Given the existing research gap as regards a qualitative linguistic perspective, we suggest a first analysis here that is less fine-grained and detailed than current research on e.g., the therapeutic alliance, given the latter's much longer research tradition (for a recent overview see Horvath and Muntigl 2018). Such a research framework permits to address the suggested components of the working alliance, the participants' bond, and their mutual agreement on (or negotiation of) tasks

2. Originally, the concept of working alliances was introduced by Greenson (1965) in his paper "The working alliance and the transference neurosis".

as well as goals and helps to gain first insights how these components interrelate in the concrete talk-in-interaction. In what follows, we propose the Basic Activity Model of Coaching (Graf 2019) for this purpose and discuss its applicability and necessary adaptation for the current purpose. The model also allows to capture the person-centeredness, process-orientation, solution-focus, and co-activity of coaching and address their influence on the local trajectory of the coaching alliance.

The Basic Activity Model of Coaching was proposed by Graf (2019) as a means to explain and analyze the activity type and discourse type 'executive coaching'. Unlike existing theoretical models of coaching, this alternative, empirically based model is set on basic activities as action units instead of phases as structural and temporal units. The basic activities center on 'what' coach and client do in coaching and 'how' they discursively and interactively realize this 'what'. The model contains the four activities 'Defining the Situation', 'Building the Relationship', 'Co-Constructing Change' and 'Evaluating the Coaching' (cf. Graf 2019: 71). These activities are realized in and through particular discursive practices that evolve around the repetitive tackling of the activity-specific communicative tasks and core components whose local functions are contextually determined. Due to their intra-activity and inter-activity variability, they allow for capturing the complex structural, interactive, and thematic loops characteristic of the discourse-based professional helping format 'executive coaching' across individual sessions and along entire coaching processes. Coach and client thereby engage in all of the four basic activities when doing coaching. Concurrently, they (can) also engage in more than one activity at a time as is the case with 'Building the Relationship', which (implicitly) permeates all interaction in the sense of a permanent task (Spranz-Fogasy 1992; Graf 2019). The working alliance is conceptualized here as drawing on all four basic activities of the model and their communicative tasks, yet with differing emphases according to the stage and specificities of the coaching interaction as well as whether bonding or agreeing on tasks and goals is in the interactional focus.

Predominantly, but not exclusively, the basic activities 'Building the Relationship' and 'Defining the Situation' and their respective communicative tasks and core components underlie the discursive and interactive establishment of the coaching alliance: Together they frame the professional (helping) interaction between coach and client on the relational, thematic, and procedural levels and build the matrix against which all other activities transpire. In particular, in 'Building the Relationship' the participants discursively establish their respective roles and identities, which are premised on the mutually dependent 'standardized relational pair' (Sacks 1972) 'coach' and 'client'. These are not preordained notions or 'brought along'; instead, they are 'brought about' in the concrete interaction (Sarangi 2001: 6) via engaging in professional and layperson practices, by coordinating these practices and, finally, by orienting towards the emerging overall relational structure of the ongoing coaching interaction. Of particular relevance in professional and lay identity building are practices related to constructing and distributing coaching-relevant knowledge and expertise (Gülich 2003; Graf and Spranz-Fogasy 2018) and participants' epistemic authority, status and stance in this context (Heritage 2011, 2013; Drew 2018). In and through these discursively established roles and identities-in-interaction, coach and client hold different interaction rights and obligations, i.e., they have a different share in negotiating and defining both their bond and the tasks, goals, and procedures of coaching.

In 'Defining the Situation', the participants – among other communicative tasks – engage in 'Methodological and Procedural Framing of Coaching', which entails the core components 'Explaining Methods and/or Procedure', 'Integrating Client's Experience with Coaching' as well as 'Negotiating the Individual Definition of Coaching' (cf. Graf 2019: 85ff.). The principal function of this basic activity, which is most prolific during the initial stage of a coaching process, is to orient clients towards the local and global layout of the encounter and thus to establish a common ground and stock of knowledge relevant to interactional tasks and goals. Such a common stock of knowledge is based on the local co-construction and distribution of coaching-relevant knowledge and expertise. This, in turn, is inextricably linked with participants' reciprocal identity constructions. I.e., whatever coach and client do when they do coaching, they do so in and for the relationship with their interactive partner. The negotiated and established frame as regards the relational, thematic, and procedural levels of coaching, i.e., the working alliance, builds the backbone against which the other basic activities (Graf and Jautz 2019) 'Co-Constructing Change' and 'Evaluating the Coaching' and their respective communicative tasks and core components transpire and, in turn, mold the working alliance.

4. Methodology and data

The analysis applies an integrative discourse analytic framework as put forth in Graf (2019), primarily drawing on Theme-Oriented Discourse Analysis (Roberts and Sarangi 2005) along with Activity Analysis (Sarangi 2005), two closely linked approaches to analyze how language constructs professional practice as situated between 'sequential description' and 'extra-situation explanation' of social encounters (cf. Sarangi 2010). For the more local management of the working alliance, concepts and categories from Conversation Analysis such as sequentiality (see Schegloff 2007), alignment and affiliation (Stivers, Mondada and Steensig 2011), epistemics (Heritage 2011, 2013; Drew 2018) and identities-in-interaction (Zimmerman 1998) are drawn on. Finally, Interactional Sociolinguistics concepts account for how the participants in coaching frame the ongoing situation and actively construct and constantly update the context of the situation (Goffman 1974; Gumperz 2001).

The data – originally in German – stem from *Emotional Intelligentes Coaching*. The entire corpus, video- and audio-recorded by the coaches themselves between 2007 and 2009, consists of 10 face-to-face, one-on-one coaching processes by two coaches, one male and one female coach, and their male and female clients, all executives from internally operating, DAX-listed organizations. The participants (i.e., coaches and clients) signed an informed consent as regards the recording of the sessions and the publication of related results. Each process contains three to nine individual sessions, which in turn last between 2 and 2.5 hours (cf. Graf 2019: 60ff.). The data has been transcribed according to GAT2 conventions (Selting et al. 2009).

For the current contribution, we choose two first sessions by the female coach with a male and a female client, which are maximally different as regards clients' experience with coaching, their expectations concerning coaching and their coaching concerns. First sessions, and specifically the initial phases we focus on here, evince specific interactional affordances, in particular as regards defining the situation, delineating the overall thematic direction of the coaching process and initiating and establishing the relationship. They are thus considered interactionally crucial for the trajectory of the ensuing professional encounter (Nowak 2010). Particularly beginnings decide on the characteristics and intensity of the (commencing) coaching alliance and thereby prepare the grounds for agreeing on goals and tasks for the coaching process.

5. Working on the working alliance: Analysis and findings

The following excerpts stem from the initial phases of the first sessions[3] between the female coach (Co) and a male (C1) and a female client (C2). C1 receives coaching as a supportive HR measure for having taken over a larger branch in the financial sector. He does not have any experience with coaching in a narrow sense. C2 has had an emotional breakdown due to a highly challenging project as senior consultant and as a consequence took part in a training on "Emotional Intelligence" (offered by the same company as the coaching), where she gained experience with the underlying methods of *Emotional Intelligentes Coaching*.

3. While these first sessions are the first face-to-face encounter, coach and clients have already had a telephone conversation. These prior-to-coaching conversations lay the foundation for coach and clients' respective identity constructions and their forming relationship. In the actual coaching, the participants refer to the phone calls and hence also orient to this pre-established relationship and their pre-established roles and identities.

To elucidate the discursive particularities of the working alliance during such an early phase, we first zoom in on how the coach designs the initiation of the coaching proper based on the clients' prior self-presentations and their experience with coaching, i.e., on how the participants get started (5.1). Next, we detail how the clients voice their expectations regarding coaching as such, the coach's role and their working relationship (5.2). Finally, we explore how the participants negotiate their expectations regarding their relationship, the goals, and tasks of coaching as well as its procedures (5.3).

5.1 Getting started

The first two excerpts illustrate how the coach as professional helper prepares the ground for the proper coaching work according to the clients' needs.

Excerpt 1. Prior to the following explanation sequence, the coach (Co) has inquired about the client's (C1) experience with coaching. C1 has elaborated that this is his first external coaching and has voiced reservations due to experiences with other HR measures.

001	Co	now as for how i proceed because you said you_re also
002	Co	wondering what what will happen right
003	Co	completely normal we
004		(0.25)
005	Co	talk to each other
006	C1	hmhm
007	Co	and there will probably also be times
008		(0.5)
009	Co	erm when we start to go into the topics in more detail
010		(0.25)
011	C1	hmhm
012		(0.75)
013	Co	er when i will ask you to just
014		(0.25)
015	Co	sense your feelings more closely
016		(0.25)
017	Co	or to
018		(0.25)
019	Co	replay situations inwardly
020		(0.5)
021	Co	which we then so to speak look at
022	Co	like in slow motion what exactly is happening [there]
023	C1	[hmhm]

The coach initiates her information-delivery sequence (Silverman 1997) via a meta-pragmatic framing strategy "now as for how i proceed" [line 1] and accounts for doing so via indirectly quoting the client and his suspense regarding the procedure. She thereby orients both to the client's epistemic status (Heritage 2013), i.e., his lack of knowledge, and affiliates with his expressed reservations, i.e., his emotional status. Next, via another meta-pragmatic framing strategy, she topicalizes her method as something ordinary via a pre-explanatory evaluation "`completely normal`" [line 3] followed by defining coaching via a normalizing strategy as having a conversation ("`we (0.25) talk to each other`") [line 3–5]; she uses the first-person personal pronoun "`we`" and frames coaching as a co-active conversation. She provides more details, describing her method in an everyday language, down-toning the therapeutic connotation of the coaching register, while also introducing her professional focus on the client's emotional experience by, e.g., using the Emotional Intelligence register ("`sense your feelings more closely`") [line 15] (Fischer 2016: 27). Moreover, the coach uses hedging and relativizing forms (such as reducing more emotion-oriented parts of coaching to single moments, e.g., "`there will probably also be times`") [line 7], as another affiliative orientation to the client, who had previously voiced insecurity.

Excerpt 2. Excerpt (2) follows right after the coach and the second client's (C 2) introductory small talk.

```
001  Co   okay ((smiles)) yes and now
002       (3.0)
003  Co   to to you to what has (say) brought
004       (0.5)
005  Co   you here
006  C2   ((laughs)) erm
007       (2.0)
008  C2   do you already know any anything from (trainer) and (colleague)
          or just the question where i have to start
009  C2   where i have to hook on
010  C2   [or shall] i just start [at ] the very beginning
011  Co   [well i  ]              [yes]
012  Co   i would
013       (0.5)
014  Co   (look) this is of course a legitimate question where to start
015       (1.0)
016  Co   i_d just say that you
017       (0.25)
018  Co   tell me whatever you think that i
019       (0.25)
020  Co   i should know
021  C2   hm
022  Co   about your background
023  C2   hm
```

Smiling and signalling availability via "`okay`" [line 1], the coach in her open concern elicitation addresses both the client as a person (second person singular pronoun "`you`") and her concern ("`what has (say) brought you here`") [line 3–5].

This thematic agenda move, which marks the transition to coaching proper, is maximally open and client-centered with little thematic pre-structuring. While the concern presentation phase is one of the very few structurally provided-for locations for clients to present their concern in their own way and in accordance with their own agendas (cf. Heritage and Robinson 2006: 49), the coach concurrently pre-empts the client's status as co-expert of coaching and its procedure (cf. Peräkylä 1995: 251). Yet, the client turns down the attributed position of a co-expert (via disaffiliating laughter, a hesitation marker and a 2-second pause), who can handle such a lack of thematic pre-structuring. Instead of providing an aligning and affiliating response regarding her concern, she thus poses a (three-part) counter question, returning epistemic authority and expert status to the coach. The client first inquires about possible shared knowledge ("do you already know any anything from (trainer) and (colleague)")[line 8] and next about where her concern presentation should start ("where i have to start") [line 8], which she reformulates using consulting language ("where i have to hook on") [line 9]; the final part of her counter questioning is a thematically closed question, again marked as an alternative ("[or shall] I just start [at] the very beginning")[line 10]. While the coach is ascribed epistemic authority regarding amount and type of knowledge necessary for coaching – and thus positioned as coaching expert –, the client claims epistemic authority, too, yet for another territory of knowledge (Heritage 2011). She does so by engaging in differentiated questioning, adopting the discursive identity of "questioner", which is the category-bound activity of the professional agent, be it coach or consultant (Rettinger 2011).

The coach – taking on the attributed role of expert – immediately sets out to respond to the last part of the question sequence, but interrupts herself and, via a self-initiated self-repair, ratifies the client's inquiry as legitimate [line 14]. She thereby uses her error correction as an interactional resource to acknowledge the client's status of co-expert. In a second start using the subjunctive form [line18, line 20], she leaves the decision of what is important to the client, thereby again attributing co-expertise to the client, while down-toning her own expertise.

Summary: Getting started

"Getting started" in coaching follows different interactional trajectories depending on the clients and their background, i.e., what experiences, expectations, and expertise they bring to coaching, and what is thus needed to collaboratively achieve a common ground for the ensuing coaching. This is shown in divergent discursive activities on the side of the coach that range from extensive defining practices to direct concern elicitation practices. In so doing, the coach positions the clients as layperson and co-expert respectively, and thereby frames the encounter and the relationship with them as more or less symmetrical or egalitarian. These practices prepare the necessary grounds for a mutual agreement on coaching tasks and goals and in their tailoring to the relevant needs of the clients, they also serve as relational practices to establish a bond between the participants and as such form part of the coach's client design.

5.2 Voicing expectations regarding coach, coaching and coaching alliance

The two clients differ markedly in their expectations regarding the coach, the coaching, and the alliance as well as in the way they implicitly or explicitly express these expectations.

Excerpt 3. The subsequent excerpt with C1 follows after Excerpt (1) and is still part of clarifying the preliminaries of the coaching process and their working together.

```
001  Co   and erm
002       (2.1)
003  Co   well naturally
004  Co   whatever you would also like to know about me or about
005       (0.5)
006  Co   my background or my procedure
007       (1.1)
008  Co   you are
009  Co   (naturally) also
010       (0.25)
011  Co   more than welcome [to find] out a bit more
012  C1                    [hmhm    ]
013       (0.25)
014  C1   okay good
015       (0.5)
016  C1   yes
017       (0.5)
018  C1   erm good i_ve just had another look at erm your cee vee again
019  C1   er [as it was]
020  Co      [hmhm     ]
021  C1   in with the [document]ation
022  Co               [hmhm    ]
023       (0.5)
024  C1   erm
025       (1.1)
026  C1   yes well
027  C1   there will almost certainly be questions at some point
          depending on the
028  C1   situation well it it [it_s not so]
029  Co                        [hmhm       ]
030  C1   important for me now to know everything that
```

```
031  C1   you_ve done [ever]ybody
032  Co               [yes ]
033  C1   you_ve er er helped
034       (0.5)
035  C1   erm i_m also
036  C1   assuming now that the bank decided to choose you and your
          pool of consultants
037  C1   with good reason [i will cer]tainly
038  Co                    [hmhm      ]
039  C1   not do the
040  Co   yes yes
041  C1   validity check once again [whether   ]
042  Co                             [((laughs))]
043  C1   it_s also okay for [yes] well i
044  Co                      [yes]
045  C1   assume that to be the case
```

After the coach has given her definition of coaching, explained her procedure and has set the temporal frame, she explicitly invites C1 to inquire about herself, her background and/ or her procedure (via a three-part list) in an explicitly affiliative manner ("more than welcome") [line 11] (see Nowak's (2010: 232f) "Offering the possibility to ask questions"). In doing so, she makes herself available both as a person and in her professional role as a coach. Concurrently, she assumes the client to have an interest in her (framing coaching as a co-active process) and indexes her understanding of coaching, and in particular the coaching alliance, as a somewhat egalitarian relationship, based on a mutual interest in one another and some shared knowledge.

Such a personal offer to ask questions makes an aligning and affiliative personal reply the preferred response (Pomerantz and Heritage 2013). C1 acknowledges this offer via hesitantly uttered agreement tokens such as "okay", "good" [line 14] and "yes" [line 16, 26] and thematically orients to the coach's CV, marking her credentials as most relevant for him. He thereby de-selects the option to learn more about her as a person and to lay the foundation for a more personal bonding. In order to avoid threatening the coach's face even more, the client very vaguely and tentatively announces possible questions on his side in the future. After this relational face-saving work, he formulates an explicit personal lack of interest in the coach's achievements and credentials. In addition and via a change of footing (Goffman 1979), the client reframes his personal responsibility, stages himself as an obedient and devoted representative of the paying organization and places all responsibility on the latter, whose decision he does not question (also shown in his terminology "[i will cer]tainly not do the validity check once again") [line 37, 39, 41].

Excerpt 4. This excerpt is the continuation of Excerpt (2), where the coach and client 2 negotiate the information necessary to start the coaching proper and thereby also negotiate their respective status as experts. The client starts reporting about the trainer she worked with during the Emotional Intelligence training prior to the coaching.

```
001  C2  <<laughing> okay>
002  C2  erm yes i was at (trainer)_s
003  C2  it was (trainer) who has recommended you
004  C2  said this might be
005  C2  that would fit well according to her intuition
006  C2  °h h° and after I have with (trainer)
007  C2  and really have to say at this point
008  C2  [actually]
009  Co  [yes hm  ]
010      (0.25)
011  C2  was really [good]
012  Co              [yes ] good
013  C2  also in the also in the small group
014  Co  [yes ]
015  C2  [well] that [was]
016  Co              [yes]
017      (0.25)
018  C2  i found this very impressive
019  C2  and there i then
020      (0.5)
021  C2  had the feeling that i can well [trust] (trainer)_s intuition
022  Co                                  [hm   ]
023  C2  [because] simply (xxx) said
024  Co  [yes    ]
025      (1.5)
026  Co  was familiar
027  C2  yes somehow yes fami familiar because i as i said
028  C2  i have the feeling that i can trust in her intuition
029  C2  [because] i had the impression there was
030  Co  [hm     ]
031      (0.5)
032  C2  somehow a good rapport
```

After reaching a mutual consent regarding the necessary information (see Excerpt (2)), C2 aligningly starts delivering which background information she considers most relevant as part of her concern presentation: She first informs the coach about which trainer she had, and that this person had recommended the coach. Next, the client details why the trainer had recommended the coach via an indirect quote and starts deviating from her concern formulation initiated by the coach's topic elicitation. C2 embarks on topicalizing the trustful and good relationship with the trainer, whom she explicitly praises – in an insertion sequence via a meta-pragmatic framing strategy – as trainer ("was really [good]", "i found this very impressive") [line 11; line 18] and as a trustworthy source for a recommendation ("had the feeling that i can well [trust] (trainer)_s intuition") [line 21]. Both, praising the trainer's work and her intuition are repeated by the client via various emotion terms and in syntactically parallel constructions. The coach minimally responds, positively evaluates the client's own positive evaluation of the trainer and collaboratively completes the client's utterance regarding trust, thereby affiliating with the client.

In her praising sequence, C2 stages herself as an emotional client, who bases judgment and decisions on emotions and who values a close bond and personal relationships. By praising the trainer and their working alliance, the client is ego-stroking the coach, yet concurrently challenging her and their relationship by implicitly raising expectations regarding the coach, her professional quality and the nature and quality of their ensuing relationship.

Summary: Voicing expectations regarding coach, coaching and coaching alliance
By explicitly and/ or implicitly conveying their expectations as regards coaching and their relationship with the coach, C1 and C2 claim specific institutional identities for themselves and concurrently project a specific counter identity on the coach in the sense of Sacks' 'standardized relational pair' (1972). The success-oriented service-taker C1 projects his envisioned working alliance with the coach as professional means to an end (Excerpt (3)); and the emotionally demanding C2 as a high-quality, trustful bond (Excerpt (4)).

The coach displays her client design, i.e., her orientation to the locally constructed client identities and their specific needs (in the sense of person-orientation), by offering the clients sufficient and thematically open discursive spaces to voice their definitions and expectations. Yet, in initiating these presentation phases, the coach as professional agent concurrently stays in control.

5.3 Negotiating the expectations

The third focus lies on how coach and client negotiate the coaching agenda and procedure based on the clients' explicitly and/ or implicitly voiced expectations and their co-constructed institutional identities.

Excerpt 5. Prior to this excerpt, C1 addresses his work-life balance and frames it as an additional concern and the coach offers the client the opportunity to explore this theme. As part of her client design, she validates the client's output orientation as regards success and development and thus thematically frames exploring the work-life balance as geared towards a good result ("what would be a good result there") (not in the excerpt).

```
001  Co   yes hmhm
002       (2.5)
003  C1   that would also be really okay
004  C1   with me if if you could tell me
```

```
005          (0.5)
006   C1     where you would subjectively say
007   C1     that that would be a good result
008          (0.5)
009   Co     hm
010   C1     because i always consider the the result only from my
             present perspective
011   C1     and whether this is ultimately a good result indeed is is
             something i don_t know
012   Co     yes
013   Co     so it_s good that you
014          (0.25)
015   Co     are telling me that i er i i rather ask questions i_ve got
016   Co     a questioning stance now right and that could be seen as
017          (0.75)
018   Co     yes
019   Co     maybe as a
020          (0.25)
021   Co     coach or counselor
022          (0.25)
023   Co     stance right
[Lines 24-61 omitted]
062   C1     well to [er ] reflect on yourself and to look inside is good
             but when you
063   Co             [yes]
064   C1     really want to make something change in yourself then that
             also includes for me having
065          (0.5)
066   C1     a different [situation or a different perspective]
067   Co                 [i do that so that you (.) right preci]sely
068          (0.5)
[Lines 69-72 omitted]
073   C1     this together i think is somehow certainly
074   Co     together
075   Co     it has to be both
076   C1     yes
```

As the client only minimally responds to her thematic agenda-move (not in the expert), she prompts the client's alignment with her offer via "yes" [line 1]. After yet another, even longer pause indicating possible interactional trouble, client 1 responds, yet in a disaligning and disaffiliative manner, and immediately shifts footing away from the prior thematic scope set by the coach to their way of interacting. He requests the coach's subjective evaluation regarding the "good result" [line 7] and accounts for his request. Client 1 thereby implicitly (and not for the first time) criticizes the procedure, indexing his definition of coaching as a means to improve his leadership skills and his resulting expectations as regards his professional collaboration with the coach. Moreover, the client attributes a different discursive and professional identity to the coach, viz. giving her opinion and acting as a consultant. This reciprocally positions himself in the role of the receiver of her opinion as part of a service encounter framework.

In her reaction to the client's request, the coach initially ratifies it and evaluates it positively. Yet, C1's request also prompts her to detail her procedure and attitude as opposing to what the client has requested. Against this re-established common ground, the coach concedes to voice her subjective perspective (not in transcript). This motivates the client to make some concessions, too: in his next turn, he first positively evaluates self-reflecting and exploring, i.e., the coach's method, and thus – at least nominally – positions the coach as professional expert for change. Yet, by talking about "real change" from a general perspective ("`when you really want to make something change in yourself`") [line 62, 64] he also claims a certain epistemic authority ("`that also includes for me`") [line 64] when providing his definition of coaching. However, next in this negotiation sequence (omitted in the transcript), C1 down-grades the significance of the coach's point of view and (again) indexes his performance orientation as well as his understanding of coaching as a service encounter. In an overlapping turn, the coach confirms to adapt her procedure ("`i do that` ...") [line 67]. In turn, C1 concludes his own turn by conceding – in a hedged and syntactically incomplete form – that both positions belong together.

Excerpt 6. Prior to this excerpt C2 elaborates on how she (tries to) practice(s) mindfulness, a method learned during the training and also an essential technique of *Emotional Intelligentes Coaching*. She thereby positions herself as an ambitious pupil and concurrently signals approval of the overall coaching methodology.

```
001  Co   great
002       (0.5)
003  Co   good very good that you put this into practice
004  C2   <<laughing> hm more or less good but
005       (0.25)
006  C2   at least i try>
007  Co   yes yes yes yes
008       (1.5)
009  Co   and of course this helps you in everyday situations a bit
010       (0.25)
011  Co   perhaps also
012  Co   to stay more with yourself or to sense yourself
013       (0.75)
014  Co   erm (this didn_t look) like this [(xxx) ]
[Lines 15-28 omitted]
029  C2   the truth but <<with stifled voice> simply doesn_t help>
030  Co   yes
031       (6.0)
032  Co   °h h° so we_ll
033  Co   also work
034       (0.25)
035  Co   with mindfulness here o[kay] if you can imagine well i will
036  C2                           [hm ]
037       (0.25)
038  Co   support you
```

```
039   Co   and well
040        (0.25)
041   Co   so that you_re more [in c]ontact with it
[Lines 42-54 omitted]
042   Co   i can help you so to speak
043   Co   to make your way there and also with the help of the questions
           erm well to discover
044   Co   a bit more and to sense a bit more as well in my experience
           the answer is is it is
045   C2   hm
046   Co   in ther[e right ]
047   C2   <<points with both arms to herself>
                     [where el]se should it be>
048   Co   <<smiling> [yes yes yes          ]>
049   C2              [where else ((laughs))]
050        (0.5)
051   Co   well naturally i know
052   Co   a few principles right i er or it_s also er er
053        (4.5)
054   Co   a i_ll also make them transparent
055   Co   for you [okay]
056   C2           [hm  ]
057   Co   and i_ll help you to slow down a bit now in this approach
[Lines 58-67 omitted]
068   C2   i know this approach in that it is
069        (0.5)
070   Co   [((laughs briefly))]
071   C2   [similar to someth ]ing that i always do as well just in a
           completely different field ((laughs))
072   Co   [yes]
```

In line 1, the coach – following the client's detailed description – explicitly praises C2's practicing via a three-part list ("great (0.5) good very good") [line 1–3] and thereby acknowledges the client's ambitious personality as part of her client design. Concurrently, she positions herself as professional expert, engaging in the category-bound activity of evaluating and assessing. In a disaligning manner – marked by laughing (Haakana 2001) – C2 partly rejects this positive evaluation and relativizes her success in practicing mindfulness. This relativization is not taken up by the coach, who instead – and linked via the coordinating conjunction "and" [line 9] – pursues her own agenda elaborating on the general benefits of practicing mindfulness for the client ("and of course this helps you in everyday situations") [line 9]. The client – in an even more explicitly disaligning manner, framed by non-verbal emotionality – rejects the coach's explanation (initiated via an emotional negation "nope") and more generally questions the benefit of the method as such ("the truth but <<with stifled voice> simply doesn_t help>") [line 29]. The coach, in turn, only minimally reacts to this resisting reaction and after a marked 6-second pause changes the footing/ thematic focus. While continuing with the topic 'mindfulness', she reframes its focus from the client's personal (negative) experience to mindfulness as their shared method in the here and now. Concurrently, she adopts a different discursive identity, i.e., that of an explainer, and thereby takes control over the interactional development. She details their mutual working "so we_ll also work (0.25) with mindfulness here o[kay]" [line 32–35] (first person plural co-active "we") in two parts: She first explains the method in a rather general manner accounting for it from her professional and experienced position ("i]n my experience") [line 44] and next, she more specifically offers to support C2 in practicing mindfulness with concrete principles that will help the client to reach her specific coaching goals.

In both parts the coach positions herself in the role of the professional helper and expert and the client in the role of the helped (in the sense of Sacks' (1972) 'standardized relational pair') (via e.g., "i will support you" and "i can help you") [line 35, 38; line 42]. This represents an interactionally and relationally delicate moment in two respects: the coach needs to prove that the method is indeed worthwhile and she must manage contested epistemic domains (Drew 2018) by honoring the client's competency (i.e., the client's epistemics of experience) and presenting herself as the true expert with whom the client can successfully practice mindfulness (based on the epistemics of expertise) (cf. Weidner 2012 quoted in Heritage 2013: 392). The client, in turn, marks the first, general information as redundant and already in her territory of knowledge both verbally (via the rhetorical question "where el]se should it be") [line 47] and non-verbally (via laughter and an expressive gesture). Yet, she can accept the second part on the following grounds: In an insertion, she also claims epistemic authority over the method, resulting from her own professional epistemic domain. The negotiation sequence is terminated by a finalizing overall ratification of the method, the procedures and the usefulness/ prospect of success of mindfulness by the client, who – in her comparison with her own work as consultant –claims different, but equally valuable epistemic authority.

Summary: Negotiating the expectations

The last excerpts showcase challenging moments for both working alliances and how these challenging moments are interactionally tackled and solved within extensive negotiation sequences. Coach and client in Excerpt (5) negotiate the client's individual definition of coaching against the backdrop of the coach's professional understanding of coaching as co-active and person-centered format, which also bears on their expectations as regards their respective institutional roles and identities. Excerpt (6) illustrates how the delicate relationship between coach and client's status of (co-)experts is negotiated in the context of the coaching concept 'mindfulness', the client's prior experience with this methodology and its importance for the ensuing coaching process.

6. The dynamics of the working alliance and client design in coaching: Summary and outlook

In this last section we will review our findings regarding the local co-construction of the working alliance by the two coach-client dyads during the beginning of their first sessions. In our summary, we particularly focus on the coach and how she attunes to the individual clients in initiating and managing the working alliance as part of her 'client design'. In analogy with 'recipient design' (Sacks et al. 1974: 727), we understand 'client design' as the multitude of respects in which coaches employ discursive practices to (a) display an orientation and sensitivity to their clients and their institutional positioning as specific clients with individual epistemics of experience, relational and emotional needs and, thereby, (b) counter-position themselves with their institutional identity as coach relative to their epistemics of expertise and their coaching agenda.

The very nature of coaching as a person- and process-oriented as well as co-active helping intervention emerges in our data in negotiation practices regarding the individual framing of coaching and in adapting the interactive layout of the encounter between the coach and her clients with their respective epistemics of expertise and experiences. The coach needs to discursively manage ensuing knowledge discrepancies (Mondada 2011: 27) as well as epistemic contests (Drew 2018: 178) with clients as regards the tasks and goals of coaching. She orients to the (lack of) knowledge of her clients in defining and framing practices, whereby she adopts changing discursive identities (such as information provider or questioner) and concurrently ascribes the respective changing discursive counter identities to her clients (e.g., information recipient or answerer). Yet, the clients may or may not take up these ascribed counter-identities and instead position themselves discursively and situationally differently as, e.g., counter-questioner and co-expert. According to Zimmerman (1998: 94), such a display of discourse identities is tied to the nuanced situated identities of the parties, i.e., the coach as professional expert and helper and clients as particular help-seekers (such as service taker and co-expert, respectively), which in turn link these local activities to the (more or less) standing social arrangement and institution of 'coaching' through the socially distributed knowledge participants have about it.

While establishing a common ground for the ongoing communicative doing is always relevant and guarantees interactional smoothness and success, this rarely happens explicitly as can be witnessed in the coaching data. As argued by Rettinger (2011) and Graf (2019), an anticipatory clarification of participation roles and the coaching procedure represents an endemic feature of first sessions in coaching. It takes place in the basic activity 'Defining the Situation', more specifically in the communicative task 'Methodological and Procedural Framing of Coaching' and concomitantly in the basic activity 'Building a Relationship' and the communicative task 'Establishing the Roles and Identities of 'Coach' and 'Client''. Client design thereby shows in, e.g., choosing specific informing practices such as normalizing, specific register use or down-toning, whereby the coach is doing "being a caring coach" who affiliates with her client's suspense. Client design also shows in NOT engaging in 'Methodological and Procedural Framing of Coaching' and instead immediately moving to the first proper thematic coaching slot and inviting the client, experienced with coaching and its methods, to present her concern via an open topic elicitation as part of the basic activity 'Co-Constructing Change' and the communicative task 'Diagnosing'. Yet, such discursive and interactive flexibility in view of diverse clients with vastly differing experiences and expectations is always confined by the coaching protocol, which ultimately guides the coach's local actions and their client design.

To sum up, client design is an essential prerequisite for the working alliance in coaching, which is not something pre-ordained and given, but something locally established in the here-and-now of the coaching interaction by the participants; concurrently, the working alliance is not – once established – a static notion, but an evolving and adapting discursive and interactive achievement along the coaching process. While insights into its initiation, negotiation and development during the first session was the focus of this contribution, its further evolvement along an entire coaching process as well as the affordances of its finalization at the end of a coaching process need further empirical investigation.

References

Behn-Taran, Angelika. 2014. *"I Am My Worst Enemy". A Linguistic Analysis of Interactive Dynamics or Relational Patterns in Business Coaching Conversations.* Dissertation. Ludwig-Maximilians-Universität München.

Böhringer, Daniela, Sarah Hitzler, and Martina Richter (eds.). 2022. *Helfen. Situative und organisationale Ausprägungen einer unterbestimmten Praxis.* Bielefeld: Transcript Verlag.

Bordin, Edward S. 1979. "The Generalizability of the Psychoanalytic Concept of the Working Alliance." *Psychotherapy: Theory, Research and Practice* 16 (3): 252–260. https://doi.org/10.1037/h0085885

Drew, Paul. 2018. "Epistemics in Social Interaction." *Discourse Studies* 20 (1): 163–187. https://doi.org/10.1177/1461445617734347

Fischer, Kerstin. 2016. *Designing Speech for a Recipient. The Roles of Partner Modeling, Alignment and Feedback in So-Called 'Simplified Registers'.* Amsterdam: John Benjamins. https://doi.org/10.1075/pbns.270

Gessnitzer, Sina, and Simone Kauffeld. 2015. "The Working Alliance in Coaching: Why Behavior is the Key to Success." *The Journal of Applied Behavioral Science* 51 (2): 177–197. https://doi.org/10.1177/0021886315576407

Goffman, Erving. 1974. *Frame Analysis: An Essay on the Organization of Experience*. Cambridge, Mass.: Harvard University Press.
Goffman, Erving. 1979. "Footing." *Semiotica* 25 (1/2): 1–29. https://doi.org/10.1515/semi.1979.25.1-2.1
Graf, Eva-Maria. 2019. *The Pragmatics of Executive Coaching*. Amsterdam: John Benjamins. https://doi.org/10.1075/pbns.303
Graf, Eva-Maria, and Sabine Jautz. 2019. "'und wie wie entsteht veränderung und damit haben_s wir ja auch mit dir zu tun' – Einblicke in die inter- und intra-aktivitätsspezifische Dimension der kommunikativen Basisaktivität 'Ko-Konstruieren von Veränderung' im Führungskräfte-Coaching." In *Pragmatik der Veränderung*, ed. by Eva-Maria Graf, Claudio Scarvaglieri, and Thomas Spranz-Fogasy, 209–237. Tübingen: Narr/ Francke/ Attempto.
Graf, Eva-Maria, and Joanna Pawelczyk. 2014. "The Interactional Accomplishment of Feelings-Talk in Psychotherapy and Executive Coaching. Same Format, Different Functions?" In *Discourses of Helping Professions*, ed. by Eva-Maria Graf, Marlene Sator, and Thomas Spranz-Fogasy, 59–89. Amsterdam: John Benjamins. https://doi.org/10.1075/pbns.252.04gra
Graf, Eva-Maria, and Thomas Spranz-Fogasy. 2018. "Helfende Berufe – Helfende Interaktionen." In *Handbuch Text und Gespräch*, ed. by Karin Birkner, and Nina Janich, 418–442. Amsterdam: Mouton de Gruyter. https://doi.org/10.1515/9783110296051-017
Graßmann, Carolin, Franziska Schölmerich, and Carsten C. Schermuly. 2019. "The Relationship between Working Alliance and Client Outcomes in Coaching: A Meta-Analysis." *Human Relations* 73 (1): 35–58. https://doi.org/10.1177/0018726718819725
Greenson, Ralph R. 1965. "The Working alliance and the transference neurosis." *Psychoanalytic Quarterly* 34: 155–181. https://doi.org/10.1080/21674086.1965.11926343
Gülich, Elisabeth. 2003. "Conversational Techniques Used in Transferring Knowledge between Medical Experts and Non-Experts." *Discourse Studies* 5 (2): 235–263. https://doi.org/10.1177/1461445603005002005
Gumperz, John. 2001. "Contextualization and Ideology in Intercultural Communication." In *Culture in Communication: Analyses of Intercultural Situations*, ed. by Aldo Di Luzio, Susanne Günthner, and Franca Orletti, 35–54. Amsterdam: John Benjamins. https://doi.org/10.1075/pbns.81.05gum
Haakana, Markku. 2001. "Laughter as a Patient's Resource: Dealing with Delicate Aspects of Medical Interaction." *Text* 21 (1 & 2): 187–219.
Heritage, John. 2011. "Territories of Knowledge, Territories of Experience: Empathic Moments in Interaction." In *The Morality of Knowledge in Conversation*, ed. by Tanya Stivers, Lorenza Mondada, and Jakob Steensig, 159–183. Cambridge: Cambridge University Press. https://doi.org/10.1017/CBO9780511921674.008
Heritage, John. 2013. "Action Formation and its Epistemic (and Other) Backgrounds." *Discourse Studies* 15 (5): 551–578. https://doi.org/10.1177/1461445613501449
Heritage, John, and Jeffrey D. Robinson. 2006. "Accounting for the Visit: Giving Reasons for Seeking Medical Care." In *Communication in Medical Care: Interaction between Primary Care Physicians and Patients*, ed. by John Heritage, and Douglas Maynard, 48–85. Cambridge: Cambridge University Press. https://doi.org/10.1017/CBO9780511607172.005
Horvath Adam O., and Peter Muntigl. 2018. "The Alliance as a Discursive Achievement: A Conversation Analytical Perspective." In *Therapy as Discourse. The Language of Mental Health*, ed. by Olga Smoliak, and Tom Strong, 71–93. Basingstoke: Palgrave Macmillan, Cham. https://doi.org/10.1007/978-3-319-93067-1_4
Hudson, Frederic. 1999. *The Handbook of Coaching*. San Francisco: Jossey-Bass.

Ianiro, Patrizia M., Nale Lehmann-Willenbrock, and Simone Kauffeld. 2015. "Coaches and Clients in Action: A Sequential Analysis of Nonverbal Interpersonal Styles in Coach-Client Interactions." *Journal of Business and Psychology* 30: 435–456. https://doi.org/10.1007/s10869-014-9374-5

Jautz, Sabine. 2017. "Immer auf Augenhöhe? Ein Blick in den sprachlichen Werkzeugkoffer im Coaching." In *Sprache in Rede, Gespräch und Kommunikation. Linguistisches Wissen in der Kommunikationsberatung*, ed. by Marcel Dräger, and Martha Kuhnhenn, 47–64. Frankfurt am Main etc.: Peter Lang.

Kilburg, Richard R. 2000. *Executive Coaching. Developing Managerial Wisdom in a World of Chaos.* Washington D.C.: American Psychological Association. https://doi.org/10.1037/10355-000

Mondada, Lorenza. 2011. "The Management of Knowledge Discrepancies and of Epistemic Changes in Institutional Interactions." In *The Morality of Knowledge in Conversation*, ed. by Tanya Stivers, Lorenza Mondada, and Jakob Steensig, 27–57. Cambridge: Cambridge University Press. https://doi.org/10.1017/CBO9780511921674.003

Neukom, Marius, Katrin Schnell, and Brigitte Boothe. 2011. "Die Arbeitsbeziehung im Coaching – ein Stiefkind der Forschung." *Organisationsberatung, Supervision, Coaching* 18 (3): 317–332. https://doi.org/10.1007/s11613-011-0242-0

Nowak, Peter. 2010. *Eine Systematik der Arzt-Patient-Interaktion*. Frankfurt am Main etc.: Peter Lang.

Peräkylä, Anssi: 1995. *AIDS Counseling. Institutional Interaction and Clinical Practice*. Cambridge: Cambridge University Press. https://doi.org/10.1017/CBO9780511597879

Pomerantz, Anita, and John Heritage. 2013. "Preference." In *The Handbook of Conversation Analysis*, ed. by Jack Sidnell, and Tanya Stivers, 210–228. Chichester, U.K.: Wiley Blackwell.

Rettinger, Sabine. 2011. "Das Coaching-Erstgespräch: 'Handlungsidentitäten' in der Beziehungsgestaltung zwischen Coach und Klient." In *Beratung, Coaching, Supervision: Multidisziplinäre Perspektiven vernetzt*, ed. by Eva-Maria Graf, Yasmin Aksu, Ina Pick, and Sabine Rettinger, 149–166. VS Verlag für Sozialwissenschaften, Wiesbaden. https://doi.org/10.1007/978-3-531-93341-2_10

Roberts, Celia, and Srikant Sarangi. 2005. "Theme-Oriented Discourse Analysis of Medical Encounters." *Medical Education* 39: 632–640. https://doi.org/10.1111/j.1365-2929.2005.02171.x

Sacks, Harvey. 1972. "An Initial Investigation of the Usability of Conversational Data for Doing Sociology." In *Studies in Social Interaction*, ed. by David Sudnow, 31–74. New York: Free Press.

Sacks, Harvey, Emanuel A. Schegloff, and Gail Jefferson. 1974. "A Simplest Systematics for the Organization of Turn-Taking for Conversation." *Language* 50 (4): 696–735. https://doi.org/10.1353/lan.1974.0010

Sarangi, Srikant. 2001. "On Demarcating the Space between 'Lay Expertise' and 'Expert Laity'." *Text* 21 (1 & 2): 3–11.

Sarangi, Srikant. 2005. "Activity Analysis in Professional Discourse Settings: The Framing of Risk and Responsibility in Genetic Counselling." *Hermès* 41: 110–120.

Sarangi, Srikant. 2010. "Practising Discourse Analysis in Healthcare Settings." In *The SAGE Handbook of Qualitative Methods in Health Research*, ed. by Ivy Bourgeault, Robert Dingwall, and Ray de Vries, 397–416. Los Angeles: SAGE Publications. https://doi.org/10.4135/9781446268247.n21

Schegloff, Emanuel. 2007. *Sequence Organization in Interaction. A Primer in Conversation Analysis*. Cambridge: Cambridge University Press. https://doi.org/10.1017/CBO9780511791208

Selting, Margret et al. 2009. "Gesprächsanalytisches Transkriptionssystem 2 (GAT2)." *Gesprächsforschung – Online-Zeitschrift zur verbalen Interaktion* (http://www.gespraechsforschung-ozs.de) 10: 353–402.

Sills, Charlotte. 2021. "Understanding the Coaching Relationship." In *The Coaches' Handbook. The Complete Practitioner Guide for Professional Coaches*, ed. by Jonathan Passmore, 68–76. New York: Routledge.

Silverman, David. 1997. *Discourses of Counselling: HIV Counselling as Social Interaction*. London: SAGE Publications.

Spranz-Fogasy, Thomas. 1992. "Ärztliche Gesprächsführung – Inhalte und Erfahrungen gesprächsanalytisch fundierter Weiterbildung." In *Kommunikationsberatung und Kommunikationstraining. Anwendungsfelder der Diskursforschung*, ed. by Reinhard Fiehler, and Wolfgang Sucharowski, 68–78. Opladen: Westdeutscher Verlag. https://doi.org/10.1007/978-3-322-85086-7_5

Stivers, Tanya, Lorenza Mondada, and Jakob Steensig. 2011. "Knowledge, Morality and Affiliation in Social Interaction." In *The Morality of Knowledge in Conversation*, ed. by Tanya Stivers, Lorenza Mondada, and Jakob Steensig, 3–24. Cambridge: Cambridge University Press. https://doi.org/10.1017/CBO9780511921674.002

Theebom, Tim, Bianca Beersma, and Annelies E. M. van Vianen. 2014. "Does Coaching Work? A Meta-Analysis on the Effects of Coaching on Individual Level Outcomes in an Organizational Context." *The Journal of Positive Psychology* 9 (1): 1–18. https://doi.org/10.1080/17439760.2013.837499

Weidner, M. 2012. "On the organization of Polish doctor–patient communication". PhD dissertation, Department of Linguistics, University of Antwerp.

Will, Theresa, Schulte, Eva-Maria, and Simone Kauffeld. 2019. "Coach's Expressed Positive Behaviour Linked to Client's Interest to Change: An Analysis of Distinct Coaching Phases." *Coaching | Theorie & Praxis* 4 (4): 1–10. https://doi.org/10.1365/s40896-019-0027-6

Zimmerman, Don H. 1998. "Identity, Context and Interaction." In *Identities in Talk*, ed. by Charles Antaki, and Sue Widdicombe, 87–106. London: SAGE Publications.

Relationship building in oncological doctor-patient interaction

The use of address forms as 'Tie Signs'

Susanne Günthner
University of Muenster

This paper studies practices of relationship building between oncologists and their patients during consultations when a diagnosis of malignancy is communicated. The analysis – with its focus on physicians' uses of terms of address – aims to provide a better understanding of the sequential construction of the doctor-patient relationship in highly sensitive consultations.

In our data, oncologists frequently address their patients by name – even when recipiency is not at issue. They use this communicative resource to contextualize the heightened attention they are giving their patients and to lend the interaction a more personal quality.

Drawing on methods of Conversation Analysis and Interactional Linguistics, I will show that relationship building is an ongoing task doctors are confronted with in the process of interactions.

Keywords: address forms, 'tie-signs', oncological consultations, affiliation, alignment

1. Introduction

Interactionally oriented approaches to communicative practices have opened new perspectives from which relationship building in everyday interaction can be analyzed. In focusing on language use as it unfolds in real time, social relationship building and acts of affiliation are studied as they are constructed, confirmed or modified in the dialogical process of ongoing social activities (Pomerantz and Mandelbaum 2005; Stivers, Enfield and Levinson 2007; Stivers 2008; Enfield 2009; Günthner 2016; Günthner and Zhu 2017; Couper-Kuhlen and Selting 2018).

Based on the analysis of authentic face-to-face interactions in a medical setting, this paper aims at contributing to our understanding of relationship building, and

https://doi.org/10.1075/pbns.331.09gun

to ways of indicating "connections between individuals constructed via communicative acts" (Scarvaglieri and Graf this volume) in highly sensitive doctor-patient interactions.[1] To be more precise, I will illustrate how physicians mobilize address forms as a communicative practice in order to align and affiliate with their patients in oncological consultations.

In oncological consultations, when patients are summoned to be informed of a diagnosis of cancer, physicians face two separate communicative tasks: (a) They must inform their patients of clinical evidence of a cancer diagnosis, i. e. they have to deliver bad news (Maynard 2003) and provide the details of their patients' life-threatening disease. (b) They must propose and negotiate physically demanding therapies. At the same time, physicians are confronted with conflicting expectations: They are expected to be honest about the life-threatening diagnosis, and also leave room for hope that treatment could prove successful.[2]

Oncological studies and medical textbooks continue to emphasize the importance of the doctor-patient alliance for 'patient contentedness' and 'compliance' as important predictors of outcome measures (Noack et al. 2007; Sator and Spranz-Fogasy 2011; Reineke and Spranz-Fogasy 2013). In a similar vein, Ribeiro et al. (2013, 295) point out: "The strength of the alliance is arguably the best and most reliable predictor of outcomes [...] and is generally considered one of the most important common factors in therapy".[3] However, as of yet, linguistic research on practices of relationship building and the construction of co-alliances in interactions between doctors and cancer patients is scarce. This is surprising, given the fact that cancer consultations and the delivery of bad news are considered to be one of the most challenging communicative situations doctors encounter in their professional lives (Fruht and Vogelhuber 2016, 3ff.).

In studying relationship building in oncological settings, the following questions arise: How do doctors affiliate with their patients in these highly challenging communicative situations? What resources do they use in order to 'do relationship building' in the process of these highly sensitive institutional interactions? In what way do address forms function as communicative devices to indicate professionals'

1. See also Kuna and Scarvaglieri (this volume); Džanko (this volume) on communicative resources employed to do relationship building in doctor-patient interactions.

2. Cf. I want to thank Prof. Dr. Martin Bentz for his information on clinical guidelines for these interactions.

3. Cf. also Muntigl and Horvath (2015, 41) who argue with regard to therapist-client interactions: "Over the last three decades, empirical research has provided robust support for the general claim that the quality of the therapeutic relationship bears ubiquitous and significant relation to treatment outcome across the breadth of client problems and variety of treatment approaches." See also Kuna and Scarvaglieri (this volume).

closer alignment with their patients?[4] These questions will be addressed here, and the analysis will show how communicative strategies contribute to relationship work as it is actively co-constructed in the ongoing interaction and how personalized orientation is "talked into being" (Heritage 1984) on a turn-by-turn basis.

First, I will outline the methodological framework and introduce the data used for the study, and then focus on uses of address forms as a resource for doing relationship work and building doctor-patient alliances. Thus, the main part of the paper is dedicated to a data-based, interactionally grounded analysis of physicians' use of addressing patients by name as a way of contextualizing social 'withness' (Goffman 1971) in oncological consultations. In contexts in which recipiency is not at issue, physicians are shown to mobilize various sequentially positioned forms in addressing their patients by name. In the conclusion, I will discuss possible implications of the analysis.

2. Methodological framework

The following study of communicative practices of relationship building and constructing doctor-patient alliances is grounded in Interactional Linguistics (Couper-Kuhlen and Selting 2001; 2018; Deppermann and Günthner 2015; Imo and Lanwer 2019) and draws on theoretical implications and methodology developed within Conversation Analysis, enriched by concepts stemming from Anthropological Linguistics (Gumperz 1982; 2001) and the Sociology of Knowledge (Luckmann 1990; 2001), in order to study forms and functions of language as systematically employed in everyday social interactions.[5] Authentic everyday (private as well as institutional) interaction is the natural habitat for investigating how social life is constructed, confirmed, and modified by participants in their unfolding interactions. To (re)construct the social actions they are engaged in, participants contextualize and display their ongoing actions to one another while simultaneously interpreting those of their co-participants (Heritage 1984). For the production and interpretation of communicative actions, participants do not treat utterances as isolated objects but relate them to the sequential context as well as to the embedded 'social field' (Hanks 2007) within which they occur.

On the basis of this strictly empirical approach, linguistic phenomena are treated as interactional resources which participants mobilize to accomplish recurrent tasks

4. See also Kuna and Scarvaglieri (this volume) on the role of address forms for relationship management in Hungarian primary care consultations.

5. Social institutions are part of everyday life; thus, institutional interactions (e.g. medical interactions) are considered part of everyday social interactions (see Schütz and Luckmann 1979).

in everyday interactions (Günthner and Luckmann 2001). Accordingly, more or less sedimented communicative practices are indicative of the ways in which social reality is constructed and modified in the process of interaction (Luckmann 2001).

This analysis of the various uses of address terms in medical consultations is part of a growing body of research which investigates the use of address forms in naturally occurring sequences of interaction and their context contingent functions (Stivers, Enfield and Levinson 2007; Günthner 2016; Raymond 2016).

The study is carried out in connection with a project financed by the Deutsche Krebshilfe (German Cancer Aid) "*Von der Pathologie zum Patienten: Optimierung von Wissenstransfer und Verstehenssicherung in der Onkologie zur Verbesserung der Patientensicherheit*".[6] The analysis examines a corpus of 40 oncological doctor-patient interactions (lasting between 5 and 31 minutes), which were audio-recorded between 2014 and 2015 at the Municipal Hospital of Karlsruhe, Germany.[7] All of these interactions were conducted in German. The data collection took place in the following departments of the Municipal Hospital: Medical Clinic I: General Internal Medicine, Nephrology, Rheumatology, and Pneumology; Medical Clinic III: Hematology, Oncology, Infectiology, and Palliative Medicine; Clinic for General and Visceral Surgery, and Women's Hospital.

The oncological consultations used here are with patients who, based on the available results from pathology. have been summoned to the Municipal Hospital. The consultations regarding the patients' cancer diagnoses were carried out by senior physicians from the respective departments. In addition to the patients and the physicians, in 22 of the 40 consultations patients were accompanied by family members or friends.[8] To keep the interactions as authentic as possible, the project staff were not present during the recordings, and consent to record the consultations and to use the transcripts for scientific purposes were obtained from all participants. All recordings were transcribed according to GAT 2, a system for transcribing talk-in-interaction (Selting et al. 2009; cf. the English translation by Couper-Kuhlen and Barth-Weingarten 2011).[9] Names and other references to the identities of the participants were anonymized.

6. See Bentz, Binnenhei, Coussious, Gruden, Imo, Korte, Rüdiger, Ruf-Dördelmann, Schön and Stier (2016); Imo (2017).

7. A total of 56 consultations were collected. As I only had 40 interactions available at the time of the study, my analysis concentrates on these 40 consultations.

8. In four consultations a ward physician or a student in her/his practical year attended the consultation.

9. Given that no video material is available, bodily expressions cannot be included in the analysis.

3. 'Doing social relationships': The use of address forms as 'Tie Signs'

In line with Social Constructivism (Berger and Luckmann 1966; Luckmann 1990), Interactional Sociolinguistics (Gumperz 1982; 2001) and Conversation Analysis (Schegloff 2007), I treat social interaction as the key site where the (re)construction, confirmation and change of social relationships occur. Interpersonal communication functions not only as the principal means for establishing social relationships, it also serves to reveal their empirically observable side.[10]

Accordingly, social relationships are not to be treated as 'things we have', and thus, as static entities, but as something which participants construct in their ongoing interactions. As Mandelbaum (2003, 207) points out: "Increasingly in the communication field, scholars are coming to recognize that the character of a relationship is built moment by moment, by interactants, in and through interaction".[11]

Drawing on an interactional perspective of relationship building in the process of interpersonal talk, the analysis will focus on the question of '*how*' relationship work 'is being done'; that is, on the methods and communicative practices participants employ 'to do relationship work' in interactions.[12] This perspective gives rise to the following question: What methods do participants in ongoing interactions apply 'to do relationship building'?[13]

As work by Goffman (1971), Goodwin (2001), Mandelbaum (2003) and Pomerantz and Mandelbaum (2005) illustrate, even though participants have a number of resources at their disposal with which to mark social relationships, they mainly use implicit cues, which are incidental to their ongoing activities (cf. Mandelbaum 2003, 209). Such "tie-signs" do not explicitly "communicate messages" but they are highly context sensitive cues providing "evidence about relationships, that is, about ties between persons [...]" (Goffman 1971, 194–195).

10. Cf. Keller, Knoblauch and Reichertz (2012); Günthner and Zhu (2017). Cf. also Enfield (2006) who claims that language is one of the central means with which to negotiate and confirm interpersonal relations.

11. See Graf, Scarvaglieri and Spranz-Fogasy (this volume) on communicative acts employed for building relationships in helping professions.

12. See also Muntigl (this volume) on issues of 'how' relationships are displayed in psychotherapeutic encounters.

13. The question of '*how*' has become central for studies in Conversation Analysis, ever since Sacks addressed the question of '*how is that social activity done*': "Harvey Sacks keeps this question in front of him by using the verb 'to do' in thinking about social activities. He refers to arguing as *doing arguing*; being embarrassed as *doing embarrassment*; exclaiming as *doing exclaiming*; questioning as *doing questioning*, etc. In this way, he tried to keep focused on the methodical ways in which social activities are produced by members of the culture" (Churchill 1971: 183).

The analysis will concentrate on one sort of "tie-sign" doctors use in oncological consultations for relationship building by addressing their patients by their names. Various studies within Conversational Analysis and Interactional Linguistics have demonstrated that participants use address forms "in the service of a variety of actions beyond addressing per se" (Clayman 2010, 163) (see also Schwitalla 1995; 2010; Lerner 2003; Rendle-Short 2007; 2011; Günthner 2016). Besides selecting next speaker (Sacks, Schegloff and Jefferson 1978), speakers in interactions employ address forms for other purposes, e.g. ensuring recipiency (Lerner 2003), launching topic shifts (Clayman 2010; Rendle-Short 2011) or signaling sequential departure (Rendle-Short 2007; 2011; Clayman 2012; Günthner 2021). As the following analysis demonstrates, doctors in oncological consultations do not only mobilize personalized address terms as a device for the management of interactive 'alignment' (e. g. for gaining co-participants' attention when shifts in the communicative agenda are at issue), but also apply personalized address terms to do relationship work (Goffman 1967; Linke and Schröter 2017) and thus, to indicate 'affiliation' in these highly sensitive situations.

The term 'alignment' refers to the structural organization of interaction and, thus, to the sequential organization of communicative projects in progress. Aligning actions are ones "facilitating the proposed activity or sequence; accepting the presuppositions and terms of the proposed action or activity; and matching the formal design preference of the turn" (Stivers, Mondada and Steensig 2011, 21; Stivers 2008). 'Affiliation', however, relates to the affective level of interaction, i.e., how utterances relate to the affective stances. Affiliative actions are "maximally pro-social when they match the prior speaker's evaluative stance, display empathy and/or cooperate with the preference of the prior action" (Stivers, Mondada and Steensig 2011, 21; Stivers 2008).[14]

4. Addressing patients by name during oncological consultations

The 40 oncological interactions (involving 40 patients and 24 of their companions, and 13 senior physicians) include 61 address forms, which are distributed as follows:

14. See Droste and Günthner (2021) for the management of alignment and affiliations by vocative uses of the German "du" (*'you'*). See also Muntigl and Horvath (2015); Muntigl (this volume) for "relational disaffiliation in therapeutic relationships". Cf. Džanko (this volume) on cultural differences in building affliliation in German and Bosnian medical encounters.

Table 1. Participants' use of address forms

Doctors addressing patients	44
Doctors addressing patients' companions	4
Patients addressing doctors	10
Patients' companions addressing doctors	2
Indistinct	1

Addressing practices in these consultations are distributed as follows among the interactive sequences:

Table 2. Address forms in different sequential contexts

Who addresses whom by name?	Opening sequence	Closing sequence	Core phase
Doctors addressing patients	13	9	22
Doctors addressing patients' companions	3	0	1
Patients addressing doctors		4	6
Patients' companions addressing doctors	1		1
Indistinct			1

As these tables indicate, doctors produce by far the greatest number of address terms (48 out of 61). Beyond opening and closing sequences, half of the physicians' addressing practices are located in the core phase of the interaction. This result is surprising in that address terms in medical encounters generally tend to be limited to the "ritual bracket of interaction" (Goffman 1971, 79), i. e. to opening and closing sequences (see Džanko 2020 on address terms in German and Bosnian doctor-patient interactions).

The core phase in these oncological consultations is comprised of various 'activity phases':[15]

- reconstruction of the previous history with regard to the pending diagnosis;
- delivery and explanation of the cancer diagnosis;
- presentation and discussion of a recommended treatment plan;
- scheduling of the therapeutic measures (Günthner 2017; 2018).

As the securing of recipiency is generally not in doubt during the core phase of the interaction, the original tasks of addressing one's co-participant by name, identifying the participants and ensuring recipiency, are not required. So, the resource

15. See Spranz-Fogasy (2005) on 'activity phases' in medical encounters; cf. also Heath (1992) on the delivery of diagnoses in medical consultations.

of addressing one's co-participant by name is available to perform other communicative functions.

As the data will show, physicians mobilize vocative forms [title + family name] during the core phase of oncological consultations to manage the following tasks:

1. to construct interactive alignment:
   This function comes close to what Rendle-Short (2011) calls "shift implicative" use. Through use of the vocative ['Frau' (Ms.) or 'Herr' (Mr.) + family name],[16] physicians gain patients' attention for shifts in the communicative agenda, for segmenting interactional phases and introducing new topics.
2. to contextualize affiliation:
   By addressing their patients by name, doctors display a more personal "orientation and sensitivity to the particular other(s)" (Sacks, Schegloff and Jefferson 1978, 43) and thus, do relationship work. Direct address forms constitute a sustainable resource in doctors' pursuit of their institutional goals and their commitment to establishing working alliances with their patients.

In the following, I will concentrate on vocative practices ['Frau' or 'Herr' + family name] doctors implement to do relationship work and thus, display being "in a 'with'" (Goffman 1971, 196) with their patients. For this paper, I have chosen a set of representative examples for a detailed analysis of how doctors do relationship work when addressing their patients by name.

As various studies claim (Lerner 2003; Rendle-Short 2007; Clayman 2012; Günthner 2016; 2021; Droste and Günthner 2020; 2021), vocatives are "positionally sensitive" (Schegloff 1996; Auer and Lindström 2016). Their interactive function is intertwined with their sequential and contextual position. While pre-positioned turn- or TCU-prefacing vocatives tend to be used to attract the addressee's attention and to establish mutual orientation, post-positioned vocatives tend to be employed as stance-markers. However, even though my data show functional tendencies for address terms depending on the sequential and syntactic context in which they are used, one cannot adhere to a strict correlation between the position of the vocatives and their functions. As the following excerpts will reveal, instead of a binary opposition between pre- and post-positioned address terms, we can observe positional tendencies as well as overlaps.

16. In my data, physicians generally address their patients by [title + family name] (i.e. 'Frau' (Ms.) or 'Herr' (Mr.) + family name] or by using the V pronoun "Sie" ('you'). Patients, however, address their physicians either by [title + professional title + family name] (i.e. 'Frau/Herr Doktor' + family name) or only by [title + professional title] (i.e. 'Frau/Herr Doktor'). They also use the V pronoun "Sie" ('you') when referring to their physicians. See also Nübling, Fahlbusch and Heuser (2012) on address forms and names in German. Cf. Droste and Günthner (2021) on vocative uses of the German pronoun "du" ('you').

Post-positioned address term

The following excerpt is taken from an oncological consultation between the physician AW and the patient Frau Wehaus (PW),[17] who was just informed about the histological finding, i.e. breast cancer. After having delivered the bad news, AW informs Frau Wehaus about the recommended therapy. The patient (who is not a native speaker of German), however, focuses more on her astonishment regarding the diagnosis (l. 235):

(1) Consultation 035–1[18]

```
234  PW:  aber WISsen sie, (-)
          but you know, (-)
235       ich bin jetzt SPRACHlos; (-)
          I am speechless right now; (-)
236       ich bin <<sehr deutlich > REgelmäßig> zur
          untersuchung [gegangen? ]
          I have always gone <<very articulate> regularly> to all
                       [check-ups?]
237  AW:               [hm,]      ]
238       (2.8)
239       ich GLAUB_S ihnen, (.)
          I believe you, (.)
240  PW:  und und bei meine FRAUeärztin,
          and and I also,
241       WAR ich auch,
          saw my gynecologist,
242       (2.7)
243  AW:  wann WAR_N sie da zuletscht,
          when did you go last,
244       (3.5)
245  PW:  also Ich hab in meine BICHle,
          well I've got it in my little notebook,
246  AW:  hm_hm,=oKE,
          hm_hm,=okay,
247       °h isch ja jetzt net so wichtig WANN genau,
          °h it's not that important right now when exactly you were there,
248       aber ISCH schon do-
          but it's quite da-
249       isch schon DOOF;
          it's quite daft;
250       ich GLAUB_S ihnen;
          I believe you;
251       isch schon schon BLÖD;
          it's really really vexing;
```

17. All of the names in the transcripts have been anonymized (the patients' surnames end with the syllable "haus"; the physicians' surnames with "berg"). The abbreviation AW refers to female doctors, AM to male doctors, PW to female and PM to male patients.

18. See Günthner (2021).

```
252    <<p> ja;> (--)
       <<p> yeah;> (--)
253    ((atmet tief ein und aus)) (2.0)
       ((takes a deep breath)) (2.0)
254    jetzt HELfe mer ihnen frau wehaus; (.)
       now we are going to help you ms. wehaus; (.)
255    verSORgen sie gut,
       take good care of you,
256    und GUCKe,
       and make sure,
257    dass mer das gut HINkriege;=hm?
       that we will manage it well;= alright?
```

Instead of responding to AW's suggestions about the planned therapy, the patient, PW, restates her bewilderment at the diagnosis (l. 234ff.), especially, in view of the seeming contradiction between the regular medical check-ups with her gynecologist and her diagnosis of breast cancer (l. 263ff.). The doctor responds by affiliating with PW's affectual stance ("ich GLAUB_S ihnen, (.)" '*I believe you, (.)*'; l. 239) and thus, conveys her understanding and empathy.

In line 240, PW reaffirms the precautionary measures she had taken. Again, AW communicates her sympathy for the patient's bewilderment (l. 237ff.; 246ff.) and displays her understanding of PW's emotional situation (cf. "aber ISCH schon doisch schon DOOF; ich GLAUB_S ihnen;" '*but it's quite da-, it's quite daft; I believe you;*'; l. 248–250).[19] With this intersubjective orientation, AW, by affiliating with the patient's consternation, indicates a "congruency of relevance systems" (Schütz and Luckmann 1979, 88). The physician bonds with her patient (see Muntigl, Knight, Horvath and Watkins 2012, 117). As Ms.Wehaus remains silent, AW repeats her emphatic assessment "isch schon schon BLÖD; <<p ja;>" ('*it's really really vexing; <<p> yeah*') and takes a deep breath (l. 252). As PW neither provides recipient tokens nor takes over the turn (cf. the pause of 2 sec.; l. 253), AW introduces a thematic shift. Already the TCU initial "jetzt" ('*now*'; l. 254) indicates a turnabout from the past stage (i.e. the bemoaning of PW's stroke of fate) to the hic et nunc, and thus, to the situation at hand: Now Ms. Wehaus will be helped and taken care of. This shift in perspective is accompanied by the post-positioned address form "frau wehaus; (.)" ('*Ms. Wehaus*'; l. 254), which marks a more personal orientation towards PW.

As Lerner (2003, 185) claims, post-positioned terms of address are generally used "to demonstrate a particular stance toward or a relationship with a recipient under circumstances where that demonstration is particularly relevant."[20] Couper-Kuhlen and Selting (2018, 23) observe that "[...] turn-final address terms accomplish important interpersonal and stance-related work and in this sense are

19. See also Kupetz (2014, 4).

20. See Günthner (2017) for the marking of "stances" employing post-positioned address terms.

far from being mere ‚noise': in short, we cannot afford to neglect them". This close connection between post-positioned address terms and stance-taking also holds for the address term which AW mobilizes in Excerpt (1): The nominal vocative form ("frau wehaus") retroactively conveys an expressive stance towards what AW has just said ("jetzt HELfe mer ihnen frau wehaus; (.)" '*now we are going to help you ms. wehaus; (.)*'), indicating that she won't abandon PW in her desperate situation.[21] This post positioned address form comes close to what Clayman (2010, 178), who studies address forms in news interviews, calls "doing speaking from the heart":

> This practice is plainly useful in a range of action environments where genuineness or sincerity becomes salient. Beyond enabling speakers to express belief in the absence of evidence (...), or in the face of contrary evidence and outright challenges (...), it also facilitates vows and promises that might otherwise come across as hollow and disingenuous.

As this segment shows, doctors in oncological consultations use address terms as "tie-signs" (Goffman 1974; 1982), which – besides marking a heightened dialogical orientation toward their co-present interlocutors – indicate their willingness to confront the fears, sorrows and wishes of each individual patient, lending "the utterance a personal and intimate quality" (Couper-Kuhlen and Selting, Online chapter F; 2018, 29).

Due to their attention-getting potential, address terms may also accomplish alignment-related work. In (1) Consultation 035–1, AW is trying to inform her patient about the recommended treatment and to discuss the therapeutic measures. However, PW drifts away from the agenda by emphasizing her "speechlessness" and bemoaning her diagnosis. The personalized address term functions to bring PW's attention back to the agenda, to the 'here-and-now' of the ongoing interaction, so that AW can continue with her explanation of the chosen therapeutic measures. In addition to its function as a stance-marker, the address term functions as a means to correct ongoing "misalignments" (Stivers 2008) and to redirect a co-participant's attention to the agenda of the ongoing consultation.

Pivot-positioned address term

Whereas the address term in segment (1) Consultation 035–1 was post-positioned and thus reflected back on the preceding talk by conveying AW's stance, the address term in (2) Consultation 007–01 pivots between two turn-constructional units and

21. Cf. also Koerfer and Albus (2018, 837) about the relevance of addressing patients by name for building good relations in doctor-patient-interactions.

can be heard as belonging to the prior TCU as an incrementally positioned vocative and, at the same time to the subsequent TCU as an initial element.

The extract is taken from the end of the oncological consultation between the patient PM (Mr. Lehaus) and the doctor AM. Once AM has informed Mr. Lehaus of his cancer diagnosis and negotiated the upcoming therapy, the patient recapitulates his last few months, which were strongly affected by his wife's illness and death.

(2) Consultation 007–01

```
670  PM:  der TOD von meiner frau,
          the death of my wife,
671       vorheriges JAHR,
          last year,
672       SAG ich mir,
          I always tell myself,
673       (-) was SCHLIMmeres kann ein_m net passIEre.
          (-) nothing worse can happen to you.
674       (---) wegen dem_hab ich IMmer gsagt,
          (---) that's why I've always said,
675       (--) was- egAl was jetzt NACHkommt,
          (--) what- no matter what happens next,
676       KANN net so schlImm sein,
          it can't be as bad,
677       wie DES im letschte jahr.
          as what happened last year.
678  AM:  (-) °h [ das::, ]
          (-) °h [ this::, ]
679  PM:         [außer es] kann mir SELber
          passieren,(--)
                 [unless it ] could happen to me, (--)
680       dass ich LETZTendlich so ende;
          that I end up the same way;
681       aber alles VORher,
          but everything before that,
682       isch IRgendwo:, (---)
          is somehow; (---)
683  AM:  ich verSTEH das.
          I understand that.
684       herr LEhaus-
          Mr. Lehaus-
685       das kann          [ich auch SEHR gut,]
          I can understand [you very well,    ]
686  PM:                    [des WAR ja irgend]wo;
                            [well it was some ]how;
687       das war auch IRgendwo so m_meine kraft;
          it was also somehow m_my strength;
688       wo ich geSAGT hab,
          when I said,
689       (--) ich hab zwar NIMMer meine frAU,
          (--) even though I lost my wife,
690       (--) aber ich HAB,
          (--) but I had,
691       ich had die KRAFT,
          I had the strength,
```

```
692        und die RÜCKmeldung von meine kinder
           gekrIEgt,
           and the support of my children,
693        (-) und des hat sehr GUT,
           (-) and that was really good,
694        es hat MIR geholfe;
           it helped me;
```

Even though recipiency is not at issue, AM in line 684 addresses his patient by name. In the immediately preceding TCU (l. 683), AM responds to the emotionally charged story of the death of the patient's wife and his struggle in dealing with this loss. The doctor displays an understanding of his patient's emotional situation ("ich verSTEH das." '*I do understand that.*'; l. 683), "while orienting to an asymmetry regarding their experiential rights and/or emotive involvement" (Kupetz 2014, 7). As Heritage (2011, 159) states, the "relationship between knowing something and having experienced it is deeply entrenched in interactional practices associated with assessment and evaluation." Thus, for AM's claim of 'understanding' PM's tragic experience during recent months represents a rather sensitive issue, as AM does not share this experience; i.e. it is PM, who as the experiencer has exclusive epistemic access. Heritage (2011, 160) argues in this context that "when persons report first-hand experiences of any great intensity [...], they obligate others to join with them in their evaluation, to affirm the nature of the experience and its meaning, and to affiliate with the stance of the experiencer toward them." AM fulfills these social, and even moral obligations with his display of being "in a 'with'" (Goffman 1971, 196). Such moments of marking "social solidarity" (Durkheim 1915) prove to be "fundamental to the creation of social relationships, to social solidarity, and to an enduring sociocultural and moral order" (Heritage 2011, 160–161).[22]

AM's statement of "understanding" (l. 683), which functions as an affiliative response based on his comprehension of PM's emotional state, is followed by the direct address form: "herr LEhaus-" (l. 684), which lends his statement a personal quality. The address term [title + family name] forms a prosodic unit in and of itself. The vocative form "Herr Lehaus" is both the coda to the first unit "ich verSTEH das." ('*I do understand that.*') and a preface to the second unit "das kann [ich auch SEHR gut,]" ('*I can understand [you very well,]*'):

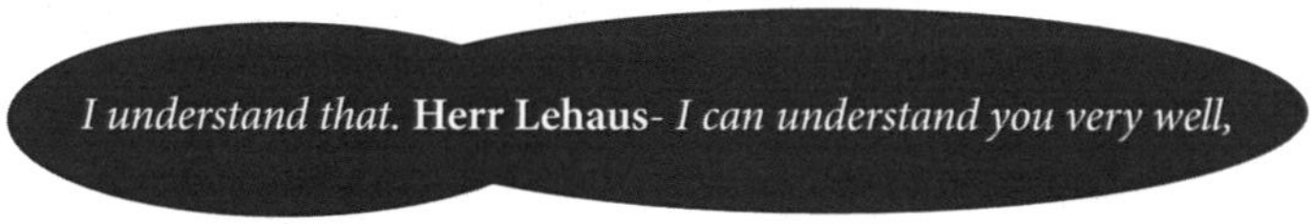

22. Cf. also Muntigl (this volume) on therapists' display of understanding and their construction of affiliation and social bonding.

With the address form in hinge position, AM reaffirms his prior "intersubjective sharing" (Tomasello and Carpenter 2007, 121), and, at the same time, projects a continuation which directs the recipient's attention to the upcoming unit. As Couper-Kuhlen and Selting (2018, 30) emphasize, pivotal address terms "permit extensions of turns in order to provide support for prior weak or vulnerable claims".

AM's explicit demonstration of understanding and "intersubjective sharing" (Tomasello and Carpenter 2007, 121), however, is a somewhat delicate issue. On the one hand, the physician conveys an understanding of what his patient is going through emotionally and marks a "person-centered relational stance" (Muntigl, Knight, Watkins, Horvath and Angus 2013, 1; Muntigl this volume). On the other hand, the postulated epistemic access to his patient's emotions can easily be interpreted as "intruding on patients' epistemic rights" (Heritage and Raymond 2005). In this sensitive context, the implementation of the address term helps to present the talk as "genuine and sincere" (Clayman 2012, 1866; see also Couper-Kuhlen and Selting 2018, 30), even though the doctor has no epistemic access to his patient's emotions.

Both Excerpts (1) Consultation 035–1 and (2) Consultation 007–01 illustrate that physicians use vocative address terms ['Frau' (Ms.) or 'Herr' (Mr.) + family name] (during the main phase of oncological consultations) not only to call upon their patients' attention for the ongoing interaction in the *hic et nunc*, but also to display "social solidarity" (Durkheim 1915) through "heightened personal orientation" (Günthner 2016).

While the post-positioned vocative in Consultation 035–1 was mobilized to index a strong commitment to AW's preceding statement, contextualizing her sincerity,[23] the Janus-faced vocative in pivot position retroactively conveys AM's expressive stance, emphasizing his understanding, and at the same time orienting his co-participant's attention to what is to follow.

Both excerpts, however, demonstrate that relationship work is being done in the ongoing process of interaction[24] by using highly context sensitive cues (i.e. "tie-signs"), which tend to be incidental to their ongoing activities (cf. Goffman 1971, 194–195; Mandelbaum 2003, 209). These findings support the idea that person reference designs are habitually employed in conjunction with social activities, which in turn are shaped by the interactional sequences and the 'social field' in which they occur.

23. See also Schwitalla (2010, 188) on speakers employing address terms to increase the "Eindringlichkeit der Äußerungen" ('*the intensity of the utterances*').

24. See Deppermann and Günthner (2015) on temporality in interaction.

Pre-positioned address term

As the next extract will illustrate, not only are post-positioned or pivotal address terms used as resources for relationship building, initially positioned address forms also reach beyond drawing a co-participant's attention to the upcoming action and are mobilized as resources to contextualize 'withness'.

The following segment is preceded by a conflict between the patient's husband LM, who accompanies the patient, and the physician AW. Subsequent to LM's statement that he expects his wife (who was diagnosed with breast cancer) to get alternative treatment instead of having breast surgery, a dispute develops between the husband and the doctor. As LM insists on trying to persuade AW about the merits of alternative medicine, AW offers to hand over a copy of the histology to the couple, so that they can consult the wife's gynecologist and talk to her in more detail about reasonable treatment options.

In line 627, the patient PW (Ms. Behaus) takes over the turn by asking the doctor, AW, if it is possible to phone the doctor to make an appointment for the recommended operation. (Neither PW nor her husband LM are native speakers of German):

(3) Consultation 069[25]

627 PW: DARF ich mit ihnen in telefonische kontakt also,
may I get in touch with you by phone that is
628 dass ich dann schon feste terMIN dann mache,
so that I can make a fixed date,
629 AW: FÜR die opera[tion,]
for the opera[tion]
630 PW: [ja;]
[yeah;]
631 AW: wir könn ihn_n GERne einen festen termin machen,
of course we can make a fixed date for you now,
632 sie können aber auch GERne nochmal, (-)
however you can also once more, (-)
633 sich nochmal mit [ihrem] FRAUenarzt beraten,
consult with [your] gynecologist,
634 PW: [ja;]
[yeah:]
635 AW: oder wenn sie eine ZWEITmeinung einholen,
or if you want to get a second opinon,
636 h° aber **frau BEhaus** ich BITte sie, (-)
*h° but **Ms. Behaus** I beg you, (-)*
637 bä_ schieben sie des NICH auf die lange bank;
pl_do not put it off;

25. See Günthner (2021).

```
638   PW:    [          ja_ja;       ]
             [   yeah_yeah;          ]
639   AW:    [weil sie haben        ]WIRKlich sUper sUper, (---)
             [because you really ] have excellent excellent, (---)
640          chAncen geSUND zu sein hin[terher;]
             chances to fully recover  [afterwards;]
641   PW:                              [ja;          ]
                                       [yeah;        ]
642          (7.4)
```

After pointing out the possibility for the patient and her husband to consult with PW's gynecologist and obtain a second opinion (l. 631–635), AW continues her turn with the initially positioned adversative conjunction "aber" ('*but*'), followed by the address term "frau BEhaus" ('*Ms. Behaus*'). This initially positioned vocative accomplishes various tasks. In the triadic conversation, it singles out a participant as selected recipient, i. e. Ms. Behaus and not her husband, who had dominated the preceding discussion on the necessity of an operation. With the address term, AW reestablishes PW as the focus of the interaction. Furthermore, the combination of the adversative conjunction "aber" ('*but*') and the address term with its attention-soliciting property contextualizes the heightened relevance (i.e. functioning as a "foregrounding strategy"; Clayman 2010, 171; see also Günthner 2016, 417) of the speaker's following action: her request. This request – "bä_schieben sie des NICH auf die lange bank; [weil sie haben] WIRKlich sUper sUper, (---) chAncen geSUND zu sein hin[terher;]" ('*pl_do not put it off; [because you really] have excellent excellent, (---) chances to make a full recovery [afterwards;]*') (l. 637–640) – introduced with the projecting construction (Günthner 2008) "ich BITte sie," ('*I beg you*') – clearly opposes the husband's position of considering alternative healing methods (which he had proposed just shortly before). With the address term, AW not only "individuates the referent" (Hanks 2007, 149), he also displays a personalized concern for Ms. Behaus.[26]

As this segment indicates, in environments in which attention-getting has already been established, the vocative form is 'free' to take on a variety of pragmatic uses. Also pre-positioned vocatives, which draw participants' attention to what is to follow, may work as stance markers which contextualize speaker's commitment to the following action and display heightened affiliation and social 'withness'.[27]

As Heritage (2004, 237) points out, institutional interaction is characterized by a prevailing *asymmetry* which results, among other things, from the tension

26. This again comes close to what Clayman (2010, 178) calls "doing *speaking from the heart*".

27. This kind of "recipient-centeredness" (Scarvaglieri 2017) works to build and manage therapeutic relationships (Graf, Scarvaglieri and Spranz-Fogasy this volume).

between (a) doctors' professional perspective of treating "the individual as a 'routine case'", and (b) patients' perspective of their "case [as] personal and unique". In a similar vein, Frommer (2014, 109) refers to the dilemma doctors and psychotherapists are faced with in their professional social action. On the one hand, physicians are (professionally) supposed to treat the patient as a "case" and to distance themselves from individual factors and from disturbing emotional intrusions. Thus, for professional medical treatment it seems necessary to eliminate individual factors, as "professionals would not be able to manage their work with clients without routine and distance" (Bergmann 2014, 429; translation S.G.). On the other hand, however, patients experience their illness as individually grounded and subjective. Accordingly, doctors are expected "to open up to the subjective experience of each patient" (Frommer 2014, 109; translation S.G.), as their patient-orientation contributes to patients' compliance. This conflict demands "an ongoing shift of perspectives from objective case-data to patients' subjective experience and expectations" (Frommer 2014, 109; translation S.G.).

In oncological consultations, doctors manage this conflict by indicating a greater, more personal orientation toward their patients and, thus, displaying social 'withness'. Hereby, addressing their patient by name (even though recipiency is not at issue) acts as an important resource. Personalized addressing lends the clinical interaction a personal and intimate quality, leaning towards patients' subjective demands (cf. Heritage 2004, 237; Frommer 2014, 109; Bergmann 2014, 429). As Bergmann (2014, 429) emphasizes: "[...] socially it makes a big difference – for example with regard to the emotional character or the thematic development of the conversation – whether the professional treats his counterpart in the interaction as an interchangeable case or as an individual client" (translation S.G.).

In my data, doctors' display of heightened personal orientation toward their patients (by addressing them by name) is primarily used for social activities such as indicating empathy, comfort and sincerity, as well as in situations in which differences of opinion (concerning the conversational alignment as well as emotional or therapeutic questions) have to be dealt with.

In the following excerpt, which is again taken from Consultation 069, the physician AW uses the vocative form "frau BEhaus" ('*Ms. Behaus*'; l. 938) to display a heightened personal orientation toward her patient.

Just before this excerpt, Ms. Behaus' husband leaves the room as a response to the ongoing conflict with the doctor (AW). When Ms. Behaus is left alone with the doctor (AW), she states that she herself prefers to undergo the required operation and wishes to make a prompt appointment:

(4) Consultation 069[28]

```
929  AW:  dann MITTwoch?
          then wednesday?
930  PW:  ja;
          yeah;
931  AW:  woll_n sie MITTwoch,
          do you want on wednesday,
932       dann ham sie noch ein bisschen (.)
          beDENKzei[t, ]
          this would give you some (.) time to think it [over,]
933  PW:            [ja;]
                                                          [yeah;]
934  AW:  und haben bisschen ZEIT          [noch,°h ]
          and it will give you some more [time,°h ]
935  PW:                                 [ja;      ]
                                         [yeah;    ]
936  AW:  mit ihrem MANN sich auseinanderzusE[tzen,]
          to discuss everything with your hus [band, ]
937  PW:                                      [ja,    ]
                                              [yeah, ]
938  AW:  aber frau BEhaus verSPRECHen sie mir,
          but Ms. Behaus do promise me,
939       sie MÜSsen      [operiert werden,]
          you have to get [the operation,  ]
940  PW:             [<<flüsternd>>ich MACH ich mach das,>]
                     [<<whispering> I will I will do it,> ]
941       waRUM, (-)
          why, (-)
942       herr XYZ kennt mich SO schon seit jahren,
          Mr. XYZ has known me for many years,
943       sag (.)komm zu UNS,
          says (.) come here,
944       ich bin (.) dank IHM zu ihnen gekommen,
          I came (.) to you thanks to him,
945       weil sie die BESte sind;=ja,
          because you are the best; =yeah,
946       und ich MACH das,
          and I will do it,
947       ob der WILL oder nicht;
          whether he wants me to or not;
```

After having proposed "MITTwoch" ('*Wednesday*') as the date for the surgery, AW adds that this date will give Ms. Behaus some time to deal with her husband (l. 936). With the initially positioned adversative conjunction "aber" ('*but*'; l. 938), AW again takes over the turn. The following address term "frau Behaus" ('*Ms. Behaus*') in combination with the projective construction (Günthner 2008) "verSPRECHen sie mir," ('*do promise me,*'; l. 938) projects the subsequent action as highly relevant and

28. Cf. Günthner (2021).

sensitive. The force of the requested 'promise' is strengthened by the prosodically marked modal verb "MÜSsen" ('*must*').

Again, the personalized address term accomplishes relationship building. It indexes affiliation, and dealing with the patient as an individual lends the clinical interaction a personal quality. Hereby, the doctor indicates that she is not treating Ms. Behaus as one case among many, but that she sincerely cares about Ms. Behaus' personal needs. This kind of individualized care bridges the distance between the physician and the patient, demonstrating the doctor's concern for her patient.

This segment also supports the observation emphasized by Graf, Scarvaglieri and Spranz-Fogasy (this volume) that doctors and other professionals employ "recipient centeredness" to "uphold an otherwise endangered working relationship". At this stage of the interaction, the physician attaches great importance to re-affiliating with her patient and reaching common interactional ground regarding the therapeutic agenda. By employing the individualized address form "frau Behaus" ('*Ms. Behaus*'), AW recalibrates relationship ties with her patient. Ms. Behaus' whispering response "[<<flüsternd>> ich MACH ich] mach das,>]" ('[<<*whispering*> *I will I will do it,*>]'; l. 940) marks her agreement and indicates her compliance with AW (despite her husband's objections).

Again, one can observe how an address term is mobilized as a tie-sign, which is not explicitly communicated, but works as a contextualization cue, indexing social 'withness'.

5. Conclusion

As Stivers, Enfield and Levinson (2007, 19) claim, "our entire motivation to communicate is in service of managing social relations". Social relations, however, are not simply given but are constructed by participants in everyday life (Berger and Luckmann 1966). Hereby, interpersonal communication plays a major role (Keller, Knoblauch and Reichertz 2012), as talk-in-interaction is the vehicle we use in order to build and strengthen our social relationships and thus the locus where social 'withness' is "talked into being" (Heritage 1984). In addition, talk-in-interaction represents the side of relationship building which can be observed and studied empirically.

As the data reveal, in oncological consultations physicians frequently employ address forms even when recipiency is not at issue. This communicative practice proves to be a multifunctional resource which lends the clinical interaction a personal quality. It can be used to repair ongoing misalignment and refocus a co-participant's attention on the agenda of the consultation. Doctors also employ vocatives as a means for contextualizing their heightened attention to their patients' needs and indexing social 'withness' (Goffman 1971). Thus, the use of personalized address forms is also a communicative practice for relationship building in clinical contexts. Personalized vocatives function as linguistic tools which allow doctors to recalibrate social bonds with their patients as they progress in talk.

Research about doctor-patient communication claims that physicians are often confronted with a dilemma (Frommer 2014, 109). On the one hand, for professional reasons, they must treat their patients as one case among many. On the other hand, they are confronted with individuals who consider their disease as a subjectively unique experience and balk at being treated as a mere clinical case. Bergmann (2014, 430) argues: "The communicative sensibility of the professional is essentially demonstrated by the fact that he or she succeeds in mediating between these poles at the level of interaction – for example, in a doctor-patient conversation in a hospital" (translation S.G.). As the data demonstrate, physicians in oncological consultations manage this shift of perspectives from treating the patient as one case among to orienting to patients' individual experiences, fears and expectations by mobilizing personalized address forms and thus, contextualizing being "in a *with*" with their patients (Goffman 1971, 196). The presented uses of address forms no longer represent vocatives in their traditional sense (i. e. as a means for securing recipiency), but resemble pragmatic markers located on the 'metapragmatic level' (Silverstein 1993), contextualizing social 'withness'. This shift from an attention-getting device to a 'tie-sign' is deeply intertwined with their inherent potential to demonstrate a speaker's heightened orientation to her/his co-participant as an individual.

Acknowledgements

I want to thank Lisa Roebuck for proofreading the English. My thanks also go to the anonymous reviewers for their helpful comments on an earlier version.

Bibliography

Auer, Peter, and Jan Lindström. 2016. "Left/Right Asymmetries and the Grammar of Pre- vs. Post-Positioning in German and Swedish Talk-in-Interaction." *Language Sciences* 56: 68–92. https://doi.org/10.1016/j.langsci.2016.03.001

Bentz, Martin, Martin Binnenhei, Georgios Coussious, Juliana Gruden, Wolfgang Imo, Lisa Korte, Thomas Rüdiger, Antonia Ruf-Dördelmann, Michael R. Schön, and Sebastian Stier. 2016. "Von der Pathologie zum Patienten: Optimierung von Wissenstransfer und Verstehenssicherung in der medizinischen Kommunikation." *SpIn: Arbeitspapierreihe Sprache und Interaktion* 72. http://krebshilfe.sprache-interaktion.de/wp-content/uploads/2016/08/Bentz-et-al.-2016-Von-der-Pathologie-zum-Patienten.pdf (last access: 15.05.2020).

Berger, Peter, and Thomas Luckmann. 1966. *The Social Construction of Reality*. New York: Free Press.

Bergmann, Jörg. 2014. "Der Fall als epistemisches Objekt." In *'Der Fall' – Studien zur epistemischen Praxis professionellen Handelns*, ed. by Jörg Bergmann, Ulrich Dausendschön-Gay, and Frank Oberzaucher, 423–440. Bielefeld: Transcript.

Churchill, Lindsey. 1971. "Ethnomethodology and Measurement." *Social Forces* 50: 183. https://doi.org/10.2307/2576936

Clayman, Steven E. 2010. "Address Terms in the Service of Other Actions: The Case of News Interview Talk." *Discourse and Communication* 4 (3): 161–183. https://doi.org/10.1177/1750481310364330

Clayman, Steven E. 2012. "Address Terms in the Organization of Turns at Talk: The Case of Pivotal Turn Extensions." *Journal of Pragmatics* 44: 1853–1867. https://doi.org/10.1016/j.pragma.2012.08.001

Couper-Kuhlen, Elizabeth, and Dagmar Barth-Weingarten. 2011. "A System for Transcribing Talk-in-Interaction: GAT 2." *Gesprächsforschung – Online-Zeitschrift zur verbalen Interaktion* 12: 1–51.

Couper-Kuhlen, Elizabeth, and Margret Selting. 2018. *Interactional Linguistics. Studying Language in Social Interaction*. Cambridge: Cambridge University Press.

Deppermann, Arnulf, and Susanne Günthner (eds). 2015. *Temporality in Interaction*. Amsterdam, Philadelphia: John Benjamins. https://doi.org/10.1075/slsi.27

Droste, Pepe, and Susanne Günthner. 2020. "'das mAchst du bestimmt AUCH du;': Zum Zusammenspiel syntaktischer, prosodischer und sequenzieller Aspekte syntaktisch desintegrierter du-Formate." In *Prosodie und Konstruktionsgrammatik*, ed. by Wolfgang Imo, and Jens Lanwer, 75–110. Berlin, Boston: De Gruyter. https://doi.org/10.1515/9783110637489-003

Droste, Pepe, and Susanne Günthner. 2021. "Enacting 'Being with You': Vocative Uses of *du* ('you') in German Everyday Interaction." *Pragmatics* 31 (1): 87–113. https://doi.org/10.1075/prag.19030.dro

Durkheim, Émile. 1915. *The Elementary Forms of the Religious Life: A Study in Religious Sociology*. London: George Allen & Unwin.

Džanko, Minka. 2020. *Rollengebundene Asymmetrie in Arzt-Patient-Gesprächen. Ein Vergleich im Deutschen und Bosnischen*. Heidelberg: Universitätsverlag Winter.

Enfield, Nick J. 2006. "Social Consequences of Common Ground." In *Roots of Human Sociality: Culture, Cognition, and Interaction*, ed. by Nick J. Enfield, and Stephen C. Levinson, 399–430. London: Berg.

Enfield, Nick J. 2009. "Relationship Thinking and Human Pragmatics." *Journal of Pragmatics* 41(1): 60–78. https://doi.org/10.1016/j.pragma.2008.09.007

Frommer, Jörg. 2014. "Therapie als Fallarbeit: Über einige Grundprobleme und Paradoxien professionellen Handelns in der Medizin". In *'Der Fall' – Studien zur epistemischen Praxis professionellen Handelns*, ed. by Jörg Bergmann, Ulrich Dausendschön-Gay, and Frank Oberzaucher, 103–123. Bielefeld: Transcript.

Fruht, Christiane, and M. Vogelhuber. 2016. *Kommunikation in der Onkologie: Überbringen schlechter Nachrichten*. Universitätsklinikum Regensburg. http://de.slideshare.net/ChristianeFruht/ueberbringen-schlechternachrichten (last access: 15.12.2019).

Goffman, Erving. 1967. *Interaction Ritual: Essays on Face-to-Face Behavior*. Chicago: Aldine.

Goffman, Erving. 1971. *Relations in Public: Microstudies of the Public Order*. New York: Basic Books.

Goffman, Erving. 1974/1982. *Das Individuum im öffentlichen Austausch. Microstudien zur öffentlichen Ordnung*. Frankfurt a. M: Suhrkamp.

Goodwin, Marjorie H. 2001. "Participation." In *Key Terms in Language and Culture*, ed. by Alessandro Duranti, 172–175. Malden, Oxford: Blackwell.

Gumperz, John J. 1982. *Discourse Strategies*. Cambridge: Cambridge University Press. https://doi.org/10.1017/CBO9780511611834

Gumperz, John J. 2001. "Interactional Sociolinguistics: A Personal Perspective." In *The Handbook of Discourse Analysis*, ed. by Deborah Schiffrin, Deborah Tannen, and Heidi E. Hamilton, 215–228. Malden: Blackwell.

Günthner, Susanne. 2008. "Projektorkonstruktionen im Gespräch: Pseudoclefts, *die Sache ist*-Konstruktionen und Extrapositionen mit *es*." *Gesprächsforschung – Online-Zeitschrift zur verbalen Interaktion* 9: 86–114. http://www.gespraechsforschung-ozs.de/heft2008/ga-guenthner.pdf (last access: 15.05.2020).

Günthner, Susanne. 2016. "Praktiken erhöhter Dialogizität: Onymische Anredeformen als Gesten personifizierter Zuwendung." *Zeitschrift für Germanistische Linguistik* 44 (3): 406–436. https://doi.org/10.1515/zgl-2016-0022

Günthner, Susanne. 2017. "Sprachliche Verfahren bei der Übermittlung schlechter Nachrichten – sedimentierte Praktiken im Kontext onkologischer Aufklärungsgespräche." *SpIn: Arbeitspapierreihe Sprache und Interaktion* 73. http://arbeitspapiere.sprache-interaktion.de/arbeitspapiere/arbeitspapier73.pdf (last access: 09.10.2021).

Günthner, Susanne. 2018. "Thomas Luckmanns Einfluss auf die Sprachwissenschaft – Kommunikative Gattungen im Alltagsgebrauch am Beispiel onkologischer Aufklärungsgespräche." In *Lebenswelt und Gesellschaft. Gedenkband für Thomas Luckmann*, ed. by Alois Hahn, and Martin Endreß, 358–400. Konstanz: UVK.

Günthner, Susanne. 2021. "Namentliche Anreden in onkologischen Aufklärungsgesprächen: Formen und Funktionen onymischer Anreden in der Interaktion." In *Linguistik und Medizin: Sprachwissenschaftliche Zugänge und interdisziplinäre Perspektiven*, ed. by Marina Iakushevich, Yvonne Ilg, and Theresa Schnedermann, 71–92. Berlin, Boston: De Gruyter. https://doi.org/10.1515/9783110688696-005

Günthner, Susanne, and Thomas Luckmann. 2001. "Asymmetries of Knowledge in Intercultural Communication: The Relevance of Cultural Repertoires of Communicative Genres." In *Culture in Communication: Analyses of Intercultural Situations*, ed. by Aldo Di Luzio, Susanne Günthner, and Franca Orletti, 55–86. Amsterdam, Philadelphia: John Benjamins. https://doi.org/10.1075/pbns.81.06gun

Günthner, Susanne, and Qiang Zhu. 2017. "Anredeformen im Kulturvergleich. Verwandtschaftsbezeichnungen als Mittel der kommunikativen Konstruktion sozialer Beziehungen in chinesischen und deutschen SMS-Interaktionen." In *Sprache und Beziehung*, ed. by Angelika Linke, and Juliane Schröter, 119–149. Berlin, Boston: De Gruyter. https://doi.org/10.1515/9783110496918-007

Hanks, William F. 2007. "Person Reference in Yucatex Maya Conversation." In *Person Reference in Interaction: Linguistic, Cultural and Social Perspectives*, ed. by Nick J. Enfield, and Tanya Stivers, 149–171. Cambridge: Cambridge University Press.

Heath, Christian. 1992. "The Delivery and Reception of Diagnosis in the General Practice Consultations." In *Talk at Work*, ed. by Paul P. Drew, and John Heritage, 235–268. Cambridge: Cambridge University Press.

Heritage, John. 1984. *Garfinkel and Ethnomethodology*. Cambridge: Polity.

Heritage, John. 2004. "Conversation Analysis and Institutional Talk: Analysing Data." In *Qualitative Research: Theory, Method and Practice*, ed. by David Silverman, 222–245. London: Sage.
Heritage, John. 2011. "Territories of Knowledge, Territories of Experience: Empathic Moments in Interaction." In *The Morality of Knowledge in Conversation*, ed. by Tanya Stivers, Lorenza Mondada, and Jan Steensig, 159–183. Cambridge: Cambridge University Press. https://doi.org/10.1017/CBO9780511921674.008
Heritage, John, and George Raymond. 2005. "The Terms of Agreement: Indexing Epistemic Authority and Subordination in Talk-in-Interaction." *Social Psychology Quarterly* 68: 15–38. https://doi.org/10.1177/019027250506800103
Imo, Wolfgang 2017. "Trösten: Eine professionelle Praktik in der Medizin." In: *Arbeitspapierreihe Sprache und Interaktion* 71. http://arbeitspapiere.sprache-interaktion.de/arbeitspapiere/arbeitspapier71.pdf (last access: 02.06.2021).
Imo, Wolfgang, and Jens Lanwer. 2019. *Interaktionale Linguistik: Eine Einführung*. Berlin: Metzler. https://doi.org/10.1007/978-3-476-05549-1
Keller, Reiner, Herbert Knoblauch, and Jo Reichertz. 2012. "Kommunikativer Konstruktivismus." In *Kommunikativer Konstruktivismus: Theoretische und empirische Arbeiten zu einem neuen wissenssoziologischen Ansatz*, ed. by Reiner Keller, Hubert Knoblauch, and Jo Reichertz, 3–22. Berlin: Springer.
Koerfer, Arnim, and Christian Albus. 2018. *Kommunikative Kompetenz in der Medizin. Ein Lehrbuch zur Theorie, Didaktik, Praxis und Evaluation der ärztlichen Gesprächsführung*. Radolfzell: Verlag für Gesprächsforschung.
Kupetz, Maxi. 2014. "Empathy Displays as Interactional Achievements – Multi-Modal and Sequential Aspects." *Journal of Pragmatics* 61: 4–34. https://doi.org/10.1016/j.pragma.2013.11.006
Lerner, Gene H. 2003. "Selecting Next Speaker: The Context-Sensitive Operation." *Language in Society* 32 (2): 177–201. https://doi.org/10.1017/S004740450332202X
Linke, Angelika, and Juliane Schröter. 2017. "Sprache in Beziehungen – Beziehungen in Sprache: Überlegungen zur Konstitution eines linguistischen Forschungsfeldes." In: *Sprache und Beziehung*, ed. by Angelika Linke, and Juliane Schröter, 1–32. Berlin, Boston: De Gruyter. https://doi.org/10.1515/9783110496918-002
Luckmann, Thomas. 1990. "Social Communication, Dialogue and Conversation." In *The Dynamics of Dialogue*, ed. by Ivana Marková, and Klaus Foppa, 45–61. New York: Harvester Wheatsheaf.
Luckmann, Thomas. 2001. *On the Methodology of (Oral) Genres*. Plenary Talk at the Symposium on Genres. Oslo: University College.
Mandelbaum, Jenny. 2003. "Interactive Methods for Constructing Relationships." In *Studies in Language and Social Interaction*, ed. by Phillip J. Glenn, Curtis D. LeBaron, and Jenny Mandelbaum, 207–219. Mahwah, NJ, London: Lawrence Erlbaum. https://doi.org/10.4324/9781410606969-18
Maynard, Douglas W. 2003. *Bad News, Good News. Conversational Order in Everyday Talk and Clinical Settings*. Chicago: University of Chicago Press.
Muntigl, Peter, Naomi Knight, Adam O. Horvath, and Ashley Watkins. 2012. "Client Affectual Stance and Therapist-Client Affiliation: A View from Grammar and Social Interaction." *Research in Psychotherapy: Psychopathology, Process and Outcome* 15 (2): 117–130.
Muntigl, Peter, Naomi Knight, Ashley Watkins, Adam O. Horvath, and Lynne Angus. 2013. "Active Retreating: Person-Centered Practices to Repair Disaffiliation in Therapy." *Journal of Pragmatics* 53: 1–20. https://doi.org/10.1016/j.pragma.2013.03.019

Muntigl, Peter, and Adam O. Horvath. 2015. "The Therapeutic Relationship in Action: How Therapists and Clients Co-Manage Relational Disaffiliation". In *The Therapeutic Relationship: Innovative Investigations*, ed. by Hadas Wiseman, and Orya Tishby, 41–59. London, New York: Routledge.

Nübling, Damaris, Fabian Fahlbusch, and Rita Heuser. 2012. *Namen. Eine Einführung in die Onomastik*. Tübingen: Narr.

Noack, Thorsten, Heiner Fangerau, and Jörg Vögele (eds). 2007. *Querschnitt Geschichte, Theorie und Ethik der Medizin*. München, Jena: Urban and Fischer.

Pomerantz, Anita, and Jenny Mandelbaum. 2005. "Conversation Analytic Approaches to the Relevance and Uses of Relationship Categories in Interaction." In *Handbook of Language and Social Interaction*, ed. by Kristine L. Fitch, and Robert E. Sanders, 149–171. Mahwah, NJ: Lawrence Erlbaum.

Raymond, Chase W. 2016. "Linguistic Reference in the Negotation of Identity and Action: Revisiting the T/V Distinction." *Language in Society* 92 (3): 636–670.

Reineke, Silke, and Thomas Spranz-Fogasy. 2013. "Arzt-Patient-Kommunikation: Allgemeine Merkmale und Besonderheiten bei Brustkrebspatienten." In *Krankheit: Lernen im Ausnahmezustand? Brustkrebs und Herzinfarkt aus interdisziplinärer Perspektive*, ed. by Dieter Nittel, and Astrid Seltrech, 444–454. Berlin, Heidelberg: Springer. https://doi.org/10.1007/978-3-642-28201-0_36

Rendle-Short, Johanna. 2007. "'Catherine, You're Wasting your Time': Address Terms within the Australian Political Interview." *Journal of Pragmatics* 39 (9): 1503–1525. https://doi.org/10.1016/j.pragma.2007.02.006

Rendle-Short, Johanna. 2011. "Address Terms in the Australian Political News Interview." In *Talking Politics in Broadcast Media. Cross-Cultural Perspectives on Political Interviewing, Journalism and Accountability*, ed. by Mats Ekström, and Marianna Patrona, 93–111. Amsterdam, Philadelphia: John Benjamins. https://doi.org/10.1075/dapsac.42.09ren

Ribeiro, Eugenia, and Antonio P. Ribeiro, Miguel M. Goncalves, Adam O. Horvath, and William B. Stiles. 2013. "How Collaboration in Therapy Becomes Therapeutic: The Therapeutic Collaboration Coding System." *Psychology and Psychotherapy* 86 (3): 294–314. https://doi.org/10.1111/j.2044-8341.2012.02066.x

Sacks, Harvey, Emanuel Schegloff, and Gail Jefferson. 1978. "A Simplest Systematics for the Organization of Turn-Taking for Conversation." In *Studies in the Organization of Conversational Interaction*, ed. by Jim Schenkein, 7–55. New York: Academic Press. https://doi.org/10.1016/B978-0-12-623550-0.50008-2

Sator, Marlene, and Thomas Spranz-Fogasy. 2011. "Medizinische Kommunikation." In *Angewandte Linguistik – Ein Lehrbuch*, ed. by Karlfried Knapp, 376–393. Tübingen, Basel: Francke.

Scarvaglieri, Claudio. 2017. "Beraten und Psychotherapie: Zur Differenzierung zweier Formate helfenden Handelns." In: *Beraten in Interaktion. Eine gesprächslinguistische Typologie des Beratens*, ed. by Ina Pick, S. 53–76. Frankfurt am Main: Peter Lang.

Schegloff, Emanuel A. 1996. "Some Practices for Referring to Persons in Talk-in-Interaction: A Partial Sketch of a Systematics." In *Studies in Anaphora*, ed. by Barbara Fox, 437–486. Amsterdam: John Benjamins. https://doi.org/10.1075/tsl.33.14sch

Schegloff, Emanuel A. 2007. *Sequence Organization in Interaction: A Primer in Conversation Analysis*. Cambridge: Cambridge University Press. https://doi.org/10.1017/CBO9780511791208

Schütz, Alfred, and Thomas Luckmann. 1979. *Strukturen der Lebenswelt*. Band 1. Frankfurt a.M.: Suhrkamp.

Schwitalla, Johannes. 1995. "Namen in Gesprächen." In *Handbücher zur Sprach- und Kommunikationswissenschaft*. Band 11.1, ed. by Hugo Steger, and Herbert E. Wiegand, 498–504. Berlin, New York: De Gruyter.

Schwitalla, Johannes. 2010. "Kommunikative Funktionen von Sprecher- und Adressatennamen in Gesprächen." In *Eigennamen in der gesprochenen Sprache*, ed. by Nicolas Pepin, and Elwys de Stefani, 179–199. Tübingen: Francke.

Selting, Margret, and Elizabeth Couper-Kuhlen (eds). 2001. *Studies in Interactional Linguistics*. Amsterdam: John Benjamins. https://doi.org/10.1075/sidag.10

Selting, Margret, Peter Auer, Dagmar Barth-Weingarten, Jörg R. Bergmann, Pia Bergmann, Karin Birkner, Elizabeth Couper-Kuhlen, Arnulf Deppermann, Peter Gilles, Susanne Günthner, Martin Hartung, Friederike Kern, Christine Mertzlufft, Christian Meyer, Miriam Morek, Frank Oberzaucher, Jörg Peters, Uta Quasthoff, Wilfried Schütte, Anja Stukenbrock, and Susanne Uhlmann. 2009. "Gesprächsanalytisches Transkriptionssystem 2 (GAT 2)." *Gesprächsforschung – Online-Zeitschrift zur verbalen Interaktion* 10: 353–402.

Silverstein, Michael. 1993. "Metapragmatic Discourse and Metapragmatic Function." In *Reflexive Language: Reported Speech and Metapragmatics*, ed. by John Lucy, 33–58. Cambridge: Cambridge University Press. https://doi.org/10.1017/CBO9780511621031.004

Spranz-Fogasy, Thomas. 2005. "Kommunikatives Handeln in ärztlichen Gesprächen – Gesprächseröffnung und Beschwerdenexploration." In *Psychosomatische Gesprächsführung in der Frauenheilkunde – ein interdisziplinärer Ansatz zur verbalen Intervention*, ed. by Mechthild Neises, Susanne Ditz, and Thomas Spranz-Fogasy, 17–47. Stuttgart: Wissenschaftliche Verlagsgesellschaft.

Stivers, Tanya. 2008. "Stance, Alignment, and Affiliation during Storytelling: When Nodding is a Token of Affiliation." *Research on Language and Social Interaction* 41 (1): 31–57. https://doi.org/10.1080/08351810701691123

Stivers, Tanya, Nick J. Enfield, and Stephen C. Levinson. 2007. "Person Reference in Interaction." In *Person Reference in Interaction: Linguistic, Cultural and Social Perspectives*, ed. by Nick J. Enfield, and Tanya Stivers, 1–20. Cambridge: Cambridge University Press.

Stivers, Tanya, Lorenza Mondada, and Jakob Steensig. 2011. "Knowledge, Morality and Affiliation in Social Interaction." In *The Morality of Knowledge in Conversation*, ed. by Tanya Stivers, Lorenza Mondada, and Jakob Steensig, 3–26. Cambridge: Cambridge University Press. https://doi.org/10.1017/CBO9780511921674.002

Tomasello, Michael, and Malinda Carpenter. 2007. "Shared Intentionality." *Developmental Science* 10 (1): 121–125. https://doi.org/10.1111/j.1467-7687.2007.00573.x

Practices of relationship building in Hungarian primary care

Communicative styles and intergenerational differences

Agnes Kuna and Claudio Scarvaglieri
Eötvös Lorand University Budapest / Ghent University

Using data from Hungarian primary-care consultations, we present linguistic features of relationship-building, focusing on the role of address forms and metapragmatic reflections. We also investigate intergenerational differences and different styles of managing doctor-patient relationships. Based on a range of evidence (discourse about doctor-patient communication in the public and in academia, participant observation of consultations, interviews with practitioners, analysis of instructional videos, questionnaire surveys), we discuss a change in doctor-patient communication at both macro (socio-cultural) and micro (interactional) levels. Factors influencing this process include general social change, digitisation and the communicative training of healthcare professionals. We conclude that physicians build different types of relationships with language, which hints at an overall shift in Hungarian society and in healthcare communication in general.

Keywords: relationship-building, primary care, metapragmatic reflection, attitude deixis, relationship styles

1. Introduction

In recent decades, attention has increasingly been devoted to the fact that the efficacy and outcome of any medical treatment is greatly influenced by the nature of the relationship between physician and patient. Models of this healing relationship have changed radically: Hierarchical medical relationships progressively give way to partnership-based, cooperative interactions (Ainsworth-Vaugh 2004; Warren 2006). In the literature, this trend is interpreted as a shift from doctor- and illness-centred treatment toward patient- and relationship-centred care (Beach 2013; Bigi 2016).

https://doi.org/10.1075/pbns.331.10kun

Our paper uses ethnomethodology and discourse analysis (Tannen et al. 2015) to investigate how such change manifests itself in patient-physician interaction. Based on a corpus of medical encounters in Hungarian primary care (Kuna 2016), interviews, and discussion in academia and in (social) media, we investigate practices of building and managing relationships, such as address forms, ways of referring to self and others, and actions such as diagnoses and discussing treatment plans. Our analysis is also supplemented by a pragmatically-oriented investigation of videos of doctor-patient communication (Bálint et al. 2014). We show that, depending on how they were trained, Hungarian physicians employ and combine these practices differently, thereby building and managing different types of relationships. We argue that these differences are not the product of a person's age, but of far-reaching societal changes of communicative tools (digitisation), patterns and norms (cf. Blommaert 2018) which overall appear to be connected to a general transformation of Hungarian society (Hambuch et al. 2018).

We start with an introduction in relationships, in general, and in primary care, in particular (Section 2). Next, we introduce our data and methods (Section 3). Focusing on address forms, attitudinal deixis and metapragmatic comments, we discuss linguistic devices in relationship building in Hungarian primary care (Section 4). In Section 5, we examine whether an intergenerational change can be detected in our data related to these devices. Furthermore, we also discuss which communicative patterns can be described in patient- and physician-centred relationship building. We end by summarising our findings and highlighting some future challenges (Section 6).

2. Relationship-building in doctor-patient consultation

Relationships and relationship-building have formed an integral part of the "art of healing" and physician-patient interaction since ancient times (Hall et al. 1981, Csabai et al. 2009, Meskó 2014, Koerfer and Albus 2018). In general terms, a relationship describes the 'state of affairs' (Merriam-Webster s.v.)[1] between people who are interacting. From an interactionist perspective, it has been shown that participants actively construe and manage relationships and that, in principle, each communicative act can affect and change a relationship (Goffmann 1959; 1966; Volosinov 1973; Locher and Watts 2008; Linke and Schröter 2017). An interpersonal relationship is thus not a simple given, but the ever-changing product of communicative acts by the interactants (including linguistic and gestural acts, body position, gaze or facial expressions). It is this overt constructionist quality

1. https://www.merriam-webster.com/dictionary/relationship (accessed 9/ 1/ 2020)

of relationships that renders them observable through established methods of the social sciences, including participant observation and discourse analysis. While relationships are overtly constructed and managed one interactive act at a time, participants build a (covert) mental model of their relationship and adapt this model according to each subsequent act (cf. Linke and Schröter 2017: 15). Thus, each communicative act, like choosing a specific linguistic form to address someone (see Section 4.1 below), can potentially change the model participants have of their relationship (e.g. whether it is hierarchical or non-hierarchical, close or distant, adversarial or consensual). While this covert mental model of a relationship is difficult to observe, our analysis shows that interactants occasionally make their assumptions about the state of their relationship apparent by commenting on communicative acts like protesting against inappropriate address forms (cf. Example (1) below).

In doctor-patient communication, the interpersonal relationship has special importance, as it is one of the factors that contribute to successful diagnosis and therapy. As suggested by Hall and colleagues (1981: 18; emphasis added), "medicine is an art whose magic and creative ability have long been recognised as residing in the *interpersonal* aspects of *patient-physician relationship*". Crucial factors that contribute to any relationship include emotions, social background, personal character traits, and the communicative situation itself. These factors are interactively construed and negotiated in a dynamic way during doctor-patient communication through verbal and non-verbal means. In relationship-building, several activities play a role, such as greetings, handshakes, conversational behaviour (e.g. simultaneous talk, interruption), knowledge construction, emotional expression, and agenda negotiation (Koerfer et al. 2018).

Reflexive language use and metalinguistic or metapragmatic reflections constitute an important part of interactions that contribute to relationship-building (Lucy 1993; Bublitz and Hübler 2007; Verschueren 2000). The term "metapragmatic awareness" refers to the reflexivity with which speakers engage in a language activity (Verschueren 2000; Silverstein 2003; Scarvaglieri 2017). One major function of metapragmatic reflections in physician-patient interaction is the construal and management of social and interpersonal relations (Kuna and Hámori 2019: 230–234, Kuna and Hámori forthc.). Metapragmatic actions thus play a key part in building both shared knowledge and rapport between physicians and patients, something we will observe and discuss in more detail in the analysis of consultations in Sections 4 and 5.

Another linguistic device that strongly impacts the way relationships are built is social (Levinson 1983: 89) or attitudinal deixis (Verschueren 1999: 20–21). This term refers to linguistic elements that construct participants' social identity and the relationship between them. These devices appear in various linguistic constructions, including address forms, greetings, personal pronouns, T/V differentiation (i.e. the use of the polite, distant (V) vs. the close (T) address form) and they play a prominent role in the linguistic elaboration of relationship building (Domonkosi 2016). Analysing relationship-building in physician-patient interactions (Section 4), we focus on the role of address forms and also touch on the use of first-person deictic elements.

Over the past few decades, the doctor-patient relationship has undergone changes at both the macro-level of society and the micro-level of concrete interaction. During this period, a shift has been described that concerns the general way relationships are established and managed. This shift is strongly connected to rights, ethics and the socio-cultural background of medication (Pilling 2004; Heritage and Maynard 2006; Bigi 2016). In Hungary, where our study was carried out, there currently is a wide-spread discussion in the general public, in social media, and in academia about changing relationships between patients and doctors. Hambuch et al. bring together three separate research projects and point out that research in medicine sociology, medicine psychology and linguistics has found evidence for a "slow shift in doctor patient interaction [...] from paternalism towards cooperation" (2018: 62–63; translation AG and CS). This shift concerns communicative processes that are vital for diagnosis and therapy, processes such as "the communication of information, decision-making and the acceptance of responsibility" (ibid, 62; translation AK and CS). Their observation of change is based on, among other things, features of turn-taking at consultations, where the number and the duration of turns by doctors and patients are shown to be approximately the same – which is a feature of symmetrical communication (ibid). Moreover, both doctors and patients engage in overlapping turns, which also indicates a symmetrical relationship (ibid, 67). The authors, therefore, find a convergence between medical communication and everyday interaction and relate this finding to general societal changes after "the democratic transformation of 1990" (ibid, 59).

The findings of these studies as well as investigations of online medical consultations (cf. Gaal, 2016; Sára et al. 2013; Pilling 2018) suggest that current doctor-patient communication in Hungary appears to be characterised by a certain degree of symmetry and a demand for non-hierarchical, cooperative relationships. The situation is however, paradoxical. On the one hand, it can be observed that younger and better-informed patients prefer to participate in decision-making, disfavouring the paternalistic model. On the other hand, Hungarian patients' evaluation of the doctor as a good communicator rests on the paternalistic model, as suggested by questionnaire surveys (Málovics et al. 2009; Vajda et al. 2012: 346).

So far though, researchers have only addressed the *current situation* of doctor-patient-interaction. No study has compared how relationship management has changed over time by examining different sets of data. In this paper, we draw on data from public discourse, interviews, questionnaires and participant observation of doctor patient communication to investigate whether the thesis about a shift towards more symmetrical interaction is backed by empirical evidence. Since data from past decades is not available, we will compare the communicative practice of different generations of doctors and will use doctors who have been trained under different societal circumstance as proxies to address questions of communicative change (Section 5). Additionally, we analyse eight video clips (Csabai et al. 2009), which are used for educational purposes in the training of physicians and psychologists. These clips were based on authentic discourse and are particularly useful to illustrate differences in relationship-building.

3. Data and methods

The research we present in this paper forms part of a comprehensive, methodologically complex study of doctor-patient communication, which started in 2012 and is still in progress (Kuna 2016; Kuna and Hámori 2019; Kuna and Domonkosi 2020). The present analysis is based on a dataset of participant observations, written notes and transcripts of conversations and interviews with physicians. Additionally, we refer to discourse in the (social) media and to a quantitative survey with physicians. Using participant observation, the communicative practice of four general practitioners was documented in detail during more than 400 encounters (for further details, see Kuna and Kaló 2014; Kuna 2016).

The study involved two junior physicians (J1, J2) with at least four years of work experience and two senior ones (S1, S2) with 20 years of service. The junior doctors had studied medical communication at university, unlike the two senior ones. We conducted semi-structured interviews with each of the doctors, discussing topics such as their motivation for choosing a medical career, their experience and social-emotional as well as communicative attitudes to patients. Additionally, we sent out a questionnaire to physicians and patients to elicit comments about address forms used in physician-patient interactions (Kuna and Domonkosi 2020). All data were originally recorded in Hungarian and translated into English (by A.K.).

We use descriptive analysis (Harris 2006, Marshall 2021) to analyse the data gathered via ethnographic observation. This approach allows minimal interpretive interventions, which fits our research question about changes in relationship-building and allows readers to engage with the data with some supporting analysis. The interviews were analysed using Qualitative Content Analysis (Mayring 2010).

Another part of our research is based on eight instructional videos recorded with professional actors, simulating doctor-patient consultations (Csabai et al. 2009).

The eight consultations portray four different scenarios, each enacted according to both the patient-centred and the paternalistic model of doctor behaviour. They are also designed to activate typical female and male role models (Bálint et al. 2014). Their entire time span is 32 minutes (3.117 words, 176 conversation turns). Two scenarios (four consultations) unfold at a G.P. surgery, with the remaining two involving psychologists and their patients (four conversations). The recorded events are, therefore, not real-life discourses. Instead, they present schematic interactional patterns which have been derived from research on paternalistic and patient-centred modes of communication in healthcare (Csabai et al. 2009). In the course of analysis, the fact that these conversations are designed to mirror such patterns (instead of being real-life discourses) is taken into account and reflected in our comments. Although the video clips show schematic discourses, they illustrate observations about linguistic patterns in the enactment of paternalistic and patient-centred relationship-building in the context of identical medical situations. This material enables a comparison between physician and patient-centred communication in interaction. Since it is based on research about natural language discourse in healthcare and basically represents a reenactment of the original recordings, we rely on this dataset to illustrate the communicative structures in question (patient-centred vs. physician-centred). Data about the material under study are presented in detail in Table 1 below.

Table 1. Meta data about the video material

Video clip ID	Duration	Model	Participants	Gender	Issue
V,1a	4:08	Patern.	Psych.-P	F-M	panic disorder, anxiety
V,1b	4:11	P-c.	Psych.-P	F-M	panic disorder, anxiety
V,2a.	4:17	Patern.	D-P	F-M	elevated glucose level, obesity
V,2b	4:53	P-c.	D-P	F-M	elevated glucose level, obesity
V,3a	4:23	Patern.	Psych.-P	M-F	chronic headache, high stress level
V,3b	4:34	P-c.	Psych.-P	M-F	chronic headache, high stress level
V,4a	2:45	Patern.	Psych.-P	M-F	pregnant woman has contracted influenza from her child
V,4b	2:57	P-c.	Psych.-P	M-F	pregnant woman has contracted influenza from her child

4. Relationship-building in doctor-patient communication: Attitudinal deixis and metapragmatic actions

In this section, we present the results of our analysis of linguistic devices of relationship-building in Hungarian primary care. We focus on attitudinal deixis, because these small linguistic devices particularly impact the (re-)construction of any relationship (cf. above Section 2; Günthner in this volume). Another reason for our emphasis on attitudinal deixis is that Hungarian is characterised by a very elaborate and unique system of address forms and that there is much public discussion about which address forms should be used in which situation (see below, Extract (1)).[2] We contextualise this section by discussing metapragmatic comments and their impact on doctor-patient relationships (Section 4.2). In the subsequent section, we investigate how the modified use of these devices has contributed to a change in communication and relationship-building between doctors and patients.

4.1 Attitudinal deixis

As mentioned, address forms play a fundamental role in relationship-building (Eckert 2006; Norrby and Wide 2015; Koerfer et al. 2018; see also Günthner this volume). The Hungarian address system features several ways to express V (see Table 2). and various socio-culturally transmitted address forms exist which encode aspects, such as intimacy, friendliness, closeness and distancing, hierarchy, power and solidarity (Bartha and Hámori 2010, Kuna and Domonkosi 2020).

Table 2. Typical constructions of T- and V-forms in Hungarian[3] (Domonkosi 2010: 34–35)

T	V
pronoun *te* in singular and *ti* in the plural	Pronoun *ön* in the singular and *önök* in the plural co-occurring with 3rd person possessives and verbs
zero pronoun all with 2nd person possessives and verbs	Pronoun *maga* in the singular and *maguk* in the plural co-occurring with 3rd person possessives and verbs
	zero pronoun with 3rd person
	tetszik + infinitive

2. General information on the Hungarian language can be found in Rounds 2001 and Havas et al. 2015.

3. According Brown and Gilman's (1960) T stands for informal, while V for formal, official, more distanced address.

The rich variety of Hungarian address forms is reflected in physician-patient relations, and may give rise to several problems. This is because particular address forms may be assigned different evaluations and identity-creating roles across individuals or communities of practice (Eckert 2006; Csiszárik and Domonkosi 2018). This becomes obvious in an anecdote that has been frequently discussed in the media and that we present here as a first example illustrating the current discussions in Hungarian society about address forms.[4]

(1) *'How are you,* ***Uncle Tibor?****', the head doctor is asking a patient.*
'I'm OK, thank you', comes the reply, followed by ***Uncle and the doctor's given name.***
*Oh no, there's going to be a scandal here, I can sense it, but no, the doctor is only asking for a small correction: '****Perhaps Mr Assistant Professor****, if you will be so kind'.*
'No problem', says the patient. 'However, could you please also address me as ***Mr Chief Engineer, or Mr Director,*** *of course only if it's not too much trouble, because that's what I am.'*[5]

Addressing patients as *bácsi* 'uncle', *néni* 'aunt', possibly *mama* 'mum', *papa* 'dad', or based on their bed numbers can be highly problematic and offensive, as such forms tend to be interpreted as highlighting asymmetry in the relationship (Csiszárik and Domonkosi 2018). The use of the auxiliary *tetszik* ('to please') followed by an infinitive is also not without problems (Kuna and Domonkosi 2020). Although it is typically intended to be a sign of politeness, it often foregrounds the gender and age of the addressee, which can imply a hierarchical relationship. In short, it is a source of communicative problems that in Hungarian, V forms are highly varied in informal communication but that none of the variants has a general enough scope or neutral social and stylistic value (Csiszárik and Domonkosi 2018; Kuna and Domonkosi 2020). Hence, as illustrated in (1), address forms aimed at creating an informal atmosphere and reducing social distance (e.g. *bácsi, néni, tetszik*) are often seen as reinforcing hierarchy/asymmetry. This is also supported by the fact that these forms are typically employed by doctors speaking to patients, with the reverse hardly ever occurring (see also (6)–(11) below).

4. Independent of the authenticity of the reported exchanges, the fact that they garner such widespread attention in the (social) media and that they are frequently commented upon illustrates that the use of address forms and its potential change constitute important topics in Hungary.

5. https://24.hu/poszt-itt/2017/05/13/dr-gyarmati-andrea-talan-adjunktus-ur-ha-szabad-kernem/ (Accessed10th June 2017; our translation)

In our data, patients consistently used the nominal address form *doktor úr, doktornő* (literally, 'Mr./Ms. Doctor') and *főorvors úr/nő* ('Mr/Ms Head Doctor') to address physicians. The V pronouns *ön, maga* ('you$_{\text{formal}}$') and the controversial *tetszik* ('to please') + infinitive form were rarely employed. By contrast, doctors addressed their patients in a much more varied way. Generally speaking, the adopted forms express a V-type relation (with only a few exceptions, when the physician and the patient were acquaintances, friends or members of the same family). As examples from the consultations we observed demonstrate, the following patterns appear in the doctors' speech: addressing by name (2), pronoun avoidance, use of the patient's surname or given name + *bácsi/néni,* the *tetszik* + infinitive construction (3), use of the V pronouns *ön* or *maga* (4), and other linguistic devices (5).

(2) 'How are you$_{\text{formal}}$, **[given name]**?' (J1,6)

(3) 'Do you take medicine for that?'
(Lit. 'Does it *[tetszik]* **please you to take** medicine for that?') (J2,14)

(4) 'Lest they give that *[Ön]* **to you$_{\text{formal}}$**' (S1,6)

(5) '**Aunt [surname], dear,** this is because...' (S2,11)

A questionnaire study about the *tetszik* + infinitive addressing pattern, involving 50 patients and 50 doctors (Kuna and Domonkosi 2020), sheds further light on the attitudes and potential problems related to address forms. As a V variant, the *tetszik* + infinitive pattern is often used by doctors in an attempt to reduce distance and create a sense of directness and politeness, primarily in interactions with elderly and/or female patients. This is illustrated by the following extracts from the questionnaire administered to physicians:

(6) 'It allows for closeness [between interlocutors], which is important in doctor-patient relationships.'

(7) 'For addressing the elderly; it is kinder, more direct, less rigid.'

On the other hand, some physicians suggest that when the pattern is consciously used to address a younger patient, it conveys an intention to teach good manners. Moreover, informants are of the opinion that the use of *tetszik* may express subordination and a hierarchical relationship:

(8) 'Sometimes there is an affirmative and pedagogical motivation behind the use of *tetszik.*'

(9) 'As if the doctor didn't regard the patient as an equal.'

Reflections offered by patients in our questionnaire survey confirm this sense of asymmetry. Informants report avoiding *tetszik* in their communication with doctors as it does not support a partnership-based relationship. Exceptional cases may arise, however, when the patient is proffering a request.

(10) 'We are equal partners with the doctor, this is not reflected by *tetszik/tessék*'

(11) '[I use it] for adding weight to a request.'

Based on questionnaire data and our observations of consultations, we found that physicians indeed use the *tetszik* + infinitive construction much more frequently than patients. In these cases, it usually functions as a general politeness marker. Nevertheless, in most cases, it contributes to the construction of an asymmetrical relationship.

Both the examples from consultations (2–5) and reflections shared in the questionnaire (6–11) or on the internet (episode 1) point to the fact that address forms play a key role in relationship-building between physicians and patients. The traditional Hungarian address forms may give rise to a variety of problems in this regard. Healthcare professionals intend to create a more intimate relation with the forms described in this section, but they might end up construing a hierarchical relationship and maintaining or reinforcing asymmetry instead. The fact that more and more patients find this disturbing, suggesting that it creates inequality and is, therefore, ill-suited to the physician-patient relationship, marks an ongoing process of change. Universities have responded to this challenge by advising medical students to ask patients about how they prefer to be addressed. In Section 5, we investigate such processes of change in relationship-building in more detail.

As part of attitudinal deixis, the use of 1st person plural can also play an important role in relationship-building (for details, see Kuna 2016). These deictic elements are often connected to metapragmatic reflections, which we discuss in the next subsection.

4.2 Metapragmatic comments and relationship-building

In doctor-patient interactions, successful knowledge transfer and shared understanding are central goals. In this process, participants need to construct common ground, coordinate their activity and collaborate jointly to create and manage meaning in conversation (Clark 1996). Particularly important tools for this coordination are reflexive language and metapragmatic reflections (Bublitz and Hübler 2007; Caffi 2016). A previous investigation (Kuna and Hámori 2019) identified four major functions of metapragmatic reflections in doctor-patient interaction: (1) support of knowledge-sharing and information management; (2) organisation of the interaction and the participants' actions; (3) construal of social relations; and (4) communicating emotions. These functions are closely intertwined in specific interaction, as is evident in Examples (12)–(14) below.

While metapragmatic comments form part of a different linguistic category than attitudinal deixis – metapragmatic comments constitute their own type of linguistic action, whereas deictica are single elements to be used within such types of action – both have the potential to contribute considerably to relationship-building and management. By commenting on their relationship, interactants can, for example, address the current state or development of their relationship, describe expectations about their relationship or express dissatisfaction. All of these acts can have considerable effects on the relationship. The following extracts from our corpus of doctor patient conversations illustrate such processes (targeted items in bold).

(12) '**I'm listening, you can tell me what it's all about.** How can I help you?' (J1, 12)

(13) '**We have talked** about this before. That is the reason, why you need breakfast.' (S1, 1)

(14) There is some diarrhea, **I'm saying this once again.** (S2, 11)

In (12), the physician emphasises that he is listening to the patient and wants to help. By explicitly commenting on his stance and presenting himself as attentive, he construes a relationship in which the patient has the possibility to voice any issue or complaint they might have.

In (13) and (14), the physicians S1 and S2 comment on the fact that they are repeating information they had expressed before. By explicitly mentioning this, they stress the importance of the information in question and they construe a relationship in which they have the right to admonish the patient, who apparently did not react appropriately to their original statement. In these cases, metapragmatic comments contribute to the construction of an asymmetrical relationship between the two parties.

These and additional Examples (15a)–(17b) demonstrate that metapragmatic reflections play a crucial role in the continuous, dynamic coordination of joint action as the construal of shared knowledge and, conomitantly with the establishment of doctor-patient relationships (see more Kuna and Hámori forthc.).

5. Changes in relationship-building

Example (1) illustrated that, in Hungary, communicative patterns seem to be changing. The doctor chooses the traditional form "uncle" that has for a long time been used to address older male patients (cf. Dzanko this volume). By using this same form to address the doctor, the patient changes the traditional pattern of greetings and address forms. The patient thereby establishes a form of equality, as both participants are addressed with the same word that anchors them within the family domain. The doctor's reaction demonstrates how unusual this behaviour is, as he insists on his professional title. Again, the patient then tries to establish an equal relationship, by asking to be addressed with his professional title as well. This exchange that was reported in the media and widely discussed on the internet, illustrates a clash between traditional hierarchical forms of addressing and interacting and a new, more equal, way of communication. It also suggests that any changes towards a more balanced[6] relationship between physicians and patients have not yet been completed, but that there is an evolving process of change and that the degree and the type of change are objects of interactive and social (in the media, on the internet) discussion and negotiation. To demonstrate this, in the subsections below we present research results based on participant observation with regard to communication by two generations of physician. This is followed by a comparison between patient- and physician-centred communicative styles supported by an analysis of discourses in instructional videos.

5.1 Changes of communicative practice: Intergenerational aspect

Since data from previous decades are not available, it was not possible to directly compare communication patterns from different decades. Instead, we investigated communicative practice of different generations of physicians that have been trained under different societal conditions. They are thus used as 'proxies' to make societal changes accessible that take place over long periods of time and are, as such, difficult to document. To demonstrate that such change is indeed taking place, in this section we sum up the results of comparative analyses of 100 encounters documented via participant observation (Kuna and Kaló 2014) and also summarise analyses of excerpts from doctor-patient consultations and interviews with doctors (Kuna and Scarvaglieri 2019).

The comparative analysis of doctor-patient consultations suggests that regardless of their age, all four doctors tend to use detailed explanations in their communication by employing, among others, questions, expressions of politeness, positive feedback and repetition. We did, however, observe differences in communication style and behaviour that support the hypotheses discussed in the literature (see above, Section 2) and in the public about changing communicative patterns. Our analyses revealed that elderly doctors display less linguistic and communicative flexibility and are more likely to adopt clichés, whereas younger doctors employ

6. Although by its very nature, physician-patient relationships will rarely be completely symmetrical, in the patient-centred model, more balanced hierarchical relationships may appear, with communication playing an essential role in their construction (Bigi 2016).

a wider linguistic repertoire (Kuna and Kaló 2014). According to the data, the decision-making and knowledge representation of senior doctors are more commonly characterised by certainty or even linguistic items that project 'infallibility'. We find, for example, senior physicians who did not address a patient's concerns about the change of her medication and the possible side-effects the new medication might have. Instead, the doctor repeatedly brushed the patient's concerns aside as "nonsense" and also rejected her claims that she did not know about the changed medication. In another example, a senior physician sent a dizzy young patient away without treatment or medication, repeating instead that he needed to eat breakfast and advising the patient about his lifestyle ("That is why you must eat breakfast. And three litres of fluids. And a regular schedule. Then you will able to find work as well."). The patients' concerns about their health situation or medication were not addressed. The physicians simply repeated their message and built a clearly hierarchical relationship.

In contrast, the communication style of junior doctors appeared more varied, depending more on the situation and its numerous factors rather than their own personality. Their behaviour was more often characterised by empathy, patience, understanding, uncertainty (the evaluation of possibility/probability ['it could be better, we will see']), involvement, and the linguistic expression of joint activity (e.g. 'we can solve that with an ambulance'). We found that junior physicians adapted towards their patients by, for example, taking up the patient's point about the need to combine alternative and Western medicine and by integrating the patient's view into their own argumentation about the need to have surgery ("I understand that you would like to try an alternative" [...] "But it is difficult to draw the line – where there is a definitive anomaly, how you can heal that with your mind, on a purely mental level"). In this connection, they demonstrated regard for the patient's perspective and succeeded in convincing the patient to accept the proposed treatment. In another example, a junior doctor explicitly told the patient that he would adapt her medication if problems occurred – a clear contrast to the first instance referred to above, in which a senior doctor brushed aside the patient's repeated concerns as "nonsense".

Doctors also expressed these differences explicitly when asked about them in semi-structured interviews on communication in medical encounters. One of the senior doctors stated, for example, that he is "more or less always talking like this" and that he "cannot act differently really". In contrast, the junior doctors emphasised the importance of communication, in general, and being able to adapt to different patients: "Communication is extremely important. It's important to strike a common chord with everybody. All sorts of people are coming to us, age, gender, skin colour, education. We have to be able to communicate with everyone."

Overall, we thus found distinct differences between the two generations. Whereas younger physicians, demonstrated and expressed a distinct willingness to adapt to their patients, members of the older generation, who had been trained under different societal conditions, adapted less to their patients and relied more on a hierarchical communication style, telling patients very distinctly what they should do and how they should behave. Our ethnography – based on participant observation and interviews – thus supports the observation in the overall public and in academic literature that there is a shift towards more egalitarian, participatory communication in Hungarian healthcare.

5.2 Change in style: physician- and patient-centred communicative patterns

In this subsection, we analyse instructional videos which were developed to specifically support the training of communicative skills and relationship-building. This makes it possible to study the linguistic features of physician- and patient-centred approaches in detail. The dataset is based on research about natural language discourse in healthcare and represents a reenactment of the original recordings. We investigated eight Hungarian discourses using conversation analytic (co-talk, turn-taking) and pragmatic criteria (speech acts, metapragmatic reflections, social deixis). Our analysis also included nonverbal communication. The results are presented below. The consultations begin with speech acts setting up social relations between doctors and patients and that typically convey politeness (greeting, introducing oneself, offering a seat) and build an initial relationship. Based on the sample under study, it can be stated that in the patient-centred style of relationship-building, these conversation-initial and conversation-final politeness acts receive more elaboration and are enacted in multiple turns (15a)–(15b) compared to the physician-centred style. It can be observed, moreover, that in the physician-centred approach, it is always the patient who initiates conversation, whereas in the patient-centred discourses, it is generally the doctor (in 3 out of 4 cases) who first engages in dialogue.

Acts of addressing the patient and reflections thereupon are highly prominent in relationship-building, especially in first encounters (see Section 4.1). Since in the Hungarian discourse community, a completely neutral style of performing such acts cannot be regarded as a given, questions about preferred forms of address constitute a key element in relationship-building. This involves explicit reflexivity in the course of relationship-building, as illustrated by (15b) in the form of a question ('How can I address you?'), followed by a reinforcing statement ('then I will do so as well'). By contrast, in (15a) the healthcare professional unilaterally decides to use the nick-name form *Marika* of the patient's first name *Mária* to address her, without any awareness of the patient's attitude to this (whether she prefers it or not, uses it only in the family, finds it too confidential, etc.).

Physician-centred	Patient-centred
(15a)	(15b)
P: 'Good morning! I am looking for doctor Békési.'	**Psy:** 'Yes. How can I help you?'
Psy: 'It is me. Welcome! Károly Békési.'	**P:** 'Good morning. I am looking for doctor Békési.'
P: 'Mária Baloghné Zombori.'	**Psy:** 'It is me. Welcome! Károly Békési.'
Psy: 'Take a seat, Marika! Do you always arrive before schedule?' (V,3a)	**P:** 'Mária Baloghné Zombori.'
	Psy: 'Take a seat! How can I address you?'
	P: 'Well, generally they call me Marika.'
	Psy: 'Fine, then I will do so as well. So. How can I help you?' (V,3b)

Although in both dialogues, the healthcare professional ends up addressing the patient as *Marika*, the two explicit reflections in (15b) allow the patient to negotiate this and to express her attitude about address forms without finding herself in a face-threatening situation (cf. Example [1]).

The presented dialogue excerpts display a variety of similarities in terms of linguistic and social actions. For example, greetings, self-introductions, welcome forms and acts of offering a seat are involved in both the patient-centred and the physician-centred approach. However, beyond the use of address forms and associated reflections, it is a key difference that relationship-building is closed by a reproach in (15a) ('Do you always arrive before schedule?'), whereas in (15b) it ends with the act of offering support as a way of commencing therapy ('How can I help you?').

In our data, efforts of building a working alliance go hand in hand with styles of knowledge sharing and information management. This process involves monitoring the participants' knowledge and adequate explanations of new information. In the example below, a general practitioner reacts to the patient's worry about heightened glucose levels.

Physician-centred	Patient-centred
(16a)	(16b)
P: 'But I don't eat any sweets, I don't even like them, and still I've become diabetic?'	**P:** 'But I don't eat any sweets, I don't even like them, and still I've become diabetic?'
D: 'Now this is not about that but rather about insulin. Insulin is not able to exert its effect as required, therefore glucose levels go up in your blood. Well then, this is it.' (V,2a)	**D:** 'Now this is not about that but rather about insulin. Insulin is not able to exert its effect as required, therefore glucose levels go up in your blood. Here I've collected a few book titles about the topic. There are some brochures here, let's see. Here you can find the things you need to know, and if you want you can also get one of the books. And if you feel that you have difficulty setting up your diet, just call me! When you have started your diet, come back after a month and we'll see how you are doing!' (V,2b)

The patient's question is the same in both dialogues. However, the doctors' answers are very different. In both cases, the healthcare professional offers an explanation of heightened glucose. In (16a), this marks the end of the relevant conversation turn, as explicitly indicated by the doctor ('Well then, this is it'). By contrast, in the patient-centred style of relationship-building, several other acts are performed, namely rendering information (both verbally and non-verbally), offering help and support, negotiating the next meeting and preparing the closing of the consultation. As a trend, it can thus be observed that in patient-centred consultations, more elaborate explanations appear.

In all consultations, we studied metapragmatic reflections (Kuna and Hámori forthc.) and person-marking devices in relation to attitudinal deixis (Kuna and Domonkosi 2022). The analysis was performed using MAXQDA. In the case of person-marking devices, we coded morpho-syntactic, pronominal, *tetszik* auxiliary + infinitive and vocative constructions in accordance with the features of Hungarian. Although the number of consultations under study does not allow for statistical measurements, as a trend it can be ascertained that in the patient-centred communicative style, physicians are more likely (with twice as many occurrences) to refer to themselves, their own feelings and knowledge. This takes the form of first person singular or plural forms, and often is combined with metapragmatic reflections ('I see', 'as I said','I'm asking because', 'I think') or the expression of shared actions ('we met', 'we can't work together'). In the patient-centred style, explicit constructions of joint attention and joint action are more common as well ('let's see', 'we'll see').

Furthermore, a clear difference was found in linguistic portrayals of the patient as an addressee. In the patient-centred style, a higher number of linguistic constructions address the patient in the doctors' speech compared to the doctor-centred style. Beyond the sheer number of references, considerable qualitative differences also appear in the construal of personal relations, as attested to by the examples in (17a) and (17b) below. At a consultation involving a male patient with panic disorder, the psychologist working with the physician-centred style of relationship-building basically constructs therapeutic work as the patient's task and responsibility (holding him accountable, *Don't you think*'). By contrast, in the patient-centred interaction, the patient's decision receives prominence, the psychologist makes inferences *('I'm sure'),* and therapy is construed linguistically by 1st person plural deictic elements as shared work *('we could think about', 'we could think it over').* In all this, attitudinal deixis plays a key role.

Physician-centred	Patient-centred
(17a) **Psy:** 'Don't you think – once you've come here – that somehow you should think differently about your condition? That you should think about – I'm just quoting as an example – your relationship with your wife?' (V,1a)	(17b) **Psy:** 'Since you decided to turn to a psychologist, I'm sure you don't think like this. It would be useful if we could think about your condition together. We could think over – I'm just quoting as – an example your, your relationship with your wife.' (V,1b)

Overall, it can thus be concluded that according to the sample under study, patient- and doctor-centred styles of relationship-building differ considerably in terms of both verbal and nonverbal communication. In patient-centred behaviour, interaction is initiated by the healthcare professional and is accompanied by eye contact between the two interactants. By contrast, in the doctor-centred model, the patient takes the initiative and eye contact is missing. In patient-centred interactions, we find a higher frequency of explanations, repetitions, and reflections about therapeutic actions and addressing practices; the physician typically bends forward, maintains eye contact with the patient, his/her facial gestures are softer, which serves to create a supportive atmosphere. By contrast, in the doctor-centred style, the healthcare professional's body is more often retracted (e.g. leaning against the chair back), with stiff facial gestures and turning away from the patient (looking at lab results or at the computer screen). Linguistically, this is frequently accompanied by expressions of reproach, expectations, instructions and typically, there is a lack of reassuring statements and reactions to the patient's emotions.

6. Conclusions and limitations

In this article, we investigated how linguistic devices like address forms, attitudinal deixis and metapragmatic comments contribute to relationship-building. Our examples illustrated the use of these communicative means in both shorter and longer stretches of speech. Based on discussions in the (social) media, a review of publications on relationships in Hungarian doctor-patient communication, interviews with physicians and our analyses of communicative practice, we were able to point out differences in how these linguistic devices of relationship-building were deployed. We discussed that, according to our analyses (Kuna and Scarvaglieri 2019), junior doctors adapted more towards the communicative needs and demands of their patients and also showed a stronger awareness of the importance of communication when asked about it. Senior physicians, in contrast, were found to be more reliant on their personal attitudes and styles of communication. They were thus more likely to adopt a paternalistic, directive style of communication, with less emphasis on the patient's concerns and needs. We also saw that junior physicians incorporated the patients' viewpoints and demands into their rhetoric and medical practice to a higher degree. These observations are supported by the fact that communicative practice is explicitly addressed in contemporary training programmes for physicians (incl. advice to ask patients how they would like to be addressed).

Based on another dataset that allowed for more detailed analysis, we were able to demonstrate differences between the patient-centred approach of communication and the physician-centred approach. We found, for example, that patient-centred communication included more explanations and repetitions as well as more pragmatical (concerning the illocution of an utterance) and lexical (concerning the proposition of utterances) involvement of the patient. We conclude that contrasting these two communication styles in this way presents a first step towards a more detailed understanding of the form and function of differences in health communication.

As our article touches on the complex and delicate subject of societal change, we want to mention a few limitations of our research. Since social processes of interactional change proceed gradually and often in partially contradicting ways, it is difficult to definitely prove that such change is taking place. We therefore speak of indicators for change that we were able to find based on different sources (public discourse, literature review, communicative practice, interview statements). Since these sources all point in the same direction – a development towards more equal relationships in primary care – it seems justified to conclude that such change is indeed occurring. Although we investigated these changes based on data from different generations of physicians, we do not hold that the differences we observed are the product of a person's age, but that they are related to far-reaching societal changes and to a general transformation of Hungarian society (cf. Hambuch et al. 2018) and to changes in healthcare communication overall (Beach 2013, Bigi 2016), i.e. not restricted to Hungary.

A further limitation of our research consists in the datasets we were able to investigate. We are currently working to increase the number of participating doctors and to include female doctors in our dataset. Increasing the sample will also allow us to widen our methodological approach and integrate quantitative-statistical analyses (cf. Mundwiler et al. 2019).

References

Ainsworth-Vaugh, Nancy. 2004. *Claiming Power in Doctor-Patient Talk*. Oxford: Oxford University Press.

Bartha, Csilla, and Ágnes Hámori. 2010. "Stílus a szociolingvisztikában, stílus a diskurzusban [Style in sociolinguistics, style in discourse: Linguistic variability and the construction of social meaning in the "third wave" of sociolinguistics]." *Magyar Nyelvőr* 134 (3): 298–321.

Bálint, Katalin, Tamás Nagy, and Márta Csabai. 2014. "The Effect of Patient-Centeredness and Gender of Professional Role Models on Trainees' Mentalization Responses. Implication for Film-aided Education." *Patient Education and Counseling* 97: 52–58. https://doi.org/10.1016/j.pec.2014.06.005

Beach, Wayne. 2013. "Introduction." In *Handbook of Patient-Provider Interactions*, ed. by Wayne Beach, 1–18. New York: Oxford University Press. https://doi.org/10.1017/CBO9781139600521.001

Bigi, Sarah. 2016. *Communicating (with) Care. A Linguistic Approach to the Study of Doctor-Patient Interactions*. Amsterdam: IOS.

Blommaert, Jan. 2018. *Durkheim and the Internet. On Sociolinguistics and the Sociological Imagination*. London: Bloomsbury. https://doi.org/10.5040/9781350055223

Brown, Roger, and Albert Gilman. 1960. "The Pronouns of Power and Solidarity." In *Style in Language*, ed. by Thomas Sebeok, 253–276. Cambridge: MIT Press.

Bublitz, Wolfram, and Axel Hübler (eds). 2007. *Metapragmatics in Use*. Amsterdam: Benjamins. https://doi.org/10.1075/pbns.165

Caffi, Claudia. 2016. "Revisiting Metapragmatics: What Are We Talking About?" In *Pragmemes and Theories of Language Use*, ed. by Keith Allan, Alessandro Capone and Istvan Kecskes, 799–821. Heidelberg: Springer. https://doi.org/10.1007/978-3-319-43491-9_40

Clark, Herbert H. 1996. *Using Language*. Cambridge: CUP. https://doi.org/10.1017/CBO9780511620539

Csabai, Márta, Ilona Csörsz, and Katalin Szili. 2009. *A gyógyító kapcsolat élménye. Kézikönyv és oktatólemez a kapcsolati készségek fejlesztéséhez*. [The experience of a healing relationship. Handbook and educational CD-ROM for the development of relationship-oriented skills]. Budapest: Oriold és Társa Kiadó.

Csiszárik, Katalin, and Ágnes Domonkosi. 2018. "A gyógyító-beteg viszonylat megszólítási változatai egy mozgásszervi rehabilitációs osztály gyakorlatközösségében. [Address form variants in healer-patient interactions in the practice community of a mosculoskeletal rehabilitation ward.]" *Acta Universitas de Carolo Eszterházy Nominatae* XLIV: 109–128.

Domonkosi, Ágnes. 2010. Variability in Hungarian Address Forms. *Acta Linguistica Hungarica* 57: 29–52. https://doi.org/10.1556/ALing.57.2010.1.2

Domonkosi, Ágnes. 2016. Perspective and Attitudinal Deixis in Hungarian. *Jezyk, Komunikacja, Informacja / Language, Communication, Information* 11: 86–98.

Eckert, Penelope. 2006. "Communities of Practice." In *Encyclopedia of Language and Linguistics*. Edited by Keith Brown, 683–85. Amsterdam: Elsevier. https://doi.org/10.1016/B0-08-044854-2/01276-1

Gaal, Ilona. 2016. "Az internet hatása az orvos–beteg viszonyra." *Orvosi Hetilap* 157 (17): 680–684. https://doi.org/10.1556/650.2016.30456

Goffman, Erving. 1959. *The Presentation of Self in Everyday Life*. London: Penguin.

Goffman, Erving. 1966. *Behaviour in Public Places: Notes on the Social Organization of Gatherings*. New York: The Free Press
Hall, Judith, Debra Roter, and Cynthia Rand. 1981. "Communication of Affect between Patient and Physician." *Health and Social Behaviour* 22 (1): 18–30. https://doi.org/10.2307/2136365
Hambuch, Anikó, Lőrinc Sárkányné, and Rita Kránicz. 2018. "Veränderung der Kommunikationsmodelle im Gesundheitswesen und ihre Widerspiegelung in den Interaktionen mit Klienten [Change of communication models in healtcare and its reflection in interaction with clients]." In *Fachbezogener Fremdsprachenunterricht – aktuelle Herausforderungen und zukünftige Chancen*, ed. by Brigita Kacjan, 59–71. Ljubljana: The Slovene Association of LSP Teachers.
Harris, Roxy. 2006. *New Ethnicities and Language Use*. Houndmills, Basingstoke: Palgrave MacMillan. https://doi.org/10.1057/9780230626461
Havas, Ferenc, Márta Csepregi, Nikolett Gulyás, and Szilvia Németh. 2015. *Typological Database of the Ugric Languages*. Budapest: ELTE.
Heritage, John, and Douglas Maynard. 2006. "Problems and Prospects in the Study of Physician-Patient Interaction: 30 Years of Research." *Annual Review of Sociology* 32 (1): 351–74. https://doi.org/10.1146/annurev.soc.32.082905.093959
Koerfer, Armin, Thomas Reimer, and Christian Albus. 2018. "Beziehung aufbauen [Constructing relationships]." In *Kommunikative Kompetenz in der Medizin: Ein Lehrbuch zur Theorie, Didaktik, Praxis und Evaluation der ärztlichen Gesprächsführung*, ed. by Armin Koefer, and Christian Albus, 814–851. Mannheim: Verl. für Gesprächsforschung.
Kuna, Ágnes. 2016. "Person Deixis and Self-Representation in Medical Discourse. Usage Patterns of First Person Deictic Elements in Communication by Doctors." *Language, Communication, Information* 11: 99–121.
Kuna, Ágnes and Ágnes Domonkosi. 2020. "Social Meanings of the Hungarian Politeness Marker *tetszik* in Doctor-Patient Communication." *Acta Universitatis Sapientiae Philologica* 12 (3): 88–104. https://doi.org/10.2478/ausp-2020-0025
Kuna, Ágnes, and Ágnes Domonkosi. 2022. "Társas deixis és a kapcsolatépítés az orvos-beteg interakcióban [Social deixis and relationship building in physician-patient interaction]." In *A deixis a magyar nyelvben*. [Deixis in Hungarian] ed. by Krisztina Laczkó, and Szilárd Tátrai. Budapest: Eötvös Collegium.
Kuna, Ágnes, and Ágnes Hámori. (forthc.). "Metapragmatics and Reflections in Support of Knowledge Transfer and Common Ground in Doctor-Patient Interaction". In *A Pragmatic Agenda for Healthcare: Fostering Inclusion and Active Participation through Shared Understanding*, ed. by Sarah Bigi, and Maria Grazia Rossi. Amsterdam: Benjamins.
Kuna, Ágnes, and Ágnes Hámori. 2019. "'Hallgatom, mi a panasz?' A metapragmatikai reflexiók szerepei és mintázatai az orvos-beteg interakciókban." ['I am listening, what is the complaint?' The roles and patterns of metapragmatic reflexions in doctor-patient interactions.]" In *Kontextualizáció és metapragmatikai tudatosság*, [Contextualization and metapragmatic awareness] ed. by Laczkó Krisztina, and Tátrai Szilárd, 260–83. Eötvös Collegium, Budapest.
Kuna, Ágnes, and Claudio Scarvaglieri. 2019. "Intergenerational Changes of Relationship Management in Primary Care." Presenation at the *IIEMCA*, Mannheim (July 2–5, 2019).
Kuna, Ágnes, and Zsuzsa Kaló. 2014. "Az orvos-beteg kommunikáció a családorvosi gyakorlatban." [Doctor-patient communication in primary care]." In *Tudomány, technolektus, terminológia. A tudományok, szakmák nyelve*, [Terminology. Language of the sciences, professions], ed. by Ágnes Veszelszki, and Klára Lengyel, 117–130. Budapest.

Levinson, Stephen. 1983. *Principles of Pragmatics*. Cambridge: CUP. https://doi.org/10.1017/CBO9780511813313

Linke, Angelika, and Juliane Schröter. 2017. "Sprache in Beziehungen – Beziehungen in Sprache: Überlegungen zur Konstitution eines Linguistischen Forschungsfeldes [Language in relationshiops – relationships in language: Reflexions on research domain of linguistics]." In *Sprache und Beziehung*, ed. by Angelika Linke, and Juliane Schröter, 1–32. Berlin, Boston: de Gruyter.

Locher, Miriam, and Richard Watts. 2008. "Relational Work and Impoliteness: Negotiating Norms of Linguistic Behaviour." In *Impoliteness in Language*, edited by Miriam A. Locher and Derek Bousfield, 77–100: de Gruyter.

Lucy, John. 1993. "Reflexive Language and the Human Disciplines." In *Reflexive Language: Reported Speech and Metapragmatics*, ed. by Lucy, John, 9–33. Cambridge: CUP. https://doi.org/10.1017/CBO9780511621031.003

Málovics, Éva, Beáta Vajda, and Péter Kuba. 2009. "Paternalizmus vagy közös döntés? Páciensek az orvos–beteg kommunikációról. [Paternalism or shared decision making. Patient about doctor-patient interaction]" In *A szolgáltatások világa*, [The world of services], ed. by Erzsébet Hetesi, Zoltán Majó, and Miklós Lukovics, 250–264. Szeged: JATEPress.

Marshall, Steve. 2021. "Navigating COVID-19 Linguistic Landscapes in Vancouver's North Shore: Official Signs, Grassroots Literacy Artefacts, Monolingualism, and Discursive Convergence." *International Journal of Multilingualism*, 1–25. https://doi.org/10.1080/14790718.2020.1849225

Mayring, Philipp. 2010. *Qualitative Inhaltsanalyse: Grundlagen und Techniken [Qualitative content analysis. Basics and technique.]*. Weinheim: Beltz.

Meskó, Bertalan. 2014. *The Guide to the Future of Medicine. Technology and the Human Touch*. Budapest: Webicina.

Mundwiler, Vera, Judith Kreuz, Daniel Müller-Feldmeth, Martin Luginbühl, and Stefan Hauser. 2019. "Quantitative und qualitative Zugänge in der Gesprächsforschung: Methodologische Betrachtungen am Beispiel einer Studie zu argumentativen Gruppendiskussionen. [Quantitative and qualitative approaches in conversation research: Methodological observations based on the example of group discussions]." *Gesprächsforschung* (20): 323–83.

Norrby, Catrin, and Camilla Wide (eds). 2015. *Address Practice as Social Action: European Perspectives*. Houndsmills, Basingstoke: Palgrave Macmillan.

Pilling, János (ed). 2004. *Orvosi kommunikáció* [Medical Communication]. Budapest: Medicina Könyvkiadó.

Pilling, János. 2018. *Orvosi kommunikáció a gyakorlatban* [Medical communication in the praxis]. Budapest: Medicina.

Rounds, Carol. 2001. *Hungarian. An Essential Grammar*. London, New York: Routledge.

Sára, Zoltán, Zoltán Csedő, Tamás Tóth, Józses Fejes. and Pörzse Gábor. 2013. "A korszerű információtechnológiai megoldások szerepe az orvos-beteg kommunikáció javításában. [The role of advanced information technology solutions in enhancing doctor-patient communication]." *Interdiszciplináris Magyar Egészségügy* 12 (4): 20–24.

Scarvaglieri, Claudio. 2017. "'Educational Landscaping': A Method for Raising Awareness About Language and Communication." *Language Awareness* 59 (5): 325–42. https://doi.org/10.1080/09658416.2017.1411358.

Silverstein, Michael. 2003. "Indexical Order and the Dialectics of Sociolinguistic Life." *Language and Communication* 23 (3–4): 192–229. https://doi.org/10.1016/S0271-5309(03)00013-2

Tannen, Deborah, Heidi Ehernberger Hamilton, and Deborah Schiffrin, eds. 2015. *The Handbook of Discourse Analysis*. Hoboken, NJ: Wiley Blackwell.
Vajda, Beáta, Sarolta Horváth, and Éva Málovics. 2012. "Közös döntéshozatal mint innováció az orvos-beteg kommunikációban [Shared decision making, as an innovation in physician-patient communication]". In *Regionális innovációs képesség, versenyképesség és fenntarthatóság*, ed. by Bajmócy, Zoltán., Lengyel, Imre. and Málovics, György. Szeged: JATE Press.
Verschueren, Jef. 1999. *Understanding Pragmatics*. London: Arnold
Verschueren, Jef. 2000. Notes on the Role of Metapragmatic Awareness in Language Use. *Pragmatics* 10 (4): 439–456. https://doi.org/10.1075/prag.10.4.02ver
Volosinov, Valentin. 1973. *Marxism and the Philosophy of Language*. New York: Seminar Press.
Warren, Ed. 2006. *B.A.R.D. in the Practice. A Guide for Family Doctors to Consult Efficiently, Effectively and Happily*. Oxford: Radcliffe Publishing.

Building (dis-)affiliative medical relationships through interactional practices of knowledge management

A comparative study of German and Bosnian medical encounters

Minka Džanko
University of Sarajevo

The goal of the current contribution is to consider and compare different aspects of (dys-)functional knowledge management indexed by a conflict involving epistemics in Bosnian and German language. My research draws on 42 audiotaped conversations of Bosnian and German doctors with their patients. The data was analyzed using Conversation Analysis.

This paper focuses first on the Bosnian data in which patients display an inability to provide the requested information or display reduced access to information they are accountable for (Heritage 2012). Interactional practices of dysfunctional knowledge management lead to misunderstandings, a break in the progressivity of the interaction, or face threatening actions such as criticism and disciplining of the patient (Holly 2001). In contrast, a focus on the German data shows a more patient-centered approach which entails more active patient participation. Furthermore, German patients display higher medical knowledge and more personal responsibility.

Keywords: doctor-patient relationship, conversation analysis, (dis-)affiliation, knowledge management, epistemics, Bosnian, German

1. Introduction

This chapter analyzes how doctors and patients turn-by-turn build their relationship around a patient's accounts of his/her current medical condition and medical history during the patient's initial problem presentation and a history-taking phase. Knowledge management between patients and doctors is considered one of the key elements of the doctor-patient interaction. A relevant task of doctors

https://doi.org/10.1075/pbns.331.11dza

during medical visits consists of delivering a diagnosis after collecting all relevant information about the patient's concerns and their history. Through the lens of Conversation Analysis, problem presentation has been studied for numerous reasons, such as the patient's accounting for her/his problem (Heritage and Robinson 2006; Heritage 2009), conveying and pursuing self-diagnoses as well as underlying fears (Beach 2011; Frankel 2001; Gill and Maynard 2006; Spranz-Fogasy 2014), and building trust and respecting a patient's self-knowledge by actively listening to and addressing the patient's concerns (Byrne and Long 1976; Chatwin 2006).

Collecting information from a patient is guided by a doctor's questions (Spranz-Fogasy 2005, 2010; Deppermann and Spranz-Fogasy 2011) which provide the agenda of the interaction (Manning and Ray 2002; Heritage and Clayman 2010). According to Boyd and Heritage (2006: 151), in addition to information about a patient's social and family background, a patient's comprehensive medical history is considered one of the foundational sources for collecting details about a patient's current medical problem. Some of the patient's answers are nonverbal signs of approval or rejection, such as a head nod, or a head shake. Others are verbal response markers such as yes/no, phrases, or narratives (Spranz-Fogasy 2010). The provided answers can vary not just in their interactional and syntactic structure but also in their degree of completeness or the self-knowledge they display. A patient's knowledge can range from a display of absolute knowledge to a display of more or less reduced access to information they are accountable for. It is conveyed to the doctor along with emotions and a psychosocial context of underlying fears and anxieties. As Löning (1993: 224) emphasizes, the doctor, in turn, has to translate the patient's complaints, which are mostly described in colloquial language, into symptoms and put them into a medical context. Rehbein (1993: 350ff) underlines the importance of the reverse transfer of knowledge in which doctors use different question types in order to invite more elaborate problem presentation or display how they understand the patient's previous turn by summarizing or recapitulating the patient's previous utterances, e.g., formulations (Ataki 2008), or minimal signals such as "hm", "yeah", "right" (Schegloff 2007).

While knowledge management between doctors and patients has been largely studied for its asymmetry and its importance for the success of the medical diagnosis and therapeutic work, less is known about different aspects of dysfunctional knowledge management indexed by a conflict involving epistemics (Heritage 2012). Generally, each and every patient is granted the epistemic authority or the epistemic access to the symptoms, processes and experiences of her/his illness. Boyd and Heritage argue (2006: 152) that a patient's responses not only provide information for the doctor, but they also display the patient's understanding of the task at hand and the opportunities and constraints it affords. In other words, the opportunity to be able to maintain epistemic primacy over her/his own domain of experience and to be regarded positively[1] requires a certain degree of reliable medical knowledge with regard to one's own health.

In this chapter I want to shed light on interactional practices of knowledge management indicated by a conflict involving epistemics which put the relationship between doctors and patients at risk as well as on different interactional practices of how disaffiliation and most importantly re-affiliation can be negotiated.

To do this, I firstly invoke the notions of affiliation and disaffiliation which are terms used within Conversation Analysis to conceptualize degrees of cooperativeness and mutual level of affect between speakers (Muntigl and Horvath 2015; Stivers 2008).[2] The researchers argue that the organization of talk is inclined towards the promotion of social solidarity, the avoidance of conflict and saving face of the speakers (Brown and Levinson 1987; Goffmann 1967; Heritage 1984). According to Heritage (1984: 265ff.) the concept of affiliation is used to describe socially solidary actions in interaction, which convey the speaker's agreement with and understanding of the prior speaker's utterances. On the other hand, the term disaffiliation describes socially divisive actions, with the consequence of straining the cooperative relationship between speakers (Heritage 1984). I also draw from Heritages (2012) concept of epistemics which is "the most influential conceptual innovation to emerge from conversation analysis (CA) in the past decade" (Lindwall, Lymer, and Ivarsson 2016: 501) argued as being the most important component in the production and recognition of action (Heritage 2012). While one speaker can have absolute knowledge on some subject and the other none, it is also possible that both speakers have the same information. Therefore, the speakers are positioned as being more [K+] or less knowledgeable [K-] about the domain in question. Both speakers have their own *territory of information* (Heritage 2012, 2013) or their *epistemic domains* (Stivers and Rossano 2010). They ultimately occupy different positions on an *epistemic gradient* which may vary in slope from shallow to deep (Heritage 2012, 2013). Epistemic status involves not just the actual possession of information on the speaker's feelings, hopes, experiences and expectations, but also the right to possess it and to articulate it (Raymond and Heritage 2006; Stivers et al. 2011). However, the epistemic status of every speaker, relative to others, can vary from domain to domain, and over time, and can also be changed from moment to moment as a result of specific interactional contributions. Epistemic stance, expressed through grammar and intonation, "concerns the moment-by-moment expression of these relationships, as managed through the design of turns at talk"

1. For a concept of *face* see Brown and Levinson 1987 and Goffman 1967.

2. For a concept of affiliation as a conversational building block of social relationships, see also Muntigl this volume.

(Heritage 2013: 376). Heritage (2013: 379) argues that epistemic congruence across turns and sequences is expressed when a speaker's epistemic stance is compatible with their epistemic status relative to some domain and some particular others. However, a variety of motives and contingencies may result in non-congruent utterances at which I will be looking in the Bosnian and German data. Consequently, I will illustrate the general patterns of how different groups of Bosnian patients (mostly, but not exclusively, chronic patients, older patients, patients from a lower social class or patients with low levels of education) display an inability to provide requested information despite their status as putatively more knowledgeable. In the corpus under examination, eight Bosnian patients (40%), display reduced access to information they should account for, such as the name of their prescribed medication, self-care routines (regular intake of medication, intake of medication on an empty stomach), providing previous medical documentation,[3] the names of previous treatments and surgeries. Furthermore, I will show that 19 out of 21 German patients show a very high level of responsibility and self-knowledge regarding their medical condition or other health related circumstances. For this chapter, I have chosen four representative examples for detailed analysis.

The research questions in this chapter are: What role have epistemics in the observable practices of knowledge management between the patients and their doctors, as well as how do such practices relate to the way doctors challenge the patient's expertise and knowledge? How do doctors and patients turn-by-turn build their (dis-)affiliative relationship around a patient's account of her/his current medical condition and medical history? In which ways is disaffiliation realized interactively and can it subsequently be repaired or not? What are commonalities and divergences in the ways in which Bosnian and German doctors and patients build a therapeutic relationship regarding functional and dysfunctional knowledge management?

Following the introduction, I will present Bosnian and German data from doctor-patient interactions (Section 2). In Section 3 the methods of Conversation Analysis will be provided. Covering different sequences from the problem presentation and history-taking in the Bosnian and German data, Section 4 assesses a relationship between what the doctor treats as being understood and what she/he still needs to find out and understand about and from the patient and her/his condition is being negotiated. The section focuses on Bosnian and German data. I concentrate first on those Bosnian sequences in which the knowledge management between patients and doctors is strained by inaccuracies and divergences of the expected self-knowledge. This leads to misunderstanding and interactional problems such as a break in the progressivity of the interaction or face-threatening actions

3. The process of implementing the electronic medical record in Bosnia and Herzegovina is still a work in progress.

towards patients. On the other hand, however, by comparing the Bosnian with the German data, the section highlights the importance of being able to maintain epistemic authority over her/his domain of experience on the patient's part in order to collaboratively achieve mutual affiliation. In Section 5, I will turn to a discussion of the findings of the comparative analysis and to the conclusion.

2. Data

The findings in this chapter are based on 42 doctor-patient-conversations. There are 21 audio-taped medical visits by four different doctors at one medical facility in Bosnia and Herzegovina. The interviews are conducted by two doctors in residency, one urologist, and one internist. The patients have different educational and socio-economic backgrounds. There are 13 female and 8 male patients, aged between 21 to 72. Sixteen encounters are first visits, five are follow-ups, and nine patients have at least one chronic illness (diabetes, hypertension, etc.). The findings in this paper are also based on 21 audio-taped medical conversations between four German private practitioners (two general practitioners, an internist, and a urologist) and their patients. There are 19 first medical interviews and two follow-ups. Four patients are chronically ill patients, 14 patients are female and seven male, aged between 20 to 70. The data has been transcribed using the minimal transcription conventions GAT (Selting et al. 2009).[4]

3. Methodology

In order to shed more light on how interactional practices of (dis-)functional knowledge management affect affiliative relationships between doctors and patients, I use the method of Conversation Analysis (CA) (Sacks, Schegloff, and Jefferson 1974). The researchers of medical conversation[5] have tried "to understand and document

4. German data has been provided by Prof. Dr. Thomas Spranz-Fogasy from the Institute for the German Language in Mannheim. The Bosnian data collection was approved by the Ethics Committee of one of the biggest University Medical Centre in Bosnia and Herzegovina. The data were collected with informed consent by the participants. To protect all participants, I have used pseudonyms and have signed the data protection statement.

5. See bibliography on medical research collected by ten Have (http://www.paultenhave.nl/medbib.htm; 545 references, 9.2.2013) and by Nowak and Spranz-Fogasy (http://hypermedia.ids-mannheim.de/pragdb/Bibliografie_zur_Arzt-Patient-Kommunikation.pdf; 5222 references, 2014)

what social actions and activities are accomplished by participants in medical encounters and *how* participants use interactional resources and sense-making practices to accomplish their goals, with the aim of identifying recurrent patterns of interaction" (Gill and Roberts 2013: 577 citing Halkowski and Gill 2010). In medical encounters interactants move through a series of activity phases in a particular order: (1) greeting and opening, (2) problem presentation and history taking, (3) diagnosis, (4) treatment recommendation, and (5) closing and farewell (Spranz-Fogasy 2005).[6] Other features of a medical encounter are the organization of activities within the different phases of the account and the sequences of action through which these activities are achieved (e.g., question-answer sequences). Generally, questions presuppose already existing knowledge and assumptions by the doctor (Heritage and Clayman 2010). Moreover, the epistemic authority of the doctor regarding the topic is considered the key element for understanding a question (Heritage and Raymond 2005). Wh-questions set a topic agenda (Manning and Ray 2002) such as symptoms, cause, time, place etc. (Spranz-Fogasy 2010). By taking an 'unknowing' epistemic stance the doctor invites elaboration and projects the possibility of sequence expansion. The more 'knowing' question formats are yes/no-questions (V-questions) and declaratives. Yes/no-questions with the finite verb in the first position of the sentence invite confirmation (Heritage and Clayman 2010). Understanding of declaratives as questions depends on prosodic, sequential, pragmatic, and epistemic features (Stivers and Rossano 2010).[7] The questions are based on presuppositions, grounded in the doctor's expert knowledge, common knowledge or in patients' prior turns (Heritage 2010; Heritage and Raymond 2012). However, the patient's epistemic status can be also challenged by question formats which encode a different epistemic stance and are directed at a topic where the patient should have primary epistemic status. Applying a conversation analytic perspective, this chapter examines and compares the practices of knowledge management indicated by epistemics in medical data from Bosnia and Herzegovina[8] and Germany.

6. Also see Byrne and Long 1976; Mishler 1984; Heritage and Maynard 2006.

7. A detailed discussion of all properties of different question formats is beyond the scope of this paper.

8. For CA research of medical encounters in Bosnia and Herzegovina, see Džanko 2020.

4. Findings

In the Bosnian corpus was observed that patients, in particular older patients, and even patients with chronic illnesses, display very limited knowledge concerning not only their medication but also other health related circumstances such as prior tests and illnesses, self-care, diet or exercise. For a patient to fail to maintain their territory of knowledge means to risk the downgrading and downplaying of their utterances and assessments and their socioepistemic role in the interaction with doctors, which ultimately strains the doctor-patient relationship. I show in the following examples that epistemic status can be dissembled by patients who deploy epistemic stance to appear more knowledgeable than they really are [K+] (Example (1)) and/or avoid any claim of epistemic authority (Example (3)). Epistemic incongruency on the patient's side causes misunderstanding and ultimately a break in the progressivity of the interaction as well as face threatening actions[9] such as accusations, criticism and disciplining of the patient. I distinguish different practices of how doctors and patients manage situations of knowledge management throughout extensive sequences of problem presentation and history-taking and present cases of collaboratively achieved (dis)affiliative relationships. The analysis of the German data (Examples (2), (4)) shows that German patients not only report on previous illnesses or examinations, but generally position themselves as reliable informants with regard to their health history, as will be shown in the examples. The German data is presented as contrasting with the Bosnian data in order to show good practices of collaboratively achieved affiliative relationships.

4.1 Knowledge of medical history

The first Bosnian extract depicts dysfunctional knowledge management despite an extensive attempt by the doctor to secure the information under evaluation. The following extract is from the conversation between a female internist and a 65-year-old male patient. The patient is visiting the internist because of swallowing problems. During the medical history taking, the patient delivers information that he had had gastric ulcers in the past for which he had been examined in Germany (not shown in the extract). The doctor begins her new turn with an alternative question based on her professional medical knowledge to find out which examination has been done (line 655). The patient declines both options and claims that the examination in Germany assumed by the doctor has not been performed for

9. See Goffmann 1967; Holly 2001.

the last fifteen or twenty years. The following extract illustrates the context of how disaffiliation evoked by a patient who claims to know more than he really does can be repaired by the doctor who uses humor as a resource to do it.[10]

(1) IA_AB_01[11]

```
655  D  did you [drink] swallow that that (-) tube with a
656  P          [yes   ]
657  D  [light    ] or did you drink that chalky fluid
658  P  [yes yes ]
659     right  but now (.) in the last fifteen or twenty years
660     nobody  swallows the tube any more
661  D  but?
662  P  (-) I don't know what [happens]
663  D                        [one  ta]kes that pill
664  P  (-) I have no idea it's done in no time
665  D  (.) aha so well yes (-) <<t>abort> that's the way
        things are being done in germany
```

At lines 655/657 the doctor begins her request for information by using professional lexis in a more informal way. She asks him if he had swallowed the tube with a light, as a reference to a gastroscopy, or if he had drunk the chalky fluid, using the latter as a comparison to indicate an abdominal x-ray. She uses two yes/no-questions with the turn-initial position of the verb which syntactically presupposes more knowledge than Wh-questions. In that way she implicitly claims to know that one of two alternative propositions will be the answer. The patient's response at lines 656: *yes,* 658: *yes yes* and 659: *right* projects at first an agreement with the doctor's assessment on the possible test but serves as a display of his own knowledge in that domain. Thus, by prefacing his turn with *right,* the speaker claims some kind of shared knowledge (AB-event known to both patient and doctor)[12] with the doctor. Moreover, at the same line he corrects the doctor by interpreting it in terms of his own presupposed [K+] knowledge of the test in Germany and making a statement about a B-event (known to a patient, but not to a doctor), in which epistemic primacy, or knowledge of personal experience, lies within the patients domain (Labov and Fenschel 1977): *but now (.) lately in the last fifteen or twenty years nobody swallows the tube any more* (line 659/60). Hence, the patient claims first-order

10. The first two letters in the examples indicate the specialization of the physician (IA = internist, UR = urologist). "D" stands for physicians, "P" for patients.

11. Due to space limits, only the English translation is shown. The original sequences in Bosnian/German are available from the author.

12. For different events of knowledge (A-, B-, AB-, O- and D-event) in relation to the local state of interaction, see Labov and Fanshel (1977).

access to it, asserting epistemic independence relative to the doctor. By doing so the patient intrudes deeply into the doctor's epistemic territory. The doctor responds from a [K-] position with: *but?* (line 661) inviting an additional explanation from the patient. After a short turn-initial delay the patient utters: *(-) I don't know what [happens]* (line 662). He uses the negation of the verb: *don't know* as a resource to modify his epistemic stance and downplay his prior claim as he may not occupy an epistemic status that is compatible with his claim. The patient's status changes within the same sequence from wishing to appear more knowledgeable to unknowing. The outcome is a serious epistemic incongruity. Interrupting with the end of his turn, the doctor reclaims her own epistemic authority and rejects the unknowing status projected at lines 659/60 with a declarative: *>one ta]kes that pill* (line 663). At line 664 after another short turn-initial delay, the patient underscores his modified unknowing status by uttering that he doesn't know how the test has been done, but with one little expansion in his answer. He includes a subjective assessment of the duration of the examination: *(-) I have no idea it's done in no time.* To fail to find out which test the patient is talking about can be understood as face threatening for the doctor. At this point in the interaction, it is not just the knowledge transfer at risk but also the speaker's relationship as they seem completely disaffiliated. The doctor then attunes to the patients utterance and responds with affiliation by displaying agreement with the change-of-state tokens: *(.) aha so* (line 665) and producing a summary formulation of the patient's previous talk in a humorous way: *well yes (-) <<t>abort> that's the way things are being done in germany* (line 665), implying that in Germany such effective tests exist which are still unknown in Bosnia and Herzegovina. Even though the doctor didn't succeed to elicit information about the gastric test in Germany, she ends the conversation with an affiliative utterance in order to overcome an interactional obstacle and achieve further progressivity of the interaction while simultaneously maintaining an affiliative dynamic in the interaction. Furthermore, the doctor may be using humor as a resource to reclaim her own epistemic authority and save not just her patient's but also her own face.

The analysis of the German data, by contrast, shows that German patients position themselves as reliable informants with regard to their health history, as will be shown in the following example. The example illustrates how a doctor displays attentiveness once the patient begins to give his account and restricts his turns to affiliative continuation signals. The following fragment is from a conversation between a urologist and an older patient who has been referred by his general practitioner based on prostate enlargement and possible surgery. In the following example the patient describes his medical history at length, giving an account of previous kidney and bladder examinations at the hospital from two years ago, their detailed values, previous diagnosis as well as of his chronic illness.

(2) UR_HD_02

```
20  P  äh (-) there äh (-) I was also examined
21     (-) (hm) (--)
22     among others my kidneys (--) as well
23     and (1.5) and the bladder (.)
24     [and there ] was partly
25  D  [mhm mhm   ]
26  P  diagnosed something else than doctor (name) has done
27     it (...)
28     was (eighty) ninety four back then there was
29     always just a little residual urine found
30  D  the doctor?
31  P  I can just say children) have (1.3) much more
32     (-)
33     three hundred or (...) [(...)  ]
34  D                         [mhm    ]
35  P  (nine hundred) ninety was found (1.0)
36     and he also believed
37     he did a cystoscopy as well
38     and he said that (--) prostate was just
39     insignificantly enlarged
40     but that I had a bladder neck obstruction (-)
41     to [(...)]
42  D     [mhm  ] mhm
```

Shortly after a greeting sequence the patient begins to report on his medical history. The patient attempts to deliver a doctorable account for him coming to see a doctor, in other words to give information "worthy of medical attention, worthy of evaluation as a potentially significant medical condition, and worthy of advice and, where necessary, medical treatment" (Heritage and Robinson 2006: 58) (lines 20–24). His account includes his examinations of kidney and bladder as well as a prior diagnosis at the hospital from two years ago. Seeing a chronically ill patient for the first time, the doctor chooses to attune to his narrative and delivers affiliative continuation signals: *mhm* (lines 25). At lines 26–29, the patient includes into his narrative two different opinions, one made earlier by another doctor and one at the hospital concerning the volume of residual urine. The doctor chooses not to utilize the pause at line 27 as possible opening to interject into the patient's narrative nor does he initiate a reply at line 28 where the patient leaves an extended pause (1.3 seconds) until the patient reaches a natural turn juncture at line 29. He then attempts to briefly seek confirmation as to whether it was a doctor who found out about the volume of the residual urine through a declarative: *the doctor?* (line 30). Since it is a recorded conversation, we can only assume that the patient non-verbally confirms his question as he continues with his own narrative concerning his past examination, diagnosis and his chronic illness (lines 31–33, 35–41) to which the doctor attunes with affiliative continuation tokens (line 34, 42). In the extract above, it can be observed that a patient who displays medically relevant knowledge concerning his medical history (previous examinations, diagnoses, chronically illness) is allowed to come to the end of his narrative in a natural way. In other words, the doctor refrains from initiating new topics or requesting more elaborative turns. The continuation signals: *mhm* are minimal responses which serve as affiliative devices to enable patients to present their own account conveying relevant details of their illness experience. The functional knowledge transfer and patient-centered approach allow collaborative interactional progressivity towards greater mutual affiliation and a more collegial dynamic between doctor and patient. Consequently, better patient outcomes are the ultimate aims of the communication (e.g. information gathering, or adherence to treatment).

4.2 Self-care related knowledge

The Bosnian data also indicates that the patients, in particular the patients with chronic illnesses display very limited knowledge concerning medical device use, self-care, or diet. In the case of chronically ill people those expectations of the doctors are even higher (Gülich 1999; Lalouschek 2008). In the following extract, we show how disaffiliation is built up around a conflict of views on the patient's diet. The following example is drawn from the same conversation as Example (1) between a 65-year-old male diabetic and a female internist. The patient from this conversation complains initially about swallowing problems, but during the problem presentation the doctor discovers that the patient doesn't know the names of his medication for diabetes, nor does he carry his prior medical records with him. The patient also claims that he doesn't eat a lot. The doctor responds with an evaluation that one would never think that according to his looks (not shown in the transcript). In response to the doctor's reaction, the patient initiates an elaboration on his daily diet (lines 361/2/3). Here, the patient's display of low knowledge and non-adherent behavior is openly criticized which puts their relationship at risk.

(3) IA_AB_01

```
361  P  [once]
362     (.) I eat around nine thirty ten at six and then till
363     tomorrow at nine nothing
364  D  that's not good anto how many times anto how many
365     times should a diabetic eat
366     YOU should tell me YOU are a diabetic you have to
367     know that better than me
368     how many times does a diabetic eat
369  P  (---) I don't know
370     (1.07)
371  D  isn't that shameful how many years do you have
372     diabetes  six
373  P  (-) yes
```

```
374  D   (.) YOU should lecture me on that how a diabetic eats
Lines 375-381 omitted
382  D   (-) this is the biggest mistake you are making for
383      eating once a day because then your body
384      keeps in a possessive way (-) everything you have
385      eaten.
386      do you understand me
387  P   yes
388  D   good anto (.) are there some other problems
```

Faced with the patients repeated display of a non-compliant[13] attitudinal stance towards his chronic disease, the doctor retreats from her action of taking history and performs instead criticism and lecturing of the patient's attitude. The doctor doesn't affiliate with the patient by confirming his diet plan but shifts the direction of talk by problematizing the patient's diet and focusing on her own "therapeutic agenda of identifying communicative patterns and relationship problems" (Muntigl et al. 2012: 124). At line 364 the doctor responds at first with a negative assessment of the patient's utterance by addressing the patient with his first name: *that‘s not good anto*. By doing so, the doctor asserts epistemic independence and supremacy relative to the speaker and performs negative assessment of his behavior. By attaching the nominal address term to her negative assessment, she emphasizes its relevance.[14] In addition to her assessment, the doctor assumes an interrogative mode with: *how many times anto how many times should a diabetic eat* (line 364/5) which clearly does not invite a response, but performs accusation. Repetitive use of the nominal address term *anto* in the mid position can be heard as emphasizing the accusation and increasing the distance between the speakers, putting the affiliation at risk of breaking down. This is underscored by her subsequent insistency and emphasized pronominal address term: *YOU should tell me YOU are a diabetic you have to know that better than me* (line 367/8). By pointing out that he is the diabetic and therefore needs to know more about it than she does, she expresses her expectation that a patient with a chronic illness should actually have specialized knowledge which includes the diabetes diet. This case demonstrates the role of attributed epistemic status by using interrogative and declarative syntax for negative assessment and criticism. The repeated question at the end of her turn: *how many times does a diabetic eat* (line 368) seems to be dedicated to controlling the patient's state of knowledge. The interrogative syntax is deployed to downgrade the socioepistemic role of the patient. After a short delay, as it becomes apparent that her interrogative signals a request and not a rhetorical question, the patient reacts with a no-knowledge

13. For compliance see Petermann 1998.

14. For address terms in medical encounters, see Sorjonen, Peräkylä, and Eskola 2001; Norrby et al. 2015; Günthner 2019; Džanko 2020. See also Günthner; Kuna and Scarvaglieri this volume.

response: *(---) I don't know* (line 369) and fails to deliver the information that the doctor is seeking. The outcome of his acceptance of the unknowing status and avoiding any claim of epistemic authority is the occurrence of dramatic epistemic discrepancies which lead to further face-threatening actions such as accusations, criticism and disciplining of the patient. After a 1.07 second delay, in which the doctor seems to process this information, she reacts with a massive intervention to devalue the patient's behavior using negative and straight interrogative syntax: *isn't that shameful how many years do you have diabetes six* (line 370/1). At this breaking point of the interaction, the speakers are disaffiliated. With her assessment she expresses both her indignation and astonishment. She conveys the stance in which she criticizes her patient by using an extreme judgement that casts the patient as unknowledgeable and irresponsible. After a short delay the patient only responds by confirming the duration of his disease: *yes* (line 373) and does not participate verbally any more until the conclusion of the doctor's next turn which is in line 386. However, the doctor produces an extended turn at talk (374–386)[15] in which she deploys new resources to challenge and criticize the patient's state of knowledge, implying that in chronic illnesses knowledge and self-management are inevitable: *(.) YOU should lecture me on that how diabetic eats* (Z. 374). At lines 382–385 the doctor uses various linguistic resources to upgrade the magnitude of his wrongdoing to express judgement, depicting him as irresponsible and unknowledgeable: *(-) this is the biggest mistake you are making for eating once a day because then your body keeps in a possessive way (-) everything you have eaten.* At line 386 she makes a shift in her action and asks the patient if he had understood her. To question the patient's understanding in a direct manner is not in accordance with politeness principles and is not recommended in a doctor-patient relationship (Brünner 2009: 175). The patient briefly confirms his understanding (line 387). The doctor then chooses to close this topic by using an acknowledgement token and a direct nominal address: *good anto.* After a brief pause, she shifts back to the complaint exploration in order to maintain further progressivity of the interaction: *are there some other problems* (line 388).

Turning now to the patient's responses, it is noted that the patient during the doctor's intense criticism does not respond to the doctor in any verbal way (from what is observed during the recording of the conversation not even by nodding). He accepts the open criticism by staying silent. With his silence he displays a silent confession. Thus, when the doctor asks if he had understood her, he briefly responds with a confirmation token: *yes* (line 387), with which he attempts to re-affiliate with the doctor. The repeated actions of disciplining have resulted in the patient

15. Due to space limits some lines are not shown.

completely submitting to the doctor and accepting the accusations she has made, so that their relationship and the therapeutic work wouldn't be put further at risk. On the other side, however, the doctor was not able or willing to get the patient to discuss the implications of his non-adherent behavior, evoked through her expressions of judgement and criticism. One can also not be sure at this point whether such interactional practices will lead to more conscious adherence to his diet plan in the future as many patients agree to a course of action suggested by a doctor when they have little or no intention of carrying it out because they want to make the interaction as free of conflict as possible (Anderson and Funell 2005: 159f.). The demonstration of the patient's deep [K-] position concerning his own health triggers a mobilization of declarative, straight, and negative interrogatives performing accusation and criticism of the patient, which disrupts the progressivity of the interaction and puts the relationship between doctor and patient at risk. Any subsequent display of non-adherent behavior represents a greater risk for the patient's life. This huge potential threat to his life allows the doctor to formulate her disagreement in a rather aggravating manner. Managing knowledge between a patient and doctor can be a very challenging task for patients and doctors. When patients appear to be more or less knowledgeable about their illness regarding various aspects (medication, previous examinations, diet) than they really are, the doctors react with a shift of the direction of talk by focusing only on their own agenda and using verbal resources at their disposal to elicit the information they need. In order to save face and re-affiliate with the doctor, the patients generally attune to the doctor's interactional guidance by accepting their agenda and even submitting themselves to criticism.

For comparison, I turn once more to the German data to see how patients display a higher level of medical knowledge with regard to their illness. I begin by showing that building an affiliative relationship throughout the interaction and gaining mutual understanding requires a certain level of knowledge on the patient's part as well as attention and guidance of the doctor. The following fragment is taken from a conversation between a German internist and an older male patient and serves as an example of how progression in the interaction as well as a collegial dynamic of the medical encounter is being collaboratively achieved. The patient with hypertension comes to a routine check. After a brief greeting sequence, the patient immediately informs the doctor that he has been regularly taking the pills prescribed by another doctor during his last visit to the practice about fourteen days ago. The doctor then orients the patient that he will shift into the physical examination and measure his blood pressure. The patient complains that his blood pressure has been lower recently (not shown in the transcript). He then informs the doctor about actions he has taken in order to lower the blood pressure (line 47).

(4) IA_MR_02

```
47  P  (and I didn't drink beer or anything like) (…)
48  D  och give yourself permission to live the life ok
49  P  yes but anyway (for seven weeks)
50     (1.4)
51  D  you didn't dare to do it
52     (---)
53  P  (until now)
54     (10.8) ((doctor measures the blood pressure))
55  D  (…)
56     (8.1) one hundred and fifty over eighty five
57     (.) very nice
Lines 58-78 omitted
79  D  the best value we have ever [had    ]
80  P                              [that's] nice
81     (---) it makes one happy then
```

The patient continues his turn elaborating that he did not drink any beer or alcohol during the therapy (line 47). His stance construction is linked to a specific action in which he took on an agentive role. The doctor responds to the patient's attitude by slightly elaborating it in a humorous way (line 48), implying that the patient does not necessarily need to adhere to such a strict lifestyle. On the other hand, the doctor seems to downplay the risks of the patient's blood pressure problem. The patient, however, first confirms the doctor's interpretation through *yes,* but then claims his epistemic independence through the adversative connector *but* and an adverb *anyway* (line 49). After a 1.4 second pause the doctor works towards affiliation with the patient's viewpoint by uttering: *you didn't dare to do it* (line 51). With this utterance, the doctor retreats from his potentially conflictual interpretation in line 48. He then attempts to secure affiliation by accepting the position of the patient as an agent who makes his own decision to overcome his health problems. Thus, after measuring the blood pressure, the doctor announces the reading: *one hundred and fifty over eighty five* (line 56) adding a positive evaluation: *very nice* (line 57). At this point, the doctor affiliates with the patient. In line 79 he uses further verbal resources to intensify his prior utterances by tending to be strongly affiliative regarding not just the positive blood pressure value but also the patient's positive attitude: *the best value we have ever [had].* A regular intake of medication as well as a lifestyle adapted to the disease/condition has led to significant improvement. The patient, in turn, affiliates with the doctor's assessment expressing agreement and satisfaction with his own health-conscious action and its outcome (line 80/1): *[that's] nice (---) it makes one happy then.*

5. Discussion and conclusion

Prior research has demonstrated that functional knowledge management in medical consultations is vital for managing therapeutic work. I argue that CA offers a practical, systematic method to explore knowledge management not only within the context of a turn's sequential position but also within the context of additional components in the production and recognition of a particular action such as epistemic status and epistemic stance (Heritage 2012). In this chapter, I have shown that building a relationship between doctor and patient is extremely sensitive to possessing and demonstrating epistemic rights.

Hence, I first focused on the questions, what role have epistemics in the observable practices of knowledge management between the Bosnian and German patients and their doctors, as well as how do such practices relate to the way doctors challenge the patient's expertise and knowledge. The study of the Bosnian data indicates that 40% of the patients, particularly older patients, patients with observable lower social or educational background and even patients with chronic illnesses, display very limited knowledge concerning their medication but also other health related circumstances such as prior tests and illnesses, or the names of their prescribed medication. More specifically, it has been shown that epistemic status can be dissembled by patients who deploy epistemic stance to appear more knowledgeable than they really are [K+] by using *extreme case formulations* (e.g. by claiming to know the previous treatments (Example (1)) and/or avoid any claim of epistemic authority by stating that they don't know the name of the previous examination, or the importance of a diabetes diet in Examples (1) and (3)). I found that when relatively unknowing patients [K-] make assertions on their medication, medical history or diet, Bosnian doctors in my data tend to challenge their epistemic status by question formats (predominantly declaratives and yes/no-questions) which encode a different epistemic stance and which are directed at the topic where the patient should have primary epistemic status in two ways: First, the doctor asserts a greater right in defining not just the topical agenda but also epistemic rights. Second, doctors retreat from their action of exploring a patient's concern or taking history and perform instead criticism and lecturing of the patient's attitude, downgrading and downplaying the patient's utterances and assessments and their socioepistemic role in the interaction. In sum, dramatic epistemic discrepancies are expressed at turn at talk when a patient's epistemic stance isn't compatible with their assumed and expected epistemic status as an "expert" regarding medication, diet, or medical history, which leads to interactional misunderstanding and a break in the progressivity of the interaction, dysfunctional sharing of knowledge and information, or even face-threatening actions.

In this research I also focused in more detail on how doctors and patients turn-by-turn build their (dis-)affiliative relationship around a patient's accounts of her/his current medical condition and medical history, in which ways is disaffiliation realized interactively and can it subsequently be repaired or not. I systematically explored longer sequences in order to be able to follow different practices of how disaffiliation and most importantly re-affiliation are negotiated when patients claim to know more than they really do, through which the progressivity of the interaction is put at risk. In the Bosnian data I focused on three ways dysfunctional knowledge management leading to disaffiliation can occur: (1) When patient's responses on topics to which they are expected to have privileged access do not meet the doctor's expectations, there is a serious risk of disaffiliation between doctor and patient. Disaffiliation can be repaired at a surface level when patients retreat from their claims and submit to the doctor's agenda. (2) Disaffiliation evoked by patients who claim to know more than they really do can be repaired by doctors who use e.g. humor as a resource to maintain an affiliative dynamic in the interaction despite dysfunctional knowledge transfer. Moreover, in one of the examples the doctor may be using humor to save not just the patient's but also her own face for not being able to elicit the information she was seeking. (3) When faced with a patient's often repeated display of non-compliant behavior towards their chronic disease, doctors tend to retreat from their action of taking history and perform face-threatening actions such as criticism and lecturing of the patient. In order to save face and re-affiliate with the doctor, patients silently submit themselves to criticism.

Last, but not least, I focused on commonalities and divergences in the ways in which Bosnian and German doctors and patients build a therapeutic relationship with regard to functional and dysfunctional knowledge management. In contrast to findings in the Bosnian data, two important differences in the German data have been extracted: (1) German patients display higher medical knowledge and more personal responsibility, which greatly impacts the management of epistemic rights related to knowledge and information between a patient and doctor (Examples (2), (4)). Patients assert primary rights to inform a doctor of their adherence to treatment plans, blood pressure level, or their medical history. In attempting to play an agentive role, patients in my German data deliver information in ways that display a medically relevant contribution. (2) German doctors seem to have adopted a more patient-centered approach which also entails more active patient participation. Thus, doctors utilize three interactional strategies: restricting their response to patient's accounts to confirmation and continuation signals; approval and positive evaluation of patient's agency; and actively listening. By doing so, doctors affiliate with patients as they convey respect for their self-knowledge and build trust. The examples in this paper reveal the general patterns found in my data of how

Bosnian and German patients and doctors through moment-by-moment interactional sequences construct relational bonds and collaboratively accomplish (re-) affiliation, and progressivity of the interaction around different aspects of knowledge management and a potential conflict involving epistemics. By comparing the interactional practices of knowledge management of doctors and patients in two different languages, I support the thesis that 'good practices' concerning affiliative relationship building in medical encounters can be generalized and applied across different languages. The cross-linguistic research of different aspects of functional and dysfunctional practices of knowledge management serves as an exercise in applied conversation analysis and encourages further CA research in medical settings in Bosnia and Herzegovina.

References

Anderson, Robert M., and Martha M. Funell. 2005. *The Art of Empowerment: Stories and Strategies for Diabetes Educators with CDROM*. 2. edition, U.S.: American Diabetes Association.

Antaki, Charles. 2008. "Formulations in psychotherapy." In *Conversation Analysis and Psychotherapie*, ed. by Anssi Peräkyla, Charles Amtaki, Sanna Vehviläinen, and Ivan Leudar. 26–42. Cambridge: Cambridge University Press. https://doi.org/10.1017/CBO9780511490002.003

Beach, Wayne A. 2011. "Lay Diagnosis: Special Issue in honour to the late Rober Hopper." *Text* 21 (1/2): 13–18.

Boyd, Elizabeth, and John C. Heritage. 2006. "Taking the history: questioning during comprehensive history-taking." In *Communication in Medical Care: Interaction Between Primary Care Physicians and Patients*, ed. by John C. Heritage, and Douglas W. Maynard, 151–184. Cambridge: Cambridge University Press. https://doi.org/10.1017/CBO9780511607172.008

Brown, Penelope, and Stephen C. Levinson. 1987. *Politeness: Some universals in language usage*. Cambridge, New York: Cambridge University Press. https://doi.org/10.1017/CBO9780511813085

Brünner, Gisela. 2009. "Die Verständigung zwischen Arzt und Patient als Experten-Laien-Kommunikation." In *Informiert und selbstbestimmt: Der mündige Bürger als mündiger Patient.* [= Beiträge zum Gesundheitsmanagement Bd. 24], ed. by Norbert Klusen, Anja Fließgarten, und Thomas Nebling, 170–188. Baden-Baden: Nomos. https://doi.org/10.5771/9783845216973-170

Byrne, Patrick S., and Barrie E. L. Long. 1976. *Doctors talking to patients: A Study of the Verbal Behaviour of General Practitioners Consulting in their Surgeries*. London: HSMO, Royal College of General Practitioners.

Chatwin, John. 2006. "Patient narratives: A micro-interactional analysis." *Communication & Medicine* 3 (2): 113–123. https://doi.org/10.1515/CAM.2006.014

Deppermann, Arnulf, and Thomas Spranz-Fogasy. 2011. "Doctors' questions as displays of understanding." *Communication & Medicine* 8 (2): 111–122. https://doi.org/10.1558/cam.v8i2.111

Džanko, Minka. 2020. *Rollengebundene Asymmetrie in Arzt-Patient-Gesprächen. Ein Vergleich im Deutschen und Bosnischen*. [Series Schriften des Europäischen Zentrums für Sprachwissenschaften (EZS)], ed. by Ludwig Eichinger et al. Heidelberg: Universitätsverlag Winter.

Frankel, Richard M. 2001. "Clinical care and conversational contingencies: The role of patients' self-diagnosis in medical encounters." *Text* 21: 83–111.

Gill, Virginia, and Douglas W. Maynard. 2006. "Explaining illness: patients' proposals and physicians' responses." In *Communication in Medical Care: Interaction Between Primary Care Physicians and Patients*, ed. by John Heritage, and Douglas W Maynard, 115–150, Cambridge: Cambridge University Press. https://doi.org/10.1017/CBO9780511607172.007

Gill, Virginia, and Felicia Roberts. 2013. "Conversation analysis in medicine." In *The handbook of conversation analysis*, ed. by Tanya Stivers, and John Sidnell, 575–92. Chichester: Wiley-Blackwell.

Goffman, Erving. 1955 (1967). "On Face-Work: An Analysis of Ritual Elements in Social Interaction." *Psychiatry* 18: 213–231. https://doi.org/10.1080/00332747.1955.11023008

Gülich, Elisabeth. 1999. "'Experten' und 'Laien': Der Umgang mit Kompetenzunterschieden am Beispiel medizinischer Kommunikation." In *Werkzeug Sprache. Sprachpolitik, Sprachfähigkeit, Sprache und Macht*, ed. by Union der deutschen Akademien der Wissenschaften zu Leipzig, 165–196. Hildesheim, Zürich, New York: Olms.

Günthner, Susanne. 2019. "Namentliche Anreden in onkologischen Aufklärungsgesprächen: eine interaktional ausgerichtete Studie zu Formen und Funktionen onymischer Anreden." *Interaktion Sprache Arbeitspapierreihe*: 1–29. http://arbeitspapiere.sprache-interaktion.de/arbeitspapiere/arbeitspapier82.pdf

Halkowski, Tim, and Virginia Teas Gill. 2010. "Conversation analysis and ethnomethodology: The centrality of interaction." In *The SAGE Handbook of Qualitative Methods in Health Research*, ed. by Ivy Bourgeault, Robert Dingwall, and Ray de Vries, 212–228. London: Sage.

Heritage, John. 1984. "A change-of-state token and aspects of its sequential placement." In *Structures of social action, Studies in conversation analysis*, ed. by Maxwell J. Atkinson, and John Heritage, 299–345. Cambridge: Cambridge University Press.

Heritage, John. 2009. "Negotiating the legitimacy of medical problems: A multi-phase concern for patients and physicians." In *Health Communication*, ed. by Dale E. Brashers, and Daena J. Goldsmith, 147–164. New York: Routledge.

Heritage, John. 2010. "Questioning in Medicine." In "*Why Do You Ask?": The Function of Questions in Institutional Discourse*, ed. by Alice Freed, and Susan Ehrlich, 42–68. New York: Oxford University Press.

Heritage, John. 2012. "Epistemics in Action: Action Formation and Territories of Knowledge." *Research on Language and Social Interaction* 45: 1–29. https://doi.org/10.1080/08351813.2012.646684

Heritage, John. 2013. "Epistemics in conversation." In *The handbook of conversation analysis*, ed. by Jack Sidnell, and Tanya Stivers, 370–394. Chichester: Wiley-Blackwell.

Heritage, John, and Douglas W. Maynard. 2006. "Introduction: Analyzing primary care encounters." In *Communication in Medical Care: Interactions between Primary Care Physicians and Patients*, ed. by John Heritage, and Douglas Maynard, 1–21. Cambridge: Cambridge University Press.

Heritage, John, and Jeffrey Robinson. 2006. "Accounting for the visit: giving reasons for seeking medical care." In *Communication in Medical Care: Interactions between Primary Care Physicians and Patients*, ed. by John Heritage, and Douglas W. Maynard, 48–85. Cambridge: Cambridge University Press. https://doi.org/10.1017/CBO9780511607172.005

Heritage, John, and Steven Clayman. 2010. *Talk in Action*, Oxford: Wiley Blackwell. https://doi.org/10.1002/9781444318135

Heritage, John, and Geoffrey Raymond. 2012. "Navigating epistemic landscapes: Acquiescence, agency and resistance in responses to polar questions." In *Questions: Formal, Functional and Interactional Perspectives*, ed. by Jan P. De Ruiter, 179–92. Cambridge: Cambridge University Press. https://doi.org/10.1017/CBO9781139045414.013

Heritage, John, and Geoffrey Raymond. 2005. "The terms of agreement: Indexing epistemic authority and subordination in assessment sequences." *Social Psychology Quarterly* 68 (1): 15–38. https://doi.org/10.1177/019027250506800103

Holly, Werner. 2001. "Beziehungsmanagement und Imagearbeit." In *Text- und Gesprächslinguistik. Handbücher zur Sprach- und Kommunikationswissenschaft*, ed. by Klaus Brinker et al., 1382–1393. Berlin, New York: de Gruyter. https://doi.org/10.1515/9783110169188.2.19.1382

Labov, William, and David Fanshel. 1977. *Therapeutic Discourse. Psychotherapy as Conversation*. New York: Academic Press.

Lalouschek, Johanna. 2008. "Ärztliche Gesprächspläne und Anliegen von PatientInnen in der chronischen Schmerzbehandlung. Arbeitspapier zum Forschungsprojekt „Schmerzdarstellung and Krankheitserzählung." http://www.univie.ac.at/linguistics/personal/florian/Schmerzprojekt/downloads/Arbeitspapier_2008_Patientenanliegen_Lalouschek.pdf

Lindwall, Oskar, Gustav Lymer, and Jonas Ivarsson. 2016. "Epistemic status and the recognizability of social actions." *Special Issue: The epistemics of Epistemics* Vol. 18 (5): 500–525. https://doi.org/10.1177/1461445616657958

Löning, Petra. 1993. "Psychische Betreuung als kommunikatives Problem. Elizitierte Schilderung des Befindens und `ärztliches Zuhören´ in der onkologischen Facharztpraxis." In *Arzt-Patienten-Kommunikation. Analysen zu interdisziplinären Problemen des medizinischen Diskurses*, ed. by Petra Löning, and Jochen Rehbein, 191–227. Berlin [u.a.]: de Gruyter. https://doi.org/10.1515/9783110880359.191

Manning, Philip, and George Ray. 2002. "Setting *the* agenda: an analysis of negotiation strategies in clinical talk." *Health Communication* 14(4): 451–473. https://doi.org/10.1207/S15327027HC1404_3

Mishler, Elliot G. 1984. *The Discourse of Medicine: Dialectics of Medical Interviews*. Norwood, N.J.: Ablex Publishing Corporation.

Muntigl, Peter, and Adam Horvath. 2015. "The therapeutic relationship in action: how therapists and clients co-manage relational disaffiliation." *Psychotherapy Research* 24 (3): 41–59.

Muntigl, Peter et al. 2012. "Client attitudinal stance and therapist-client affiliation. A view from grammar and social interaction." *Research in Psychotherapy: Psychopathology, Process and Outcome* 15(2): 117–130.

Norrby, Catrin et al. 2015. "Interpersonal relationships in medical consultations. Comparing Sweden Swedish and Finland Swedish address practices." *Journal of Pragmatics*: 121–38. https://doi.org/10.1016/j.pragma.2015.05.006

Petermann, Franz. 1998. *Compliance and Selbstmanagement*, Göttingen: Hogrefe Verlag.

Raymond, Geoffrey, and John Heritage. 2006. "The epistemics of social relations: Owning grandchildren." *Language in Society* 35(5): 677–705. https://doi.org/10.1017/S0047404506060325

Rehbein, Jochen. 1993. "Ärztliches Fragen." In *Arzt-Patienten-Kommunikation. Analysen zu interdisziplinären Problemen des medizinischen Diskurses*, ed. by Petra Löning, and Jochen Rehbein, 311–364. Berlin [u.a.]: de Gruyter. https://doi.org/10.1515/9783110880359.311

Sacks, Harvey, Emanuel A. Schegloff, and Gail Jefferson. 1974. "A simplest systematics for the organization of turn-taking for conversation." *Language* 50: 696–735. https://doi.org/10.1353/lan.1974.0010

Schegloff, Emanuel A. 2007. *Sequence Organization in Interaction: A Primer in Conversation Analysis*. Cambridge: Cambridge University Press. https://doi.org/10.1017/CBO9780511791208

Selting, Margret et al. 2009. "Gesprächsanalytisches Transkriptionssystem 2 (GAT 2)." *Gesprächsforschung – Online Zeitschrift zur verbalen Interaktion* 10: 353–402.

Sorjonen, Marja-Leena, Anssi Peräkylä, and Kari Eskola. 2001. *Keskustelu lääkärin vastaanotolla (Conversationata Doctor's Consultation)*. Tampere: Vastapaino.

Spranz-Fogasy, Thomas. 2005. "Kommunikatives Handeln in ärztlichen Gesprächen." In *Psychosomatische Gesprächsführung in der Frauenheilkunde. Ein interdisziplinärer Ansatz zur verbalen Intervention*, ed. by Mechthild Neises, Susanne Ditz, and Thomas Spranz-Fogasy, 17–47. Stuttgart: Wissenschaftliche Verlagsgesellschaft mbH.

Spranz-Fogasy, Thomas. 2010. "Verstehensdokumentation in der medizinischen Kommunikation: Fragen und Antworten im Arzt-Patient-Gespräch." In *Verstehen in professionellen Handlungsfeldern*, ed. by Arnulf Deppermann et al., 27–116. Tübingen: Narr Verlag.

Spranz-Fogasy, Thomas. 2014. *Die allmähliche Verfertigung der Diagnose im Reden. Prädiagnostische Mitteilungen im Gespräch zwischen Arzt und Patient*. Berlin, Boston: de Gruyter. https://doi.org/10.1515/9783110363296

Stivers, Tanya. 2008. "Stance, alignment and affiliation during storytelling: When nodding is a token of affiliation." *Research on Language and Social Interaction* 41 (1): 31–57. https://doi.org/10.1080/08351810701691123

Stivers, Tanya, and Federico Rossano. 2010. "Mobilizing response." *Research on Language and Social Interaction* 43 (1): 3–31. https://doi.org/10.1080/08351810903471258

Stivers, Tanya, Lorenza Mondada, and Jakob Steensing. 2011. "Knowledge, morality and affiliation in social interaction." In *The morality of knowledge in conversation*, ed. By Tanya Stivers, Lorenza Mondada, and Jakob Steensing, 3–26. Cambridge: Cambridge University Press. https://doi.org/10.1017/CBO9780511921674.002

How are you getting on with these?

Fostering clients' involvement in the therapeutic alliance in email counseling

Franziska Thurnherr
University of Basel

This contribution explores how a counselor uses requests to encourage clients to actively participate in email counseling. Applying positioning theory and relational work from interpersonal pragmatics, I answer the following research questions: How does the counselor use requests to position clients as active participants? How do affordances of the medium influence the counselor's efforts in such requests? I analyze five naturally occurring email counseling exchanges through content and discourse analysis, adding insight from a practitioner interview. The examined requests aim to improve joint understanding, foster reflection, elicit solutions, and elicit feedback on coping techniques. Results show that the counselor uses intricate relational work that constructs clients as active participants. The counselor employs medium affordances such as asynchronicity or emoticons.

Keywords: online counseling, email, interpersonal pragmatics, relational work, identity, requests, ehealth

1. Introduction

Various studies have reported that a good relationship between counselor and client – i.e. the therapeutic alliance – benefits the outcome of counseling in significant ways (cf. Ackerman and Hilsenroth 2003; Cook and Doyle 2002; Horvath et al. 2011). Krupnick et al. (1996: 532) define the therapeutic alliance as "the collaborative bond between therapist and patient."[1] This collaborative bond is essential in

1. In some therapy or counseling contexts, the interactants are called patient and therapist. In others, they are called counselor and client. In my data, they are called the latter, which is why I adhere to these nomenclatures.

https://doi.org/10.1075/pbns.331.12thu

face-to-face as well as online counseling (cf. Berger 2017; Simpson and Reid 2014; Sucala et al. 2012). Berger (2017: 519) argues, however, that "research on individualized e-mail ... therapy is still very limited." He (Berger 2017: 521) advocates for an "in-depth understanding of specific mechanisms of change and of qualitative [aspects of] relationships." Ackerman and Hilsenroth (2003: 29) state that

> (...) the most promising strategy for future research [on the therapeutic alliance] may be to examine the interpersonal exchanges between the [client] and [counselor] that impact alliance development. Investigating these in-session interactions may deepen our understanding of the nature of alliance development and the specific variables impacting it.

Interpersonal pragmatics examines the "relational/interpersonal [aspect] of interaction" (Locher 2015: 6) and is therefore predestined to examine counseling in the way that Berger (2017) as well as Ackerman and Hilsenroth (2003) suggest. Locher (2015: 8) explains that interpersonal-pragmatic aspects are best researched at "crucial moments within the composition of [...] texts" because "subtle negotiations of positionings" occur in these moments. Instances in which a counselor requests something from a client are crucial moments in counseling, because they explicitly foreground the collaborative and interpersonal nature of counseling. In the present study, I shed light on the relational/interpersonal aspect of the counselor's requests in email counseling exchanges. I thereby contribute to research on interpersonal pragmatics and (online) counseling.

In a first step, I will introduce the theoretical background of the research niche: interpersonal pragmatics and online counseling discourse. It goes beyond the scope of this paper to give an exhaustive overview of these research fields (for such an overview cf. Thurnherr 2022). Instead, I will briefly discuss interpersonal pragmatics and review some of the studies focused specifically on (online) counseling and requests (Section 2). I will then provide an overview of the data and the methodology (Section 3). In Section 4, I present and discuss the results of my analysis. Finally, I will offer concluding remarks and suggestions for future research in Section 5.

2. Theoretical background and literature review

2.1 Interpersonal pragmatics

In a nutshell, interpersonal pragmatics aims to explain that "people adjust their language to their addressees and the situation in order to achieve interpersonal effects" (Locher and Graham 2010: 2). According to Locher and Graham (2010: 2), interpersonal-pragmatic research

> (...) explore[s] facets of interaction between social actors that rely upon (and in turn influence) the dynamics of relationships between people and how those relationships are reflected in the language choices that they make.

I apply two concepts that are prominent in interpersonal pragmatics: (1) relational work and (2) identity construction. Locher and Watts (2008: 96) define relational work as "all aspects of the work invested by individuals in the construction, maintenance, reproduction and transformation of interpersonal relationships". Previous studies (cf. Bolander 2013; Lindholm 2017; Locher 2006; Thurnherr 2022; Zayts and Schnurr 2013) have examined relational work in a range of social practices, including health practices. For example, Locher (2006) identified a range of relational strategies that a team of health experts uses in an online advice column. They employed strategies such as appealing and displaying empathy, the use of humor, praising or boosting. Zayts and Schnurr (2013) have shown how relational work is used to accomplish non-directiveness in prenatal counseling in Hong Kong. These previous studies have documented subtle differences in the use of relational work depending in which context it occurred. I examine relational work in email counseling, which is a social practice that has as of yet not received much attention from researchers interested in relational work.

The second focus within interpersonal pragmatics I foreground in my study is identity construction. Identity is an integral part of counseling as clients often struggle with issues that are linked to their identity. In addition, the therapeutic alliance is an especially salient avenue for research focusing on identity as identity is inherently relational. The notion of identity is often approached from a constructionist perspective in interpersonal pragmatics. I view identity as "a social, discursive, emergent and relational phenomenon" (Thurnherr et al. 2016: 451). I thereby follow Davies and Harré's (1990) and Bucholtz and Hall's (e.g. 2005) take on identity. Davies and Harré (1990: 48) foregrounded the notion of "positioning" and defined it as "the discursive process whereby selves are located in conversations as observably and subjectively coherent participants in jointly produced story lines." Bucholtz and Hall (2005: 586; italics removed) refined Davies and Harré's approach and stated that identity is "the social positioning of self and other." Previous studies examined identity in various contexts, including a health context (cf. Gygax and Locher 2015; Hamilton and Chou 2014; Harvey and Koteyko 2013; Locher and Schnurr 2017; Mullany 2009). For example, Locher (2006: 184) illustrated how an expert identity is created in an online advice column by using humor, providing information that is accurate, or using a specific type of vocabulary. In Thurnherr et al. (2016), we demonstrated how advice-seekers and -givers use narratives to create specific identities. And in Rudolf von Rohr et al. (2019), we uncovered a range of linguistic strategies that are used to create an expert identity.

Interactants employed strategies such as providing step-by-step suggestions, showing unconditional positive regard or predicting future developments. In this paper, I examine identity in a social practice that has not received much attention from an interpersonal-pragmatic perspective.

Identity is inherently relational and is therefore closely linked to relational work and the creation of relationships. This link has been given more attention in recent years. Several authors have explicitly advocated to combine research on identity and relational work (cf. Hall and Bucholtz 2013; Locher 2013; Locher 2015). Locher (2013: 146) specifically explains that "the work [people] invest, i.e. the choices they make in interaction in situ, is what we term relational work, and the result of their choices is identity construction." In Thurnherr (2022), I demonstrated how this link between identity and relational work can be analyzed in the social practice of email counseling. I illustrated how specific relational strategies such as appealing for and displaying empathy are used to create the clients' identities as advice-seekers. The counselor, on the other hand, employs encouragement and praise to create her identity as a supportive listener, for example. In this paper, I further zoom in on the counselor's use of requests. More specifically, I demonstrate how interactants use relational work within such requests to create specific identities for the interactants. I provide a more detailed analysis of the interpersonal-pragmatic aspect of the language used in requests within the social practice of email counseling and thereby deepen our understanding of "specific mechanisms of change and of qualitative aspects of the therapeutic alliance]" (Berger 2017: 521).

2.2 (Online) counseling

Counseling and psychotherapy have received attention from diverse linguistic approaches that studied a wide range of phenomena. Face-to-face counseling and psychotherapy have, for example, been studied by conversation analysts who investigated sequential turn-taking. A prominent example of such research is Peräkylä et al. (2008), in which various conversation analysts report on topics such as formulations (Antaki 2008), optimistic questions (MacMartin 2008), or resistance (Vehviläinen 2008). Online counseling has been studied less extensively, but has garnered more attention over the past 10 years. In particular, three research groups have analyzed online counseling more closely (for detailed information cf. Thurnherr 2022).

Several studies examined the Australian counseling service *KidsHelpline*. Danby et al. (2009) compared opening sequences in a telephone and online context. Harris et al. (2012) focus on counselors' attempts to convince clients to switch from email to telephone counseling. Both studies found that there is a clear orientation towards the therapeutic alliance and that counselors seem aware of the importance of the relationship they create with clients in telephone as well as online counseling. Danby et al. (2009) documented, however, that the interaction in email counseling differs from the interaction in telephone counseling. Looking at turn-taking, for example, Danby et al. (2009: 98) demonstrated that interactants used minimal responses far more frequently in telephone than in email counseling. Instead, email counseling sees "extended turns" (Danby et al. 2009: 98) more frequently. Danby et al. (2009) report that in some cases, interactants even commented on such extended turns, showing an awareness that this seems to be different in email counseling.

Stommel and colleagues examined online counseling that is provided to clients who suffer from mild anxiety and depression as well as chat counseling that focuses on delivering "accurate information about alcohol and drugs" (Stommel and te Molder 2015: 281). Studies that focus on the first type of online counseling were dedicated to recipient design (Stommel 2012), the presentation of problems (Stommel and van der Houwen 2015) or how self-directedness can be fostered in clients (Lamerichs and Stommel 2016). In studies that examined the alcohol and drug information service, Stommel and colleagues looked at pre-closing devices (Stommel and te Molder 2015) and on meta-communicative acts with which counselors tried to handle interactional trouble (Jager and Stommel 2017).

Finally, the third group that has looked extensively into online counseling are Ekberg and colleagues, who specifically focused on examining online cognitive behavioral therapy (CBT). Ekberg et al. (2013) studied therapists' responses to clients' input in early sessions of online CBT. The authors reported that therapists moved quickly into "a task-focused direction" (Ekberg et al. 2013: 12) instead of waiting for a minimal response by the clients. This demonstrates how the medium of instant messaging can influence the turn-by-turn interaction in online counseling. Ekberg et al. (2016) examine counselors' references to clients' emotional experiences. They found that counselors used, for example, affective inferences to demonstrate their understanding of clients' emotions. Ekberg and colleagues illustrated that counselors working online can readily respond to clients' needs of feeling understood, but that they can also move the counseling process forward in a speedy fashion.

All three of these groups have analyzed online counseling from a conversation-analytic perspective. They have provided us with vital insights into the turn-taking organization of online counseling, including differences and idiosyncrasies compared to face-to-face or telephone counseling, as well as idiosyncrasies of the specific medium that is used. Some of these studies have also taken the interpersonal nature of the interaction into account. My study aims to complement this research by specifically focusing on the relational work that is used and the identities that are created. This allows us to deepen our understanding of requests in email counseling from different perspectives.

2.3 Interpersonal speech activities: From questions to requests

Different types of speech activities have been researched in a counseling or psychotherapy context, such as formulations (Antaki 2008), problem presentation (Stommel and van der Houwen 2015), or resistance (Vehviläinen 2008). Further ones are proposals for behavior change (Ekberg and LeCouteur 2012), reinterpretative statements (Bercelli et al. 2008), or self-disclosure (Pawelczyk and Erskine 2008). Among such speech activities, requests or questions have received slightly less attention from researchers (cf. Kabatnick et al. this volume on solution oriented questions). Four studies are of relevance to my own study: MacMartin's (2008) analysis of optimistic questions, Ekberg and LeCouteur's examination of interrogatives (2012) as well as their study of information-soliciting questions (2014), and Kabatnik et al.'s research on solution oriented questions (this volume).

To begin with, Ekberg and LeCouteur (2012 and 2014) examined 20 one-on-one sessions of cognitive behavioral therapy in a face-to-face setting by employing conversation analysis. Ekberg and LeCouteur (2012) identified three strategies that therapists used to propose behavioral change, among them interrogatives. They reported that therapists employed interrogatives to present proposals so that clients could reject them. In other words, it was the clients' epistemic right to either ignore, simply acknowledge or implement the proposals. Ekberg and LeCouteur (2012: 237) found that this type of proposal "can lead to localised client resistance." In Ekberg and LeCouteur (2014), the focus lies on information-soliciting questions. Ekberg and LeCouteur (2014: 64) state that therapists use such questions to "co-implicate clients in the accomplishment of [behavioral change]." These questions seem to succeed in facilitating change in clients. Ekberg and LeCouteur (2014) revealed the intricate work therapists conduct in such information-soliciting questions.

MacMartin (2008) examines counselors' optimistic questions and clients' responses. She demonstrates how such questions "asked clients about their strengths, abilities, and success in addressing the issues that brought them to therapy" (2008: 80). Focusing on the clients' reactions, the study disclosed that clients mostly misaligned with optimistic questions. They did so either with answer-like responses or with non-answer responses. MacMartin thereby reveals how seemingly simple and well-meant questions can have an undesired effect on clients. Instead of focusing on positives, the clients reiterated their troubles in order to legitimize their need for help. However, MacMartin also illustrates that resistance can still be relevant for further collaborative work. The therapist recognizes that the clients' troubles need further attention.

Kabatnik et al. (this volume) research solution oriented questions in early sessions of psychodiagnostic interviews. They demonstrate that such questions occur frequently in their data and specifically at particular times within the interviews, i.e. towards the end of a discussed topic. Kabatnik et al. address in particular how carefully the therapists design such questions in order to help move patients from a focus on their problems towards solutions. Kabatnik et al. show how patients at first resist such a perspective change. However, through the therapists' careful intervention following the questions, they manage to increase patients' cooperativeness. Similar to MacMartin, therefore, Kabatnik et al. demonstrate that face-threatening practices such as posing solution oriented questions can still result in therapeutic progress by attentively negotiating the therapeutic alliance.

I want to add to existing research on questions, or more precisely on requests, by answering the following research questions:

1. How does the counselor use requests to position clients as active participants in the therapeutic alliance?
2. How do affordances of the medium of email influence the counselor's positioning efforts in such requests?

Due to the scope of this paper, I will not be able to analyze counselors' requests as well as clients' reactions. Instead, I will focus on the ways the counselor uses relational work to create specific identities within requests.

3. Data and methodology

The present study analyzes naturally occurring email counseling exchanges collected from 2013 to 2014. These exchanges took place between students of a British university and a counselor employed by the university's counseling service. The exchanges consist solely of written text. All counseling is administered as short-term therapy. In the case of email counseling, short-term means that the counselor and the client exchange between six to twelve emails. All exchanges are one-to-one and private messages (Herring 2007). The service labeled its counseling as well-being counseling. In other words, interactants focus on a variety of topics that center around the clients' emotional well-being, such as anxiety, depression, self-esteem or relationship troubles.

During the process of data collection, the counseling service that provided the data changed the way that interactants sent messages. Therefore, the corpus consists of two types of email counseling exchanges. On the one hand, two of the five exchanges consist solely of emails in which the counseling content is written directly in the body of the email. On the other hand, the participants of the other three exchanges sent a password-protected document back and forth via email. The counseling content is written in this document rather than in the email itself.

Instead of email exchanges, I will therefore call an entire counseling exchange between one counselor and one client a thread, defined by Harris et al. (2012: 25) as "a series of chained email exchanges between a counselor and a client over an extended timeframe." Hence, the corpus is made up of five threads by five different clients with the pseudonyms Anna, Ellie, Chris, Mel, and Taylor. Each of these five clients has a private thread with the same counselor. The threads consist of ten to twelve emails. In total, there are 57 emails and around 52,000 words. As some participants used an additional document instead of an email for the content of the counseling, I use the term 'entry' rather than 'email' to talk about a specific message within a thread.

Previous studies revealed that the type of counseling that is applied influences the way that language is used (cf. Beckwith and Crichton 2014; Fitzgerald and Leudar 2012). The counselor in my data applies a humanistic perspective and practices solution-focused brief therapy (SFBT) and cognitive behavioral therapy (CBT). Common to these approaches or therapies is a focus on solutions and clients' resources rather than their problems (cf. Calkins et al. 2016; Comer 2010; De Shazer and Berg 1997; Gingerich and Wabeke 2001). In addition, the collaborative process is foregrounded (Comer 2010: 84). This is relevant as it demonstrates the counselor's awareness of how important the therapeutic alliance is.

In addition, I conducted an interview with the counselor, following Pick's (2011: 74; my translation) call to "include [the counselor's] perspective in the analysis" to give the counselor the opportunity to "share impressions, expectations and so on about the interaction" (Pick's 2011: 74; my translation). During the interview, I presented some of my findings to the counselor and asked her to provide her interpretation of these findings. For example, I specifically asked the counselor to interpret some of the requests that she made in the threads. In addition, I questioned the counselor about some of my broader observations and about (online) counseling in general. I will intersperse my findings with some of the counselor's comments to incorporate a participant perspective in the analyses of specific examples in the following section.

To examine the threads, I use a mixed methodology that consists of content analysis (Locher and Thurnherr 2017; Miles et al. 2014; Saldaña 2013), discourse analysis (Locher and Thurnherr 2017; Johnstone 2000; Schiffrin et al. 2001) and the use of the interview as secondary data. I applied the concept of discursive moves in the content analysis. Miller and Gergen (1998: 192) define a discursive move as "the kind of contribution that the entry made to the ongoing interchange." In other words, the focus lies on the function of the entry. Other studies focusing on identifying interpersonal-pragmatic phenomena (cf. Bolander 2013; Locher 2006; Morrow 2012; Placencia 2012) have also used this approach. These studies have identified discursive moves such as apologies, advice-giving, assessment, or requests for information. For the present paper, I utilized the content analysis in order to zoom in on a specific set of text passages in which the counselor poses requests (for detailed information about how I identified such requests, cf. Thurnherr 2022). Using discourse analysis, I analyzed these requests from an interpersonal-pragmatic perspective and supplemented my findings with the counselor's interpretations gained from the interview. This mixed methodology allows me to complement the findings from previous studies (such as the ones reviewed in Section 2).

Throughout my research, I have adhered to several ethical guidelines that I set up based on various sources (Bolander and Locher 2014; McKee and Porter 2009; Pick 2011). For example, the counselor contacted all clients, so that their personal information would neither be revealed to the readership of my publications nor to myself. The counselor anonymized all of the exchanges and sent them to the clients to check with them whether the exchanges could be sent along to me in the anonymized form. In addition, the counselor (in my name) gained informed consent from the clients. Further, I have presented my findings to various groups of counselors including the counselors working at the university that provided the data. In this way, I have tried to provide the counselors with the results and thereby let them benefit from my study.

4. Results

The counselor used 192 requests (see Thurnherr 2022 for a detailed description) to check whether she correctly understood the clients or whether the clients understand her, to get more information, or to uncover progress. In other words, the counselor uses requests for a variety of reasons. Common to all of them is that they explicitly invite clients to enter into a dialogue with the counselor. In this paper, I specifically look at four types of requests and highlight the interpersonal-pragmatic aspects that the counselor carries out with the help of these requests. The four types of requests are:

1. Requests to improve joint understanding
2. Requests to foster reflection
3. Requests to elicit solutions
4. Requests to elicit feedback on the application of suggested coping techniques

These four types of requests are by no means the only ones that are present in my data. They are the ones that occur most frequently, however. They cannot always be clearly differentiated from each other. Their boundaries are fuzzy and can overlap at times. My aim here is not to give an exhaustive and complete list or numerical distribution of different types of requests. Rather, I want to show the relational nuances that are created through them. In what follows, I highlight what kind of relational work is done and how it creates the counselor's and the clients' identities.

4.1 Improving joint understanding

The first type of request is used to improve the joint understanding of the clients' troubles. The counselor positions the clients as having privileged knowledge in such requests. In other words, the counselor positions the clients as experts of their own troubles. Such requests often appear after the counselor's use of formulations (cf. Antaki 2008). Example (1) shows one of the counselor's requests in Ellie's thread.

(1) It sounds as if, now you are home, everyone else is thinking 'phew, now I can take a break', and have stepped right back. *Have I understood this right Ellie?*

Formulations often position the counselor as an expert. The counselor formulates the clients' troubles in specific ways to facilitate the counseling process (Antaki 2008). By asking the clients to confirm whether she has understood them correctly, the counselor positions the clients as experts on their own troubles. In Example (1), the counselor depicts herself as the recipient of the information (subject position of the mental verb *understand*). In addition, the request provides the client with an opportunity to disagree. In this way, the expertise of the counselor is downplayed, while the importance of the clients' active participation in accomplishing the joint understanding of the client's troubles is foregrounded.

The counselor also uses more extended requests to arrive at a joint understanding of the clients' troubles. Often, these requests start with the construction *help me to* followed by a post-predicate clause. Example (2) shows such a request from Chris' thread.

(2) *Help me to get a clearer sense Chris of the nature of these anxious thoughts.*

Previous to this statement from the counselor, Chris talked about unhelpful thoughts and their negative impact on his anxiety. The counselor wants to know more about them. By using the facilitative verb *help* in connection with the accusative personal pronoun *me* and the infinitive *to understand*, the counselor positions herself as the recipient of the information that she wants Chris to provide. Chris, meanwhile, is positioned as the provider of the information. This presupposes that Chris has access to this knowledge, which positions him as an expert on his own troubles. As in Example (1), the counselor foregrounds the client's expertise and thereby positions him as an important participant in ensuring that the counselor and the client understand the client's troubles in the same way. Graf and Jautz (this volume) have also found that coaches in a coaching context invest particular effort to highlight clients' expertise on their own experiences. In addition, the counselor commented on achieving joint understanding of the clients' troubles during the interview:

> I think it's really important to reflect back to the client so they know that you've heard them. I want them to know that I'm doing my best to understand and to give them that voice that they never really had to say what's on their mind.
>
> (Interview)

The counselor expresses her awareness that it is vital for the clients to feel heard and understood. This demonstrates the importance of such requests. While both examples aim to improve joint understanding, the confirmation (Example [1]) or explanation (Example [2]) does not follow immediately due to the asynchronicity of email communication. This results in the counselor continuing with her reply without having received an answer to her requests yet and as a result without knowing whether joint understanding was or will be achieved. This pattern clearly differs to the interaction ensuing in face-to-face counseling.

4.2 Fostering reflection

The second type of requests are used to foster reflection. Locher (2006), too, documented that the team of health experts on an online advice column used interrogatives to foster reflection. Solution-focused therapy foregrounds the importance of the resources that clients already have at their disposal (De Shazer and Berg 1997; Gingerich and Wabeke 2001). In my data, the counselor repeatedly utilizes requests that foster reflections in clients to, for example, uncover resources that are not overtly recognized or not yet utilized by the clients. Or the counselor requests clients to view their troubles from a different perspective or to observe their emotions during particular situations. As with the first type of requests, this type positions clients as experts on their own experiences. The clients' expertise elicited through the first type of requests focused on their troubles, whereas the clients' expertise evoked by the second type of request focuses on their resources and their positive experiences.

Example (3) illustrates how the counselor tries to elicit examples of supportive resources from a client who struggles to deal with the debilitative physical illness of her mother:

(3) *I'm wondering what support you have?*

By using the mental verb *to wonder*, the counselor positions herself as the agent of a thought process. In addition, the progressive aspect adds a sense of immediacy. This downplays the asynchronicity of the interaction, as it signals that the counselor is wondering about this question right now despite the fact that the client might read this request days after the counselor wrote it. At the same time, the indirect form mitigates the force of the request. This is especially salient as the counselor states that the client already has support, rather than asking what new support she could possibly find. Despite the mitigation, the counselor clearly puts the responsibility to uncover supportive resources in the hands of the client. The counselor does not suggest supportive resources herself. Clearly, the request aims to foster reflection in the client, who is positioned as an active and necessary participant in the therapeutic alliance.

Previous to the counselor's request shown in Example (4), the client expressed her dislike of herself and her wish to change. The counselor responds with the following request:

(4) *What might this Mel look like? What is she wearing, what is she doing, what expression does she have etc?*

The counselor aims to focus the clients' reflection on a positive image rather than the negative image the client currently has of herself. While the first request is mitigated through the use of the modal verb *might*, the following requests are direct and in progressive aspect. I argue that this emphasizes the immediacy of the task's content and aims to help the client to conjure a clearer image of who she would like to be. As with Example (3), the counselor carefully constructs the requests in a way that lays the responsibility of providing the answers in the client's hands. She does not provide an image of what an ideal person would look like. Both Examples (3) and (4) demonstrate that the counselor does not simply tell clients what resources to access or what to think. Instead, the counselor positions the clients as resourceful themselves. At the same time, the counselor positions herself as a facilitator who encourages clients to access and find their own resources.

4.3 Eliciting solutions

The counselor uses requests to elicit solutions from the clients rather than providing them herself. They resemble the information-soliciting questions that Ekberg and LeCouteur (2014) found. These requests go a step further than requests that foster reflection. Requests that aim to elicit solutions aim to trigger concrete solutions for a specific problem. They are, therefore, often more direct or contain more details than the requests that foster reflection.

In Example (5), the counselor asks the client to provide suggestions as to where she could practice voicing her opinion. The counselor suggested specific instances already, but asks the client to provide her own suggestions as well.

(5) *What are your ideas where you could practice this?*

By using the construction *your ideas*, the counselor invokes the therapeutic alliance. She has provided ideas already. As partners in the therapeutic alliance, the client is asked to provide her ideas. Similar to findings in Kabatnik et al. (this volume), the counselor thereby foregrounds the egalitarian epistemic level between herself and the client. While the request is in direct form (i.e. present simple *are*), the activity (*practicing*) is written in modal form (i.e. *could*). This clearly demonstrates the counselor's awareness that the suggested activity (voicing her own opinion) is difficult for the client. In other words, the counselor's request carries the potential to threaten the client's face and the counselor's linguistic choices demonstrate that she aims to avoid such an effect. Damaging the client's face would possibly affect the therapeutic alliance in a negative way, because it could be interpreted as an activity that is neither collaborative nor one that supports the bond between client and counselor. At the same time, the direct request clearly positions the client in a way that enforces the necessity of an answer. This balancing act of requesting an answer and demonstrating an awareness of the difficulty of the suggested activity illustrates the counselor's careful use of language in constructing requests (cf. Kabatnik et al.: this volume).

Example (6) demonstrates how the counselor facilitates the client's preparation for a discussion with her boyfriend. The client expressed a need to be able to spend more time by herself. She told the counselor that her boyfriend does not readily comply with this need. Since both the client and the counselor agree that spending time alone would be beneficial to the client, the next step is providing the client with the tools to accomplish this goal. The counselor supports the client in finding a way to fulfill her expressed need of time apart.

(6) *How could you present this idea to your boyfriend in a way that would help him to see it as a positive, rather than you not wanting to spend time with him?*

Importantly, the counselor does not simply request that the client propose an idea. Rather, she suggests that the client should present the idea in a way that elicits a positive reaction from the client's boyfriend. Through suggesting this change of perspective, the counselor manages to gently direct the client towards a specific type of answer. She provides the client with a specific tool – the perspective change – that allows the client to accomplish the goal that the counselor and the client identified together. The counselor thereby positions herself as an expert who provides vital suggestions to the client who can then accomplish the task with the tools the counselor presented. At the same time, she clearly positions the client as the one who has the ability to provide the answer to this request. Example (5) as well as Example (6) display how the counselor positions clients as active participants in the therapeutic alliance who can provide solutions for their own troubles. Especially Example (6) has revealed how attentively the counselor chooses her words to convey these interpersonal effects. In addition, both examples also demonstrated the counselor's awareness of designing her answers specifically to the client's current stage of progress within the counseling process. Alas, the counselor in my data shows similar recipient design to the coaches in Graf and Jautz (this volume), indicating that helping professionals are specifically attuned to the therapeutic alliance.

4.4 Eliciting feedback on applications

Through the course of the counseling process, the counselor suggests various coping techniques that the clients can try out. These suggestions are interlaced with requests to trigger feedback from the clients. Due to the asynchronicity (Herring 2007) of email communication, clients are not forced to immediately respond to requests. At times, but by all means not every time a client does not provide an answer, the counselor follows up on her suggestions or requests. These follow-ups often aim to elicit feedback on the application of the suggested coping techniques. Such requests are very complex with regard to relational work and to the construction of identities as Example (7) illustrates. In a previous entry in Mel's thread, the counselor suggested that Mel should write a list with positive qualities and achievements. The counselor asked Mel to share some examples. Mel responded neither to the suggestion nor to the request. While the counselor might simply wait for a response to the request in a face-to-face context, the counselor does not have this option in email counseling. In email communication, clients can more readily just ignore requests. However, not answering the request could potentially threaten the counselor's face as well as stall the progression of the counseling process. In a next entry, the counselor writes the request shown in Example (7):

(7) ☺ *How are you getting on with these Mel, and how does it feel looking back at your growing list of achievements?*

The counselor does not comment on the potential face-threat the client committed by not answering the previous request. I argue that the counselor does not want to damage the client's face by explicitly pointing out her lack of a response. Rather, she utilizes a smiley emoticon (Dressner and Herring 2010: 256) to start her inquiry. This mitigates the potential threat to the client's face as the counselor asks Mel a second time about the suggested coping technique without having received any feedback the first time. The counselor seems to deliberately steer clear of mentioning the face-threat that was committed by the client when not giving an answer. Instead, the counselor tries to shine a positive light on the suggested coping technique.

The first clause focuses on the application of the suggested coping technique. The counselor asks Mel how she is *getting on with* them. The progressive aspect is of considerable importance. It hints towards the activity type of the suggested coping technique: Writing a list is something that one actually does. The progressive aspect brings the immediacy of an action into focus. Further, it also suggests that Mel is currently executing the activity. Due to the asynchronicity of email communication, the counselor's use of the progressive form occurs at a different time than the client's reading of it. The lexical choice of the phrasal verb *to get on* further highlights that this activity is not a one-time activity. Rather, it is an activity that should be carried out over an extended period of time. This further mitigates the direct question and, at the same time, encourages Mel to continue with writing the list.

Presented with this example during the interview, the counselor argues that she tries to give the clients an opportunity to say that they have not tried the suggested coping technique:

> I mince my words carefully because hopefully my intention will come across to clients. When I ask them whether they've tried out a technique I suggested, I try to phrase my question so it's ok if they have or haven't tried it out. My intention is they're allowed to say they haven't. (Interview)

Clearly, the counselor aims to make the clients comfortable enough that they feel they can answer whatever they would like. Example (7) also shows, though, that the construction the counselor uses (*How are you getting on...*) could arguably result in a dispreference for a negative response such as "I'm not getting ahead." In other words, the counselor's linguistic choices could prevent clients from answering truthfully and thereby hinder the counseling process as well as damage the therapeutic alliance.

In the second clause of Example (7), the counselor moves towards Mel's potential emotional reaction during and after the activity. The counselor possibly aims to display the therapeutic effect writing the list can have on the client. In this way, the counselor carefully tries to motivate Mel and supports her in fulfilling this task. The supportive aspect of the therapeutic alliance is foregrounded in that the counselor predicts Mel can write the list. The counselor displays her faith in Mel's ability to recognize positive qualities and accomplishments. However, the request can also be potentially face-threatening to clients who do not manage to write down at least some achievements or positive qualities. Since the counselor suggests that clients are able to do this, clients who cannot manage might feel they have failed the task. Thereby, the goal of the task is not achieved and Mel might feel discouraged about her own therapeutic progression. Importantly, the counselor's choice of the adjective *growing* in connection with the list highlights that writing the list is by no means an activity of the past or present, but rather one that is continuous. This might mitigate the potential face-threat slightly as it can be argued that clients might progress better with this activity in the future. Example (7) illustrates expertly how intricate the relational work and resulting identities are in requests.

5. Conclusion and outlook

This paper illustrated how the counselor in my data uses requests for a range of interpersonal reasons. While the differences are subtle, they explain various interpersonal effects that are created and how they impact the therapeutic alliance. In several instances, I showed how the affordances of the medium of email influence the counselor's use of requests. Especially the asynchronicity of the medium allows the counselor to use certain linguistic devices that would carry much more face threatening potential for a client's face in face-to-face encounters. Therefore, the counselor uses the affordances of the medium to her advantage. Overall, both the data and the interview with the counselor have displayed how aware the counselor is of the therapeutic alliance and how intricate the relational work is that she uses to create her own and the clients' identities.

In addition, my findings support those of Kabatnik et al. (this volume) as well as Graf and Jautz (this volume) in that the helping professionals design their input carefully towards each help-seeking individual respectively and thereby practice what researchers have called 'recipient design' (cf. Graf and Jautz this volume for a definition). Kabatnik et al. have found that therapists use solution oriented questions usually at the end of topic development, whereas Graf and Jautz demonstrated how carefully coaches negotiate the epistemics of experience and expertise. Both chapters also highlight how these careful choices by helping professionals directly impacts the therapeutic alliance as an interactional achievement. My findings also foreground the collaborative and interactional nature of the therapeutic alliance and show how the relational work is specifically employed to negotiate the therapeutic alliance.

Through my study, I was able to both contribute to ongoing research on interpersonal pragmatics and online counseling. I analyzed a social practice that has so far received little attention from an interpersonal-pragmatic perspective. This is especially salient as counseling is a social practice in which the relational aspect is highly salient to the goal of the practice itself. I provided further detail in the ways that relational work can create specific identities. I thereby added to research that is especially interested in the link between these two prominent notions in interpersonal pragmatics. Further, I have provided a detailed analysis of one specific practice in a type of online counseling that has not received as much attention yet: email counseling. I demonstrated throughout my paper how certain affordances such as the use of emoticons or the asynchronicity can be used to the counselor's advantage. On the other hand, I also showed that the counselor deals with certain difficulties that are specific to the medium of email, such as the clients' option of simply ignoring requests the counselor has made. Importantly, I could also complement vital previous work from for example conversation analysts on online counseling by providing a further perspective – interpersonal pragmatics – that has so far not paid much attention to online counseling.

At the same time, I want to briefly list some shortcomings of my study and some future avenues of research that can be pursued. Due to the scope of this paper, only the counselor's requests and not the clients' reactions to such requests could be analyzed. Secondly, due to the fuzzy category boundaries of the different types of requests, I was not able to quantify the analysis of the 192 requests that I found in my corpus. Thirdly, I only examined counseling exchanges by one counselor. And finally, I only applied one perspective in my analysis, namely an interpersonal-pragmatic one. I argue that the complexity of the situated practice of email counseling would merit an examination of different perspectives within linguistics and in combination with researchers from other professions and practitioners. Future research could tackle all three of these shortcomings. An examination that would include the clients' responses could further carve out the interactional achievement that is necessary to create identities (cf. Thurnherr 2022). This would be especially fruitful as clients can react in various ways to the different types of requests, but seem to, for example, give more positive responses to the requests that elicit feedback, while they sometimes struggle more with answering requests that foster solutions. However, the clients also differ individually in how they respond to the requests. A broader study that incorporates different counselors, different approaches to counseling as well as more clients (that are also not only students) would certainly broaden our understanding of the social practice of email counseling overall. Finally, an interprofessional approach to the study of email counseling could shed further light on aspects such as the influence of specific counseling approaches on linguistic choices by the interactants.

References

Ackerman, Steven J., and Mark J. Hilsenroth. 2003. "A Review of Therapist Characteristics and Techniques Positively Impacting the Therapeutic Alliance." *Clinical Psychology Review* 23: 1–33. https://doi.org/10.1016/S0272-7358(02)00146-0

Antaki, Charles. 2008. "Formulations in Psychotherapy." In *Conversation Analysis and Psychotherapy*, ed. by Anssi Peräkylä, Charles Antaki, Sanna Vehviläinen, and Ivan Leudar, 26–42. Cambridge: Cambridge University Press. https://doi.org/10.1017/CBO9780511490002.003

Beckwith, Andrew, and Jonathan Crichton. 2014. "Homework Setting in Cognitive Behavioral Therapy: A Study of Discursive Strategies." *Communication and Medicine* 11(2): 91–102. https://doi.org/10.1558/cam.v11i2.16169

Bercelli, Fabrizio, Federico Rossano, and Maurizio Viaro. 2008. "Clients' Responses to Therapists' Reinterpretations." In *Conversation Analysis and Psychotherapy*, ed. by Anssi Peräkylä, Charles Antaki, Sanna Vehviläinen, and Ivan Leudar, 43–61. Cambridge: Cambridge University Press. https://doi.org/10.1017/CBO9780511490002.004

Berger, Thomas. 2017. "The Therapeutic Alliance in Internet Interventions: A Narrative Review and Suggestions for Future Research." *Psychotherapy Research* 27 (5): 511–524. https://doi.org/10.1080/10503307.2015.1119908

Bolander, Brook. 2013. *Language and Power in Blogs: Interaction, Disagreements and Agreements*. Amsterdam and Philadelphia: John Benjamins. https://doi.org/10.1075/pbns.237

Bolander, Brook, and Miriam A. Locher. 2014. "Doing Sociolinguistic Research on Computer-mediated Data: A Review of Four Methodological Issues." *Discourse, Context and Media* 3: 14–26. https://doi.org/10.1016/j.dcm.2013.10.004

Bucholtz, Mary, and Kira Hall. 2005. "Identity and Interaction: A Sociocultural Linguistic Approach." *Discourse Studies* 7 (4–5): 585–614. https://doi.org/10.1177/1461445605054407

Calkins, Amanda W., Jennifer M. Park, Sabine Wilhelm, and Susan E. Sprich. 2016. "Basic Principles and Practice of Cognitive Behavioral Therapy." In *The Massachusetts General Hospital Handbook of Cognitive Behavioral Therapy: Current Clinical Psychiatry*, ed. by Timothy J. Peterson, Susan E. Sprich, and Sabine Wilhelm, 5–14. New York: Springer. https://doi.org/10.1007/978-1-4939-2605-3_2

Comer, Ronald. J. 2010. *Abnormal Psychology*. New York: Worth Publishers.

Cook, Jonathan E., and Carole Doyle. 2002. "Working Alliance in Online Therapy as Compared to Face-to-Face Therapy: Preliminary Results." *CyberPsychology and Behavior* 5 (2): 95–105. https://doi.org/10.1089/109493102753770480

Danby, Susan J., Carly Butler, and Michael Emmison. 2009. "When 'Listeners Can't Talk': Comparing Active Listening in Opening Sequences of Telephone and Online Counseling." *Australian Journal of Communication* 36 (3): 91–113.

Davies, Bronwyn, and Rom Harré. 1990. Positioning: The Discursive Production of Selves. *Journal for the Theory of Social Behaviour* 20 (1): 43–63. https://doi.org/10.1111/j.1468-5914.1990.tb00174.x

DeShazer, Steve, and Insoo Kim Berg. 1997. "'What Works?' Remarks on Research Aspects of Solution-Focused Brief Therapy." *Journal of Family Therapy* 19: 121–124. https://doi.org/10.1111/1467-6427.00043

Dresner, Eli, and Susan C. Herring. 2010. "Functions of the Nonverbal in CMC: Emoticons and Illocutionary Force." *Communication Theory* 20: 249–268. https://doi.org/10.1111/j.1468-2885.2010.01362.x

Ekberg, Katie, and Amanda LeCouteur. 2012. "Negotiating Behavioural Change: Therapists' Proposal Turns in Cognitive Behavioural Therapy." *Communication and Medicine* 9 (3): 229–239. https://doi.org/10.1558/cam.v9i3.229

Ekberg, Katie, and Amanda LeCouteur. 2014. "Co-implicating and Re-shaping Clients' Suggestions for Behavioural Change in Cognitive Behavioural Therapy Practice." *Qualitative Research in Psychology* 11 (1): 60–77. https://doi.org/10.1080/14780887.2012.709917

Ekberg, Stuart, Rebecca Barnes, David Kessler, Alice Malpass, and Alison Shaw. 2013. "Managing the Therapeutic Relationship in Online Cognitive Behavioural Therapy for Depression: Therapist's Treatment of Clients' Contributions." *Language@Internet* 10: article 4.

Ekberg, Stuart, Alison Shaw, David Kessler, Alice Malpass, and Rebecca Barnes. 2016. "Orienting to Emotion in Computer-mediated Cognitive Behavioral Therapy." *Research on Language and Social Interaction* 49 (4): 310–324. https://doi.org/10.1080/08351813.2016.1199085

Fitzgerald, Pamela, and Ivan Leudar. 2012. "On the Use of Formulations in Person-centred, Solution-focused Short-term Psychotherapy." *Communication and Medicine* 9 (1): 13–22. https://doi.org/10.1558/cam.v9i1.13

Gingerich, Wallace J., and Todd Wabeke. 2001. "A Solution-focused Approach to Mental Health Intervention in School Settings." *Children and Schools* 23 (1): 33–47. https://doi.org/10.1093/cs/23.1.33

Gygax, Franziska, and Miriam A. Locher. 2015. "Introduction to Narrative Matters in Medical Contexts Across Disciplines." In *Narrative Matters in Medical Contexts Across Disciplines*, ed. by Franziska Gygax, and Miriam A. Locher: 1–16. Amsterdam and Philadelphia: John Benjamins. https://doi.org/10.1075/sin.20.01gyg

Hall, Kira, and Mary Bucholtz. 2013. "Epilogue: Facing Identity." *Journal of Politeness Research* 9 (1): 123–132. https://doi.org/10.1515/pr-2013-0006

Hamilton, Heidi E., and Wen-Ying S. Chou. 2014. "Introduction: Health Communication as Applied Linguistics." In *The Routledge Handbook of Language and Health Communication*, ed. By Heidi E. Hamilton, and Wen-Ying S. Chou, 1–12. London and New York: Routledge.

Harris, Jessica, Susan Danby, Carly W. Butler, and Michael Emmison. 2012. "Extending Client-centered Support: Counselor's Proposals to Shift from E-mail to Telephone Counseling." *Text and Talk* 32 (1): 21–37. https://doi.org/10.1515/text-2012-0002

Harvey, Kevin, and Nelya Koteyko. 2013. *Exploring Health Communication: Language in Action*. London: Routledge.

Herring, Susan C. 2007. "A Faceted Classification Scheme for Computer-mediated Discourse." *Language@Internet* 4: article 1.

Horvath, Adam O., A. C. Del Re, Christoph Flueckiger, and Dianne Symonds. 2011. "Alliance in Individual Psychotherapy." *Psychotherapy* 48 (1): 9–16. https://doi.org/10.1037/a0022186

Jager, Margot, and Wyke Stommel. 2017. "The Risk of Metacommunication to Manage Interactional Trouble in Online Chat Counseling." *Linguistik Online* 87 (8): 191–212. https://doi.org/10.13092/lo.87.4179

Johnstone, Barbara. 2000. *Qualitative Methods in Sociolinguistics*. Oxford: Oxford University Press.

Krupnick, Janice L., Stuart M. Sotsky, Sam Simmens, Janet Moyer, Irene Elkin, John Watkins, and Paul A. Pilkonis. 1996. "The Role of the Therapeutic Alliance in Psychotherapy and Pharmacotherapy Outcome. Findings in the National Institute of Mental Health Treatment of Depression Collaborative Research Program." *Journal of Consulting and Clinical Psychology* 64 (3): 532–539. https://doi.org/10.1037/0022-006X.64.3.532

Lamerichs, Joyce, and Wyke Stommel. 2016. "'But How Often Does this Happen?': Problem Reducing Responses by Coaches in Email Counselling." In *The Palgrave Handbook of Adult Mental Health*, ed. by Michelle O'Reilly, and Jessica N. Lester, 287–307. London: Palgrave Macmillan. https://doi.org/10.1057/9781137496850_16

Lindholm, Loukia. 2017. "'So now I'm Panic Attack Free!': Response Stories in a Peer-to-Peer Online Advice Forum on Pregnancy and Parenting." *Linguistik Online* 87 (8): 25–41. https://doi.org/10.13092/lo.87.4171

Locher, Miriam A. 2006. *Advice Online: Advice-giving in an American Internet Health Column.* Amsterdam and Philadelphia: John Benjamins. https://doi.org/10.1075/pbns.149

Locher, Miriam A. 2013. "Relational Work and Interpersonal Pragmatics." *Journal of Pragmatics* 58: 145–149. https://doi.org/10.1016/j.pragma.2013.09.014

Locher, Miriam A. 2015. "Interpersonal Pragmatics and its Link to (Im)politeness Research." *Journal of Pragmatics* 86: 5–10. https://doi.org/10.1016/j.pragma.2015.05.010

Locher, Miriam A., and Sage L. Graham. 2010. "Introduction to Interpersonal Pragmatics." In *Interpersonal pragmatics*, ed. by Miriam A. Locher, Sage L. Graham, 1–13. Berlin and Boston: de Gruyter Mouton. https://doi.org/10.1515/9783110214338.0.1

Locher, Miriam A., and Stephanie Schnurr. 2017. «(Im)politeness in Health Settings." In *The Palgrave Handbook of Linguistic (Im)politeness*, ed. by Jonathan Culpeper, Michael Haugh, and Daniel Z. Kádár, 689–711. London: Palgrave Macmillan. https://doi.org/10.1057/978-1-137-37508-7_26

Locher, Miriam A., and Franziska Thurnherr. 2017. "Typing Yourself Healthy: Introduction to the Special Issue on Language and Health Online." *Linguistik Online* 87 (8): 3–24. https://doi.org/10.13092/lo.87.4170

Locher, Miriam A., and Richard J. Watts. 2008. "Relational Work and Impoliteness: Negotiating Norms of Linguistic Behavior." In *Impoliteness in Language: Studies on its Interplay with Power in Theory and Practice*, ed. by Derek Bousfield, and Miriam A. Locher, 77–99. Berlin and Boston: de Gruyter Mouton.

MacMartin, Clare. 2008. "Resisting Optimistic Questions in Narrative and Solution-focused Therapies." In *Conversation Analysis and Psychotherapy*, ed. by Anssi Peräkylä, Charles Antaki, Sanna Vehviläinen, and Ivan Leudar, 80–99. Cambridge: Cambridge University Press. https://doi.org/10.1017/CBO9780511490002.006

McKee, Heidi, and James E. Porter. 2009. *The Ethics of Internet Research: A Rhetorical, Case-based Process*. New York: Peter Lang.

Miles, Matthew B., A. Michael Huberman, and Johnny Saldaña. 2014. *Qualitative Data Analysis: A Methods Sourcebook* (3rd ed.). Thousand Oaks: Sage.

Miller, John, and Kenneth J. Gergen. 1998. "Life on the Line: The Therapeutic Potentials of Computer-mediated Conversation." *Journal of Marital and Family Therapy* 24: 189–202. https://doi.org/10.1111/j.1752-0606.1998.tb01075.x

Morrow, Phillip R. 2012. "Online Advice in Japanese: Giving Advice in an Internet Discussion Forum." In *Advice in Discourse*, ed. by Holger Limberg, and Miriam A. Locher, 255–279. Amsterdam and Philadelphia: John Benjamins. https://doi.org/10.1075/pbns.221.16mor

Mullany, Louise. 2009. "Introduction: Applying Politeness Research to Health Care Communication." *Journal of Politeness Research* 5: 1–10. https://doi.org/10.1515/JPLR.2009.001

Pawelczyk, Joanna, and Richard Erskine. 2008. "Expressing the Unexpressed: Self-disclosure as Interactional Achievement in the Psychotherapy Session." *Communication and Medicine* 5 (1): 35–48. https://doi.org/10.1558/cam.v5i1.39

Peräkylä, Anssi, Charles Antaki, Sanne Vehviläinen, and Ivan Leudar (eds.). 2008. *Conversation Analysis and Psychotherapy*. Cambridge: Cambridge University Press. https://doi.org/10.1017/CBO9780511490002

Pick, Ina. 2011. "Praxisnahe Erforschung von (Beratungs-)Gesprächen: Ablauf eines sprachwissenschaftlichen Forschungsprojektes." In *Beratung, Coaching, Supervision*, ed. by Eva-Maria Graf, Yasmin Aksu, Ina Pick, and Sabine Rettinger, 69–83. Wiesbaden: Verlag für Sozialwissenschaften. https://doi.org/10.1007/978-3-531-93341-2_5

Placencia, Maria E. 2012. "Online Peer-to-Peer Advice in Spanish Yahoo!Respuestas." In *Advice in Discourse*, ed. by Holger Limberg, and Miriam A. Locher, 281–305. Amsterdam and Philadelphia: John Benjamins. https://doi.org/10.1075/pbns.221.17pla

Rudolf von Rohr, Marie-Therese, Franziska Thurnherr, and Miriam A. Locher. 2019. "Linguistic Expert Creation in Online Health Practices." In *Analyzing Digital Discourse: New Insights and Future Directions*, ed. by Patricia Bou-Franch, and Pilar Garcés-Conejos Blitvich, 219–250. London: Palgrave Macmillan. https://doi.org/10.1007/978-3-319-92663-6_8

Saldaña, Johnny. 2013. *The Coding Manual for Qualitative Researchers* (2nd ed.). London: Sage.

Schiffrin, Deborah, Deborah Tannen, D. and Heidi E. Hamilton (eds.). 2001. *The Handbook of Discourse Analysis*. Malden and Oxford: Blackwell.

Simpson, S. G., and Corinne L. Reid. 2014. "Therapeutic Alliance in Videoconferencing Psychotherapy: A Review." *Australian Journal of Rural Health* 22 (6): 280–299. https://doi.org/10.1111/ajr.12149

Stommel, Wyke. 2012. "Salutations, Closings and Pronouns: Some Aspects of Recipient Design in Online Counselling." *Communication and Medicine* 9 (2): 145–158. https://doi.org/10.1558/cam.v9i2.145

Stommel, Wyke, and Hedwig te Molder. 2015. "Counseling Online and over the Phone: When Preclosing Questions Fail as a Closing Device." *Research on Language and Social Interaction* 48 (3): 281–300. https://doi.org/10.1080/08351813.2015.1058605

Stommel, Wyke, and Fleur van der Houwen. 2015. "Counseling and New Media Technologies: A Comparison of Problem Presentations in E-mail and in Chat." *Communication and Medicine* 12 (2–3): 243–256. https://doi.org/10.1558/cam.18298

Sucala, Madalina, Julie B. Schnur, Michael J. Constantino, Sarah J. Miller, Emily H. Brackman, and Guy H. Montgomery. 2012. "The Therapeutic Relationship in E-therapy for Mental Health: A Systematic Review." *Journal of Medical Internet Research* 14 (4): 110–187. https://doi.org/10.2196/jmir.2084

Thurnherr, Franziska. 2022. *Interpersonal Pragmatics and the Therapeutic Alliance: The Collaborative Work in Email Counseling*. NIHIN Studies: Freiburg.

Thurnherr, Franziska, Marie-Therese Rudolf von Rohr, and Miriam A. Locher. 2016. "The Functions of Narrative Passages in Three Written Online Health Contexts." *Open Linguistics* 2: 450–470. https://doi.org/10.1515/opli-2016-0024

Vehviläinen, Sanne. 2008. "Identifying and Managing Resistance in Psychoanalytic Interaction." In *Conversation Analysis and Psychotherapy*, ed. by Anssi Peräkylä, Charles Antaki, Sanna Vehviläinen, and Ivan Leudar, 120–138. Cambridge: Cambridge University Press. https://doi.org/10.1017/CBO9780511490002.008

Zayts, Olga, and Stephanie Schnurr. 2013. "'[She] Said: 'Take the Test' and I Took the Test': Relational Work as a Framework to Approach Directiveness in Prenatal Screening of Chinese Clients in Hong Kong." *Journal of Politeness Research* 9 (2): 187–210. https://doi.org/10.1515/pr-2013-0009

Twitter as a helping medium

Relationship building through German hashtag #depression

Susanne Kabatnik
University of Greifswald

This article analyzes the German discourse space #depression on Twitter regarding relationship building. The data basis is a corpus of German #depression tweets as well as follow-up communication. In the German #depression discourse space, users initiate social exchange. This is realized interactively through narration, the formulation of wishes, questions or requests, which evoke further reactions of the community. The basis for the relationship building, which will be demonstrated in a case study, are the technical affordances provided by the medium and the resulting potential for interaction.

Keywords: relationship, interaction, social media, hashtag, #depression, Twitter, German

1. Introduction

In this article, German #depressions posts on Twitter are analysed with regard to the relationship constitution among users. The tweets on depression are in German, but the disease is perceived as an epidemiological phenomenon and described by the WHO and in the ICD-10 in terms of general symptoms. According to a study by the Robert Koch Institute, in 2019 9.2% of the German population suffered from depression (Hapke, Cohrdes and Nübel 2019: 65) and thus belong to a minority in Germany. The illness is stigmatized and those suffering from it experience discrimination and exclusion, e.g. from social groups, activities or the job market (Richter et al. 2006: 704). In addition, experiences of stigmatization and discrimination lead to secrecy and to difficulties in maintaining or initiating essential interpersonal relationships (Baer et al. 2016: 4). However, a stable social environment and relationships in different areas of society are essential for those suffering from the illness and can improve their symptoms. A lack of a social

https://doi.org/10.1075/pbns.331.13kab

environment and permanent exclusion from private and professional spheres can have serious consequences and even lead to suicide (see Hapke et al. 2019). In western societies, speaking about depression is a taboo and therefore it is only predestined for a few specific communication situations in face-to-face communication (see Andalibi et al. 2017: 1493f.).[1] What experiences people have with depression often remains unknown and is largely inaccessible to research that is not primarily psychological-psychotherapeutic, such as linguistics. So how can practices of relationship building of people suffering from depression be studied when the content is so private and protected?

On social media platforms on the Internet, the boundaries of what can be said are more fluid and they open up communicative spaces to talk about tabooed and highly private content (for disabilities see Cochrane 2017), also including depression. By using the hashtag #depression, a discourse space is created, in which the users form social groups and thus practice relationship building (see Andalibi et al. 2017) without analog contact (see Döring 2003; Ali-Hasan and Adamic 2007; Wellman 2001). However, building relationships on social media differs from that in the analogous face-to-face situation, because it is based on different framework conditions, so-called technical affordances, i.e. the technical possibilities provided by the medium (see Marx 2019a: 111/122; Marx 2017: 10). Moreover, on this medium building relationships is based primarily on the exchange of written language. Categories of relationship are either explicitly identifiable on the linguistic surface or are displayed implicitly (but reconstructably) (see overview in Linke and Schröter 2016; Kabatnik and Spranz-Fogasy in this volume).

The field of what can be said on the internet expands successively, highly private and sensitive information is shared in quasi-public space and bundled under hashtags, such as #depression (Marx 2019b; Marx 2019a; 126; Bucher 2019; Andalibi et al. 2017). People suffering from depression connect with other people seeking help and support on Facebook, Twitter or Instagram (see Andalibi et al. 2017; Scherr and Schmitt 2018; Choudhury et al 2013a, b; 2014). For Instagram, the hashtag #depression has already been confirmed as a valid communication link for investigating experiences of depression (see Andalibi et al. 2017: 1490). By sharing meaningful emotional experiences and exchanging them with others, they can be positively reinterpreted and re-contextualized (cf. Rimé 2009; Muth

1. These findings are to be considered in the Western cultural context, which affects how depression is talked about. The study by Al Zidjaly (2017) shows how mental health is being discussed in Oman: mental illnesses are also constructed in the Islamic context as supernatural and cured by religion rather than as illnesses treated by medical and psychological intervention. So, we get a very different picture and the influence of culture and religion on the understanding of mental health concerns becomes apparent.

Andersen 2017). Under the same hashtag, the topic of depression represents a common space of discourse that documents the experience between the interactors and thus makes it accessible for linguistic analysis (Marx 2019a: 123/126; Marx and Weidacher 2019). In consequence, new aspects of private interaction as well as practices for constituting and maintaining interpersonal relationships can be observed (Marx 2017: 15).

Studies of online platforms in the medical field indicate that those suffering from a disease can benefit from the social support offered by the forums, which can lead to reduce the symptoms (Finn 1999; Galegher, Sproull and Kiesler 1998; Schultz 2002; Park, McDonald and Cha 2013):

> This result suggests that using the Internet to talk with close ties prompts improved psychological well-being, just as shown in the literature on offline communication with close ties. (Bressiere et al. 2008: 60)

In addition, negative emotional experiences, e.g. in relation to the act of revelation, require cognitive effort, stimulate social exchange and activate the attachment system (Rimé 2009), so that group membership on social network sites can emerge through the disease as a common thematic reference point (Bucher 2019; Reimann 2019: 202). The positive effects of social interaction on the Internet for people with clinical depression include improved psychological adjustment, increased treatment effectiveness and resilience, and reduced mortality (Mattson and Gibb Hall 2011; Bressiere et al. 2008: 60f.). However, the use of social media in personal emergency situations is also viewed critically. After all, the exchange in online forums on, for example, anorexia or self-harm can promote harmful behavior by validating disease-promoting practices (Haas et al. 2011). In addition, those individuals would neglect other social contacts as a result of their relationship constitution on the Internet (see Bressiere et al. 2008: 61). If, however, no social resources are available at all, the Internet is the only medium of communication and thus also the only possibility for building relationships.

Studies of communicative behavior on social networking sites of English-speaking people suffering from depression show specific linguistic behavior in postings that can be used for diagnostic purposes. For example, Twitter data is collected for the prediction and diagnosis of various mental illnesses such as bipolar personality disorder, post-traumatic stress disorder and depression (Choudhory et al. 2013a and b; Coppersmith et al. 2014, 2015). Significant for English speaking users with depressions is, for example:

- the frequent use of filler and curse words
- distinctive language styles, such as a strongly developed self-reference through pronouns

- expression of social and medical concerns
- increase or persistence of a negative affect
- a lower active or passive participation in the network
- nocturnal online activity patterns
  (see Reece and Danforth 2017: 8f.; Nguyen et al. 2017: 10661; Choudhury et al. 2013b: 128; Vedula 2017: 127)

Increased posting frequency seems to express the need to communicate, expressing the desire for conversations and relationships. Emotions can be expressed through filler and curse words as well as sad images, and reactions of compassion and sympathy can be elicited (see Andalibi et al. 2017: 1489). Postings about depression on social networking sites contain personal stories, information about the disease, self-doubt, reports of experiences with medications as well as explicit requests for support. They can be classified according to their type of speech action, such as questions, answers, advice or self-revelations, but can also be subcategorized as (not) empathic (Andalibi et al. 2017: 1486/1493; Nguyen et al. 2017: 10660; Davison, Pennebaker and Petrie 1997; Finfgeld 2000). From an interactional perspective, these postings elicit reactions, such as the adjacency pairs question – answer, request for support – advice / information or self-revelation – counter-revelation (see Schegloff and Sacks 1973: 299; Gülich and Mondada 2008: 53–58) and thus promote disease-related exchange with and about other sufferers. The hashtag #depression has not yet been studied in German, and there are no studies on the communicative behaviour of German users on social media platforms.[2]

Based on the above, the following research questions can be derived: How are relationships in the discourse space #depression on Twitter initiated? And could Twitter function as a helping medium for people in crisis situations? The data basis of the investigation is a corpus of tweets with the hashtag #depression, the generation and constitution of which is described in detail below (Chapter 2). I will focus on initial tweets and first analyze their Twitter-typical interaction potentials (Chapter 3) and will then focus on the level of speech action as conclusions can be drawn about the relationship initiation potential of initial tweets from the subsequent follow-up communication (Chapter 4). Finally, I will demonstrate how relationship is constituted by using an example of a beginning relationship in the interaction space #depression, which is created by the hashtag and the search query #depression.

2. Iakushevich (under review) and Iakushevich and Stelter (in prep.) conduct research on German depression profiles on Instagram, but Iakushevich focuses her study on selected profiles from a discourse-linguistic perspective rather than an interactional or relationship-constitutive one.

2. Data and method

The data consists of publicly available Twitter postings on the hashtag and search query #depression, which were streamed with the software Rstats in April and May 2020. The data collection includes 47.175 postings in 31 languages, such as English, German, French, Dutch, Italian or Polish. For the study, the German tweets were extracted and generated into a corpus (Corpus 1),[3] to which contributed 299 different tweeters. Based on Corpus 1, a second corpus was manually created (Corpus 2) containing the comments of tweets marked as relevant by the community. The corpora serve different research questions and are summarized in Figure 1 and Table 1 (below).

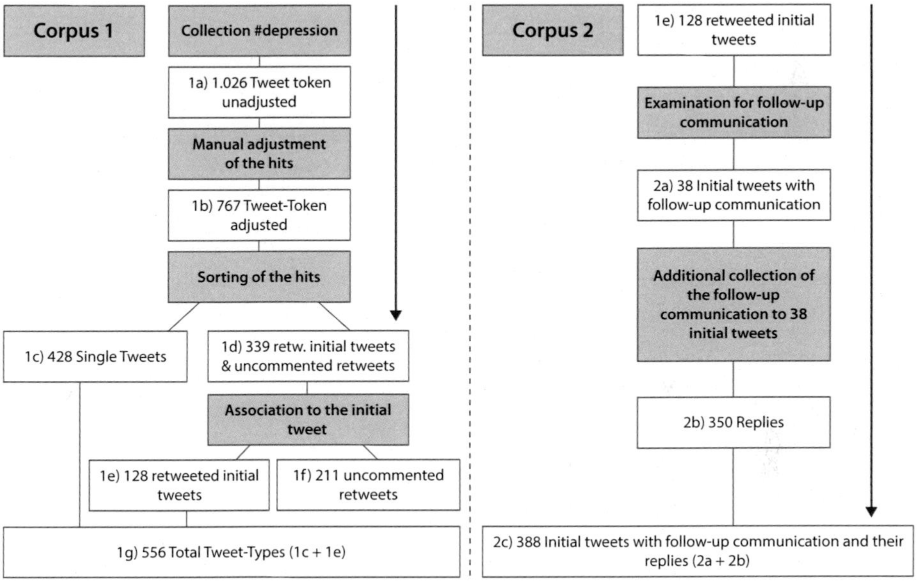

Figure 1. Data collection and processing

On data collection Corpus 1: The corpus includes 1.026 Twitter posts with 26.608 text words (see Figure 1; 1a). The data was manually purged and sorted. Manual purging of hits resulted in 767 postings (19.891 text words) for further analysis (1b). Sorting refers to the classification of tweets into initial tweet, (commented) retweet and reply. The categorization of the tweets can be derived from the collected metadata, such as Twitter handle, creation date and time, and tweet type.

3. I would like to express my sincere thanks to Sascha Wolfer (Leibniz Institute for the German Language, Mannheim) for his support in building the corpus.

Because uncommented retweets are quotes from existing tweets, the corpus also should be searchable without these redundancies. Therefore, identical tweets, i.e., uncommented retweets, were separated from the rest of the data. Sorting reveals 428 singularly occurring initial tweets, replies, and commented retweets in the corpus on the one hand (1c). And 339 retweeted initial tweets and their quotes on the other hand (1d), which are split into 128 initial tweets (1e) and 221 uncommented retweets (1f). Excluding these 221 uncommented retweets results in 556 tweet types (1g).

On data collection Corpus 2: Because the kind of data is a real-time stream on #depression, the data represents a segment of the #depression timeline at the moment it is updating. Therefore, the postings cannot be read in the corpus as a coherent text in their sequence-logical order. The replies situated there appear detached from their initial tweets. Furthermore, neither the number of retweets, likes or replies nor the follow-up communication itself can be recorded, because this only takes place after the timeline has been updated. The 128 retweeted initial tweets from Corpus 1 can be interpreted as salient due to their high retransmission by the Twitter community and therefore are the basis for Corpus 2. Retweeted initial tweets without redundancies were checked for follow-up communication, which was identified in 38 of 128 retweeted initial tweets (2a). This follow-up communication was collected manually (2b). For 38 initial tweets, 350 replies were realized (2b), i.e. a total of 388 initial tweets and their replies.

Table 1. Corpora 1 and 2 – number of twitter postings and text words

Corpus 1: Stream //depression tweets[1]	**Total hits**	**Text words**
a. Total tokens unadjusted	1.026	26.608
b. Total tokens adjusted	767	19.891
c. Single tweets	428	11.099
d. Retweeted initial tweets and uncommented retweets	339	8.792
e. Retweeted initial tweets	128	3.320
f. uncommented retweets	211	5.472
g. Total Tweet Types	556	14.419
Corpus 2: Follow-up communication[2]		
a. Initial tweets with follow-up communication	38	874
b. Replies	350	8.055
c. Initial tweets and their replies	388	8.929

Essential for the study of relationship formation on Twitter are the technical affordances provided by the medium (cf. Marx 2019a: 111/122; Marx 2017: 10), such as the possibility to retweet or comment, because they open up potentials for interaction in the discourse space #depression, for which Corpus 1 was studied. For the investigation of interaction potentials, the postings and replies in Corpus 2 were functionally subcategorized according to speech action types (see also Andalibi et al. 2017). Methodologically, the present study combines the inventory of corpus linguistics with qualitative research methods of interactional linguistics regarding the derivation of categories of relationship co-construction on Twitter. This includes the direct addressing of other users, the tagging by hashtags and the discourse spaces opened by this, as well as the conditional relevancy in the sequence of initial tweets (cf. Dang-Anh et al. 2013: 81–85, Imo and Lanwer 2019: 177). Tweets are copyrighted artworks that I address for gaining scientific knowledge; I quote them in their original form and provide them in English translation. Original data is in German. Since the data contains highly sensitive content, it has been anonymized for ethical reasons. The anonymization concerns both nicknames as well as personal data.

3. Twitter-specific interaction potentials

The study of how people with depression constitute relationships on Twitter pursues the principle question if there is interaction in the hashtag #depression. The categorization of #depression tweets in Corpus 1 according to their type into initial, (annotated) retweet, and reply indeed suggests the activity of users in the #depression discourse space on Twitter. By reproducing and commenting tweets about depression, 237 interactions between different users can be identified in 767 #depression tweets, which split as follows.

Table 2. Categorization of the cleaned #depression tweets into tweet types

Corpus 1: Stream depression tweets	Total hits	Initial tweets	Commented retweets	Uncommented retweets	Reply	Rest
b. Token total adjusted	767	428	41	211	68	19

(Un)commented retweeting represents a reference to other posts by multiplying already existing postings, allowing users to express common views and their appreciation as well as to maintain their contacts within the network (cf. Demuth/Schulz 2010: 33/43).

Thematically, the #depression tweets could refer, for example, to medication using antidepressants (1), psychotherapy (2), withdrawal from interpersonal relationships (3), lack of motivation as well as difficulties in coping with everyday tasks (4), reactions of the environment (5), and the experience of receiving the diagnosis (6):

(1)

05.05.2020, 11:29 p.m.	User1	Day 6 Discontinuation of the barely effective antidepressant after 6 years of taking it: – Positive effect: - – Negative effect: Empty and all pointless. Actually like most of the rest of the time. Hardly bearable permanent condition. However was mostly also with tablets like that. #notjustsad #depression 'Tag 6 Absetzen des kaum wirksamen Antidepressivums nach 6 Jahren Einnahme: – Positiver Effekt: – Negativer Effekt: Leer und alles sinnlos. Eigentlich wie großteils sonst auch. Kaum erträglicher Dauerzustand. War jedoch auch mit Tabletten meist so. #notjustsad #depression'

(2)

15.05.2020, 1:26 p.m	User2	The therapy talk this morning went great. I guess my childhood has shaped me a lot and that's why it's so hard to get out of the hole (protective shield). #Depression #SocialPhobia #notjustsad 'Das Therapie-Gespräch heute morgen lief super. Meine Kindheit hat mich wohl sehr geprägt und darum ist es auch so schwer aus dem Loch (Schutzschild) rauszukommen. #Depression #SozialePhobie #notjustsad'

(3)

01.05.2020, 6:32 a.m	User3	CN #depression Also explains why it is so exhausting to maintain contacts. I sometimes have just one chat open in WhatsApp a day, haven't communicated with anyone else all day. 'CN #depression Erklärt auch warum es so anstrengend ist Kontakte aufrecht zu halten. Ich hab zum Teil gerade mal einen Chat in WhatsApp offen am Tag, habe sonst mit niemanden kommuniziert den ganzen Tag über.'

(4)

26.04.2020, 9:02 p.m	User4	#depression #weekend No shower for 7 days No brushing teeth for weeks Garbage overflows Cigarettes, coke, coffee and Nutella bread Laundry piles up

Fresh air for 2min on the balcony for a cigarette.
Medication against the mind theater

Well, that' s how a depression can be! [...]

'#Depression #wochenende 7 Tage nicht duschen
Wochenlang keine Zähne putzen
Müll quillt über
Kippe,Cola,Kaffee und Nutella Brot
Wäsche stapelt sich
Frische Luft für 2min auf dem Balkon für eine Kippe.
Medikamente gegen das Kopfkino

Tja so kann eine Depression sein! [...]'

(5)

04.05.2020, 7:17 p.m	User5	As my father commented on my #depression, "No thanks, I don't need to read up on it. My common sense is enough for that." And bang, his common sense quickly came up with a revolutionary solution: "You just need to get your act together!" 'Wie mein Vater sich zu meiner #Depression äußerte: „Nein danke, ich muss mich darüber nicht informieren. Dafür reicht mein gesunder Menschenverstand." Und zack, sein gesunder Menschenverstand hatte schnell eine revolutionäre Lösung: „Du musst Dich einfach nur zusammenreißen!"'

(6)

01.05.2020, 10:44 a.m	User6	the day before yesterday i got the diagnosis #depression in passing.now i have to deal with it. the wonderful @UserA will help me as best as he can. [...] 'vorgestern habe ich im vorbeigehen die diagnose #depression rübergereicht bekommen.now i have to deal with it. der wunderbare @UserA wird mir dabei helfen, so gut er kann. [...]'

The Examples (1)–(6) thematically show a connection to disease processes, accompanying circumstances or symptoms of depression: Example (1) addresses consequences of discontinuing antidepressants – one of the main treatment methods for depression (cf. Hautzinger 2013: 422–429). User1 describes the sixth day after discontinuing the six-year-old and *barely effective* medication. Example (2) is about a positive experience of a therapy session (*went great*) and the author's realization about a childhood conditioning. In Example (3), the author's social withdrawal is addressed, which is a concomitant of depression (cf. Summer 2008: 34f.). Due to *just one chat open in WhatsApp a day*, the communication behavior on WhatsApp is considered to be low. However, through this post on Twitter, a willingness for interpersonal contact – even if only on Twitter – is indicated. Example (4) is a description of everyday tasks that presumably can no longer be accomplished due to a lack of motivation as one of the main symptoms of depression (cf. Hautzinger 2010: 1). Example (6) is about a negative reaction to the depression from the family circle of the author of the tweet, which is reproduced by direct speech, thus creating immediacy, closeness, and authenticity (cf. Günthner 2000: 4). The father of the diseased man advises to pull himself together, which is ironized by *revolutionary* to criticize the father's unability to empathize. User6 reports his experience of the diagnosis being passed to him, expressing stunnedness at the brevity of the diagnosis message, which is reinforced by *now I have to deal with it* (English in original). User6 then tags UserA, which is described as *wonderful*. Because of this positive external attribution and the direct addressing, a – probably close – relation is made public and updated. This tweet can be interpreted as a public confession of an already existing relationship. This example is relevant to the present paper because categories of relationship building can be derived from it, such as positive external attributions, explicit relationship confessions and direct addressing.

Direct addressing of other users can be found in 83 of 577 #depression tweets, thus creating potential for interaction. Users are informed about the addressing by Twitter and can react in the form of likes, retweets or replies. Through addressing the following tweet contains offers of relationship on different levels:

(7)

03.05.2020, 9:58 p.m	User7	@UserB is relatively new on Twitter and maybe some of you want to become his #follower. He writes like me about the not easy life with #depressions. I can empathize well with his tweets. #nightshift #depression ‘@UserB ist relativ neu bei Twitter und vielleicht hat der eine oder andere Lust sein #Follower zu werden. Er schreibt wie ich über das nicht leichte Leben mit #Depressionen. Ich kann mich gut in seine Tweets einfühlen. #nachtschicht #depression‘

In Example (7) the new UserB is addressed and presented by User7. This is followed by a positioning of User7 by characterizing their Twitter channels as similar and thus emphasizing the commonality of the users. This can be interpreted as relationship-constituting behavior (see Köhler 2012: 259ff.). Furthermore, this Tweet contains an invitation to follow UserB by introducing the user and his channel. This can be understood as an integrating action (cf. Köhler 2012: 260ff.), which is made possible by the technical affordances of the social media platform.

In addition to the #depression hashtag, this tweet (7) also contains three more hashtags, namely #follower, #depressions and #night shift. The extension of other hashtags can be observed in 422 of 577 documents (without redundancies) and is therefore significant for #depression tweets. Two (128/577), three (80/577) or more than three hashtags (214/577) can be used. The hashtags can be implemented initially, medially (see also Zappavigna 2018) or, as in the following Example (8), in a series of final hashtags:

(8)

15.05.2020, 2:06 a.m	User8	The moment when you eat at night around 2 chips and YouTube brings YouTube slimming advertisement #Borderline #Depression #cptsd #Suicidal thoughts #fromtheloonybin #notjustsad 'Der Moment wenn man nachts um 2 Chips isst und YouTube abnehm Werbung bringt #Borderline #Depression #kptbs #Suizidgedanken #ausderklapse #notjustsad'

Example (8) is about the nightly consumption of chips and YouTube. User8 believes that the weight loss advertisements are in conflict with the eating behavior. The six following hashtags link User8's statement with #Borderline #Depression #cptsd[4] #Thoughts of suicide # fromtheloonybin, #notjustsad (English in the original) and locate them both pathologically and spatiotemporally in the medium (see Zappavigna 2018: 41ff.), which makes the thematized conflictual behavior more urgent. Due to the hashtags used in (8), this tweet can be received in six discourse spaces on crisis situations, which increases the probability of eliciting a reaction from other users. Not only the followers of User8 get the possibility to react to the tweet, but also the recipients, who move in the discourse spaces #Borderline, #Depression, #cptsd, #suicidalthoughts, #fromtheloonybin and #notjustsad. In 576 tweet types, 1.864 hashtags were realized. The hashtag #depression is frequently used to refer to other mental disorders such as borderline, burnout, complex post-traumatic stress disorder, but also to emotional and conscious states, such as suicidal thoughts, stress or anxiety (see Küchenhoff et al. 2017: 13 ff.). In addition, treatment options or places of treatment, such as (interpersonal) psychotherapy or psychiatry, are also discussed. Further prominent keywords in combination with depression on Twitter are the hashtags #NotJustAMood and #NotJustSad, which emphasize depression as a recognized disease instead of perceiving it as a temporary sadness or mood.

---

4. Abbreviation for complex posttraumatic stress disorder.

#depression tweets contain connecting elements, such as direct addressing, reception in different discourse spaces through multiple keywording or disease-related experiences, which open up the potential for interaction and enable follow-up communication on Twitter. The private content on disease-related topics of the #depression postings suggest an open communication space in the #depression discourse space.

4. Interaction potentials at the level of speech action

In Corpus 1, 128 initial tweets could be identified, which were marked as relevant by their further distribution in the discourse space #depression (see Demuth/Schulz 2010: 32). What these tweets have in common is that users contribute support and information (9, 10), seek social contacts (14), activate the network (12, 13), are emotionally expressive (15) and seek social exchange through narration (16) or social comparison (11) (see categorization in Andalibi et al. 2017: 1491):

(9)

01.05.2020, 09:13 a.m	User9	#Mentaldisorders: An increasing number of Germans are diagnosed with #Depression https://t.co/5uAtyi2TGS [...] '#PsychischeStörungen: Immer mehr Deutsche bekommen eine #Depression diagnostiziert https://t.co/5uAtyi2TGS [...]'

(10)

17.05.2020, 9:41 p.m	User10	Very difficult but also important topic Twitch and depression discuss it in the comments at @UserC #twitch #depression #twitchstreamer #discussion https://t.co/fIO9KomOPz 'Sehr schweres aber auch wichtiges Thema Twitch und Depression diskutiert doch mal fleißig mit in den Kommentaren bei @UserC #twitch #depression #twitchstreamer #diskussion https://t.co/fIO9KomOPz'

Example (9) is about the increasing number of diagnosed depressions in Germany. The hashtag #Mentaldisorders provides the framework for the article in which #depression is taken up and specified (see Dang-Anh 2013: 83ff.). The tweet contains a link to an article in an online science magazine with the same title, which summarizes the results of a psychological study. The tweet has a purely informative function due to its objectivity and is not marked as emotionally supportive (19/128; see Demuth and Schulz 2010: 21ff.; Andalibi et al. 2017: 1491).

In Example (10), a life stream on Twitch about depression is pointed out and readers are invited to join the discussion. Depression is evaluated as a very serious and important topic (see Schwarz-Friesel and Consten 2014: 140). The platform Twitch and the streamer UserC are thus promoted (cf. Demuth and Schulz 2010: 28ff./45). Concurrently, the Twitch stream of UserC provides information about the disease and, through the possibility of synchronous exchange, also emotional support (27/128; see Andalibi et al. 2017: 1491).

(11)

07.05.2020, 7:10 p.m	User7	"Giving meaning to #depression is better than letting depression give you a meaning." #quote Benno Blues '"Der #Depression eine Bedeutung zu geben ist besser, als sich von der Depression eine Bedeutung geben zu lassen." #Zitat Benno Blues'

Example (11) includes a quote on depression, expressing that it is better to attach a positive function to the disease than to be socially stigmatized by the disease. Thus, through the comparison of personal and social self-image social exchange is sought (38/128; see Andalibi et al 2017: 1491), in which the active attribution of meaning to depression is positively framed.

(12)

18.05.2020, 11:43 a.m	User7	Today I have such terrible #depressions that I feel like I can't get off the couch. I feel like there are tons on my body. #Fuck #Depression! 😫 'Ich habe heute so schreckliche #Depressionen, dass ich das Gefühl habe, nicht mehr von der Couch zu kommen. Ich fühle mich so, als würden Tonnen auf meinem Körper sein. #Fuck #Depression! 😫

Example (12) is a personal narrative of User7's current state of illness. The user is currently severely depressed and can't get off the couch, describing his depression-related lethargy and negative feelings. This highlights the perceived helplessness and illustrates the symptoms of the disease. The hashtag #Fuck and the emoji with the face surrendering 😫 marks the user's feelings (see Havryliv 2017: 31). By describing the current situation, this tweet can be classified as a depression narrative (9/128; see Demuth and Schulz 2010: 32; Andalibi et al. 2017: 1491), in which affected persons describe their everyday life with depression and thus provide insights into their everyday and emotional worlds.

(13)

06.05.2020, 11:49 p.m	User1	Since a perceived eternity again self-harmed and for heavvvven's fucking will, that feels good!!! It is so liberating. How can something be bad that helps so much? As if the bad was flowing out of me instead of the blood. It's unleashing. #notjustsad #depression 'Seit einer gefühlten Ewigkeit wieder selbst verletzt und um Himmmmells fucking Willen, tut das gut!!! Es ist so befreiend. Wie kann etwas schlecht sein, dass so sehr hilft? Als würde das Übel anstelle des Blutes aus mir herausfließen. Es ist entfesselnd. #notjustsad #depression'

Example (13) describes the self-harming behavior of a user, which is temporally located after a phase of abstinence and thus set to be relevant. Self-harm can be associated with depression (Hautzinger 2010) and is a socially taboo subject (see Baer et al. 2016). The user describes her self-harm as a liberating and unleashing event and uses euphemistic markers, such as *for heavvvven's fucking will, that feels good* and the character iteration *!!!*, which contrasts the positive feelings to the maladaptive pattern of self-harm. This is illustrated by the question *How can something be bad that helps so much?*, with which she emphasizes the relief of psychological suffering through self-harm, questions the avoidance of self-harming behavior and seeks approval and legitimization. *As if the bad was flowing out of me instead of the blood* describes bleeding as a result of self-harm, which is attributed the function of being a vent for bad things.

Through the thematization of a taboo, the relevance markings and euphemisms as well as the detailed description of the self-harm, the tweet can be described as emotionally highly expressive (17/128; Andalibi et al. 2017: 1491). In face-to-face communication, it would be almost impossible or only in some circumstances possible to address the positive characteristics of self-harming behavior (see Andalibi et al. 2017: 1493f.), so that on the one hand it is reasonable to conclude that there is an open communication space in the anonymous discourse space #depression. On the other hand, such strong emotional expressions interactionally evoke reactions, for example in the form of requests for well-being, offers of help or information about places to go.

(14)

10.05.2020, 07:47 a.m	User11	Please read. @UserD · May 10th Depression: Being honest with yourself and communicating this to the outside world. [...] #depression #photo #photography #mask #help #INFO #Iamherelikethis #depressed #notjustsad

‘Bitte lesen.

@UserD · 10. Mai
Depression: Ehrlich zu sich selbst zu sein und das auch nach außen hin kommunizieren. […]
#depression #Foto #fotografie #Maske #hilfe #INFO #ichsohierso #depressed #notjustsad‘

(15)

15.05.2020, 12:10 p.m	User12	I want to go to the sea! Alone. #depression #homegroundedwithhusband #andingeneral […]
		‘Ich will ans Meer! Allein. #depression #hausarrestmitehemann #undüberhaupt […]’

Example (14) is a commented retweet, which asks the followers of User11 to read the tweet of UserD. This retweet marks the tweet from UserD as relevant and establishes contact with UserD. Retweeting UserD’s contribution while at the same time requesting the followers to read it shows that User11 publicly professes his relationship to UserD (cf. Demuth and Schulz 2010: 38). He spreads the view of UserD, implicitly expressing that he is of the same or similar opinion. UserD is also informed about sharing and recommending his contribution, which also informs him about User11’s attitude towards his contribution. This creates a relationship through the technical affordance of retweeting in two ways: firstly, UserD is notified that User11 has read UserD’s contribution, considers it relevant and recommends it to his followers. Second, the retweet and the activation of the network stimulates the relationship between UserD and the followers of User11 (7/128; see Andalibi et al. 2017: 1491).

A network activation also occurs in Example (15): The author expresses her wish to go to the sea alone via the verb *want* (see Demuth and Schulz 2010: 24). The postulated restriction *Alone.*, which is marked as completed by the full stop, can be seen as a relevance mark. However, the hashtags #depression, #homegroundedwithhusband and #andingeneral give this expression a specific framing. With the hashtag #depression a thematic attribution is increased, which is opposed to a simple wish to relax at the sea from stressful everyday life. The hashtag #homegroundedwithhusband reflects an apparent contradiction, as a marriage should not be like a prison, but rather a place of security. The third hashtag #andingeneral, contrasts with the two previous hashtags because of its semantic emptying and symbolizes a beginning language crisis, a reluctance to explain further. The accumulation of contradictions has the potential to evoke reactions from the network, even if they only ask empathic questions about the marriage. In this way, the network is implicitly activated through a search for support.

(16)

16.05.2020, 10:34 a.m	User13	#depression does anyone know this? The eyesight decreases severely in a depression. '#depression kennt das jemand? Die Sehkraft lässt bei einer Depression schwer nach.'

In Example (16) the hashtag is used to initiate the post and address the community. This is followed by the question to the discourse space, if someone knows about it (see also Demuth and Schulz 2010: 24ff.). Since the subject of the tweet, decreasing ability to see in depression, is only introduced afterwards, *this* is used cataphorically in *does anyone know*, which creates tension (Thomsen 1997). The seclusion of *The eyesight decreases severely in a depression* and the marking by the conclusion indicates that it is not this utterance that is up for discussion (cf. Androutsopoulos 2019: 81ff.), but rather experiences of the Twitter community on the worsening of vision in depression. By asking the community and addressing them, the author's awareness of the recipients is revealed (3/128; cf. Andalibi et al. 2017: 1491).

In the digital discourse space, interactants generate resonance in the community. From an interactional point of view, tweets with (supporting) information demand distribution in the community, which is confirmed by the uncommented retweeting of such documents in this data. Reflections on personal or social self-image require the consent of the community. Thus, the users react to Example (11) approving, e.g. with *Amen Bro. Amen.* or *Yes, it is a nice thought.* [...]. The depression narration *I have such terrible #depressions that I feel like I can't get off the couch* in (12) is followed by recovery wishes from users, such as *Wish you much strength!* or *I wish you a quick and lasting improvement!* Users react to emotionally expressive tweets, as in (13), with shocked reactions and their own self-revelations, such as *Can you please stop? I am bleeding right now with you* 😒. UserD thanks User11 for the recommendation by *many thanks for sharing ! and thanks for your comment !* (see also Demuth and Schulz 2010). Since wishes interactionally demand their fulfillment, users react to the wish of a trip to the sea in (15) with digital wish fulfillments in the form of images of beaches. Questions set answers conditionally relevant (cf. Imo and Lanwer 2019: 177), such as *It is the same for me* as a reply to the question about experiences with decreasing eyesight during depressions in (16).

The replies to 38 #depression tweets were examined for their speech action type. Commented tweets already contain a relationship-building action. Speaking or writing to someone means per se attention, care and an offer of a relationship (cf. Androutsopoulos 2004: 178, for HIV/AIDS see Chariatte 2017). The comments to the tweets make further follow-up communication possible:[5]

5. The tweets cannot be coded with several codes at the same time. These codes are defined as mutually exclusive.

Table 3. Categorization of replies

Category	Example	Number of 350
Agreement	Amen Bro. Amen. 'Amen Bro. Amen.'	26
Partial agreement	Yeah, maybe. But here it is so that you are directly labeled if you have psychological problems. Then everything else is psychosomatic. I don't have any more confidence in that. So definitely no doctor. 'Ja vielleicht. Aber hier ist es so, dass man direkt abgestempelt ist, wenn man psychische Probleme hat. Dann ist alles andere psychosomatisch. Habe da kein Vertrauen mehr. Also definitiv kein Arzt.'	4
Elaboration	#Sugar is in so many processed #foods without us even realizing it. We absorb this indirectly. I take a look at the #list of ingredients in the food. If I cook myself, I know what is in it. '#Zucker steckt in so vielen verarbeiteten #Lebensmitteln ohne das wir es merken. Diese nehmen wir indirekt auf. Ich schaue mir die #Zutatenliste der Lebensmittel an. Wenn ich selber koche. weiß ich was drill ist.'	17
Expression of counter position	That does not fit together so well now. I am not aware of any depression that is the cause of vision loss. 'Das passt jetzt nicht so gut zusammen. Mir ist keine Depression bekannt, die Ursache fur Sehkraftverlust ist.'	23
Pictorial	<3	17
Positioning	I did not know that, that is interesting. 'Das wusste ich nicht, ist ja interessant.'	26
Advice	You should have your drug dose adjusted! 'Du solltest deine Medi – Dosis neu einstellen lassen!'	16
Gratitude	Dear User, thank you for taking the time for this thread [...] 'Lieber Nutzer, danke, dass Du Dir die Zeit fur diesen Thread genommen hast [...]'	14
Compassion	Sometimes simply everything becomes too much. I think an admice [sic] can be appropriate. Especially because you get in touch with people instead of isolating yourself further. The described situation is obviously difficult enough. All the best – if desired, with a hug! 'Manchmal wird einfach alles zu viel. Ich finde, da kann cm Rant [sic] angemessen sein. Besonders, weil man so in Verbindung tritt, anstatt sich weiter zu isolieren. Die beschriebene Situation ist offensichtlich schwierig genug. Alles Liebe – wenn gewünscht, gerne mit Umarmung!'	20

(continued)

Table 3. (*continued*)

Category	Example	Number of 350
Counter-revelation	One of my key moments was when I realized that underneath my anger lies helplessness and I can't stand it at all, things became clearer for me. 'Einer meiner Schlüsselmomente war, als ich rausgearbeitet hatte, das unter meiner Wut Hilflosigkeit liegt und ich diese partout nicht ertragen kann, wurde einiges klarer für mich.'	44
Quotes and phrases	If "everything" is somehow already hanging on the silk thread, it will break at an additional tension. 'Wenn „alles" irgendwie schon am seidenen Faden hängt, reißt dieser bei einer zusätzlichen Spannung.'	21
Information	And once again the study to the video https://psychiatrie.charite.de/forschung/neurobiologisches_labor/studieninformation_fuer_interessenten_der_mino_trd_studie/ 'Und noch einmal die Studie zum Video https://psychiatrie.charite.de/forschung/neurobiologisches_labor/studieninformation_filer interessenten der mine trd studie/'	3
Request	Explain it. […] 'Erklär das mal. […]'	1
Wish	I wish you a quick and lasting improvement! 'Ich wünsch dir eine schnelle und nachhaltige Besserung!'	13
Question	What do you do about it? 'Was machst du dagegen?'	8
Rest	-	10

In this way, the commentators express their empathy, appreciation and encouragement and support with useful information and instructions. They encourage the writers to accept help and point out that they are not alone, which indicates a sense of community through the caring support offered by the community in the #depression discourse space.

5. A case example

The positive social support in the discourse space #depression on Twitter and the comments that there are people with similar experiences indicate the existence of relationships in this discourse space (see Andalibi et al. 2017: 1496), whose emergence I demonstrate using the already introduced Example (16) on the question of vision loss in depression. The interaction is introduced with *#depression does anyone know this?* by User13.

(16)

16.05.2020, 10:34 a.m	User13	#depression does anyone know this? The eyesight decreases severely in a depression. '#depression kennt das jemand? Die Sehkraft lässt bei einer Depression schwer nach.'

(17)

16.05.2020, 10:58 a.m	UserE	#depression does anyone know this? The eyesight decreases severely in a depression. '#depression kennt das jemand? Die Sehkraft lässt bei einer Depression schwer nach.'

(18)

16.05.2020, 1:29 p.m	User14	@User13 and @UserE https://www.praxisvita.de/depressive-sehen-schlechter-wie-das-gehirn-den-koerper-krank-macht-11726.html

The initial tweet (16) is retweeted by UserE after 24 minutes without comment and thus marked as relevant (see Demuth and Schulz 2010: 26ff.). This is followed by a response from User14, which contains an external link to a health site on the Internet with information on the connection between vision and depression. User14 thus implicitly agrees with User13's statement. This statement represents supportive behavior with regard to the constitution of the relationship (see Andalibi et al. 2017: 1492), see the following answers:

(19)

16.05.2020, 1:27 p.m	User14	@User13 and @UserE I have the same problem. In depressive phase [sic] I can hardly read because everything is blurred. My eyes are fine. I have been told several times that this is related to depression. 'Ich habe das Problem auch. In depressiven Phase kann ich kaum lesen weil alles verschwimmt. Meine Augen sind in Ordnung. Mir wurde mehrfach gesagt, dass dies im Zusammenhang mit der Depression steht.'

(20)

16.05.2020, 2:10 p.m	User15	@User13 I thought I was nuts. Can hardly see some days. Blurred and as if through fog. Can't read at all then. The letters literally dance. I can't see like I did when I was 20, but since I've gotten psychologically worse, my eyesight has also started to fade. 'Ich dachte schon, dass ich spinne. Kann manche Tage kaum sehen. Unscharf und wie durch Nebel. Lesen geht dann gar nicht. Da tanzen die Buchstaben förmlich. Sehe grundsätzlich nicht mehr wie mit 20. Aber seit es mir psychisch schlechter geht, schwindet auch die Sehkraft.'

(21)

16.05.2020, 2:11 p.m	User15	@User15 and @User13 And on particularly "bad" days I see particularly badly. So it does seem to be somehow connected. 'Und an ganz besonders "schlechten" Tagen sehe ich besonders schlecht. Scheint also tatsächlich irgendwie zusammen zu hängen.'

(22)

16.05.2020, 3:07 p.m	User16	@User13 Likewise 'Auch'

(23)

16.05.2020, 10:18 p.m	User17	@User13 I sometimes have the feeling of having no energy left to focus my eyes on particularly depressive questions [sic!], then everything becomes blurred. But fortunately for me it is usually very short. Is that what you mean or does it last longer with you / is it different? 'Ich habe manchmal an besonders depressiven Fragen [sic!] das Gefühl, keine Energie mehr zu haben, um mit den Augen zu fokussieren, dann verschwimmt alles. Ist aber bei mir zum Glück meist sehr kurz. Ist es das, was du meinst oder hält das bei dir länger an / ist anders?'

(24)

16.05.2020, 10:59 p.m	User13	@User13 @User14 and @UserE I myself am strongly affected by this. I haven't read a normal book for a long time. There is no special print with glossy [sic!] writing. [...] 'Bin selbst stark davon betroffen. Normales Buch lesen schon länger nicht mehr. Es gibt ja kein Spezialdruck mit gtoßer [sic!] Schrift. Verwirrtes Gesicht Besorgtes Gesicht'

In their answers, different users admit to the worsening of vision by their own experiences. The answers can be minimal, as *likewise* in (22), or extend over several replies as an elaborate answer to User14's question, as in (20–21). User15 introduces her contribution with *I thought I was nuts*, indicating the uncertainty about a similar experience, marked by *nuts*.[6] This is followed by a detailed description of the user's experiences on vision, which contains almost no typing errors and is orthographic, which can be interpreted as an indicator of objective interest (see Storrer 2018: 235). On some days, User15 can hardly see or read, which is illustrated by the metaphors like seeing through fog and dancing letters.

After relativizing the possible correlation between the author's age and eyesight, User15 connects the dwindling eyesight with the deterioration of her mental condition, which leads her to agree with User14's question. In the second part of the answer, User15 reports on her vision on *particularly "bad" days*, whereby she continues her agreement. With regard to relationship, this could mean that two users have come into contact here who share similar experiences, both on the overarching theme of depression and the effects of the illness on vision. User14 reacts by confirming the experiences with *I feel the same way*, thus acknowledging the similarity of the two users.

User15 continues with the decision question on other symptoms related to hurting eyes (*Do your eyes sometimes burn so terribly? As if you are totally overtired or have a fever?*), inviting User14 to elaborate on her experiences. After User14's brief agreement *Yes, I know*, User15 also reacts with a *Wh*-question about countermeasures, which makes an elaborated answer conditionally relevant. Two replies are used by User14 to list various countermeasures, such as sleep, an antiallergic or a cooling washcloth, with which the user shows him/herself highly cooperative. This is because the disclosure of personal actions functions like a piece of advice, similar to communication in self-help forums (see Hünniger 2019: 28; Lindholm 2017). She concludes her answer with *I think you have to look for yourself. Sometimes*

6. Original German is *ich spinne*.

one thing helps, then another, referring to the advice, but at the same time limiting its effectiveness to individual needs.

Further advice from other users can be identified in this thread, e.g. to adjust the font size (*setting Kindle font size larger would be an option?* User14, 21.05.2020, 11:06 p.m), to go to the doctor (*but go to the ophthalmologist anyway and maybe also to the family physician therefore.* User19, 16.05.2020, 2:24 p.m) or to take a certain medicine (*Maybe you could try Astaxanthin. Astaxanthin also strengthens the eyesight.* User19, 16.05.2020, 5:15 p.m), thus the users not only show support but also signal empathy and compassion (see Andalibi et al. 2017: 1492). Offers of help and support represent relationship-constituting behavior, because the helpers have to put themselves in the position of the person seeking help and offer solutions to problems (cf. Hünniger 2019: 33ff.).

The advice of users to go to the doctor is followed by a discussion on the attitude of doctors towards psychological problems. User15 reacts first with *yes perhaps* (16.05.2020, 2:34 p.m) partially agreeing with the advice, whereby she deals with the proposition, but announces doubts about this suggestion. Due to her experience that doctors judge people with psychological problems quickly, she has lost confidence in doctors and finally rejects the advice. These experiences with physicians are shared by users User19 and User13, which they can relate to through *I can sympathize with you* (16.05.2020, 7:04 p.m) and the revelation of years of similar experiences and *trust is not my thing either. There are only a few doctors I trust* (16.05.2020, 3:09 p.m). They agree with User15 and position themselves accordingly (see Lucius-Hoene and Deppermann 2004: 169). User13 then leads back to the initial topic: Her ophthalmologist has diagnosed a deterioration of vision. She confirms this diagnosis by reporting her experience that on some days she can hardly see or read anything. She thus refers to User15's first answer lexically recurrent, thereby acknowledging the similarity in the symptoms of the two users. This is reinforced by the concluding praise for the description of the symptoms (*you describe it really well.* User 13, 16.05.2020, 3:09 p.m).

This is followed by two self-revelations of User15 and User13, in which they share their positive emotions about the commonalities. User15 writes *You know, this makes it easier for me right now* (16.05.2020, 3:12 p.m), through which she addresses User13 directly and reveals herself to her. This insight into the emotional world of the author establishes an interactionally shared state of knowledge and generates intersubjectivity, which leads to a common orientation (see Günthner 2016: 18ff.). The *you-know*-construction functions here as a metapragmatic means of coordinating attention and is conspicuous at this point because it marks proximity and privacy between two interactants (cf. Günthner 2016: 21). Concurrently, this is created in public space on Twitter between two users who were (probably) previously unknown to each other (cf. Chenault 1998). Through this, User15 expresses her relief about the common ground, which is followed by the smiling and embracing Emoji 🤗 (16.05.2020, 3:20 p.m), that expresses counter-joy. This is followed by expressions of familiarity, such as in which both users commit themselves to the helping function of Twitter through the open communication space and the emerging interest and suffering-groups.

(25)

16.05.2020, 3:20 p.m	User13	@User15 and @User19 It is good to read that others also have such difficulties. Sometimes I just get laughed at. That scratches then very much at my psyche. 'Es tut gut, wenn man liest, das andere auch solche Schwierigkeiten haben. Ich werde manchmal nur belächelt. Das kratzt dann sehr an meiner Psyche.'

(26)

16.05.2020, 3:28 p.m	User15	@User13 and @User19 There are some things I have never told anyone. For this reason. If you are dismissed for a year by all the doctors and therapists with severe shortness of breath and pain only with psychosomatics, you don't say anything so quickly anymore. […] 'Ich habe manches noch nie jemand erzählt. Aus diesem Grund. Wenn man ein Jahr von sämtl. Ärzten und Therapeuten bei schlimmer Atemnot und Schmerzen nur mit Psychosomatik abgetan wird, sagt man nicht mehr so schnell was. […]'

The case study shows how a question addressed to the community and an answer required by conditional relevance elicit replies from the community about vision and depression. The answers include consent, revelations about one's own problems, and advice, and address other difficulties associated with depression. The author of the initial tweet and the commentators find support, compassion, understanding, as well as other people with the same problems, thus raising the problem from an individual to a systematic level – the problems are no longer individual isolated cases but are recognized as part of the syndrome depression. Twitter thus acquires thoroughly helpful functions for people in crisis situations through the social support of the community in the #depression discourse space, which is explicitly addressed by the community.

6. Discussion and conclusion

In the German discourse space #depression on Twitter interaction occurs between its users. The technical affordances provided by the WWW offer opportunities to create relationships with other interactants. Through the open communication space on Twitter, highly private and sensitive information is shared in a quasi-public space. People suffering from depression network with other help and connection seekers on Twitter under the hashtag #depression. The hashtag can thus be confirmed as a valid communication interface for investigating the experience of people suffering from depression. #depression tweets contain points of reference, such as direct addressing, reception in different discourse spaces through multiple keywording or disease-related experiences, which open up the potential for interaction and enable follow-up communication on Twitter. Through (un)commented retweeting, direct addressing and multiple keywording using hashtags, users can express common views and their appreciation, maintain their contacts within the network and be heard in different spaces of discourse.

In #depression postings stigmatized or painful topics are addressed. Users share their stories about current sensitivities, concerns and experiences with the disease. Users can contribute support and information, establish social contacts, activate the network, express emotions and search for social exchange through narration or social comparison. Replies from the community are elicited through the conditional relevance of the initial tweets, i.e. underlying social rules exist irrespective of the medium used. The replies contain agreement, revelations about own problems and advice. Users find support, compassion, understanding, and sympathy. Commentators thus express their empathy, appreciation and encouragement and support with useful information and instructions. They encourage the writers to accept help and point out that they are not alone with their problems, which indicates a sense of community through the caring support offered by the community in the #depression discourse space. The problems can be raised from an individual to a systematic level and then become visible to the community as part of the syndrome of depression.

The investigation of the discourse space #depression on Twitter indicates that those suffering from depression benefit from the social support offered by the medium. By sharing meaningful emotional experiences and exchanging them with others, they can be positively reinterpreted and re-contextualized. Twitter thus has a helping function for people in crisis situations through the social support of the community in the #depression discourse space.

Acknowledgements

I would like to express my sincere thanks to Konstanze Marx for her revision, suggestions and support in the conception of this paper.

References

Ali-Hasan, Noor F. and Lada A. Adamic. 2007. "Expressing social relationships on the blog through links and comments." In *Proceedings of the International Conference on Weblogs and Social Media (ICWSM)*. Boulder, CO.

Al Zidjaly, Najma. 2017. "Mental health and Islamic religion online: An intertextual analysis." *Linguistik Online* 87(8): 167–189. https://doi.org/10.13092/lo.87.4178

Andalibi, Nazanin, Pinar Ozturk, and Andrea Forte. 2017. "Sensitive Self-disclosures, Responses, and Social Support on Instagram: The Case of #Depression." In *Proceedings of the 2017 ACM conference on computer supported cooperative work and social computing*, ed. by Charlotte P. Lee et al., 1485–1500. New York, NY: Association for Computing Machinery. https://doi.org/10.1145/2998181.2998243

Andersen, Elisabeth Muth. 2017. "Typing yourself accountable: Objectifying subjective experiences in an online health forum." *Linguistik Online*, 87(8): 43–68. https://doi.org/10.13092/lo.87.4172

Androutsopoulos, Jannis. 2004. "Online-Gemeinschaften und Sprachvariation. Soziolinguistische Perspektiven auf Sprache im Internet." *Zeitschrift für Germanistische Linguistik* 31(2): 173–197.

Androutsopoulos, Jannis. 2019. "Digitalisierung und soziolinguistischer Wandel. Der Fall der digitalen Interpunktion." In *Deutsch in Sozialen Medien. Interaktiv – multimodal – vielfältig Reihe: Jahrbuch des Instituts für Deutsche Sprache*, ed. by Konstanze Marx, Henning Lobin and Axel Schmidt, 77–94. Berlin, Munich, Boston: De Gruyter.

Baer, Nadja, Claudia Sikorski, Melanie Luppa, Steffi Riedel-Heller, Steffi, and Georg Schomerus. 2016. "Das Stigma Depression–eine Interaktion zwischenöffentlichem Diskurs und Erfahrungsberichten Betroffener." *Psychiatr Prax* 43(03): 1–8.

Bressiere, Katherine, Sara Kiesler, Robert Kraut, and Bonka Boneva. 2008. "Effects of Internet Use and Social Resources on Changes in Depression." *Information Communication and Society* 11(1): 47–70. https://doi.org/10.1080/13691180701858851

Bucher, Hans-Jürgen. 2019. "Politische Meinungsbildung in sozialen Medien? Interaktionsstrukturen in der Twitter-Kommunikation." In *Interaktion und Medien*, ed. by Konstanze Marx, and Axel Schmidt, 287–318. Heidelberg: Winter.

Chariatte, Nadine. 2017. "HIV/AIDS in South Africa: Graphic signs countering the stigma and silence." *Linguistik Online* 87(8), 127–150. https://doi.org/10.13092/lo.87.4176

Chenault, Brittney G. 1998. "Developing Personal and Emotional Relationships Via Computer-Mediated Communication." *CMC Magazine* 5(5).

De Choudhury, Munmun, Scott Counts, and Eric Horvitz. 2013a. "Social media as a measurement tool of depression in populations." *Proceedings of the 5th Annual ACM Web Science Conference*, 47–56. https://doi.org/10.1145/2464464.2464480

De Choudhury, Munmun, Scott Counts, and Eric Horvitz. 2013b. "Predicting postpartum changes in emotion and behavior via social media." *Proceedings of the ACM SIGCHI Conference on Human Factors in Computing Systems*, 3267–3276. https://doi.org/10.1145/2470654.2466447

De Choudhury, Munmun, Scott Counts, Eric J. Horvitz, and Aaron Hoff. 2014. "Characterizing and predicting postpartum depression from shared facebook data." In *Proceedings of the 17th ACM conference on Computer supported cooperative work & social computing*, 626–638. New York, NY: Association for Computing Machinery. https://doi.org/10.1145/2531602.2531675

Cochrane, Leslie E. 2017. "An imagined community of practice: Online discourse among wheelchair users." *Linguistik Online* 87(8): 151–166. https://doi.org/10.13092/lo.87.4177

Coppersmith, Glen, Mark Dredze, and Craig Harman. 2014. "Quantifying mental health signals in Twitter." In *Proceedings of the workshop on computational linguistics and clinical psychology: From linguistic signal to clinical reality*, 51–60. Baltimore, MD: Association for Computational Linguistics. https://doi.org/10.3115/v1/W14-3207

Coppersmith, Glen, Mark Dredze, Craig Harman, Kristy Hollingshead, and Margaret Mitchell. 2015. "CLPsych 2015 shared task: Depression and PTSD on Twitter." In *Proceedings of the 2nd Workshop on Computational Linguistics and Clinical Psychology: From Linguistic Signal to Clinical Reality*, 31–39. Denver, CO: Association for Computational Linguistics. https://doi.org/10.3115/v1/W15-1204

Dang-Anh, Mark, Jessica Einspänner, and Caja Thimm. 2013. "Mediatisierung und Medialität in Social Media: Das Diskurssystem „Twitter"." In *Sprache und Kommunikation im technischen Zeitalter: Wieviel Internet (v)erträgt unsere Gesellschaft?*, ed. by Konstanze Marx, and Monika Schwarz-Friesel, 68–88. Berlin: DeGruyter.

Davison, Kathryn, James Pennebaker, and KJ Petrie. 1997. "Virtual narratives: Illness representations in online support groups." In *Perceptions of health and illness: Current research and applications*, ed. by Keith J. Petrie, and John A.Weinman, 463–486. London: Psychology Press.

Demuth, Greta, and Elena K. Schulz. 2010. "Wie wird auf Twitter kommuniziert? Eine textlinguistische Untersuchung." In *NET.WORX* 56, 1–52.

Döring, Nicola. 2003. "Virtuelle Identitäten – Cyber-Beziehungen – Online-Gemeinschaften?" In *Die neue Kommunikationswissenschaft*, ed. by Martin Löffelholz, and Thorsten Quandt, 235–254. Wiesbaden: VS Verlag für Sozialwissenschaften. https://doi.org/10.1007/978-3-322-80405-1_13

Finfgeld, Deborah. 2000. "Therapeutic groups online: the good, the bad, and the unknown." *Issues in Mental Health Nursing* 21(3): 241–255. https://doi.org/10.1080/016128400248068

Finn, Jerry. 1999. "An exploration of helping processes in an online self-help group focusing on issues of disability." *Health & Social Work* 24(3): 220–231. https://doi.org/10.1093/hsw/24.3.220

Galegher, Jolene, Lee Sproull, and Sara Kiesler. 1998. "Legitimacy, authority, and community in electronic support groups." *Written communication* 15(4): 493–530. https://doi.org/10.1177/0741088398015004003

Gülich, Elisabeth, and Lorenza Mondada. 2008. *Konversationsanalyse. Eine Einführung am Beispiel des Französischen*. Tübingen: Niemeyer (= Romanistische Arbeitshefte 52). https://doi.org/10.1515/9783110974058

Günthner, Susanne. 2000. "Zwischen direkter und indirekter Rede." *Zeitschrift für germanistische Linguistik* 28(1): 1–22. https://doi.org/10.1515/zfgl.2000.28.1.1

Günthner, Susanne. 2016. "Diskursmarker in der Interaktion – Formen und Funktionen univerbierter *guck mal-* und *weißt du-*Konstruktionen." In *Diskursmarker im Deutschen. Reflexionen und Analysen*, 103–130. Göttingen: Verlag für Gesprächsforschung, 103–130.

Haas, Stephen M., Meghan E. Irr, Meghan, Nancy A. Jennings, and Lisa M. Wagner. 2011. "Communicating thin: A grounded model of Online Negative Enabling Support Groups in the pro-anorexia movement." *New Media & Society* 13(1): 40–57. https://doi.org/10.1177/1461444810363910

Hapke, Ulfert, Caroline Cohrdes, and Julia Nübel. 2019. "Depressive Symptomatik im europäischen Vergleich – Ergebnisse des European Health Interview Survey (EHIS) 2." *Journal of Health Monitoring* 4(4).

Hautzinger, Martin. 2010. *Akute Depression*. Göttingen: Hogrefe.

Hautzinger, Martin. 2013. *Kognitive Verhaltenstherapie bei Depressionen*. Beltz: Weinheim.

Havryliv, Oksana. 2017. "Verbale Aggression: das Spektrum der Funktionen." In *Linguistik Online Sprache und Gewalt/Language and Violence* 82: 27–48. https://doi.org/10.13092/lo.82.3713

Hünniger, Julia. 2019. *Selbsthilfeforen als Ressource sozialer Unterstützung. Eine qualitative Studie sozialer Unterstützungsprozesse in Liebeskummerforen*. Wiesbaden: Springer. https://doi.org/10.1007/978-3-658-25166-6

Iakushevich, Marina (under review). "'Immer mehr Menschen fallen in Depressionen.' Mediale Konstruktionen einer Volkskrankheit." In *Linguistik und Medizin. Sprachwissenschaftliche Zugänge und interdisziplinäre Perspektiven (= Sprache und Wissen)*, ed. by Marina Iakushevich, Yvonne Ilg, and Theresa Schnedermann. Berlin/Boston: De Gruyter. https://doi.org/10.1515/9783110688696-023

Iakushevich, Marina, and Judith Stelter. In prep. *Zwischen Selbstdarstellung und Selbsttherapie: Psychische Erkrankungen auf Instagram*.

Imo, Wolfgang, and Jens P. Lanwer. 2019. *Interaktionale Linguistik: Entstehung und theoretische Annahmen*. Stuttgart: Metzler. https://doi.org/10.1007/978-3-476-05549-1

Köhler, Sina-Mareen. 2012. *Freunde, Feinde oder Klassenteam? Die Suche nach habitueller Gemeinsamkeit und persönlicher Gemeinschaft in der Peerbeziehung*. Wiesbaden: Springer SV. https://doi.org/10.1007/978-3-531-19719-7

Küchenhoff, Joachim (ed.). 2017. *Depression (= Analyse der Psyche und Psychotherapie. Band 16)*. Gießen: Psychosozial-Verlag.

Lindholm, Loukia. 2017. "'So now I'm panic attack free!': Response stories in a peer-to-peer online advice forum on pregnancy and parenting." *Linguistik Online* 87(8), 25–41. https://doi.org/10.13092/lo.87.4171

Linke, Angelika, and Juliane Schröter (eds.). 2016. *Sprache und Beziehung*. Berlin/Boston: de Gruyter.

Lucius-Hoene, Gabriele, and Arnulf Deppermann. 2004. "Narrative Identität und Positionierung." *Gesprächsforschung – Online-Zeitschrift zur verbalen Interaktion* 5: 166–183.

Marx, Konstanze, and Georg Weidacher. 2019. *Internetlinguistik*. Tübingen: Narr Francke Attempto. https://doi.org/10.33675/2019-82537869

Marx, Konstanze. 2017. *Diskursphänomen Cybermobbing. Ein internetlinguistischer Zugang zu [digitaler] Gewalt*. Berlin/New York: de Gruyter. https://doi.org/10.1515/9783110561609

Marx, Konstanze. 2019a. "Kollektive Trauer 2.0 zwischen Empathie und Medienkritik: Ein Fallbeispiel." In *Alternative Öffentlichkeiten. Soziale Medien zwischen Partizipation, Sharing und Vergemeinschaftung*, ed. by Stefan Hauser, Roman Opilowski, and Eva L. Wyss, 109–130. Bielefeld: transcript. https://doi.org/10.1515/9783839436127-005

Marx, Konstanze. 2019b. "Von #Gänsehaut bis #esreicht – Wie lässt sich ein Territorium neuer Sagbarkeit konturieren? Ein phänomenologischer Zugang." In *Neues vom heutigen Deutsch. Empirisch – methodisch- theoretisch. Jahrbuch 2018*, ed. by Ludwig Eichinger, and Albrecht Plewnia, 245–264. Berlin/New York: De Gruyter. https://doi.org/10.1515/9783110622591-012

Mattson, Marifran, and Jennifer Gibb Hall. 2011. *Health as communication nexus: a service-learning approach*. Kendall/Hunt Publishing Co.

Nguyen, Thin, Bridianne O'Dea, Mark Larsen, Dinh Phung, Svetha Venkatesh, and Helen Christensen. 2017. "Using linguistic and topic analysis to classify sub-groups of online depression communities." *Multimedia Tools and Applications* 76(8): 10653–10676. https://doi.org/10.1007/s11042-015-3128-x

Park, Minsu, David W. McDonald, and Meeyoung Cha. 2013. "Perception Differences between the Depressed and Non-Depressed Users in Twitter." In *Proceedings of the International AAAI Conference on Weblogs and Social Media* 7(1), 476–485.

Reece, Andrew G., and Christopher M. Danforth. 2017. "Instagram photos reveal predictive markers of depression." *EPJ Data Science* 6(15): 1–12.

Reimann, Sandra. 2019. "«Und hab total den Heulanfall bekommen » – Emotionskulturen im Netz am Beispiel der Selbsthilfeplattform." In *Mediale Emotionskulturen*, ed. by Stefan Hauser, Martin Luginbühl, and Susanne Tienken, 201–218. Berlin: Peter Lang.

Richter, Dirk, Bernhard Eikelmann, and T. Reker. 2006. "Arbeit, Einkommen, Partnerschaft: Die soziale Exklusion psychisch kranker Menschen." *Gesundheitswesen* 68(11): 704–707. https://doi.org/10.1055/s-2006-927288

Rimé, Bernard. 2009. "Emotion elicits the social sharing of emotion: Theory and empirical review." *Emotion Review* 1(1): 60–85. https://doi.org/10.1177/1754073908097189

Schegloff, Emanuel A. 2007. *Sequence organization in interaction. A primer in conversation analysis*. Cambridge: Cambridge University Press. https://doi.org/10.1017/CBO9780511791208

Scherr, Sebastian, and Marlene Schmitt. 2018. "Passive Facebook-Nutzung, selektive Selbstdarstellung und negative Wahrnehmungen des eigenen Lebens: Mehrgruppen Cross-Lagged Panelanalysen zu differentiellen Effekten im Kontext psychologischen Wohlbefindens." *M&K Medien & Kommunikationswissenschaft* 66(1): 58–74. https://doi.org/10.5771/1615-634X-2018-1-58

Schultz, Pamela N. 2002. "Providing information to patients with a rare cancer: using Internet discussion forums to address the needs of patients with medullary thyroid carcinoma." *Clinical Journal of Oncology Nursing* 6(4): 219–222. https://doi.org/10.1188/02.CJON.219-222

Schwarz-Friesel, Monika, and Manfred Consten. 2014. *Einführung in die Textlinguistik*. Darmstadt: WBG (Wiss. Buchges.).

Storrer, Angelika. 2018. "Interaktionsorientiertes Schreiben im Internet." In *Sprache im kommunikativen, interaktiven und kulturellen Kontext*, ed. by Arnulf Deppermann, Arnulf, and Silke Reineke, 219–244. Berlin/Boston: De Gruyter. https://doi.org/10.1515/9783110538601-010

Summer, Elisabeth 2015. Macht die Gesellschaft depressiv?. *Alain Ehrenbergs Theorie des »erschöpften Selbst« im Licht sozialwissenschaftlicher und therapeutischer Befunde*. transcript-Verlag.

Thomsen, René Sehested. 1997. *Kataphorik. Eine empirische Untersuchung pronominaler Kataphern aus rezeptiver Sicht*. Ph.D. Dissertation. Aarhus.

Vedula, Nikhita, and Srinivasan Parthasarathy. 2017. "Emotional and linguistic cues of depression from social media." In *Proceedings of the 2017 International Conference on Digital Health*, 127–136. New York: Association for Computing Machinery. https://doi.org/10.1145/3079452.3079465

Wellman, Barry. 2001. "Computer Networks as Social Networks." *Science* 293: 2031–2034. https://doi.org/10.1126/science.1065547

Zappavigna, Michele. 2018. *Searchable Talk: Hashtags and Social Media Metadiscourse*. London: Bloomsbury.

Relational dimensions of organized helping

Findings and implications

Claudio Scarvaglieri and Eva-Maria Graf
Ghent University / Klagenfurt University

The contributions in this volume set out to investigate relationships between help-providers and clients across a variety of helping interactional contexts and different media. While sharing a processual and interactive perspective on relationship building within the confines of a linguistic approach, the theoretical discussions and analyses in these contributions zoomed in on diverse phenomena on the micro and meso-level of helping interactions. To carve out the pragmatics of relationship building in helping contexts, this last chapter juxtaposes the contributions as regards overarching relational dimensions and offers these as a potential meta-language of linguistically researching helping relations.

The dimensions covered include the participants who engage in a helping interaction; the verbal and non-verbal techniques and methods of establishing and managing relationships; the theoretical and empirical connection between relationships and the purpose of communication in organized helping (i.e. the need for helpful change or support in the client or the person seeking help); the development of relationships over time from abstract socio-historical perspectives to the confines of a particular dyad; and the medium of interaction – especially electronic and social media – and its effects on the relationship. Given that several contributions investigate the distribution of roles related to relationship management and the use of categories of social identification in their connection to relationships, another dimension is the linguistic co-construction of roles in organized helping.

Based on the volume's contributions, we distinguish the following empirical dimensions of research on relationships in helping professions:

– Relationships between whom? – Personal dimension
– Relationships how? – Linguistic and discursive dimension (practices and strategies of relationship building)
– Relationships why? – Functional dimension (relationships and change)
– Relationships when? – Temporal dimension (the development of relationships over time)

https://doi.org/10.1075/pbns.331.14sca

- Relationships where? – Medial dimension (the communicative medium and its influence on relationships)
- Relationships who? – Identity dimension (the influence of social categories on relationship building)

In this summarizing chapter, we describe each of these dimensions in more detail, basing our discussion on the contributions to this volume and broadening our argumentation with the help of related research. We end with some thoughts on the future of linguistic research on relational management in organized helping.

Before discussing the dimensions of relationships below, the following briefly summarizes our understanding of relationship. As outlined in the introductory chapter (Graf et al. this volume) and supported by the contributions represented in this volume, we define relationship as a connection between individuals constructed via communicative acts which are performed and concomitantly perceived by the interacting individuals (cf. Spencer-Oatey 2007; Locher and Watts 2008; Arundale 2010). Based on these communicative acts, participants construct a mental model of their relationship. This model perceives of the relationship as e.g., close vs. distant, cordial vs. formal, cooperative vs. confrontational or symmetrical vs. asymmetrical. As the interaction proceeds, interactants not only perform communicative acts, they also concomitantly monitor each act regarding its impact on the relationship and adapt their model of the relationship accordingly. As shown by Guxholli et al., Muntigl, and Pawelczyk and Faccio in their contributions, in psychotherapy this means that any single utterance by the therapist can impact the relationship and that such impact has to be managed as well as weighed against other possible communicative or therapeutic consequences of the utterance. Managing the relationship is thus a permanent task (Spranz-Fogasy's "Daueraufgabe" (1992)) or a basic activity (Graf 2019) to be tackled concurrently with all other interactive tasks; the relationship can, on the one hand, be affected and altered by every communicative act, but will, on the other hand, also impact how each communicative act is understood and reacted to by the participants. Participants who assume their relationship to be cordial and cooperative, will react to a challenging utterance in a more relaxed and accepting way than participants who perceive their relationship as already complicated and strained. As suggested by Pomerantz and Mandelbaum (2005) and evidenced by Muntigl (this volume), it is possible to identify sequence types that locate relationships within a certain category (like 'close' or 'intimate') and that entail expectations regarding future interaction (like telling about one's own problems). These sequence types and the interactive expectations they create can be utilized by (professional) helpers to express e.g., empathy and support. Specific relationships thus bring with them interactional expectations and the way participants respond to these expectations in turn influences how their relationship develops along the interaction. Relationship and talk-in-interaction prove to be deeply interconnected and highly influential on one another.

1. Relationship between whom?: Personal dimension (the helper and the 'helped')

Our first empirical dimension concerns the individuals that participate in the interaction and construct and manage a relationship. In most parts, the contributions examine relationships that evolve between a (professional) agent who works for a helping institution and a client who seeks help. In its clear demarcation of who is helping and who is being helped, this kind of relationship is covered by the majority of the contributions. Yet, the presented studies also reveal that it is not the only type of relationship relevant for and in helping interactions. For one, we have witnessed that clients will refer to their relationship with a third party (partner / husband, friend, co-worker) and turn this into a topic of their treatment (specifically in psychotherapy (Guxholli et al.; Pawelczyk and Faccio)) (see also Graf 2019 for triadic constellations within the dyadic coach-client relationship). Within the dyad of helper and helped, another relationship can thus become thematically and interactionally relevant. As Pawelczyk and Faccio illustrate, therapists can use the patient's relationship with somebody else to manage their own relationship with the client through the way they comment on it. The relationship to a third person can be turned into the topic of interaction within the helping dyad and can even be turned into a means to manage the helping relationship.

Furthermore, as especially the contribution by Kabatnik details, the interactive role of the subject and the object of helping need not be pre-established and fixed. Similar to group or systemic therapy and formats like intervision or coaching (Graf 2019), within the #depression community on Twitter a person lending help in one situation can, in another situation, be the one who seeks and receives help. In such instances (and particularly in this medium, see below), relationships emerge as much more flexible and reciprocal than in traditional institutional helping arrangements with pre-established and fixed roles and boundaries and asymmetries attached to them.

Similar to such dynamics of switching roles within a relationship, the roles of 'helper' and 'helped' within relationships can also be acted out in different, flexible ways. Graf and Jautz talk about the 'client-design' in coaching relationships (cf. recipient-centeredness (Scarvaglieri 2017) for therapy), which means that coaches "display an orientation and sensitivity to their clients" and "counter-position themselves with their institutional identity". Coaches thus construct a specific helping role for themselves and thereby open up a relational space within the communicative dyad that can be occupied by their clients.

The contributions also elaborate how agents and clients create more or less formal and close or distant relationships. Depending on where any specific relationship is situated along such formality and distance scales, the interactants perceive of their own roles and identities differently. The article by Buchholz specifically tackles this phenomenon under the idea of moments of "fusion" in therapy. These are moments in which the participants appear to transcend a dyadic understanding of their relationship – that is a perception of two distinct entities interacting with each other – to a "meeting of the minds" (cf. Peräkylä 2008) in which they feel to be experiencing or perceiving the same things. In such moments, participants move beyond established portrayals of relationships and create a common "we" that, for a short term, appears to go beyond the involved individuals and creates a bond facilitating further therapeutic work (see below relationship and change). "Doing we" – as termed by Buchholz – thus takes the relationship on a different level and allows for new insights as well as a different mode of interaction.

All in all, the question who is involved in relationship building triggers responses that feature much more variance than might initially be expected. When investigating relationships, we thus need to take into account how interactants perceive of themselves, which roles they create and maintain for themselves and their counterparts and how these processes are negotiated.

2. Relationships how?: Linguistic and discursive dimension (practices and strategies of relationship building)

A dimension of relationship management tackled by most, if not all, of the volume's contributions comprises the discursive and communicative practices by which interactants establish and manage relationships. The studies of this volume thereby offer insights into multiple ways of linguistic and discursive relationship-management.

As any relationship is verbally initiated by the first words exchanged between the interactants, several contributions focus on address forms or person references and their immediate impact on relationship building. These contributions argue that e.g., clinicians use personal or personalized address forms to create closeness and intimacy (Muntigl) or social 'withness' (Günthner) and thus reduce the institutional asymmetries that are fundamental for institutions in helping professions. Address forms and person references thus provide simple, yet powerful linguistic tools that allow help-providers to create more equal relationships and to reduce interpersonal distance. They also allow for a re-focusing of the personal aspect of the medical or psychological 'case' at hand. At the same time, these tools need to be used carefully, as too much closeness or an inappropriate form of intimacy may be rejected by the patients (Kuna and Scarvaglieri) or communicative partners.

Most communicative practices employed by help-providers do not focus on relationship management per se, but pursue goals related to immediate institutional or situational purposes (e.g., the patient's cure, the client's development). Questions that aim to elicit solutions for the patient's problems, for example, are in essence a tool to help the patient reflect on their goals and to re-focus their mindset from problems to possible solutions. However, clinicians may formulate solution-oriented questions in a way that foregrounds the patient's own experience and communicates support and cooperation; moreover, these questions convey patients that they are capable of finding their own solutions to their problems (Thurnherr; Kabatnik et al.). Solution-oriented questions are thus regularly put forward in ways that strengthen the clients' self and also promote a good working relationship between practitioner and client. In a similar vein, when dealing with possible face-threatening interventions by therapists, both patient and therapist do considerable interactional work to preserve face while at the same time advancing the therapeutic process and maintaining relational affiliation (Guxholli et al.). These contributions thereby showcase that relationship management is usually not at the forefront of the interaction, but something that interactants need to constantly monitor and consider, even when they are foregrounding other interactional and institutional goals. Relationship management thus often consists less in the 'what' than in the 'how' of the interaction. As suggested by our definition above, relationship here reveals itself as ever-changing and therefore as in constant need of monitoring and (micro-)managing.

This dimension of relationship becomes especially poignant when focusing on instances of opposition to interventions or episodes of disaffiliation or confrontation between the involved parties. In these moments, it is vital for participants – the professional helpers in particular – to broker ways of re-affiliation. To achieve this, helpers use diverse means, including changing the footing and thematic focus (Graf and Jautz), incorporating the client's viewpoint into their own argumentation without retreating (Pawelczyk and Faccio; Kuna and Scarvaglieri) and accepting the other's standpoint (Winkler; Muntigl) or even mirroring their position and reformulating it (Muntigl). The contributions demonstrate that agents in organized helping put a strong emphasis on re-affiliating with their clients and invest much interactional work in pursuit of this goal. They regularly leave the interactional path they had been following, retreat from their initial position or adapt it to achieve re-affiliation. Even if they appear to be insisting, professional helpers make sure to modify their utterances in a way that makes them easier to accept for the client (Winkler). Thereby, agents themselves attest to the importance they put on stable and functioning relationships with their clients. After all, a relationship that cannot be re-affiliated and thus remains permanently strained, will lead to serious doubts on the client's side about the agent's professional commitment (Muntigl) or may have other detrimental consequences and thus puts the entire process of organized helping at risk.

One way to remedy a (heavily) strained relationship is by explicitly addressing it and thus to leave the modus of covert relationship management (Mandelbaum 2003). The contributions showcase that participants will comment on their relationship to voice their own expectations (Graf and Jautz), to get a clearer understanding of their counterpart and their perception of the situation (Muntigl; Graf and Jautz) and to create a common interactional ground (Kuna and Scarvaglieri; Graf and Jautz). Topicalizing the relationship can be used to initiate a joint reflection on prior communicative action(s) and about the status of the relationship, it can thus allow for transparent and conscious management of the relationship. In this regard, such explicit thematization differs from other means of relationship management which stay more implicit, without both parties becoming fully aware of them. A meta-pragmatic topicalization of the relationship can be used as a means to address and potentially rectify problematic developments, to explain preceding interaction to create common ground and to make further joint work possible (Graf 2019).

The chapters in this volume hence draw attention to the linguistic and communicative intricacies of establishing and maintaining relationships in organized helping discourse. Although Guxholli et al. (this volume) focus on the patient's efforts to mitigate potential damage to the therapeutic relation, most contributions find the helping agent overtly or covertly engaged in maintaining or repairing the working alliance. They thus highlight that help-providers are especially mindful of the fact that, as laid out above, each communicative act affects their relationship with the client and help-providers take great care to preserve a good rapport with the client. Even though most communicative actions do not specifically focus on relationship management, helping professionals make sure to implement them in a way that allows for upholding a good relationship. If this fails, help-providers will use a number of interactional means to re-affiliate with the client and to repair their relationship.

The multi-faceted and complex nature of the communicative practices that build and manage relationships thus demonstrate the importance of the relationship as such, the core relational responsibility that (professional) helpers carry as well as its situationally and processually changing nature.

3. Relationships why?: Functional dimension (relationships and change)

Clinicians and other help-providers first and foremost aim to achieve specific goals through communication. These goals consist of clients' personal and professional development, their physical or mental well-being, or furthering their understanding of their current (health) situation and possibilities of its future evolution. Interaction in organized helping is thus geared towards change in the patient/client (cf. Graf et al. 2019; Pawelczyk and Graf 2019) that is prepared, supported or triggered through the communicative processes investigated in the current volume. As argued by several contributions, a working relationship constitutes the basis and precondition for a successful helping process and functions like an "infrastructure for therapy" (Peräkylä 2019: 273) and other helping formats. The data discussed by Kuna and Scarvaglieri (this volume), for example, indicate that patients appear more compliant when doctors set up a symmetric relationship and communicate in non-hierarchical ways. In psychotherapy, the therapeutic relationship is commonly seen as the single most important factor for successful therapy:"the relationship can heal" according to Norcross and Lambert (2018: 311) (cf. Ardito and Rabellino 2011; Ribeiro et al. 2013;). Despite its general importance for setting off helpful change in the patient/client, the interconnectedness between supporting change and maintaining a good relationship with the patient/client can at times be difficult if not contradicting (cf. Scarvaglieri 2020). Therapists and coaches will, for example, attempt to make clients aware of mental or behavioral structures they were previously unaware of. This may threaten the clients' epistemic primacy as well as their face and thereby also strain the relationship (Guxholli et al.; Pawelczyk and Faccio; Graf and Jautz). At the same time, in therapy, just like in coaching and doctor-patient communication, achieving helpful change often also means changing the patients' knowledge, specifically their perspective on themselves and their biographical situation. Therapists and other help-providers therefore regularly engage in communicating new information to the clients and accept the interactional risks inherent to communicative acts such as interpretations or confrontations. As discussed in the previous section, they voice these utterances in a way mindful of their relationship and they leave, reformulate, or adjust their original statement as well as use various other communicative means to preserve or re-establish the working relationship with their clients.

Regarding the functional dimension of relationships, the chapters display communication in organized helping as a complex balancing act of pursuing interactional and institutional goals while establishing and maintaining a stable working relationship.

4. Relationships when?: Temporal dimension (the development of relationships over time)

The aspect of change also bears on the development within a helping interactional dyad and thus on the temporal or historical dimension of relationships. As clients change, so will their relationships with their agents. This dimension is accounted for in the contributions by Graf and Jautz as well as Kuna and Scarvaglieri. Graf and Jautz focus on the internal dynamics that underlie coaching processes and on the pivotal phase at the beginning of the first coaching sessions. They argue that the initial establishment of a coaching relationship largely impacts on its further development as well as on the coaching process at large; methodologically then, any relationship is best understood from its interactive starting points. Kuna and Scarvaglieri focus on the socio-historical dimension of relationships in Hungarian primary care and discuss socio-cultural changes in the way relationships between doctors and patients are established and maintained. They argue that, related to general social changes in Hungary specifically but also in correspondence with changes in healthcare communication overall, doctor-patient relationships appear to have undergone change, too, and have become more symmetrical, transparent and egalitarian.

The chapters that address the temporal dimension thus evidence that relationships are not fixed entities in time, but dynamic constructs that must be understood from their temporal positioning and development. Furthermore, these communicative and inter-individual processes appear to be connected to larger socio-cultural structures and thus appear to mirror changes to these extra-linguistic structures to some extent (cf. Blommaert 2018). We hold that the temporal dimension of relationships, particularly their interdependence with socio-cultural changes, is so far under-investigated and requires more research.

5. Relationships where?: Medial dimension (the communicative medium and its influence on relationships)

Some of the contributions also demonstrate how the communicative medium impacts processes of interaction in general and relationship building in particular. In face-to-face interaction, communication proceeds simultaneously and synchronously (i.e., communicative acts are perceived while they are being performed), sequentially (i.e., participants react immediately towards each other, building up sequences of interaction), multimodally (i.e., participants use multiple modes of communication, such as gesture, facial expression, voice etc. (Mondada and Schmitt 2010)) and fleetingly (i.e., communicative acts 'disappear' once performed). These characteristics carry certain affordances, for example the chance to quickly signal, and possibly rectify, non- or misunderstandings and to simultaneously use verbal, non-verbal and para-verbal means and thereby also communicate very nuanced layers of meaning (see e.g., Ehlich 1994; Deppermann and Spranz-Fogasy 2001; Deppermann 2008).

Computer-mediated communication is in great parts structured by different affordances, which also impact the way relationships are constructed and managed online (see e.g., Stommel and te Molder 2015; Locher and Thurnherr (eds.) 2017; Kysely et al. 2022; Thurnherr in press/2022). As mentioned above, within the Twitter community surrounding the hashtag #depression, participants will regularly occupy both, the role of the helper and the 'helped' (Kabatnik). The medium thus affects the distribution of roles among users, allowing for a more symmetrical and egalitarian discourse, as those, who are providing help to someone or are contemplating doing so, may be needing and receiving help from the same people at another point in time. The tweets documented by Kabatnik reflect this flexible participant structure, with users regularly referring to their own experiences when giving advice to other participants. Participants thus position themselves not as medical or therapeutic experts, but as experts with regard to their subjective personal experiences with the illness. "Helping" in such online, peer-to-peer or one-to-many relationships thus seems to entail a more reciprocal sharing of experiences and mutual self-disclosure of the participants (cf. Pawelczyk and Graf 2011). Another affordance of the medium is anonymity. When setting up an account on twitter, individuals can choose to disclose their proper name, stay anonymous (by choosing an obvious fake name) or use a pseudonym. Unlike in traditional face-to-face discourse in organized helping, recipients and readers of tweets therefore often have no way of knowing who they are communicating with or if the tweets are even sent by a real person (and not a bot). While the anonymity of the medium can have problematic consequences (cf. Marx 2018), in the case of mental illnesses, which are still frequently treated as taboo, it concurrently lets people open up and share their experience "in public". The medium then allows both for a more open and wider discourse about mental illness, while its anonymity may at the same time hamper creating stable and trustful relationships among interactants, who do not know much, if anything, about each other.

The far-reaching consequences of the medium of communication on relationships are also illustrated by Thurnherr in her analysis of email counselling. Unlike in the twitter community, participants here know each other personally and build up a unique one-on-one relationship. Doing so, they however need to manage communicative asynchronicity that distinguishes this medium (e-mail communication) from traditional helping discourse. Such communicative asynchronicity allows the counsellor to use linguistic devices that would appear more face threatening in face-to-face communication – the affordances of the medium thus facilitate to uphold a working relationship while pursuing other communicative goals (see above). On the other hand, asynchronicity may also create problems for the counsellor and the ensuing exchange, as clients can simply ignore requests etc. and act non-responsively, i.e., ignore the progressivity principle. This may lead to repetitious questions by the counsellor, which may seem overtly insisting and thus potentially affect the relationship in a negative way.

Overall, the studies evince that the medium of communication largely impacts on relationship building. It affects not only the linguistic and communicative devices that participants employ to build and maintain relationships, but even more fundamentally, it can also influence their roles within the helping process and who they are to each other on a personal level. Due to its (lack of) synchronicity, the medium also entails a temporal dimension, even if understood in terms different from the ones laid out above (socio-historical, development within the dyad). Finally, as participants evince diverse interaction patterns and may build alternative relationships online, the medial dimension thereby also impacts the identity dimension.

6. Relationships who?: Identity dimension (the influence of social categories on relationship building)

Contributions to the volume also lend attention to the identity dimension of relationships. This dimension refers to (discursively) established social categories communicatively applied to characterize and group people (cf. Sacks 1995) and their local influence on the respective helping relationships. Categories explicitly addressed in this volume include gender (Pawelczyk and Faccio), age or generation (Kuna and Scarvaglieri), culture (Džanko) and professional status 'expert' vs. 'layperson' (Graf and Jautz). While all participants bring these categories to the interaction at hand, they are only discursively put center-stage in specific situations and for specific purposes. Participants thereby create, negotiate or contest forms of (non-)belonging to different specifications within a category (i.e., man vs. woman) and attribute different character traits and behaviors to groups and individuals. The contributions that address these categories document how help-providers make them relevant to build relationships and support their communicative and institutional goals. In Pawelczyk and Faccio's contribution, a woman therapist at times accepts highly stereotypical characterizations of men and women by her woman patient. By partly aligning with the patient on gender issues, the therapist avoids potential conflict, is able to bond with the patient and reinforce their relationship and to thereby build a more stable basis for future therapeutic work. While the therapist in this case accepts the categorization drawn by the patient at least partly, Graf and Jautz present a coach putting forward and negotiating the dichotomy of layperson vs. expert and positioning the client as a co-expert. The coach thereby frames the relationship in a more egalitarian way and thus creates a more cooperative and relaxed atmosphere that supports future work.

Džanko's study points out differences in how Bosnian and German doctors manage knowledge in their respective interactions with patients. She concludes that German conversations appear more patient-centered, elicit more active participation, and allow for more subjective and experiential knowledge on the side of the patient, who are better informed and more knowledgeable as regards their own illnesses. Kuna and Scarvaglieri with their focus on doctor-patient interactions from different generations in a Hungarian context also argue that differences of this kind should be less understood in terms of ethnicity or fixed traits of a certain language group or culture, but should be interpreted within the context of socio-historical processes that influence communicative behavior. The studies by Džanko as well as Kuna and Scarvaglieri thus demonstrate that it is possible to detect variance of communicative behavior and patterns of relationship building across language groups or generations. Categories of the identity dimension are not applied in an essentialist manner that ascribes fixed traits to specific groups, but are grounded in a conception that interconnects micro-linguistic observation of communication with societal process and structure (cf. Blommaert 2018) and thereby allows to detail how participants' discursively performed identities matter in relationship building.

Future directions

Regarding research on relationship management in formats of organized helping, we would like to end with sketching out possible future directions.

Firstly, from a purely interaction analytical perspective, it seems worthwhile to address more elaborately the interconnectedness of implicit and explicit relationship management. Specifically important are questions about how metapragmatic comments emerge within the usually implicit, covert management of relationships, how they are performed and handled by the interactants and how participants end such overt sequences and return to a tacit handling of relationships. It would also be interesting to analyze the impact of such meta-discursive practices on the overall quality of the helping relationship and to investigate whether certain formats of organized helping recur more regularly to explicitly addressing the relationship.

Secondly, since relationships are both mental and interactional phenomena, a combination of interaction analysis with methods and tools from cognitive linguistics (like the frame concept laid out by Ziem 2014) seems a worthwhile and promising undertaking. This approach could be expanded to include psychological works that cover, for example, aspects of the mentalization of relationships (Bateman and Fonagy 2015) or bring in studies on inter-individual attachment (Mercer 2006; Bowlby 2012) and its performance in interaction. A combined application of these approaches would result in a promising comparative perspective; in the context of helping professions, such a perspective would not only investigate them from different methodological angles, but would also allow to contrast different types of professional helping interactions and the way relationships are constructed and managed across these formats (cf. Pick and Scarvaglieri 2022, Graf and Scarvaglieri in prep.)

Thirdly, a fruitful avenue in the investigation of relationships consists in relying on applying quantitative and mixed-methods and techniques of visualization more frequently and in more nuanced ways (cf. Winkler, this volume). Such procedures would be particularly stimulating for applied and transdisciplinary settings, where insights into the emergence, development and character of helping relations could be feedbacked to helping professionals and integrated in trainings and supervision to further professionalize the work of the respective helping agents.

References

Ardito, Rita B., and Daniela Rabellino. 2011. "Therapeutic Alliance and Outcome of Psychotherapy: Historical Excursus, Measurements, and Prospects for Research." *Frontiers in Psychology* 270: 1–11. https://doi.org/10.3389/fpsyg.2011.00270

Arundale, Robert B. 2010. "Relating." In *Interpersonal Pragmatics (Vol. Handbooks of Pragmatics)*, ed. by Miriam A. Locher, and Sage L. Graham, 137–167. Berlin: Mouton. https://doi.org/10.1515/9783110214338.1.137

Bateman, Anthony W., and Peter Fonagy (eds). 2015. *Psychodynamische Therapie. Handbuch Mentalisieren*. Gießen, Lahn: Psychosozial-Verlag.

Blommaert, Jan. 2018. *Durkheim and the Internet: On Sociolinguistics and the Sociological Imagination*. London: Bloomsbury. https://doi.org/10.5040/9781350055223

Bowlby, John. 2012. *The Making and Breaking of Affectional Bonds. Routledge Classics*. Hoboken: Taylor and Francis. https://doi.org/10.4324/9780203441008

Deppermann, Arnulf. 2008. *Gespräche analysieren: Eine Einführung*. Wiesbaden: Verlag für Sozialwissenschaften. https://doi.org/10.1007/978-3-531-91973-7

Deppermann, Arnulf, and Thomas Spranz-Fogasy. 2001. "Aspekte und Merkmale der Gesprächssituation." In *Text- und Gesprächslinguistik. Linguistics of text and conversation: Ein internationales Handbuch zeitgenössischer Forschung. An International Handbook of Contemporary Research*, ed. by Klaus Brinker, Gerd Antos, Wolfgang Heinemann, and Sven F. Sager, 1148–1161. Berlin: de Gruyter. https://doi.org/10.1515/9783110169188.2.17.1148

Ehlich, Konrad. 1994. "Funktion und Struktur schriftlicher Kommunikation." In *Handbücher zur Sprach- und Kommunikationswissenschaft: Vol. 10,1. Schrift und Schriftlichkeit: Writing and Its Use: Ein interdisziplinäres Handbuch internationaler Forschung: An interdisciplinary Handbook of International Research*, ed. by Hartmut Günther, and Otto Ludwig, 18–41. Berlin, New York: de Gruyter. https://doi.org/10.1515/9783110111293.1.1.18

Graf, Eva-Maria. 2019. *The Pragmatics of Executive Coaching. Pragmatics & Beyond New Series.* Amsterdam: Benjamins. https://doi.org/10.1075/pbns.303

Graf, Eva, and Claudio Scarvaglieri. In prep. *Psychotherapy and Coaching – A Discourse-analytic Focus on Communalities and Differences.*

Graf, Eva-Maria, Claudio Scarvaglieri, and Thomas Spranz-Fogasy (eds). 2019. *Pragmatik der Veränderung. Problem- und lösungsorientierte Kommunikation in helfenden Berufen.* Studien zur Pragmatik. Tübingen: Narr.

Kysely, Andrea, Brian Bishop, Robert T. Kane, Maryanne McDevitt, and Rosanna Rooney. 2022. "Couples Therapy Delivered through Videoconferencing: Effects on Relationship Outcomes, Mental Health and the Therapeutic Alliance." *Frontiers in Psychology.* https://doi.org/10.3389/fpsyg.2021.773030

Locher, Miriam A., and Richard J. Watts. 2008. "Relational Work and Impoliteness: Negotiating Norms of Linguistic Behaviour." In *Impoliteness in Language. Studies on its Interplay with Power in Theory and Practice*, ed. by Derek Bousfield and Miriam A. Locher, 77–99. Berlin: Mouton de Gruyter.

Locher, Miriam A., and Franziska Thurnherr (eds). 2017. *Special Issue: Language and Health Online: Typing yourself Healthy.* Bern: Linguistics Online 87.8/17.

Mandelbaum, Jenny. 2003. "Interactive Methods for Constructing Relationships." In *Studies in Language and Social Interaction*, ed. by Phillip J. Glenn, Curtis LeBaron and Jenny Mandelbaum, 207–220. Mahwah, NJ: Lawrence Erlbaum. https://doi.org/10.4324/9781410606969-18

Marx, Konstanze. 2018. "Hate Speech – ein Thema für die Linguistik." In *Hamburger Schriften zum Medien-, Urheber- und Telekommunikationsrecht: v.12. Recht & Netz*, ed. by M. Albers, and I. Katsivelas, 37–57. Baden-Baden: Nomos Verlagsgesellschaft. https://doi.org/10.5771/9783845293288-37

Mercer, Jean. 2006. *Understanding Attachment: Parenting, Child Care, and Emotional Development.* Westport: Praeger Publishers.

Mondada, Lorenza, and Reinhold Schmitt. 2010. "Zur Multimodalität von Situationseröffnungen." In *Studien zur deutschen Sprache: Vol. 47. Situationseröffnungen: Zur multimodalen Herstellung fokussierter Interaktion*, ed. by Lorenza Mondada, and Reinhold Schmitt, 7–51. Tübingen: Narr.

Norcross, John C., and Michael J. Lambert. 2018. "Psychotherapy Relationships that Work III." *Psychotherapy* 55 (4): 303–315. https://doi.org/10.1037/pst0000193

Pawelczyk, Joanna, and Eva-Maria Graf. 2011. "Living in Therapeutic Culture: Feminine Discourse as an Agent of Change." In *Living with Patriarchy – Discursive Constructions of Gendered Subjects Across Public Spheres*, ed. by L. Holmgreen, and I. Lassen, 273–302. Amsterdam: John Benjamins. https://doi.org/10.1075/dapsac.45.15paw

Pawelczyk, Joanna, and Eva-Maria Graf (eds). 2019. "Understanding Change in Helping Professions." Special Issue for *Communication & Medicine* 16(2), 1–195.

Peräkylä, Anssi. 2008. "Conversation Analysis and Psychoanalysis: Interpretation, Affect and Intersubjectivity." In *Conversation analysis and psychotherapy*, ed. by Anssi Peräkylä, Charels Antaki, Sanna Vehviläinen, and Ivan Leudar, 100–119. Cambridge: Cambridge University Press. https://doi.org/10.1017/CBO9780511490002.007

Peräkylä, Anssi. 2019. "Conversation Analysis and Psychotherapy: Identifying Transformative Sequences." *Research on Language and Social Interaction* 52 (3): 257–280. https://doi.org/10.1080/08351813.2019.1631044

Pick, Ina, and Claudio Scarvaglieri. 2022. "Helfen im Gespräch: Empirischer Vergleich der Hilfe in Rechtsberatung und Psychotherapie." In *Helfen: Situative und organisationale Ausprägungen einer unterbestimmten Praxis*, ed. by Daniela Böhringer, Sarah Hitzler, and Martina Richter, 163–192. Bielefeld: Transcript.

Pomerantz, Anita, and Jenny Mandelbaum. 2005. "Conversation Analytic Approaches to the Relevance and Use of Relationship Categories in Interaction." In *Handbook of Language and Social Interaction*, ed. by Kristine L. Fitch, and Robert E. Sanders, 149–171. Mahwah, NJ: Lawrence Erlbaum Associates.

Ribeiro, Eugenia, Antonio P. Ribeiro, Miguel M. Goncalves, Adam O. Horvath, and William B. Stiles. 2013. "How Collaboration in Therapy Becomes Therapeutic: The Therapeutic Collaboration Coding System." *Psychology and Psychotherapy* 86 (3): 294–314. https://doi.org/10.1111/j.2044-8341.2012.02066.x

Sacks, Harvey. 1995. *Lectures on Conversation: Volumes I & II*. Oxford: Blackwell. https://doi.org/10.1002/9781444328301

Scarvaglieri, Claudio. 2017. "Beraten und Psychotherapie: Zur Differenzierung zweier Formate helfenden Handelns." In *Beraten in Interaktion. Eine gesprächslinguistische Typologie des Beratens*, ed. by Ina Pick, 53–76. Frankfurt am Main: Lang.

Scarvaglieri, Claudio. 2020. "First Encounters in Psychotherapy: Relationship-Building and the Pursuit of Institutional Goals." *Frontiers in Psychology* 11. https://doi.org/10.3389/fpsyg.2020.585038

Spencer-Oatey, Helen. 2007. "Theories of Identity and the Analysis of Face." *Journal of Pragmatics*, 39 (4): 639–656. https://doi.org/10.1016/j.pragma.2006.12.004

Spranz-Fogasy, Thomas. 1992. "Ärztliche Gesprächsführung – Inhalte und Erfahrungen gesprächsanalytisch fundierter Weiterbildung." In *Kommunikationsberatung und Kommunikationstraining*, ed. by Reinhard Fiehler, and Wolfgang Sucharowski, 68–78. Opladen: Westdeutscher Verlag. https://doi.org/10.1007/978-3-322-85086-7_5

Stommel, Wyke, and Hedwig te Molder. 2015. "Counseling Online and over the Phone: When Preclosing Questions Fail as a Closing Device." *Research on Language and Social Interaction* 48 (3): 281–300. https://doi.org/10.1080/08351813.2015.1058605

Thurnherr, Franziska. In press/2022. *Interpersonal Pragmatics and the Therapeutic Alliance: The Collaborative Work in Email Counseling*. NIHIN Studies: Freiburg.

Ziem, Alexander. 2014. *Frames of Understanding in Text and Discourse: Theoretical Foundations and Descriptive Applications*. Amsterdam: Benjamins. https://doi.org/10.1075/hcp.48

Index